COUNTDOWN

To Marian

With Best Winds

Frank Born

24 July 1989

COUNTDOWN

AN AUTOBIOGRAPHY

FRANK BORMAN WITH
ROBERT J. SERLING

Silver Arrow Books
William Morrow
NEW YORK

Library of Congress Cataloging-in-Publication Data

Borman, Frank, 1928–
  Countdown : an autobiography.

  Includes index.
  1. Borman, Frank, 1928– . 2. Astronauts—
United States—Biography. I. Serling, Robert J.
II. Title.
TL789.85.B67A3   1988   629.45'0092'4   [B]   88-15642
ISBN 0-688-07929-6

Printed in the United States of America

First Edition

1 2 3 4 5 6 7 8 9 10

BOOK DESIGN BY RICHARD ORIOLO

To Susan, Fred, and Edwin, who not only
counted down but flew every mission with me, this
book is dedicated with love and gratitude.

CONTENTS

PART THREE 1970–1988

PROLOGUE

December 21, 1968 . . .

It was still dark, but the spotlights illuminated the gigantic Saturn V—363 feet tall, the height of a thirty-six-story building. I had looked at that monster and its embracing gantry many times, but this morning it was different. I was used to having all the ground crews and technicians bustling noisily around Pad 39—on a typical day at the Cape, it was like being at an outdoor factory.

Not today. Except for the three technicians assigned to us, the pad was deserted; the very absence of humans, the very silence, seemed to accentuate the size of the gleaming white cylinder.

It was starting to get light when we entered the gantry's elevator, the dawn of a cold but sunny, absolutely clear morning. The trio of technicians and the crew were the only ones riding to the top, and the technician helping me was an old friend—an Air Force sergeant who had worked with me at Edwards Air Force Base when I was an instructor and test pilot.

"Like old times, Colonel." He grinned and I smiled back.

I entered the center hatch first, grabbing a bar just inside and swinging myself into the traditional left seat of a command pilot. My two fellow crew members followed, the technicians closed the hatch, and we cranked it down.

Five twenty-four A.M.

The countdown for *Apollo 8*, man's first trip to the moon, began.

We were alone, almost 400 feet in the air on top of a Goliath that seemed to have a life of its own. It swayed slightly in the early morning breeze and I heard the gurgles of the fuels being routed for ignition. It was like listening to the digestive system of an overfed giant whose stomach is acting up.

Outside our windows we could see seagulls lazily twisting and turning above us, oblivious to what man had created. The ambiguity of this idyllic scene hit me—the peacefulness of nature compared to the potential violence of that white giant we were sitting on. But I didn't have much time for introspection.

Only an astronaut can appreciate the ambivalence of a launch countdown. It is tension blended with anticipation. There's a kind of fear, but it's fear of failure. You're afraid not for yourself but for the Mission. You acknowledge danger, yet in a curiously oblique way—death would be resented more than feared, an illogical embarrassment after all the years of training and preparation. It would be a kind of "this shouldn't be happening" reaction.

The countdown went on. There were more than four hundred items on the prelaunch checklist. Hydrogen and oxygen supply to the fuel cells locked open . . . electrical systems all GO . . . batteries connected . . . tape recorder functioning normally . . . every switch and lever checked . . . a seemingly endless readout of instruments pertaining to launch . . .

We were tense, all business, conversation limited to the countdown procedures. There would be moments of humor later, even under stress when a laugh would do a lot for morale, but not when we were awaiting launch. Too much was at stake and the three of us were concentrating on that long checklist.

Seven twenty-eight A.M.

All unnecessary communications circuits were turned off. I took one final glance at the handle next to my left knee. This was the abort control; it had been activated, and if I rotated it counterclockwise it would fire three small rockets separating the command module from everything else. It was strictly a last resort and a theoretical one at best. I had helped design the escape system and it had been well tested, but no amount of testing can anticipate the specific nature of every emergency.

CapCom's laconic voice, a verbal cash register ticking off the final seconds, banged against our eardrums.

"T minus five . . . four . . . three . . . two . . . one . . ."

One of many countdowns in my life.

PART ONE

1928–1962

GO WEST, YOUNG MAN

The year I was born, 1928, quite coincidentally happened to be the year Eastern Airlines was founded.

The date was March 14; the place was Gary, Indiana. I was the first and only child born to Edwin and Marjorie Borman, who named me Frank Frederick Borman II after my paternal grandfather.

My paternal great-grandfather, Christopher Borman, had come to the United States from Hanover, Germany, around 1860 and found employment as a tuba player in a traveling circus. During the Civil War he had no loyalties to either side, and to get away from the fighting decided to travel to Texas. He and a friend boarded a train heading west but got no further than Indiana.

The train stopped at Tolleston, a suburb of Gary, at which point the conductor bellowed, "All immigrants get off here!" Christopher and his friend dutifully obeyed; they had no concept of the distance to Texas and probably figured they had reached their destination. Thus did my father's grandfather settle in this tiny Indiana community, where he eventually opened a trading post and the town's first post office.

My dad was Grandfather Borman's only son. He was an automobile buff almost from boyhood, but his father insisted that he get a college education and he enrolled at Wittenberg College in Springfield, Ohio, where he played fullback on the football team. A stocky, broad-shouldered youth with reddish hair, he was known to all as Rusty, which my mother calls him to this day. She was a Wittenberg coed when they met; her family had owned a shoe-manufacturing company in Bath, England, and her father eventually settled down in Crestline, Ohio, near Cleveland, where he established a firm that made surreys and carriages.

Mother was never really happy in Gary, where they moved after marrying. A devout Methodist, she had come into a close-knit Germany family with a strict Lutheran background, and although she joined the Lutheran Church she wasn't comfortable with it. I never became a Lutheran myself; when I was old enough to take catechism, Mother balked and convinced my dad that the teachers were unprofessional.

My earliest recollection of the slightly more than five years we lived in Gary concerns my grandfather. When he was running for county recorder for the first time, I was paraded onstage at a political rally, and in a quavering voice told the audience to vote for him. I was four years old.

I remember my first major toy, an American Flyer electric train—it was a replica of America's first streamliner, the *Burlington Zephyr*. That train ran second in my affections, however, to what became a perpetual infatuation with model airplanes and flying.

I was only five when this love affair began. One of my childhood treats was driving from Gary to Dayton, Ohio, to visit relatives on my mother's side. The latter included a widowed aunt who worked at Wright Field and was dating some of the Army pilots stationed there. On one such visit, Dad took me for a five-dollar ride with a barnstorming pilot in an old biplane. I sat next to Dad in the front seat, with the pilot in the cockpit behind us, and I was captivated by the feel of the wind and the sense of freedom that flight creates so magically.

Then my aunt introduced her awestruck nephew to a short, dark Army lieutenant named Albert Hegenberger who presented me with some airplane models and a children's book about airplanes that I still have and treasure—*The Red Eagle*. The name Albert Hegenberger meant nothing to me until I was old enough to realize I had met a genuine celebrity. A month after Lindbergh flew the Atlantic, Hegenberger and Lieutenant Lester Maitland had completed the first nonstop flight between Oakland and Hawaii, in an Army F-2 Fokker trimotor; Hegenberger had been the navigator.

I was a sickly kid, afflicted with sinus problems and infected mastoids. I always seemed to be catching cold and my chronic ailments reached a family crisis stage when a doctor informed them I had to get out of that Midwest climate. Dad had a going garage business with deep roots in Gary. We weren't wealthy by any means, but we had reasonable financial security even in the Depression years, and now my parents were faced with a difficult choice.

It took more than courage to make the decision. It took love and a spirit of self-sacrifice. The outcome was a tortuous verdict: Mother would take me to Arizona and Dad would stay in Gary until he could sell his interest in the garage for enough money to make a fresh start in Tucson, recommended to Mother by a sister who once had lived there.

A half century ago, Arizona's second-largest city was primarily a residential community still retaining a frontier atmosphere—even today, you can carry a gun on your person legally in Tucson, provided it's kept in open sight. At the time my mother took me there, it had no industry, a single high school, and a way of life that can be described only as relaxed.

I loved it from day one. I loved the desert, the freedom, and the exhilaration of its unspoiled, spacious beauty. Tucson was far less sophisticated than Phoenix, its big neighbor 110 miles to the north. Maybe some of the streets were still unpaved and the citizenry rather provincial, but growing up there was the best thing that could have happened to me. Most important, I wasn't sick anymore—the clean, unspoiled air, the mild temperatures even in midwinter, were nature's own antibiotics. The only sour note was missing my father, although for a six-year-old the loneliness was sporadic.

Dad sold his interest in the garage about a year later and drove out to Tucson in his 1929 Dodge sedan. It had wooden spokes that dried out quickly in the Arizona heat and clattered with every turn of the wheels—you could hear that Dodge coming three blocks away. Jobs in Tucson were scarce, but Dad managed to obtain a lease on a Mobil service station at the corner of Campbell and Sixth Street. It wasn't very far from the house he later rented—an adobe-style dwelling at 2315 East Sixth Street, near the University of Arizona.

This was where I grew up in Tucson, the fortunate beneficiary of two loving parents who gave me an idyllic boyhood despite our economic problems. Retaining the Mobil lease was predicated on meeting monthly pumping quotas, and Dad had rough going, Tucson provincialism being the major obstacle. People tended to patronize businesses that were well established, usually operated by longtime residents. Newcomers were regarded with some suspicion, which compounded the risks for any new venture in the depressed economic environment.

No matter how hard Dad tried, no matter what long hours he worked, he couldn't meet his assigned quotas, and eventually he lost the lease. To support us, he got a job changing tires and doing odd chores at a garage, and finally wound up driving a laundry truck. And Mother, her proud British spirit undaunted, took in roomers for a time. Yet while neither ever let me forget the value of a hard-earned dollar, they never pleaded poverty when it came to giving me something within reason that I really wanted.

Once I came home from Sam Hughes Elementary School and disclosed my burning ambition to play the violin. Dad promptly went out and bought me a secondhand violin for twelve dollars. My practice efforts resembled the squeals of a tortured tomcat, and I suppose Dad was just grateful that I didn't want to emulate Great-grandfather Borman's skills on the tuba.

Music was the only subject that gave me trouble in school. I was an A student from second grade on, and was one of those lucky kids who never had to study hard or cram so I always seemed to have time for other activities. These included sports; I played soccer in elementary school and liked baseball. Our bats were broken ones acquired from the university; we taped them up and played with balls that were made of tightly wrapped string secured with black electrician's tape.

My best friend was Wayne Crutchfield, whose father was a high school teacher and lived in back of us. We could walk downtown from the house and often did, although the bus ride cost only ten cents. Saturday morning was movie time; a ticket was twenty-five cents, and the feature was usually a Western, followed by a serial.

It was a halcyon existence. We dug holes in the ground to serve as miniature caves. We caught horned toads and gophers and my folks were never sure what I might bring home for a pet. Once I showed up with a goat, and at various intervals Mother had to put up with an assorted menagerie that included guinea pigs, rabbits, a Gila monster, and a huge tarantula that got out of its cage and almost gave my father a heart attack. For a long time, I kept a family of gophers in a makeshift pen on our back porch; the only well-behaved, reasonably domesticated creatures in the Borman zoo were two dogs.

Mother was the dominant one in the family. Dad was easygoing, in many respects as much an older brother to me as a parent. I can't remember his ever spanking me; it was Mother who handed out necessary punishment via a switch from a tamarisk tree. It was a long way from severe punishment, but to a seven- or eight-year-old, it was decidedly effective as a disciplinary tool.

I needed occasional discipline. I was rather small in stature, and like many undersized kids I tried to compensate by being feisty and maybe a bit too aggressive. In Gary, the kindergarten teacher had told my mother I didn't always get along with other children. The consensus among my peers there was that I was too bossy and assertive, a complaint that carried over to my adult years.

In childhood and during my early teens, I was closer to Dad than Mother. He loved to hunt and took me duck hunting even when we lived in Gary. After he joined us in Tucson, the hunting expeditions became more frequent. When I was eleven years old Dad bought me a used .410 shotgun. I financed the ammunition by going out in the desert and capturing Gila monsters, which I sold to the university.

While hunting was an occasional delight, building model airplanes became our principal joint hobby and one that I still pursue. At first we flew rubber-band-powered models almost every Sunday, and when church competed with this activity, the model airplanes won.

The challenge of constructing them was as much fun as flying them—they were made of balsa wood, the wings and fuselage covered with gossamer-thin tissue paper that had to be stiffened with a dope coating. The first one I completed and flew was a Cleveland Cloudstar, manufactured by the Cleveland Model Company, and I still have the plans Dad and I worked from.

We'd build the planes on a card table in our living room, mostly at night during the week after I finished my homework. That left the weekends free to fly them. Eventually, I was to graduate to gas-powered models, which I'm still building and flying almost fifty years later. Although I had plenty of friends my own age to play with, none of them were especially interested in model airplanes. Making models and hunting were the main activities I shared with that big kid who happened to be my father.

As I grew older, touch football became my favorite sport. From

Sam Hughes Elementary I went to Mansfield Junior High on Sixth Street, where I tried out for a team called the Blue Devils. I wasn't good enough, so a group of us rejects went out and formed our own team, playing in jerseys furnished by a local jewelry store that must have had a great civic spirit to sponsor youngsters whose parents definitely were not jewelry prospects. We weren't very good but we had a lot of fun—and fun was the theme that dominated my boyhood.

America entered World War II when I was thirteen, and this meant an improvement in the family finances. Dad went to work for a new Consolidated Vultee plant in Tucson, a modification center for B-24 bombers. Mother also got a job at Consolidated driving flight crews back and forth between the airplanes and the operations office.

I developed maturity and an appreciation of the work ethic by earning my own money. Like so many kids, I started out with a paper route, about the time I entered junior high school. It was the first of several jobs I had in Tucson and in some ways the toughest. I delivered the *Arizona Daily Star* seven days a week to more than a hundred customers. It was a morning paper, so it meant getting up no later than 5 A.M. In the summer, I also delivered the afternoon paper, the *Citizen*.

My folks never gave me an allowance. When I wanted or needed anything they considered justified or truly important to me, somehow they found a way. The paper route, however, gave me my first real feeling of the independence and pride that comes from contributing one's share.

So did my second source of income: peddling subscriptions to *The Saturday Evening Post* and *Ladies' Home Journal*. I solicited from door to door with a sample copy of each magazine and a carefully rehearsed sales pitch.

Dad returned to Gary once in his wheezing '29 Dodge and came back a few weeks later with a used 1937 two-door Dodge. My grandfather helped him pay for it, and also sent me something I had been saving for: a High-Speed Bullet model airplane engine, my first venture into the gas-powered field. I was more excited about this treasure than the '37 Dodge. Those engines cost between twelve and sixteen dollars and it seemed to me I had been saving for one forever.

So that was my childhood and early adolescence. Looking back, I realize how magnificent my parents were: unselfish, caring, and so instinctively wise in molding the character of a boy approaching young manhood. I was blessed with a father who was also a companion and friend. I was blessed with a mother who gave me the discipline I so sorely needed, yet was also fiercely protective. Equally important, they were supportive—even when I decided I wanted to fly.

I was only fifteen when I learned how.

My parents were dubious, but they didn't forbid my taking lessons, although paying for them was way beyond their means. The cost was nine dollars an hour for dual instruction and I had to earn every penny of the fees myself.

I raised the money by working before and after school, starting with my sophomore year at Tucson High. I was a bag boy at Safeway, pumped gas at a service station, and worked at Steinfeld's Department Store, then Tucson's best. For $2.50 a week, I'd arrive at the store between 6 and 7 A.M. each morning and sweep out the whole bottom floor. I must have been a hell of a sweeper, because Steinfeld's promoted me to clerk in the sporting goods section and increased my salary to $18.00 for a forty-eight-hour week.

The flying lessons began at Gilpin Airport, a small field northwest of Tucson where I signed up with Bobbie Kroll, my first instructor. The fact that Bobbie Kroll was a woman didn't bother me in the slightest. She was a damned fine pilot, and blessedly patient with this fifteen-year-old neophyte. We started out in a brand-new Taylorcraft, a single-engine, fixed-gear airplane—easy to fly and forgiving of rookie mistakes. Bobbie turned me loose for a solo after eight hours of dual instruction; the seeds of a future Air Force career were planted and gestated that day.

I wasn't too bad for someone my age. More important, after soloing and defeating the fear of that first flight alone, I wasn't afraid to face any unexpected challenge in an airplane—and that is a vital cornerstone in the making of an airman. A short time later, I was returning to Gilpin after a short flight when a nasty thunderstorm swept in faster than I expected. I just managed to beat the heart of the storm back to the airport, but I was still getting kicked around by turbulence. I landed in a crosswind that felt as if a giant fist were shoving against the side of the tiny plane. I was more tense than scared, and it was a kind of tension that was coupled with sheer excitement. I was being challenged. I wasn't thinking, *This is dangerous and I might get killed.* No, I was thinking, *I'm gonna land this bird in one piece. . . .*

It's hard to describe the feeling of satisfaction that swept over me; it was like nothing I had ever experienced before, not even after the first solo, but it would be repeated countless times throughout my flying career. It was not quite, but almost, a sense of pride, falling short of pride only because landing that Taylorcraft safely had been something expected of me—facing and then conquering a situation that called for disciplined judgment and automatic employment of acquired skill. I knew I was a hell of a long way from being a good pilot, but I also knew right then and there I could be one.

Armed with my student pilot's license, I joined a Tucson flying club that owned a Porterfield, an almost identical twin to the Taylorcraft. It cost members seven dollars an hour to fly, so I didn't fly it very often. The guy who checked me out in the Porterfield was one of those screamers that almost all pilots encounter at some stage of their careers. A nervous Nellie with a hog caller's voice, he could have rattled Baron von Richthofen and he sure rattled me, even though I finally won his grudging approval.

I was too young to become close friends with most of the pilots flying out of Gilpin, but there was one I got to know years later. He was older, a pre-med student at the University of Arizona—a lanky, soft-spoken guy with an ingratiating grin. Neither of us had any idea that Frank Borman and Tom Davis would someday head two major airlines: I would be at Eastern, and Davis the founder and president of Piedmont.

So I was juggling a lot of balls while I attended Tucson High School (THS)—working, flying, socializing, school, and football. THS was still the only high school in the city then, and also the only unsegregated public school. The several junior highs, while segregated, fed into THS, so high school years were an open society. We didn't know about racial prejudice and I had several close black friends, especially Morgan Maxwell, who now owns a successful real-estate appraisal firm in Tucson. He was not only a football teammate, but we shared a room in the summer of 1945 when we both worked at Yosemite National Park.

My official football career began when I became the first-string quarterback on the junior varsity. The JV coach was a warmhearted man named Jason Greer, but the guy all players simultaneously respected and feared was varsity head coach Rollin T. Gridley, for whom I played in my senior year.

Compared to what Gridley threw at us, all previous discipline in our young lives had been about as tough as oatmeal. He looked like someone chosen by Central Casting to play a football coach—a six-footer with a steel girder of a frame to match, gruff and hard-nosed. We were petrified by him, yet adored him.

He set rules and would not tolerate the slightest infraction. If anyone was caught drinking, using profanity, or smoking, good-bye uniform—the boy was off the squad. Gridley demanded a 110 percent effort and he expected us to play hard, but heaven help a kid who played dirty football. We were warned to keep up with our studies and he meant it, even to the point of disciplining a boy for cutting so much as a single class.

One thing about Gridley, he didn't hold a grudge; once you served your punishment time, you were back in his good graces unless you goofed again. And he liked the way I played. I wasn't much of a quarterback in most respects—I ran like I was treading water and I couldn't complete a pass against the Little Sisters of the Poor—but I had instinctive football sense and I wasn't afraid to hit or get hit.

We opened the season with me as second-string varsity quarterback. We had a damned good team, actually a great team with players who ranged from average to good. It was Grid, as we all called him, who supplied the mysterious alchemy that transformed thirty-five individuals into a single entity known as the Team. That 1945 squad went undefeated, with eleven consecutive victories that left THS unbeaten and untied in thirty-two games—still the longest winning streak in the history of Arizona high school football.

Our first-string quarterback was Lee Carey, a gifted six-foot athlete with legs like barrels and an arm like a howitzer. In the second quarter of our first game, Lee broke his arm; he would be out for most of the year. Gridley, undoubtedly with unspoken misgivings and fervent if silent prayers, put me in.

We won that game, 15–0. Over the eleven-game season, we racked up 228 points against our opponents' 39, and won the state championship. Probably because our cheerleaders could throw better than I, we were strictly a running team—I think I tried four passes all year and didn't complete one.

But I did score once through sheer improvisation. In the huddle I called a play Gridley had sent in—an off-tackle slant with our fullback, Karl Eller, carrying. But when we broke the huddle, I noticed that the Bisbee High School linebackers were playing wide and the guards were split, leaving a huge hole up the center. Our center,

Tom Fridena (he's now a supervisor of Pac-10 officials and a successful business manager), snapped the ball. I did a half pivot to hand off, but pulled the ball back just as Eller shot by. Then I took off.

Those 76 yards to the Bisbee goal line were the longest distance I've ever covered in my whole life, including the 220,000 miles to lunar orbit on *Apollo 8*. I was horribly slow and only my panting blockers saved me. Fridena always insisted that our linemen had to knock down some Bisbee players three different times before I got into the end zone. And Eller, who went on to become board chairman of the Circle K Corporation, still feels he would have scored if I had given him the damned ball.

Against North Phoenix High School in the very next game, locked in a scoreless tie late in the first half, we were backed up to our four-yard line on fourth down. I called a fake punt and threw a pass.

Naturally, it was incomplete. I trotted to the sidelines (I felt more like crawling) where Gridley awaited his daring but erring quarterback, arms folded and a look of total disbelief on his face.

"Sorry, Coach," I gulped.

"That," he said in a voice coated with steel slivers, "was an unnecessary risk."

Being exposed to Gridley's iron, no-compromise discipline was to help me not only at West Point but throughout my entire life. We all felt that way. Once we played a game in Douglas, Arizona, and stopped to eat at a hotel where the manager quietly informed Morgan Maxwell and the other blacks on the squad that they couldn't eat with their white teammates in the hotel restaurant. Morgan said nothing about this discrimination to Gridley, but the coach found out anyway. He summoned us.

"Everybody eats together," he announced.

He ordered box lunches and we ate at the ball park. Together.

There are very few giants in one's lifetime. Rollin T. Gridley was one of mine. He is still alive as of this writing, a robust eighty-five.

Like so many teen-agers, I also developed an infatuation with cars. Dad and I went around looking for a clunker and we finally bought a junked 1929 Chevrolet for twenty-five dollars, which Dad put into reasonable running condition. He also taught me how to change plugs, install rings, and so on, which led to my establishing a small repair business on the side. Most of my customers were fellow students, so I sure didn't get rich on this venture.

In spite of my extracurricular activities I still managed to get mostly A's in school. I avoided most kinds of trouble at an age when trouble could come naturally. High school kids of my era weren't as sophisticated as they are today, but there still were temptations.

Our major distraction/temptation was girls. One of them, Susan Bugbee, was a sophomore, blond, beautiful, and brainy. I was a senior varsity football player, but I was struck by a sudden onslaught of shyness mixed with plain cowardice.

We danced at informal parties several times, but any *savoir-faire* I possessed evaporated in the heat of instant infatuation. I wanted desperately to ask her for a date but I didn't have the guts.

In this crisis, I turned to my buddy Wayne Crutchfield.

"You call her," I pleaded, "and say you're Frank Borman and you'd like to go out with her."

Wayne thought I was nuts, but damned if he didn't do it, and Susan accepted. Later, when I confessed, she thought it was funny.

Susan's father had passed away when she was thirteen. He'd been a surgeon who had come to Arizona from New Jersey for his health and established a large private practice in Tucson. When the war came and so many doctors entered military service, he'd literally worked himself to death. Ruth Bugbee, Susan's mother, was a strong-willed, assertive woman, yet very caring and protective. She was Tucson's first female dental hygienist and established the public school system's first and very successful dental hygiene program. Susan's brother, Frank, two years older, became an accomplished artist.

Susan was down to earth and unselfish, with a maturity beyond her years. We didn't start going steady right away. We dated others for a while, then gradually drifted into a more exclusive understanding. Somehow I knew she was going to be the most important person in my life. She still is.

That senior year was hog heaven for me—varsity quarterback, honor student, flying, and finding the right girl. My classmates, apparently just to keep me from getting too cocky, tagged me with the nickname Squarehead—an unflattering reference to the general contours of my cranial structure. Almost twenty-five years later, when Tucson gave me a parade after the *Gemini 7* flight, members of the class of 1946 paid for a large billboard erected on top of the Pioneer Hotel along the parade route.

WELCOME HOME, SQUAREHEAD, it proclaimed.

The war was over when I graduated in June 1946. I still wanted to be an Air Force pilot, however; at first I considered getting an aeronautical engineering degree, but down deep I knew it was futile. My folks didn't have the money to send me to an out-of-state university, neither the University of Arizona nor Arizona State offered a top-notch aeronautical engineering program at the time, and I had to be realistic about getting a football scholarship—there were no college scouts parked on the doorstep of 2315 East Sixth Street. Who wanted a rather undersized quarterback with an arm like Shirley Temple's?

As I saw it, I had two choices: I could either volunteer for military induction and serve the required eighteen months that would qualify me for three years of college tuition under the GI Bill, or try for West Point; the Air Force Academy didn't exist then.

By the time I realized how badly I wanted West Point, it was apparently too late. To stand any chance, I should have talked to my congressman at the end of my junior year and then applied. I didn't start thinking about it seriously until I was well into my senior year.

One of my favorite books is Ernest Gann's *Fate Is the Hunter,* its theme being that fate really plays a major role in determining the outcome of events, and that pilots, more than anyone else, truly believe in this view of life. I know I do. Maybe fate is merely a synonym for luck, but however one defines either word, I know that all my life I've gotten breaks I didn't produce myself; unexpected interventions, like someone pushing unseen buttons to determine or at least influence the course of my destiny.

There was a judge in Tucson whose teen-age son was getting into trouble in and out of school; let's call them Judge Jones and Jimmy. Jones somehow heard I was fairly expert at building and flying model planes and called me one day.

"My son's on the verge of becoming a juvenile delinquent," he said bluntly. "I'd like to get him interested in some hobby like yours. Would you be willing to work with him? I'll buy the kits, of course."

Building model airplanes I didn't have to buy myself? I grabbed at the chance. So for several weeks, I worked with Jimmy at least two nights a week.

He not only responded well but we got to be friends, and I confided I wanted to go to West Point but that it was out of the question. One night after we finished a model airplane session, Judge Jones asked me into his study.

"Frank, I understand you're interested in going to West Point," he said.

"Yes, sir, but it's too late so I'm going into the Army. I've already volunteered. I'll have the GI Bill benefits so I can go to college."

He smiled. "Well, I may have a solution. Congressman Dick Harless happens to be a good friend of mine. He told me he has a third alternate appointment open—the guy who had the appointment decided he'd rather be a dentist. If you're really interested, I'll talk to him about you."

I suspected he had already talked to Representative Harless about me. I said, "Great, but I don't think I'll make it."

"Why not?"

"There's the first alternate and the second alternate ahead of me, Judge, not to mention the principal appointment. I'd be fourth in line. But I'd sure like to try."

"I'll put your name in," Judge Jones said.

He did. Next thing I knew, I was told to go out to Davis-Monthan Air Force Base in Tucson and take my preliminary West Point physical. I was worried because I had acne problems, particularly on my back, and the Davis-Monthan doctors took pictures to see if I was too badly scarred. Meanwhile, I rode a bus to Phoenix and took my pre-induction physical for the Army, which couldn't have cared less about acne. I had actually received orders to report to Fort MacArthur in Los Angeles immediately upon graduation from high school, when I also got a letter telling me I was to take the entrance exams for West Point on June 10 at the academy. Those three guys ahead of me had dropped out, and I had gotten the appointment. So one way or another, I was heading for a uniform—either khaki or gray.

The tests lasted a whole week. Spelling gave me the most trouble, but I struggled through this educational obstacle course and then was told to wait around for the results.

Although we still were civilians we stayed in West Point barracks, and one memorable morning they called us all out and lined us up. An officer intoned, "The following candidates, take one step forward."

He recited a long list and my name wasn't on it. That was it, I thought—the ones whose names had been called were the lucky guys who had made it. I was still feeling a little sorry for myself when the officer announced, "All you who stepped forward, I'm sorry but you didn't make it. Those still in line, congratulations!"

I had told my folks and Susan to expect me home in about three weeks. I wasn't to see them again for another year. On July 1, 1946,

I was sworn in as a cadet in the United States Military Academy, Class of 1950.

The boy was about to become a man, molded and forged in the traditions of a 152-year-old institution whose sacred motto was Duty, Honor, Country.

And that first night as a cadet, I opened my copy of *Bugle Notes*, the plebe "bible," and read its first page:

> *Dedicated to you who join the Corps in 1946. Preserve the traditions compiled herein; they are your heritage.*

2

DUTY, HONOR, COUNTRY

You're a plebe during the first year at West Point and a yearling in the second year; juniors are called second classmen and lordly first classmen are the seniors.

But anyone who has gone through the United States Military Academy is likely to remember best the category known as Beast Barracks.

Beast Barracks is the two months a new cadet spends getting acclimated before the regular plebe year begins in September. "Getting acclimated" is a euphemism for being deliberately subjected to physical and mental pressure of fierce intensity. It doesn't test courage and strength as much as willpower and desire.

Few cadets are really prepared for the ordeal. I know I wasn't, but a dogged sense of commitment saved me. The Class of '50 was older than most, which made it somewhat tougher on me—I was eighteen, while many of my classmates were veterans of World War II. I had to put out to catch up.

The upperclassmen in charge during those two months couldn't touch you, but they still could make your life miserable. Twenty push-ups for a minor infraction or even at somebody's whim may not seem like the Spanish Inquisition, but when twenty push-ups are ordered after you're already about to collapse from regular drills, you've got trouble.

There were moments when I wasn't sure that what seemed like impossible demands on the human body were worth it—*Hell,* I thought, *all this crap is a long way from flying, so why do I have to take it?*

Then a single incident helped turn me around. It involved one of my football heroes, Arnold Tucker, who was quarterback on Army's powerhouse team, which had been savaging college opponents for the past two seasons. He was a first classman in my plebe year, and one day he came around to Beast Barracks and talked to us about what West Point really meant, especially the honor system on which the entire four-year experience was based. He said that we were different from conventional college students because we had to meet higher standards, and the honor system was part of those standards.

It was heavy stuff for an eighteen-year-old from a small Arizona high school, but it really took. I was not only indoctrinated but inoculated—if a guy like Arnold Tucker believed in what he had said, it was easy to accept.

Even Susan had to take a backseat that was more like the rear of the bus. After writing that I'd be seeing her in three weeks, now I had to write that I wouldn't be home until next June—there were no furloughs for plebes, not even at Christmas.

The pressure eased when Beast Barracks ended, but not by much. I was assigned to Company H-1 when plebe year officially began and I stayed in H-1 the whole four years, a period when West Point was undergoing some worthwhile changes. The faculty and non-commissioned cadre were mostly battle-hardened men who knew what it was all about. The academy's superintendent was General Maxwell Taylor, who had commanded the 101st Airborne Division in Europe and later became Army Chief of Staff.

There were four cadets to a room during plebe year, and frankly, I didn't become really close friends with any of them. But there was an interesting first classman who lived across the hall from me. He was distinguished mostly by his easygoing indifference to almost everything. He never seemed to study, never bothered us plebes, and was known for getting in more sack time than the rest of Company H-1 combined. All the plebes liked him because he refused to join in any hazing. His name was Al Haig.

Another fellow in H-1 went on to earn a different kind of fame.

He always was in trouble, and in my yearling year he was kicked out of West Point. He somehow finagled an appointment to Annapolis, from which he graduated. The Navy gave him command of the *Vance,* a small destroyer that he took into the Vietnam war zone, and he subsequently was relieved of command after the Navy discovered he had been filing false position reports, writing fictional press releases about his alleged exploits, and forcing his officers to recommend him for the Silver Star. He retired from the Navy in disgrace, following an unsuccessful attempt to claim he was a victim of a dastardly mutiny.

Thus did former cadet Marcus Aurelius Arnheiter become a real-life version of the fictitious Captain Queeg, and the subject of a devastating book, *The Arnheiter Affair,* written by Neil Sheehan of *The New York Times.*

West Point was pretty efficient at purging itself of oddballs and misfits like Arnheiter; usually the system caught up with them by the end of their yearling year, and this included the handful of sadists who regarded hazing as a license for cruelty and browbeating. Personally, I found hazing relatively mild and harmless after Beast Barracks. In retrospect, it was even beneficial in the sense that plebe year, like Beast Barracks, was a testing ground for the mental, physical, and moral stamina of young men still in a formative stage.

Hazing to me meant inconvenience more than anything else. Its worst facet was during meals, when plebes had to eat in a braced sitting position and then be interrupted constantly by questions from whatever upperclassmen were sitting at the table. I actually lost weight that first year and so did most plebes; answering questions often left insufficient time to finish a meal.

While hazing generally didn't bother me, there was a notable exception. One upperclassman who took a dislike to me tried to make my life miserable. His own classmates thought he was strictly bad news but that didn't save me—it was rare for an upperclassman to intervene publicly on behalf of a plebe. One day I was standing in ranks and he came up to me.

"Mr. Borman, those shoes don't look too good."

I gritted my teeth. "Yes, sir!"

"But now they're going to look worse."

He lifted his heel and jammed it down on my foot.

I said very quietly, "You son of a bitch, if you ever do that again, I'll kill you."

There was dead silence in the ranks—a lowly plebe had not only challenged an upperclassman, but insulted him in front of other cadets. But the bastard just turned away, and he never bothered me again. He eventually washed out.

Hazing couldn't match a far more difficult ordeal I had to face. I had never learned to swim, and to my consternation I discovered that I couldn't graduate from West Point without being able to swim 200 yards in five minutes. I couldn't swim twenty yards in five minutes and the swimming instructor quickly ascertained that I'd probably drown anyway before transversing the twenty yards.

So I was put into a special swimming class and two or three nights a week I had to report to the post gymnasium and take lessons. One of the happiest events of plebe year was passing that special swimming class; it was one more example of achieving something simply because I wanted it so badly.

One thing I didn't achieve was playing football for West Point. I went out for the plebe team and even at that level I couldn't compete. But head coach Earl Blaik took me on as an assistant manager. My duties consisted largely of picking up socks and jockstraps, along with chasing footballs, but at least I got to associate with the legendary Blaik and the players, like Tucker, Blanchard, and Davis.

Knowing and working under Earl Blaik was an experience to be treasured. He always reminded me of Douglas MacArthur, someone whom you approached with instinctive diffidence. Everyone, including the assistant coaches, always addressed him as "Colonel." He was austere yet never pompous, possessing tremendous charisma. Blaik cared about people and kept in touch with his players long after they graduated, including ex-managers whose sole claim to Army football glory had been picking up jerseys and jockstraps.

I had no problem scholastically, although for the first time in my life I had to study. Elective courses were almost nonexistent at West Point, but we did have a choice of foreign languages. The academy offered French, German, Russian, Spanish, and Portuguese; a cadet could list any two as his preferences and take only one. "Preferences," however, were strictly theoretical—you were just as likely to get a language you didn't want. We heard from friendly upperclassmen that Spanish and Portuguese were the easiest, so I listed these and was lucky to get the latter. A lot of guys put down Spanish and Portuguese and wound up taking German or Russian.

We were paid fifty dollars a month but we never saw the money. Plebes were given scrip books to buy essentials like shaving cream and soap; most of the fifty bucks went for the uniform allowance and textbooks. My chief extravagance was ice cream, which I'd buy for fifteen cents a pint. As we progressed beyond plebe year, the academy began putting a bigger percentage of our salaries into a special account that was held for us until graduation, so we'd have some dough when our Regular Army careers began.

Each company was like a college fraternity; cadets tended to establish most of their close friendships within the confines of their own units. The Class of '50 was the first to break some ugly traditions of prejudice and bigotry by welcoming black cadets to dances. There had been a few blacks admitted to West Point prior to 1946, but they weren't allowed to attend dances, nobody would eat with them, and they were generally ostracized. To us, they were fellow cadets, not black cadets. They wore the same gray uniform we did, so eating and rooming with them came as naturally as breathing. We didn't tolerate them, we accepted them as equals, and frankly I think the Army after World War II reformed faster than the rest of our society.

Midway through plebe year, I broke up with Susan. It could have been the biggest mistake of my life, although I didn't think that way at the time. I was not only enjoying West Point, I was absolutely gung-ho about it. I was absorbing this monastic, totally dedicated life right into my bloodstream and brain. I remember the overwhelming feeling of pride when I marched with the full corps of cadets for the first time at a football game, and again the following year when we went to Washington and marched down Pennsylvania Avenue in President Truman's inaugural parade. It was bitterly cold but I didn't give a hoot.

By the time Christmas vacation came around and I knew we couldn't go home, I realized I wasn't that sorry about it. I missed my family and my girl, but somehow I arrived at the conclusion that my commitment to that one girl was interfering with my commitment to the military.

So I wrote Susan and explained, not too well I'm afraid, that West Point demanded everything of me. That I had found my career, that I was going to be an Air Force general some day, that I was going to be here for four years, and that I didn't want to be unfair to her so we should probably cool it.

Actually, Susan was simply an indirect victim of the West Point mystique that infects every cadet to some extent, or there wouldn't be a West Point. Once you accept the institution's Honor Code as sacred and inviolate, you have established the priorities and principles that will guide your career and your life.

The code is simple yet powerful. It decrees that "a Cadet will not lie, cheat, nor tolerate those who do." That code is West Point's biggest cornerstone. It's what the academy is all about, and it has survived nearly two centuries in which cynicism and compromise tried to challenge its values. The academy doesn't teach arrogance; it teaches qualities like integrity and perseverence.

If rigid adherence to such a code seems unrealistic, old-fashioned, or even corny, so be it. Maybe only a West Pointer could grasp what happens to a kid who's not only exposed to it but branded with it, imposing standards and guidelines from those four years at West Point on the rest of one's life. They placed on me the blinders of duty, oblivious to all else except the mission ahead. Seeds of the future were planted at West Point in plebe year, when I put on those blinders for the first time, broke up with Susan, and discovered that, even at Christmas, the academy in its own way had become my home.

When plebe year ended, I was fairly certain that I was going to make it through the next three. I finished in the upper third of my class. I felt I belonged. I had also changed, more than I realized, and I found this out when I went home to Tucson on my first furlough.

We were given thirty days' leave after June Week (graduation), and I found Tucson a different place from the one I had left a year ago. Many of my former classmates had gone into the Army, and I seemed more mature than the friends I saw again. Other than my family, I had no roots there anymore. They had been mysteriously transferred 2,000 miles away, and although I enjoyed being home, I discovered I really wasn't home. I missed West Point. Like all young cadets, I had been counting the days to that first furlough. Now here I was counting the days to when I could go back. The thrill of strutting around in my uniform disappeared after the first day home and I was restless. I dated a few times but didn't even try to see Susan.

The one thing plebe year hadn't changed was my Air Force ambitions; I had acquired an inbred loyalty to what West Point stood for, but not to the Army as such, and I still wanted flying as my military career.

One great thing about yearling year was being elevated out of the status of second-class citizen. The shoe was on the other foot—the hazee became the hazer. Most of us weren't bullies by instinct or choice, but there was this irresistible temptation to lord it over some hapless plebe—it's inevitable when the memories of twelve months of indignities are still fresh. Anyway, hazing West Point style isn't bullying. Kept within reasonable bounds, it is part of the mental conditioning that makes a youngster who has never known real discipline accept it automatically.

From yearling year on, we applied the most pressure on plebes we felt didn't belong at the academy. We deliberately tried to make things difficult to see how badly a kid really wanted to stay at West Point. We started off being tough on all plebes, and over the course of twelve months the more savvy upperclassmen could judge pretty well which plebes both needed and deserved the most pressure.

Studying became easier in the second year. I studied hard, yet I never had to crack a book after taps, nor did I find it necessary to study over weekends. I had more free time than a lot of guys and I really enjoyed most of my classes. West Point had an admirable practice of inviting top-notch outside speakers to lecture us, such as George Kennan, who talked on geopolitics, an enlightening experience. Engineering was a favorite subject; I not only showed aptitude for it, but I knew it would help me in aviation.

Yearlings had a chance to go home for Christmas leave, but this presented a problem for cadets whose hometowns were west of the Mississippi. Flying was the only way to get home in a hurry and get back on time, but few of us had the dough for airline tickets and it was no time of the year to try bumming rides from the Air Force.

One of my friends at West Point was Ross Mayfield, also from Arizona, and we concocted the idea of chartering a plane for a small group of cadets in the same transportation bind we were in. We contacted an outfit called Coastal Cargo, one of those shoestring non-scheduled operations that proliferated after the war.

Ross and I rounded up twenty-seven fellow poverty-stricken cadets from as far away as San Francisco and got them in on the deal we arranged with Coastal Cargo: $55 per man for a one-way flight from Teterboro Airport in New Jersey to San Francisco via Atlanta, Dallas, Phoenix, and Los Angeles. If they wanted a round trip, the fare was $110. As the entrepreneurs in this venture, Ross and I went free.

We took off late because of weather in a war-weary C-47 (DC-3) and landed in Atlanta around 2 A.M. to refuel. The fixed base operator who was supposed to provide the gas wouldn't let the captain charge it to the airline—it seems Coastal Cargo's credit standing ranked a notch lower than that of a bankrupt horse player.

"Then take my own Esso credit card," the pilot pleaded.

"For eight hundred gallons of gas? You think I'm crazy?"

The chastened captain reported the impasse to entrepreneurs Borman and Mayfield. "I'm sorry, guys, but I guess we're stuck here."

"The hell we are," I said. "We'll take up a collection."

The "collection" didn't raise enough dough to fill a Volkswagen's tank. In desperation, I said I'd try to get somebody at Esso to vouch for the captain's credit card. This offer resulted in a long series of phone calls before I reached the right man—none other than the president of Standard Oil of New Jersey.

By this time it was long after 3 A.M. It took more than an hour to reach the president after I started out by calling some night emergency number at Esso headquarters, and finally talked someone into giving me his home phone.

"My name is Frank Borman and I'm a cadet at West Point," I began when he groggily answered his phone. "I'm sorry to bother you at this time of night, sir, but I'm in charge of a load of cadets flying home for Christmas. We're stuck in Atlanta because the fixed base operator here won't let the pilot charge the gas to his airline."

"What the hell do you expect me to do about it?" he demanded.

"Well, sir, the pilot wants to use his Esso credit card and they won't honor it."

"Who did you say this was?" he asked in an incredulous tone.

"Cadet Borman, sir."

"Let me talk to that fixed base guy," he sighed.

I spent a month the following summer as one of a dozen Portuguese-speaking cadets flown to Rio de Janeiro as part of an exchange program with the Brazilian government. After our return, we got two weeks' leave at home and then went to Camp Buckner, near West Point, where cadets are introduced to the Army's various branches for the first time. I got to drive tanks and jeeps, and qualified on different types of weapons. We had every Wednesday afternoon off, dances every Saturday, and plenty of intramural sports—all pretty loose compared to a regular school year.

But exposure to such ground warfare items as tanks and artillery had no effect on my own goals. As I headed into my third year, the Wild Blue Yonder was the only horizon in sight.

* * *

West Point is a perfect example of one of life's truisms: The longer you stick out a tough situation, the easier it becomes. In the process of overcoming difficult challenges, you have to mature, harden, and adjust. The challenges are actually just as hard—they seem easier because you're better able to cope with them.

That's why my third and fourth years at the academy, especially the latter, I remember as two of the happiest years of my life. As a second classman, I made cadet corporal and I kept climbing in class academic standing—I ranked eighth when I graduated.

At the end of the third year, I was among a dozen cadets chosen to fly to Europe for a firsthand look at postwar Germany. The Berlin airlift was just winding down, and after changing planes at Frankfurt, we flew into West Berlin sitting on sacks of coal. We spent six weeks touring Germany, and this included visits to the infamous concentration camp at Dachau, the bomb-pulverized city of Cologne, and a displaced persons facility that had more pitiful DPs still there than we wanted to see.

I don't think anyone can adequately describe the impact of a sight like Dachau, with its extermination ovens and ominous, ugly gallows deliberately left intact as visual evidence of Nazi cruelty to human beings whose only sin was their religion. Cologne was bad enough, a magnificent city reduced to rubble, but Dachau left the most lasting impression on us; we had been schooled in the art of war and now were being exposed to some of its horrors.

From Germany, the Air Force flew us to Rome and then Greece for a firsthand look at the Greek Civil War, then in progress—the anti-Communist forces were using American weapons and American military advisers. It occurred to me more than once during the trip that my average college contemporary was concerned with such things as fraternity parties, whereas we were seeing a large and often unpleasant chunk of the real world. West Point changed my life, giving me unique opportunities to broaden my horizons.

They were to broaden a bit more when we returned and I was assigned to Beast Barracks as a cadet officer in charge of one company, about 150 new cadets. It was my first exposure to command. I didn't allow unnecessary or excessive hazing, and if I thought another upperclassman had gone too far, I'd have a little talk with him. But I didn't pull any punches with those future plebes, either. When it came to rules and discipline there was no buddy-buddy stuff from me and I didn't expect any in return.

All in all, that final year gave me a good exposure to leadership. I was appointed H-1's company commander and also made cadet captain, which put me in charge of about one hundred cadets who ranged from green plebes to fellow first classmen.

The best thing about senior year was becoming head football manager. This time I got to go on all the road trips and I felt more a part of the squad than ever before. We were undefeated that season and we had more than good players—Blaik's assistants included Vince Lombardi, who coached the backfield. I learned a lot about intensity from Lombardi, for even then the man with the alligator teeth was highly emotional and as much a disciplinarian as Blaik himself.

The team ate in a special section of the mess hall and could get pretty raucous and unruly. As varsity manager I was in full charge, and being a cadet captain didn't hurt. I wouldn't take any BS from anybody and that included the stars. I once reamed out Arnold Galiffa, our All-American quarterback, for throwing food. I'll admit I didn't report him, but he never gave me any trouble after that, nor did anyone else on the team. They knew I would turn in anybody if one warning didn't make him behave.

Nostalgia is a bittersweet emotion; you tend to savor memories of happy times while simultaneously missing them because you know they were once-in-a-lifetime experiences. I particularly feel that way about senior year. There was a very special pride in being a first classman; even the officers, our awesome superiors, seemed to accept us as men who had already achieved enough to command their respect and even a kind of cautious camaraderie. I remember that our TAC officer, a Regular Army colonel supervising H-1, toward the end of that final year, would knock on our door, march in—and then squat on a desktop and shoot the breeze with us for an hour. If he was also inspecting us, we never knew it.

By graduation time, I felt I was prepared for the next step in my chosen career. I had put in a tentative preference for the Air Force when I was a second classman. West Point didn't offer any guarantee—only the top graduating cadets were fairly well assured of getting the branch of service they wanted. But I wasn't worried on that score; by senior year I was in the upper 2 percent of my class.

Came that day in May 1950 when all the first classmen marched into the auditorium where they had posted the various branches and the number of available openings. Each cadet walked up to the big bulletin board and listed his first three choices in order of preference.

With fingers mentally crossed, I put down Air Force, engineers, and infantry.

I was on Cloud Nine at 20,000 feet when the postgraduation assignments were handed out—I'd made it. The metamorphosis from that lonely rookie of Beast Barracks to a cadet captain and company commander was complete—and now, assuming I could pass the Air Force physical, my future career seemed assured.

There was only one problem.

Susan.

I can't pinpoint the precise moment when I realized I had really goofed by breaking up with her. I know it began the summer before my final year, just after I returned from the European trip. I had two weeks' leave before reporting to Beast Barracks and those two weeks were not happy ones. The circle of detachment that had begun during plebe year was closed. Even more starkly than on my first leave, I felt out of place in a civilian environment. The ties of boyhood and adolescence had been severed completely, and except for my parents, Tucson and Arizona had lost their appeal. I actually felt like a stranger in my own hometown and it didn't help when I found that Susan was going with some guy.

We had at least kept up an unproductive correspondence, and when she'd entered the University of Pennsylvania to study dental hygiene, she had come up to West Point a couple of times. They hadn't been successful dates, unfortunately, but my juices had started flowing again. She had matured into a beautiful young woman, but she had also acquired a whole new set of boyfriends. By the time I decided I had made one hell of a mistake, she had already reduced this platoon down to one special suitor.

In the spring of senior year, I wrote to Susan that I had been a dumb cluck, let's take up where we left off, and how about coming to West Point for June Week and my graduation?

I received in return a very nice letter, the gist of it being thanks, but no thanks, so get lost. My parents arrived for graduation, and although I was both glad and proud they had come, I envied my classmates. The place was crawling with upperclassmen's girlfriends and fiancées, Flirtation Walk looked like a Los Angeles freeway during rush hour, and I was so stricken with unrequited love that I wouldn't go to any June Week social events, including the dances.

It helped a little, but not much, that I was the proud owner of my first brand-new automobile. First classmen were allowed to order new cars from nearby dealers at a special discount. I ordered a new Olds Rocket 88—sky-blue, with a V8 engine and a stick shift. It cost just under two thousand bucks and most of this came from my grandfather and parents as a graduation gift. I had also saved about six hundred dollars, but I spent three hundred of that nest egg to buy Susan a small engagement ring—one I had actually ordered by mail earlier that year, when I confidently figured I'd be getting married like so many graduating cadets.

I doubt if any of the other 669 new second lieutenants paid any more attention to the graduation speaker than I did. What I do remember most is the corps passing in review before the graduates; I had tears in my eyes and I'm not ashamed to admit it. To this day I get emotional thinking about West Point. It has been an anchor all my life, and when I die I want to be buried there.

I had mixed thoughts that day. Thoughts about tomorrow and the life ahead of me, the chance to put all I had been taught and had assimilated into an actual career. But also thoughts about Susan. Winning her was a mission yet unaccomplished and I was determined to convince her that she, too, had made a mistake.

Mother, Dad, and I drove back to Tucson in the Olds. I had sixty days' leave before reporting for flight training, and less than thirty days into that leave I found how lucky the cadets who had chosen the Air Force were. The North Koreans had crossed the 38th Parallel. We were at war again and criminally unprepared, as it turned out.

Susan was in Tucson when we got home. She had earned her dental hygiene degree at the University of Pennsylvania and was planning to spend the summer in Tucson before getting a liberal arts degree at the University of Arizona. The first thing I did was to call her and talk her into going out.

"We need to talk," I pleaded.

We went out that night and it was as if nothing had happened—my impetuous letter breaking things off, the few disappointing dates at West Point, her cool rejection of the June Week invitation, or, for that matter, the guy she was dating. My proposal was accepted in an Italian restaurant on the outskirts of Tucson. The owner must have noticed we were not only having a wonderful time but were obviously in love, because he kept putting coins into the jukebox and flooding the place with dreamy music.

I went through the formality of asking Susan's mother for her approval—this was 1950 when such things were considered not only proper but essential. So most of that summer leave was spent getting ready for the wedding. On July 20, 1950, Susan Bugbee became Mrs. Frank Borman; her mother gave us a beautiful wedding in an Episcopal church, St. Philip's in the Hills, and friends from both West Point and our high school days attended. Wayne Crutchfield was best man.

We had a one-week honeymoon before I was to report to my first duty station, Perrin Air Force Base in Sherman, Texas. We spent our wedding night in Phoenix, then drove the Olds north to the rim of the Grand Canyon and on to Las Vegas. On the way to the canyon, we stopped at an Indian reservation and I bought Susan, as my own wedding gift, three pieces of Indian jewelry—a turquoise necklace, bracelet, and ring.

I'm afraid we never discussed or even thought about the problems Susan might have as a military wife, married to a brand-new second lieutenant subject to constant transfers for years to come—life with no roots, and with friends as peripatetic as we. No, we went charging forward without worrying about possible, even probable, difficulties ahead.

We had embarked on a whole new adventure, wearing the armor plate of youth, optimism, enthusiasm, and love. The marriage we launched almost four decades ago still is intact and our love remains as strong as it was then. Maybe even stronger, because it has been tested so often and tempered in so many crucibles.

And one of those crucibles was a life in which death became an ever-present companion of the living.

Most airmen, if they're honest with themselves, believe in fate. They will lie about, rationalize, and deny the fact that they are not always in complete control, but in their hearts they know this to be the truth. They insist that pilots who are killed simply made mistakes, and usually unforgivable mistakes. This apparent callousness toward the tragedies that always seem to hit the other guy is merely an airman's defense mechanism—the wishful thinking, the whistling-by-the-graveyard conviction that it only happens to somebody else.

Pilots talk themselves into believing they're impervious, but I don't know of a single one who really believes it. I include myself. In my own gut, I knew this was a mere fabrication. I could glibly explain away someone else's accident, but I knew damned well it could happen to me. I've disparaged and criticized the poor shmuck who

"bought the farm," but even while I was calling him a dumb bastard, I wasn't kidding myself. Half the time we denied the existence
of fate to reassure not only our worried wives but ourselves. The
philosophy of "it won't happen to me" breeds complacency, and
complacency has killed more pilots than cancer.

And as I began my Air Force career, death would form the heavy,
invisible cross Susan was to carry on her shoulders for the next twenty
years.

3

HOW TO BE A FIGHTER PILOT IN A FEW HUNDRED LESSONS

On a hot, muggy August day at Perrin AFB, I was introduced to the first Air Force plane I ever flew. The North American T-6 basic trainer, known as the Texan, intimidated me at first. To my inexperienced eyes it seemed so huge, such a complicated monster, I wondered if I'd ever be able to master it. Yet by the end of the nearly six months I spent in basic flight training, the Texan had become a winged baby carriage.

Until the newly independent Air Force got its own academy, the Pentagon was sending it 25 percent of each West Point and Annapolis graduating class. But being a service academy alumnus didn't get anyone in our group a free set of wings or special treatment. The attrition rate, in fact, was brutal—more than 50 percent washed out. A lot of egos were bruised to such an extent that some washouts claimed the Air Force had discriminated against service school graduates. A short time after I left Perrin, I was called to testify before a commission investigating the discrimination charge. I said there hadn't been any discrimination that I could see.

"Do you think these men should be given a second chance?" one officer asked.

"No, sir, I don't."

They didn't attach much importance to my testimony, because the washouts got another shot. And I heard later almost every one of them had a serious or fatal accident after graduating.

The T-6s at Perrin had all been built during the war and most of them were showing signs of age. If you were lucky enough to draw a fairly new Texan, you were in clover; if you got one of the war-wearies, you prayed hard that your instructor had climbed out of the right side of his bed that morning—a T-6 with high mileage could have given Lindbergh gray hairs.

I was taking an aerobatic check ride one morning in a T-6 whose engine had seen better days. The Pratt and Whitney R-1340 engine on the Texan was rated at a healthy 550 horsepower, but this particular one was suffering from overage pistons and other internal ailments. My instructor on this occasion was a second lieutenant named Gay who had just gone through Perrin himself.

One of the maneuvers required during an aerobatic check was a loop, and to complete the loop you were supposed to keep your manifold pressure at a prescribed level, never deviating from that setting—in other words, don't touch the throttle because the book says do it by the numbers. Well, I started into the top of the loop and the damned plane stalled out.

"That's not the proper entry technique," Gay scolded over the intercom. "I'll show you how it's done."

He went into a loop and completed it perfectly. But I had been watching him carefully and I noticed that as he'd neared the top of the loop, he had added more throttle—which wasn't doing it by the numbers.

"Sir," I said meekly, "would you mind showing me that again?"

"Sure," Gay agreed cordially. "Like I said, there's nothing to it if you do it right."

He began his second loop. He forgot, however, that the T-6 had dual controls moving simultaneously. And as the plane approached the loop's peak, I grabbed *my* throttle, holding it so tightly that he couldn't move *his*. Caught by surprise, he couldn't react in time to override what I had done.

The inevitable happened. Gay stalled out, too. He never said another word and gave me an excellent rating.

We had fun at Perrin. The instructors were decent and helpful, we did a lot of socializing, and I even resumed building and flying model airplanes. We had rented a one-bedroom house and the only un-happy moment came when Susan had a miscarriage. Except for los-ing the baby, the six months in Texas went well and quickly. The top students earned a special privilege: their choice of the branch of Air Force flying they preferred. I picked fighter training, for which my instructors had recommended me, and was duly notified to re-port to Williams Air Force Base in Chandler, Arizona, just outside of Phoenix. I was a firm believer in the old Air Force saying "There are only two kinds of airmen—fighter pilots and targets."

So we headed for Williams in the Olds.

It was at Williams that Lieutenant and Mrs. Frank Borman got their first real taste of the downside of military life. The national housing shortage that had developed after World War II was still very much in evidence and the Korean War hadn't eased the situa-tion. So we ended up in a rather dingy trailer—the polite term was *mobile home*—whose only virtue was its proximity to the base. Su-san was pregnant again, cursed with morning sickness, but she never uttered a word of complaint about the sorry living conditions.

I reported to the group training commander at Williams—the meanest, toughest, most ornery son of a bitch I've ever met in my whole life. His name was Leon Gray; a full colonel, he was a Uni-versity of Arizona graduate who had played football at Tucson High under Gridley.

On our first day of duty at Williams, we were called into the base auditorium to hear Gray welcome his new Air Force officers, most of them newlyweds, to fighter training. He glared at us and began, "Now all you bastards know there's a war on, so I don't give a damn about your personal problems. I don't wanna hear about them. As far as I'm concerned, your wives are government property who should be turned in at each base and a brand-new one checked out at the next base.

"If you screw up in an airplane, don't give me any crap about being distracted because your wife had morning sickness or her men-strual period—that's your problem, not mine. All I'm interested in is turning you into the best fighter pilots in the world. Take a good look around you, because chances are the guy next to you is either gonna be washed out or dead."

He paused, a tiny sliver of a smile peeking out from the corner of his stern lips.

"Those of you who still want to stay," he finished, "welcome to Williams Air Force Base!"

Gray wasn't a big man—he was about my height, in fact—but he was powerfully built, with a jaw shaped like the prow of a battleship. I couldn't count the number of times he emptied the officers' club at Williams with a fistfight. But the guy could fly—he was the quintessential fighter pilot, a loner personifying what was then the USAF's unofficial motto: Every Man a Tiger.

During World War II, he'd flown P-38 reconnaissance missions in Elliott Roosevelt's squadron, and only his friendship with the president's son protected him from brass wrath when he got into scrapes. He was the kind of guy you'd want on your side during war, but in peacetime nobody knew what to do with him. Gray used to stand at the end of the runway at Williams and throw rocks at anyone who made a poor landing. He was one of the few pilots I ever knew who wasn't afraid of thunderstorms—he'd take an airplane up in the middle of one and buzz the field back and forth.

How he avoided constant reprimand was a mystery. Maybe it was because Gray's immediate boss, General Moe Spicer, also was from Arizona and cut roughly out of the same cloth. The general, our base commander, was a big guy with a handlebar mustache who had mellowed somewhat by the time I got to Williams, but we heard plenty of stories about his previous exploits.

Spicer, too, subscribed to the Every Man a Tiger creed that seemed to be embodied in the training curriculum itself. Even routine approaches were supposed to be conducted with a hell-bent flair, yet now as I look back on my Williams experience, I think this kind of philosophy in training was pretty dumb. And eventually the Air Force also got to think that way. Carried too far, it didn't produce better fighter pilots and it killed a few, too. This attitude was not altogether bad, because a certain amount of cockiness and confidence goes with the territory, but it could be dangerous. Gray used to look daggers at you if you preflighted an airplane—inspected it before takeoff—and he set the example for the instructors. I was only too ready, willing, and eager to be as much of a tiger as the next guy, a habit I fortunately outgrew gradually.

We started ground school, but Gray figured we had too much idle time, so he put the whole class to work painting latrines and mowing grass. Most of my classmates were furious. Here they were, officers in the United States Air Force, doing menial chores that would have teed off an enlisted man. You could hear the gripes all the way back to the Hudson River, and this teed *me* off. I told one of the guys, "Look, if I gotta paint a latrine, I'll paint the goddamned thing and I'll do it right."

"It's degrading," he sputtered.

"The hell is it," I retorted. "It's a job."

We were introduced to another military airplane at Williams—the T-28 Trojan, also a North American Aviation product about the same size as the T-6 but almost seventy miles per hour faster under full throttle.

We spent three months flying Trojans and then made a quantum leap up to our first jet: the Lockheed F-80, which in 1951 was still a first-line fighter and pretty hot stuff for us greenhorns.

One of our training missions was a flight to Nellis Air Force Base in Las Vegas, Nevada. We were cruising along, enjoying the scenery, when from out of nowhere came a group of snarling P-51 Mustangs, probably the best piston-engine fighters of World War II. They jumped us, a mock dogfight ensued, and there were P-51s and F-80s twisting and turning all over the sky, everyone trying to get on the other guy's tail.

We had jet speed on our side, but those Mustangs could turn on a dime and give you change. I got one all lined up in my sights when he just rolled away and gave me nothing but empty air to look at. We were too inexperienced to really dominate them, but even so we gave those Mustangs some healthy competition, and when we landed at Nellis their flight leader walked over to me.

"Nice show, lieutenant," he grinned. "My name's Alex Butterfield."

I was to remember that name years later. Alex Butterfield became head of the Federal Aviation Administration during the Nixon regime and was the man who first revealed the existence of the White House Watergate tapes.

Our baby was due in October and I was due to graduate in late August. I ranked second in my class, giving me my choice of where I'd take advanced fighter training before being sent to Korea. There were two nearby bases from which to choose—Luke AFB in Phoenix and Nellis. We naturally preferred Phoenix, and luckily we found an apartment for when the baby arrived. I also bought unfinished baby furniture, which I painted, and we were all set.

After I graduated I was assigned to temporary duty in headquarters, and one day Colonel Gray marched in.

"Borman," he ordered, "schedule Joe Jones [not his real name] for a check ride."

"Yes, sir."

I got the guy's folder, did a double take, and went into Gray's office. "Colonel, Jones has already graduated."

"I don't give a damn!" Gray barked. "Didn't you hear what I said? Schedule him for a check ride."

"Look, Colonel, he's not only graduated but he's just waiting to go to Nellis."

Gray turned purple. "Borman, I'm not gonna tell you one more goddamned time. Put that jerk in an airplane. I wanna go flying with him this afternoon."

There was no use in arguing the point further, so I contacted Jones. "You have to take a check ride with Colonel Gray this afternoon."

"But I've already graduated," Jones said logically.

I sighed. "I don't know why, but you'd better show up for that ride or it's your butt."

Gray took him up that same day and washed him out. I found out later that Gray had been told Jones was a malingerer, and added to this report was a letter Gray had received from some congressman, complaining that Jones, a reserve officer, should have been given a regular commission.

Many years later, when I was senior vice president of Operations at Eastern, our chief pilot came into my office.

"We've got a real bad actor flying for us," he informed me. "He's a deadbeat, a malingerer, and a lousy pilot. With your permission, I'd like to get rid of him."

"Who is it?" I asked.

"Captain Joe Jones. Incidentally, he's been demanding to see you and I hope you won't."

My memory bell clanged. I said, "I think I'll have a talk with him."

When Jones showed up, he didn't recognize me. He started telling me he was being persecuted, and I finally interrupted.

"Let me tell you something, Captain Jones. You don't remember me, but I remember you. I'm the guy who set you up for that check ride you botched with Leon Gray. You were a deadbeat then and I understand you're still a deadbeat. So don't bother me with your complaints."

In requesting assignment to Luke, I had also put in for a thirty-day leave so I could be with Susan when the baby was born. It was early September when we moved into the new apartment and all I had to do was sweat out the next month—I thought.

One day I went out to Luke to see if any mail had been forwarded from Williams. It was a Saturday morning and I walked up to a sergeant in the orderly room.

"I'm Lieutenant Borman, Sergeant. I'll be reporting to Luke in a few weeks and I just dropped by to check on whether there's any mail for me."

He gave me a curiously sympathetic look. "Lieutenant," he said, "you shouldn't have come out here today."

"Why not?"

"Because I've got orders to grab the first four new officers I can find and transfer 'em to Nellis. You're to report there Monday morning."

"Wait a minute," I protested. "I've got orders assigning me to Luke."

He shrugged. "Excuse me, sir, but those orders don't mean a thing."

I went home and told Susan the bad news. "You're going to have to stay here," I added.

"I won't," she said defiantly. "Frank, you're going to Korea in another four months and I refuse to be separated from you until you leave."

We rented a U-Haul trailer, notified our landlord we were surrendering our apartment lease along with the advance payment, and late that same Saturday night we were on the way to Las Vegas. We got there around 6 A.M. and found a motel where I got Susan settled, then I went out to buy a local newspaper. I found only one apartment for rent listed in the classified section, called the number, apologized for waking the landlady who answered, and told her we'd take it.

So here I was at Nellis with a wife eight months pregnant and some very tough training ahead. The Every Man a Tiger attitude so prevalent at Williams was even worse at Nellis, and the result was the highest accident rate in the Air Force. Nellis, in fact, was losing more pilots in training than the Air Force was in Korean combat.

I had never fired a gun during my entire six months at Williams. Now I had to learn how to use the airplane as a deadly weapon. Dive bombing, skip bombing, air-to-air targets, either with camera guns or firing live ammunition at towed target sleeves. Low-level strafing. Combat formations and combat maneuvers.

We flew F-80s equipped with wingtip tanks, usually holding 165 gallons but some of them large enough to accommodate 230 gallons. The bigger tanks caused trouble—they didn't have baffles installed at first, and if you took off without a full load, the fuel would start sloshing around and the aircraft's critical center of gravity (CG) would go back and forth like a horizontal Yo-Yo.

Over the Labor Day weekend while we were there, six guys were killed in accidents. But the intensive training went on, every practice mission as dangerous as the next. The theory was that if you were put through the worst in training, you were better able to survive combat. There was some merit in this—it's the philosophy behind Marine, paratrooper, and ranger training—but applying it to a 600-mph airplane manned by inexperienced pilots is another matter.

Our son Frederick was born October 4, 1951. I was flying night and day, but I was at the hospital when he was born. The first time I saw my son, a big smiling black GI wearing combat boots was holding him up for my inspection, looking just as proud as I was.

I graduated on December 4 of that year, and naturally I wanted to get in some more flying time before my Korean orders came through. Foolishly, I took an F-80 up on a practice dive-bombing mission when I had a bad cold, and ruptured an eardrum.

The flight surgeon told me I was grounded for at least six weeks, and furthermore, I would be held at Nellis until the eardrum healed.

"The hell with that," I argued. "I want to go overseas with the guys I trained with." We were supposed to go to Camp Stoneman, California, the embarkation point where Korean-bound pilots were processed, and then to Travis AFB near San Francisco for air transportation. But my orders were to proceed only to Stoneman and wait for the next available sea transportation; those same orders included the dreaded words "No flying."

I took Susan and the baby back to Tucson, where they'd stay with her mother until my Korean tour of duty was finished. I was to report to Stoneman no later than December 19, which meant no Christmas leave, and when I said good-bye to my wife and infant son it was the saddest day of my young life.

I waited until the last minute to leave for Stoneman, forcing me to take an unpressurized commercial flight instead of the bus. We made two landings between Tucson and San Francisco, further damaging the eardrum.

At Stoneman, I found my orders had been changed. The Pentagon had decided to stop sending new fighter pilots into the Korean combat zone until they had received additional training with squadrons based in Japan, Okinawa, or the Philippines.

On December 20, I boarded the transport USS *Ainsworth*—a lonely second lieutenant in a dark mood, with a busted eardrum and a flying career hanging by a thread.

I was heading for the Philippines.

It took the *Ainsworth* twenty-one days to crawl from San Francisco to Manila.

We docked in Honolulu on December 24, and our Christmas Eve present was four hours ashore. I found my way to the Royal Hawaiian Hotel—it was the only Honolulu public landmark I knew of, and hotels had public phones. Into a lobby phone booth I went, armed with a fistful of coins. I was so anxious that I left the booth door open.

"I'd like to place a person-to-person call to Tucson, Arizona," I told the operator.

"I'm sorry, sir, but Christmas Eve calls to the mainland have been booked for months. There's no way you can get through."

"I've got almost four hours to wait," I assured her.

"Four weeks is what you'd need" was her response.

I left the phone booth and stood morosely in the lobby for a few seconds. Just as I was about to walk toward the exit, I felt a tap on my shoulder. I turned to find a well-dressed, middle-aged man smiling at me.

"Lieutenant, is there anything wrong?"

I'll never know why I suddenly unburdened myself to a complete stranger—maybe it was because he just looked so damned sympathetic—but I told him my story.

"I've only got three more hours before my transport leaves," I added. "All I wanted to do was wish my wife a merry Christmas."

He nodded sympathetically. "Look, son, I'm the manager of the Royal Hawaiian. Give me that phone number you were trying to reach. Meanwhile, you just stay right here and don't you dare move until I get back."

He returned five minutes later and handed me a key. "Lieutenant, you go up to this room and just pick up the phone. Incidentally, you can talk for the whole three hours if you want to."

I followed his instructions, picked up the phone, and started to ask for the long-distance operator when a voice interrupted.

"Hello, darling."

It was Susan.

We talked for more than an hour, one of the most precious hours in my life. Then I went down to the manager's office and tried to pay him for the call, but he refused.

I disembarked in Manila with four other pilots—the rest were going on to Okinawa and Japan. I had been assigned to the 44th Fighter/ Bomber Squadron based at Clark Field, the only operational fighter outfit in Southeast Asia because everything else was in Korea. The 44th's primary mission was to fly patrols around the Philippines, mostly looking for Russian submarines, but the squadron also flew a regular schedule of practice missions, starting with a week of air-to-air gunnery. The second week it was air-to-ground, and the third week involved dropping live bombs. Every fourth week the 44th stood fighter alert over Formosa. It was a fighter pilot's heaven, but my eardrum hadn't been cleared through the pearly gates yet.

I reported in to one of the most remarkable officers I've ever known. The 44th's commander was a major named Charles McGee, a man who has remained a good friend to this day. He had more combat time than I had flying time—during World War II, McGee had served in an all-black squadron that fought with distinction in the Italian theater.

All five of us new pilots marched into his office, saluted, and stood at attention. McGee looked us over and said calmly, "I'm glad to have you people. Our job is to teach you to get ready for Korea. We have a good squadron here and we run it tight. I know you've been in a lot of outfits where they tell you, 'You play ball with me and I'll play ball with you.' Well, gentlemen, we don't do it that way here. My rule is simply, You play ball with me or I'll ram a bat up your ass."

McGee, knowing my determination to get back into the air, gave me permission to see the flight surgeon, who informed me I had the worst ear he had ever seen and added, "You're never going to fly again."

With my flying career handed a death sentence, I volunteered as a forward air observer in Korea. Rejected. Then I asked for a transfer back to the Army—I couldn't see myself staying in the Air Force flying a desk. Rejected again. So the fighter pilot without wings spent the next nine months assigned to Clark Field's facilities squadron.

I was in charge of about fifteen hundred soldiers and civilians responsible for Clark's maintenance—roads, grounds, plumbing, painting, and carpentry. I drilled the troops in perimeter defense, served on a board investigating thefts of cameras from the PX, and once kept a lovesick sergeant from marrying a known prostitute. I was miserable, yet I worked hard at whatever they gave me.

One of my tasks was to check on the readiness of some heavy equipment stored in a huge warehouse—bulldozers, trucks, graders, and so forth. It was supposed to be available quickly if needed, but when I went to the warehouse for an inspection, there wasn't a vehicle or a piece of equipment that wasn't in deplorable shape—most of it unusable without major overhauls. The stuff had been there since the end of the war and obviously hadn't been touched since.

The captain in charge of the warehouse asked me to sign off the material as being in good condition. I not only refused but did some asking around, and learned he spent most of his time playing golf. Furious, I went to his top boss, a colonel, and demanded that the SOB be court-martialed.

The colonel just laughed. "Don't worry about all that junk, Lieutenant. Captain Green [not his real name] happens to be an excellent officer who simply has too much to do, and he didn't have time to worry about that old warehouse."

"Captain Green has plenty of time to play golf," I retorted.

The smile on the colonel's face dissolved into a frown. "Borman, you're just an eager young pup. I want all that stuff written off and you can forget about it."

This was the dark side of the military, that minority of officers whose indifference and sheer laziness set a pathetic example for the enlisted personnel under their command, not to mention their fellow officers.

I talked to Susan periodically on the armed forces shortwave network, and when I felt established enough, I sent for my little family. The procedure for married officers was to request housing, and if this could be arranged, my wife and son could come over by boat— and only by boat if they were traveling at government expense.

As soon as I located a house, I called Susan and warned that if she didn't get to Manila by a certain date, I'd lose it. At this point Fred became seriously ill, and by the time he recovered, our timetable was demolished.

"Susan, sell the damned car," I told her. "That'll bring enough to pay your air fare from Tucson to Manila."

She sold our Olds for fifteen hundred dollars and bought a one-way ticket on Pan Am; suddenly the world became a great deal brighter. Our house, right on the base, was small but comfortable, and I was promoted to first lieutenant. The only dark cloud was my non-flying status.

As the flight surgeon patiently explained it, the eardrum is a three-ply affair and the rupture that had occurred in my left ear had torn all three plies, destroying two of them completely.

"What you have left is a single ply. You've built up a protective deposit over that remaining ply, but it's still too narrow and thin. You'd pop the drum the first time you flew."

"What the hell can I do about it?" I implored. "Isn't there some kind of new treatment? Even if it's experimental, I'll try anything."

"Well, there's a Filipino doctor you might see. She studied radiology at the Curie Institute in Paris. You could ask her to try radium treatments, though frankly, Lieutenant, I don't think it'll do a damned bit of good."

So six times over the next month and a half, I rode a GI bus to the clinic where the physician had her office. Then I went back to the flight surgeon, who examined the ear again and shook his head.

"It's very hard to tell whether the radium made that much difference. The layer's intact but I still think it'll pop again if you fly."

I went to McGee and pleaded my case.

"Look, Major, they admit my ear's healed, but they claim it'll rupture again if I fly. I'm in a Catch-22 bind—the flight surgeon won't give me permission to take up a plane, yet if I don't try it, I'll never know for sure. Sir, I need an airplane ride in the worst way."

McGee, God bless him, didn't hesitate. "Okay, first I'll take you up in a T-6 and see how that goes."

We flew around in the old trainer for about an hour and my ear felt fine. The next day we took a second ride, same result. Then McGee took me up in a T-33 and put the jet through the wringer. Still no problem. After we landed, McGee gently suggested, "Better go see the flight surgeon again. And tell him the truth."

I didn't tell him the truth right away. I just asked him to check the ear once more. After the examination, all I got was the same head shake and dubious expression. "Well, the ear looks the same. At least that layer's intact, but I still feel . . ."

I interrupted his familiar refrain. "Doc, you might as well know I've been flying with McGee, once in a T-33."

To his credit he didn't regard my announcement as an insult to his medical abilities. All he did was smile a little grimly. "I'll need verification from McGee on that T-33 ride."

On November 7, 1952, the commanding general of the Far East Air Forces received the report of a flying evaluation board that had "convened at Clark Air Force Base on 22 September 1952, in the case of First Lieutenant Frank Borman, 20116A." It concluded that "subject officer has been returned to flying status."

My flying career had been saved.

I hadn't flown solo since late 1951 and McGee brought me along gradually and very patiently, until he felt I was ready to become a full-fledged member of the 44th.

Yet that damn tiger in me still wasn't satisfied. I volunteered for combat duty in Korea and was turned down because F-80 pilots weren't needed there. I applied to join an F-86 Sabrejet squadron and I struck out again; to fly the F-86, I'd have to go back to Nellis for transitional training, and the Air Force already had enough Sabrejet pilots. That added up to four futile attempts to get to Korea and I decided it just wasn't meant to be.

So I settled down with the 44th Squadron, and it wasn't a bad life. One of our jobs under a new commander was ferrying reconditioned F-80s from Japan to Clark. McGee by this time had been transferred out, much to everyone's disappointment, although the new commander was a good man.

His deputy commander, however, was a Major Roberts (not his real name), an airline pilot who had been called back into the Air Force from the reserves. Relatively old for his rank, he had a lot of flying hours yet virtually none in jets. When I drew one of the ferry missions, he invited himself along. We were supposed to ferry back a couple of overhauled F-80s from Katchatawa AFB to Clark via Itazuki in Japan, Okinawa, and Tainan in Formosa.

I was flying Roberts's wing and he was supposed to be navigating as the lead pilot. We didn't have any VOR or radio range equipment, just automatic direction finders (ADF), and things went to hell in a hurry when we ran into a huge thunderstorm belt that had us flying into turbulent pea soup.

I was trying to backstop his navigation but I had to give it up—I was having too much trouble staying on his wing because he was wandering all over the sky. It was getting very bumpy and I finally called him on my radio.

"Tomato One, how are you doing?"

"We're doing fine," he reassured me.

A few minutes later, he called me.

"Tomato Two, take the lead."

"What's wrong, Tomato One?"

"My ADF's out."

I glanced at my own ADF. It was spinning wildly—we were smack in the middle of the storm area, our F-80s bucking so hard I couldn't read the instruments.

"Tomato One, my ADF is out, too. Where are we?"

"I'm not sure."

Our VHF radios had eight channels and I tried all of them; all I could get were reports from other planes in trouble. I tried the emergency channel to report we were lost, but all I heard was static.

By now we were running low on fuel and I decided it was time to push the panic button. I assumed the lead (and his call letters) and over the emergency channel transmitted the first SOS of my brief career.

"Mayday! Mayday! This is Tomato One. Unsure of our position and we're low on fuel."

Through all the unsympathetic and unheeding static came an Australian voice.

"Tomato One. Hey there, mate—don't worry. We have excellent VHF-DF [radio director finder] capability here and we'll vector you in."

"Where's here?"

"Iwakuni, mate, right outside Hiroshima."

"Roger, but my ADF's haywire."

"No problem, mate. Just keep transmitting and we'll put a DF on your signal."

Hiroshima was halfway to Itazuki. By homing in on my transmitter signal, the Aussie could triangulate it with the direction finder and give us the right heading into Iwakuni. The weather was still foul, but the major managed to hang on to my wing and our Australian savior finally handed us over to ground-controlled approach (GCA), which began talking us down. GCA limits were a 200-foot ceiling and a quarter mile of visibility, but we didn't have 200 feet to work with when we came in.

We broke out of the overcast at about 100 feet, and I positioned the F-80 to land between what appeared to be runway markers. Just in time I recognized them for what they really were—the boundaries of a seaplane lane that paralleled the runway. I came within fifty feet of flying both of us into the water, for the totally dependent major was right behind me.

I got out of my plane after we landed and let the deputy commander of the 44th Fighter/Bomber Squadron know exactly how I felt.

"You're a dumb son of a bitch and you almost got us killed," I growled. "From now on maybe I'd better lead this flight unless you have some objection."

"Lieutenant," he said, "I couldn't agree with you more. Let's go get a drink."

"Not until I buy that Aussie controller a bottle," I said.

We walked into the operations office on shaky legs, made arrangements for refueling, then went out and bought a couple of fifths of Scotch for our Australian friend and the GCA operator who had talked us down. The next morning we heard that five pilots had been killed flying in the same storm.

I figured it all made for a happy ending, but I didn't count on my major screwing up again. We waited overnight at Iwakuni for the weather to clear, flew to Itazuki without incident, and were supposed to stay there until an SA-16 Dumbo—a patrol plane—showed up to escort us to Okinawa. We were told there'd be no SA-16 available for a week, so we left anyway, refueled at the historic island, and took off for Tainan in southern Formosa.

We were cruising at 35,000 feet in clear weather when all of a sudden the major's radio communications ceased. I flew closer to Tomato Two and saw that his cockpit canopy was completely frosted over. Just when I was wondering what in the hell had gone wrong this time, he wrote with his finger on the frost, backward so I could read it: BAT [battery] OUT.

He had lost his generator, which on an F-80 meant he'd also lost the electric boost pump that transferred fuel. All he had available was the fuel in his tip tanks, which he had been using up rapidly, and there was no way he could transfer fuel from the wing tanks. Now we were in deep manure again.

I knew we couldn't get into Tainan with the fuel he had left, so I diverted to a closer base in central Formosa. I assumed he realized that, with his fuel so low, he'd have to get down in a hurry, straight in.

I went in first, then pulled up with my gear and flaps down, and circled slowly so he could land as quickly as possible ahead of me. The dumb bastard put *his* gear and flaps down and followed me around in that slow circle. He finally landed and ran out of fuel as he was rolling down the runway.

Looking back on the two years I spent in the Philippines, I'd have to say they were a mixture of fun and frustration. At one stage, I was appointed squadron gunnery officer, putting me in charge of making sure our F-80 guns fired where they were supposed to fire. It wasn't a simple matter, because we had to take into account so-called harmonizing—coordinating the airspeed with the aircraft's deck angle so the bullets would hit at 1,000 feet right where our line of sight intersected with the target.

While I'd been at Nellis, I had seen a fighter newsletter outlining the best way to harmonize aircraft guns. But when I got to the Philippines, no one had heard of the adjustment technique. The newsletter had suggested that the airplane be jacked up to the angle reached at 360 knots, the airspeed judged the most effective for correct harmonizing. At the 44th, they were still boresighting with mirrors, and that's a very ineffective way to aim a machine gun.

I sold the squadron on the airplane-jacking procedure, but in order to see whether the bullets were hitting properly, we needed something to catch the slugs. I asked the engineering construction battalion to build us an abutment. I filled out enough requisition and justification forms to paper Grand Central Station and sent them to the construction battalion.

Back came the verdict: "Disapproved."

I called a guy at the battalion and asked why.

"Because we're building a golf course for the commanding general," he told me. "We haven't the time for your abutment."

Our second son, Edwin, was born July 20, 1953, in a Quonset hut that served as Clark Field's hospital. The labor room was in a separate Quonset hut and from there Susan was wheeled along an open-air walkway into the main hut, where the delivery room was located.

Toward the end of my Philippine tour, they made me squadron baseball coach—why, I'll never know, because my grasp of baseball strategy was limited to knowing that Babe Ruth wasn't a candy bar. We had one really good player, our squadron clerk, who had some semipro experience. He broke his ankle sliding into second base, and while the injury didn't keep him from his clerking duties, I had to fill out the requisite ground safety report.

When I came to the line "Cause of accident," I wrote in, "Act of God."

This terrifies people in the safety business because they don't believe there is such a thing as an act of God. In due time, I was summoned to appear before the Clark Field ground safety officer, a beefy major who couldn't have done two laps around his own living room.

He waved my report in front of my face. "Lieutenant, this won't do."

"What's wrong with it, sir?"

"You cannot attribute an athletic accident to an act of God. You have to blame it on inadequate training or improper equipment."

"Sir, the man's a former semipro baseball player and he just caught his spikes on the bag. Ninety-nine times out of a hundred it wouldn't have happened, so that's why I called it an act of God."

"Unsatisfactory," he declared firmly. "I won't accept anything as nebulous as an act of God."

"Fine, sir. You tell me what to write under 'Cause of accident' and I'll write it. Then I'm going over to the inspector general's office and inform them you made me fill out an improper report."

His face turned tomato-red. He hemmed and hawed and finally said, "All right—make it an act of God."

I felt very self-righteous about the whole thing, but without realizing it, I had shot myself in the foot. It turned out the major was also a transportation officer and the SOB didn't forget my name. When it came time to leave the Philippines, instead of going by air like most of the pilots and their families, Susan and I were assigned to a troopship.

4

CHANGE OF COURSE

". . . Subject officer is to report to Moody AFB, Valdosta, Georgia, to teach instrument flying. Housing at this base is unavailable to personnel with families and housing in Valdosta is extremely tight so it is recommended that said officer travel without his family."

Susan and the kids came along anyway, in a secondhand Olds my father had picked out for me. We stayed in a Valdosta motel until our money ran out, spent a month in a sleazy tourist camp with a single central toilet and bathing facility, and then found a tiny prefab house. We paid seventy dollars a month in rent and we were being overcharged; some landlords around military bases have a propensity for screwing servicemen, and Valdosta was no exception.

The prefab was located on the edge of a snake-infested swamp and the neighbors warned us not to let the kids play in the backyard. Even without the snakes, the yard wasn't much of a play area anyway—during the rainy season, it turned into a small lake.

There were no curtains in the house, so we hung khaki GI blankets over the windows. And all the while, under these miserable living conditions, Susan never uttered one word of complaint. We stayed there three months and finally were able to rent a reasonably priced

home—small but modern, with a backyard overlooking a cornfield;
I repainted all the rooms, added a small screened porch that I built
myself, and also ruined a new lawnmower clearing the backyard.

Valdosta in 1953 was a red-neck town, typical of the Deep South
of that era. The segregated black school there was such a disgrace
that a number of officers' wives at Moody got together and tried to
fix it up—a gesture that went unappreciated by the white community.

I came out of the house late one morning to go to work on the
afternoon shift and was talking to some of our neighbors when a
car roared through the subdivision doing about seventy miles an hour.
I chased it in my own car through God knows how many stop signs,
and finally forced it over to the curb. The driver seemed to be in his
twenties and he was blind drunk, one of those belligerently unpre-
dictable drunks.

I wasn't sure what the bastard would do if I hauled him out of
the car, so I just took down his license number, went to the police
station, and reported the incident. A potbellied policeman checked
the license number and just chuckled.

"Oh, that's ole Billy Bob's son. He has a little drinking problem,
but he ain't hurt nobody yet."

"That drunken ape could have killed children!" I sputtered.

The cop smiled, but it was a tight, humorless smile that suddenly
dissolved with the narrowing of his eyes.

"You're just a Yankee Air Force officer," he drawled. "If I was
you, son, I'd just go home and forget it."

And that was what stood for justice in a southern town in the
1950s.

I worked hard at Moody, even accepting double shifts so I could
make up for all the flying hours I had missed while I was grounded.
I did catch up, in spades, and in the process I became a damned
good jet instrument instructor. I discovered, however, that Air Force
training still hadn't changed much. We had a lot of accidents at
Moody, and we lost some people for reasons we never really knew.

Susan was coming out of the base commissary one morning and
saw an F-89 Scorpion fighter collide with a T-33 head on. Both were
two-seater aircraft and she watched as only three parachutes came
down, one of them just partially open.

She figured this was about the time I'd be taking off, leading a
group of students on an overnight cross-country training mission.

She drove to the nearby farmer's field where she had seen the chutes drop, and was climbing over the fence when an enlisted man grabbed her arm.

"Lady," he said not unkindly, "get your ass home."

Numbly, she obeyed. My commanding officer, Major Ken Taylor, and his wife, Shirley, lived next door to us and Susan drove to their house first.

"Shirley, I just saw a midair and I think the planes were from our squadron. I want to find out if Frank was in one of them."

Shirley had been through this before.

"No, Susan," she said softly. "You have to sit and wait it out."

So wait Susan did, until she finally got word that I hadn't been involved in the collision. She told me later that she had seen it happen, but she might as well have been relating an unusual shopping experience.

She was an Air Force wife who knew how much her husband loved flying, and that he didn't want to be doing anything else. As a pilot, I actually enjoyed those risks as an exciting aspect of my job; she accepted them as part of hers.

Part of the instrument flight course I was teaching involved thunderstorm penetration techniques. A thunderstorm is normally something to be avoided by a pilot, not penetrated, but military flying is supposed to be an all-weather operation, and the Air Force felt that justified teaching penetration. So I had to take students up in T-33s and deliberately fly into boiling, angry black caldrons of clouds at just the right airspeed and attitude to keep us from getting torn apart.

One day I took a student up in a T-33 and we flew into a thunderstorm over northern Florida at 28,000 feet. All was routine until, without warning, the engine quit. It was the first jet flameout I had ever experienced, but I wasn't particularly worried.

I tried to restart the engine, and when that failed, I asked Moody for a vector back to the base, intending to glide in.

"I can't see the ground," I radioed, "so let me know when radar shows us over open ground and I'll drop the wing tanks." (I still had a lot of fuel in those tanks, and for a dead-stick landing I needed to lighten our load as much as possible.)

Then Moody advised us the field was down to absolute ceiling and visibility minimums, thus requiring a GCA landing. I knew we didn't stand a chance trying to land a powerless jet under GCA guidance, which called for precise course, altitude, and airspeed changes, so I tried something else. I waited until the T-33 had dropped to 6,000 feet and went through the engine relight procedure again.

This time it caught, and GCA talked us down to the runway. I got out of the plane trying to appear nonchalant, but I don't think I fooled my student one bit.

I had one kid who was petrified of instrument flying. He wasn't too bad as long as he could see outside the airplane, but that wasn't the way to fly instruments. Once I had a hood over his cockpit so he had no visual references except the panel in front of him, he came apart.

Finally I put him into a T-33 and took the plane down to only a hundred feet over an ugly-looking, snake-infested swamp—the last place in the world anyone would want to be near in an airplane. I told him to close the hood and snapped, "Now *you* fly the damned plane!"

It was remarkable how fast his instrument flying improved.

I flew even when I didn't have to. One Friday afternoon, just as I was leaving to go home, headquarters asked if I'd fly some full colonel to Andrews AFB near Washington.

"He has to attend a very important meeting and must get there as quickly as possible," I was told. "We can get somebody else if you have plans."

"No need to," I assured headquarters. "I'll be glad to take him."

I informed Susan I wouldn't be home that night and had a T-33 waiting on the flight line when the colonel arrived. He climbed out of a jeep and ordered an enlisted man to stuff a golf bag into the nose of the plane. So much for the very important meeting, I thought.

I said, "Sir, you can ride in the front seat."

"Fine, Lieutenant. I'd like to do the flying."

"As you wish, sir," I said unhappily.

He was a terrible pilot, handling that T-33 like a kid struggling through his first driving lesson. I didn't say a word until we were nearing Andrews, and he began screwing up a simple GCA approach. There was no way I was going to let him land the plane, and as we began to let down I yelled, "I've got it!"

When we got out of the plane, he glared at me. "Lieutenant, I could have done that landing."

I looked him right in the eye. "Sir, I'm sorry but I'm the aircraft commander and I didn't think you could."

He didn't say another word. So long as I was in charge of that airplane I outranked him, and that rule makes the Air Force, in its own way, a more democratic branch of service than any other. It is a relationship that enhances safety, because if I had succumbed instinctively to the authority those silver eagles represented, the damned fool might well have splattered a T-33 over several thousand feet of Andrews runway.

I got my first taste of test work at Moody. We always had been warned never to try an intentional spin in a T-33 because the airplane invariably would not recover. But engineers came up with the idea of putting strips on the leading edge of the wing, changing the airfoil just enough to allow recovery in a spin. I was elected to take a modified T-33 and intentionally spin it. The modification worked, but while the test flight was a lot of fun, it was just another flying assignment; becoming a test pilot was not yet on my list of preferred occupations.

I wasn't unhappy in my job at Moody. I was logging plenty of flying time and each additional hour was like acquiring more life insurance in the form of valuable experience. Teaching itself, as a matter of fact, was the best way to learn. But I still wanted to fly fighters, kept putting in requests, and after a year at Moody wangled a transfer to the fighter weapons school at Nellis—a two-month course that qualified me as a fighter weapons instructor. I figured this would get me assigned to an operational fighter squadron, but the Air Force shipped me right back to Moody to teach instrument flying again.

Overall, our tour of duty at Moody lasted eighteen months, and I devoted most of those months to trying to get transferred. At least the work load lessened so I didn't have to work double shifts, and I even found time to resume building model airplanes, including wire-controlled jobs. The kids in the neighborhood would come around to our backyard and watch me fly them. I should say, watch us fly them, for Susan got interested and began flying the models herself. Much to my chagrin, she also became more skilled at it than I was.

I had heard that a new fighter weapons school was opening at Luke AFB, a base close to my parents in Arizona, and would need instructors. I kept applying to become part of the new instructor cadre, and the long-awaited orders finally came through.

This was the summer of '55 and we found an attractive little house in Goodyear, Arizona, conveniently close to Luke, for ninety dollars a month, easily the nicest place we had lived in since our marriage. I marched confidently into the office of Colonel Deke Childs, group commander in charge of flight operations at Luke and an informal guy who called everyone "cousin."

He looked over my service folder. "Lieutenant, I see where you've been teaching instrument flying at Moody."

"Yes, sir."

"Good. I'm gonna put you to work here in basic flight school, teaching instruments."

I was stunned. "Sir, I was assigned here to teach gunnery and with all due . . ."

I never got to finish my protest. "Borman," Childs barked, "I'm running this goddamned group and you'll teach what I tell you to teach!"

It was teaching instruments again for another three months. Then I started out flying straight-wing F-84s on training missions with three students behind me, and finally got assigned to a fighter weapons school equipped with the swept-wing F-84F Thunderstreak, the hottest airplane I had flown to date. Not only was I flying a high-performance airplane, but I was instructing the cream of the Air Force's young pilots.

Some of us instructors didn't always practice what we preached. I was taking three students on a very long, low-level cross-country mission at night—a simulation of penetrating Russian airspace at an altitude that radar couldn't pick up. Because of the mission's length, the F-84s' huge tip tanks were loaded with 400 gallons of fuel, which called for a takeoff rotation speed of at least 160 knots and using all the runway available.

I was in the lead plane, started my takeoff role, and hit 160 knots when I was only halfway down the runway. I knew something was wrong—I had never before flown a F-84 with so much thrust—so I aborted the takeoff and returned to the ramp, where I discovered the reason. I had done a poor preflight check—there was no fuel in the tip tanks.

Another time, I was leading three student pilots back to Luke after finishing a gunnery mission at the Gila Bend firing range. We were at 8,000 or 9,000 feet, doing 300 knots in a restricted area where there wasn't supposed to be any other traffic, so I wasn't paying much attention to the view outside. All of a sudden I happened to look up and there was an old Air Rescue B-17 right in front of me.

"Bogey, twelve o'clock!" I yelled, and simultaneously shoved the stick forward. The three students close behind me also dove, or all four of us might have plowed into that B-17. I didn't miss the bomber by more than five feet when I dove under him. I don't know what made me look up just in time.

We also had a lot of foreigners training with us at Luke, and one day an old GI bus wheezed to a stop at the base, disgorging a bunch of guys with khaki uniforms but no insignia.

They all looked older. They were war-hardened Luftwaffe pilots, the nucleus of West Germany's postwar air force, sent to Luke to train on F-84s. Most of us felt patronizing toward them—too old, we thought, to be fighter pilots.

It took them only two hours of flying to show us how wrong we were. West Germany had sent us the best of its surviving pilots. We established great rapport with them, drinking beer together at the officers' club and listening to their stories of wartime combat, including the tactics used by Soviet pilots. It took a little while to get used to the physical appearance of one pilot—both his ears had been burned off in a crash.

The Germans were at Luke just long enough to check out in the F-84s. There were some good pilots from other countries, too—Italians, Greeks, Turks, French, and a number of South Americans—but those Luftwaffe guys as a group were the best.

There was one bunch we couldn't keep away from the whorehouses, and another that couldn't have licked a squadron of unarmed Piper Cubs—one of them shot up a target tow plane and almost killed its pilot. The Turks were good, but we always wondered if it was wise to send them up with live ammunition when the Greeks were flying anywhere in the same area.

Luke was one of my happiest tours of duty. I finally made captain and I was becoming a well-rounded, versatile pilot; I also got a chance to do some experimental weapons work. Because I was good at math and its practical applications, I became part of a project to adopt F-84 bombsights to forward-firing rockets for greater accuracy. We actually did develop the hardware and it worked—we had a class act and a tremendous amount of esprit de corps.

Whenever we had a class graduating we'd throw a party, and our graduation parties were never occasions for sobriety. We were in the middle of one the night a nationwide practice air-defense alert was called, and Luke got orders to scramble every F-84 on the base to Kirtland AFB in Albuquerque.

I don't think there was a completely sober pilot who climbed into an F-84 that night. We took off about 1 A.M., and it has always been a mystery to me how our flight leader even found Kirtland.

Approaching the field, he let down too fast, right through the F-84's Mach red line. The excessive speed caused his nose to pitch up, which came as a complete surprise to the rest of us—we were flying in a very tight formation and when he inadvertently pitched up, so did we; it was like having the driver of a fast-moving car ten feet in front of you suddenly slam on the brakes.

Like everyone else, I broke formation to avoid a chain reaction of mass collisions. There we were, in the middle of the night, with F-84s scattering in every direction. It took us fifteen minutes to re-group and land.

Crazy and stupid? Sure, but also exciting. It was part of the fighter pilot's own mystique of one man and one machine, together chal-lenging the exhilarating environment of danger that in his own mind never seems quite tough enough to defeat him.

Then, without warning, it all came to an end.

It was late spring of 1956 when the unexpected telegram arrived from Washington. I was being assigned to West Point as an instruc-tor in mechanics, tentatively starting the 1957–1958 academic year, contingent on my first obtaining a master's degree in aeronautical engineering. I was further instructed to proceed to Wright Field in Dayton for counseling on a choice of school for the aeronautical engineering program. I took the telegram into Deke Childs's office, showed it to him, and when he handed it back with nothing but a cold, wordless stare, I figured it was time I made things perfectly clear.

"Colonel, I don't want any part of this. I think I'm doing a pretty good job here and I've decided to turn it down."

The stare turned into a glare. "What do you mean, turn it down? Remember, Borman, when you put your hand up at West Point, you gave your ass to the service."

"Colonel, I don't want to teach. I want to fly fighters."

"And I don't give a damn what you want. If the service wants you to be an instructor at West Point, that's exactly what you're gon-na do."

I was desperate enough to continue the argument, but not for very long. His final words on the subject: "Captain, as far as I'm con-cerned you're nothing but Government Issue. What the government says, you do. So get your ass out of here and you go to Wright, like those orders state!"

I flew a T-33 to Wright, where I met with a counselor in charge of assigning officers to civilian schools. My grades at West Point had been high enough to get me into almost any graduate school I wanted, but most master's programs were for two years, and there was no way I was going to spend two years qualifying for a non-flying duty that would last at least another three years. He recommended the California Institute of Technology, which had a one-year program.

So in the summer of 1956, I moved my family again. Cal Tech is in Pasadena and we were fortunate to find a small house in nearby Temple City. I wasn't even sure I could cut the mustard in a scholastic environment. I had been out of school for almost six years, and for all I knew what study habits I had once possessed could have atrophied.

Cal Tech turned out to be the most difficult scholastic challenge I had ever faced. I had seen some gung-ho achievers before, but at Cal Tech virtually everyone was that way.

The curriculum itself was a unique experience—unstructured, almost entirely theoretical. I had always imagined aeronautical engineering, or any other type of engineering for that matter, to be scientifically precise. But here there was very little slide-rule usage and a great deal of theory. I got only two A's in my entire year there, and neither was earned in an engineering course.

Stimulating as Cal Tech was, I couldn't have endured it without flying whenever I could. I'd go out to a nearby air base on weekends and borrow any airplane that was available. Just before Thanksgiving, a fellow officer at the school confided he wished he could fly to Washington, D.C., and spend Thanksgiving with his girlfriend.

"So go," I said.

"No space available on commercial flights, and besides, I don't have the dough."

"Hell," I offered, "I'll take you there myself."

I scrounged up a T-33, flew him to the nation's capital, and ate my Thanksgiving dinner at Andrews Air Force Base, 3,000 miles from my uncomplaining family. It wasn't Frank Borman at his best, but it was Frank Borman doing what he liked best—flying.

Cal Tech awarded me a master's degree in June 1957, thus qualifying me for the teaching assignment at West Point. I had arranged in advance for living quarters at West Point, although we were at the bottom of the totem pole when it came to housing. We got the last house on the post and it wasn't even a house, just a grubby, spartan apartment in an eight-unit building that looked like a converted barracks. But by the time Susan finished scrubbing, improvising, and decorating, the place was not only liveable but actually attractive. I added my bit by building a back portico.

I enjoyed teaching. My immediate superiors in the mechanics department were two magnificent officers—Colonel Val Heiberg, the department head, and Colonel Harvey Fraser, who was his chief assistant. Fraser had been one of my instructors when I was a cadet. Heiberg had been a brigadier general, but took a reduction in rank to join the West Point faculty. Quiet and reserved, he came from a family that had been producing Army officers for generations.

In personality, Fraser was just the opposite—tough, profane, fiery, and feisty. He had served with the combat engineers at the Battle of the Bulge and had more ribbons on his chest than a South American general. Fraser's voice produced decibels that at an airport would have called for noise abatement procedures, and he employed it most effectively at Army football and baseball games, where you could hear him berating a referee or umpire even if he was sitting in the last row of the upper stands.

I loved the guy, but I'll never forget the time he chewed me out when he spotted a hole in one of my socks.

"Look at that goddamned hole!" he roared. "What kind of an example are you setting for your cadets, Borman?"

That was the last pair of torn socks I wore in my entire three years of teaching.

Yet for all his bombast, Fraser was a brilliant, inspiring leader and teacher. Men like Fraser and Heiberg were giants, typical of the West Point faculty cadre serving the academy during my cadet and instructor years. They came to West Point out of love for the academy and what it stood for.

The subjects I taught, with the academic status of assistant professor, were thermodynamics and fluid mechanics. I taught only second classmen and one of my students was Pete Dawkins, an All-American back who won a Rhodes scholarship and eventually retired as a brigadier general; he's now a top executive at the Lehman Brothers investment firm. Even as a young cadet, Dawkins was the kind of kid you just knew was going to make it in life.

In the classroom, I tried not to be too stiff, consciously emulating the Fraser of my own cadet days when he'd been about the most irreverent instructor I had. If I caught a student sleeping in class, I'd throw an eraser at him instead of reporting him—and I got pretty good at getting someone's attention that way.

One of the things I wanted in the lab was a smoke tunnel, so the students could see for themselves the efficiency of various airfoils. We bought a small wind tunnel from Alexander Leipish, designer of Germany's Messerschmitt 163—the world's first rocket plane. Leipish was in Cedar Rapids, Iowa, working for Collins Radio, and I went to see him before ordering the tunnel. I spent a fascinating afternoon with this renowned aeronautical engineer, discussing not only the small tunnel we needed but aerodynamics in general.

It made no difference to me that he had once served the enemy—he loved flying as much as I did. He especially liked gliders, which I had tried flying only once when I was at Cal Tech, because to him a powerless aircraft was the epitome of good aerodynamic design. We also talked about the war. I was complaining about the bureaucratic frustration every military man encounters and Leipish smiled.

"Captain," he said, "if you think the bureaucracy in this country is something, you should have seen how bureaucratic and screwed up wartime Germany was. Even the smallest decision had to be made in Berlin. Believe me, my friend, always have decisions made at the lowest possible level and have trust in the people at that level."

We rotated teaching assignments at West Point, where classes were divided according to ability. The outstanding students were in the first section, descending in order of scholastic skill to a bottom section, and I spent most of my time teaching either the first or the bottom group.

The instructors were graded, too. Fraser would pop in unannounced at frequent intervals and sit through a class, observing how we were teaching, and we were given efficiency ratings just as I had been in the Air Force.

My fears of not being able to fly proved groundless. On weekends, I'd take a T-33 up from nearby Stewart AFB and fly target missions for the Air Defense Command. There was an air defense radar unit at Stewart that would track me as I flew all the way up to Maine, usually solo, and then come back over the North Atlantic in a simulation of a Russian penetration of our airspace. A lot of this was at night.

During one summer, I flew a T-33 over Camp Buckner to give the cadets a taste of low-level strafing and bombing. I didn't drop any bombs, of course, but strategically placed charges of dynamite under my flight path provided the realism. Some of my old classmates at West Point were in the Buckner cadre and I took an awful ribbing from them, the gist of it being, "Where the hell was the Air Force in Korea when we really needed support?"

One guy in particular was constantly on my back and I finally invited him on a sunrise low-level mission. I did everything but turn that T-33 inside out and ended up turning *him* inside out—on some of my high-speed banks we were up to five or six Gs, and I never saw a man get so sick.

"Jesus, let's go home," he kept pleading.

"Not yet, Chuck. I still haven't finished the demonstration for the cadets."

When we finally landed, his cockpit was a disaster area and his face the color of an unripe banana. He staggered out of the plane and surveyed the mess.

He groaned, "My God, what are we going to do about this?"

"Chuck, I'm not gonna do anything. You made the mess, and in the Air Force the guy who throws up cleans up."

During our next to last summer at the academy, I volunteered to go through the Air Force Survival School. I figured I had to do it. I felt teaching aerodynamics had taken me out of the mainstream of my flying career and I needed a fresh challenge. The Air Force had established the survival school at Reno-Stead AFB in Nevada, largely because of too many Korean War instances where captured crews had cracked under the diabolically applied pressures of prisoner-of-war camps. The survival course was required for all Air Force combat personnel, and I reasoned that if I ever got back to fighters, I was going to have to go through it anyway.

The school's cadre, composed entirely of former POWs, could have turned a Mafia hit man pale. The seventeen-day curriculum started with two days of lectures on North Korean torture techniques. Then we were put into a painfully realistic replica of a Korean prison and the cadre interrogated us relentlessly, refusing to let us sleep or eat for long periods. They skipped actual physical beatings but they came damn close, pushing us around until we were ready to start punching. They had one torture device that had to be experienced to be believed. It was a wall locker with sliding horizontal slats, allowing the height of the locker interior to be changed. They'd adjust the height so you couldn't stand up or sit down and they'd leave you in there for hours. When they finally opened the locker, you were completely immobilized.

They had another clever little twist to the locker. They'd put it out under the hot sun, and while you were crouching inside, your muscles protesting with excruciating cramps, they'd beat on it with sticks until your eardrums were ready to break. I saw one man crack like a piece of dry wood, screaming that he couldn't stand it anymore. Common sense told us nobody was going to get killed, but sometimes common sense wasn't enough to ward off sheer panic and fear.

Another exercise was putting you into a real coffin, closing the lid, and lowering it into an open grave. Then they'd start throwing dirt on the coffin, and before long the dull thumps of the falling dirt sounded like a drumbeat of forthcoming death. I lay there for God knows how long, actually wondering if I was going to be buried alive.

After the simulated prison came a simulated escape. The idea was to teach survival in case you were lucky enough to get away, or if you had to bail out over enemy terrain, by living off the land while you found your way back to friendly territory. They sent five of us into the rugged Sierra Nevada mountains for eleven days with the following equipment:

- A package of hardtack food, but only enough to last a few days at the most.
- One parachute per man, to simulate the load we'd have to carry if we bailed out; chutes made good shelters.
- One live rabbit.
- One live instructor, whose sole duty was to make sure nobody got lost permanently or killed.

We were told to stay together until the last day, at which point the instructor would hand each of us a map showing the pickup point we were supposed to reach individually without getting caught. They taught us evasion tactics and how to set snare traps for rabbits, although we weren't actually supposed to trap any—the regular wildlife was off limits, hence the live rabbit. No weapons were allowed.

We all thought the rabbit bit was ridiculous. Who'd be cruel enough to kill, let alone eat, the cute bunny assigned to our expedition? We named him Peter and he was our friend, a pet companion we carried up and down the mountains and through the streams.

The survival food ran out about the fifth day. On the eighth day, we killed Peter and ate him.

One of our group was from Brooklyn originally, a tough, street-smart product of the slums who had gone through a rough boyhood in those cement jungles. But nothing in his past had prepared him for eleven days and nights in the Sierra Nevada wilderness. The pitch-black of nighttime and the incessant howls of coyotes turned him into a basket case.

He managed to endure so long as he was with our group, but when they turned him loose on his own on the final day, he folded. He went looking for the cadre to let them catch him, and they made him go through the ordeal all over again.

Survival school was one of those experiences worth a million dollars to have gone through, and also one of those experiences you wouldn't take a million dollars to repeat. I lost twelve pounds taking the course.

It took years before I had the courage to tell Edwin the story of the martyred Peter. My youngest son took after his father when it came to animal adoption. Just as I had once done, he was always bringing home assorted species of wildlife and more than once suffered bites requiring medical attention. It got so bad that the nurses at the base hospital would spot Edwin approaching and sigh, "Here comes the Borman kid again—get out the tetanus shots."

The boys loved West Point as much as Susan did. The academy had an excellent school for the children of its personnel and the kids enjoyed access to numerous facilities such as the gym and swimming pool when they weren't being used by cadets. They liked to watch the cadet formations, their young eyes wide at the perfect cadence, the majestic symmetry of the long gray line. Their dreams of being future West Pointers were born during those three years at the USMA.

Our relatively tiny apartment became the happiest, most stable home environment my family had known. Susan could have stayed at West Point forever, yet she was as oriented to my career as I was. Never once did she say, "I don't want to leave here—West Point is best for me and the boys."

While I was teaching at West Point, the Convair company advertised in *The New York Times* for a qualified aeronautical engineer and added that a Convair representative would be interviewing applicants in a New York hotel on a certain date.

I went for an interview and was offered three times what I was making as a captain plus a long list of fringe benefits. The representative was reciting all the virtues of living in San Diego—climate, great place to raise a family, excellent schools, and so on—when I cut him off.

"I'm sorry," I said, "but I just realized I don't really want to leave the Air Force. I'm just wasting your time."

When I told Susan I just couldn't handle a civilian job at this point in my life, she nodded and said something to the effect that it was my life.

It was during our second year at West Point that I began to change my thinking about where I was headed in the Air Force.

On October 4, 1957, only a month after I returned to West Point, the Soviet Union launched *Sputnik 1*—the world's first artificial earth satellite. It was a scientific achievement that shook our complacent society to its very roots. *Sputnik 1* was only a twenty-three-inch aluminum sphere with two radio transmitters powered by chemical batteries. But it still was the first step toward the stars, and the fact that Russia had taken that step ahead of the United States was a major blow to our national pride.

Naturally we talked a lot about *Sputnik 1* and other space program developments within our engineering department, finding it hard to believe that the Soviets were setting the pace. Up to then I hadn't thought much about space travel except as something you'd read about in science fiction. Rocketry itself was relatively new and novel to most of the military, even though we had been firing airborne rockets from fighters for a long time. We had studied the use of Germany's V-2 missiles against Britain during World War II, but while frightening and devastating, they hadn't changed the course of the war and their connection with space travel was nebulous at best.

Yet in the immediate post-*Sputnik* years, it began to dawn on me that my Air Force future lay in flight test technology, not fighters. By now I had acquired an excellent academic background and considerable experience in aerodynamics; conversely, I had been away from those glamorous fighters for four years. I possessed a technical background few pilots could match, and it became increasingly obvious that when my three-year tour of duty at West Point ended, returning to fighters might be the wrong direction in which to fly.

The names of the first seven Mercury astronauts were announced April 9, 1959, during my second spring at West Point. They were among the more than five hundred test pilots screened before the choices had been made, but I can't honestly say that their test pilot backgrounds influenced me to go this route—at that point, I was interested in experimental test flying, not space exploration.

I applied and was subsequently approved for the test pilots' school at Edwards Air Force Base in California. To celebrate, I traded in our current Chevy for a two-door 1960 Chevrolet, gray with a dazzling red interior. I proudly showed the new car to Colonel Fraser, who surveyed the red interior.

"Jesus Christ, Borman, that thing looks like a Chinese whorehouse!"

His unflattering description notwithstanding, in June of 1960 the new Chevrolet started west with the Borman family, consisting of a wife who hated to be going but stuck her pretty chin out and said nothing, two somewhat dubious little boys excited about the trip but wondering what lay in store . . .

And a husband who didn't know he was about to take his first step toward the stars.

5

BEYOND THE WILD BLUE YONDER

Edwards Air Force Base squats like a huge concrete Band-Aid on the flesh-colored hide of the desolate, windswept Mojave Desert.

Located 150 miles northeast of Los Angeles, it consists mostly of some 30,000 acres of sun-baked clay, sand, and scrub; for scenery, living conditions, and climate, being stationed on the moon would be just as appropriate. Death Valley, a geographical neighbor, is only slightly less hospitable.

Edwards has been a military installation since 1933, when the old Army Air Corps established a practice bombing range at Muroc Dry Lake, also known as Rogers Dry Lake. The unfriendly environment was offset by two virtues: year-round flying conditions and an enormous flat terrain that lent itself to long runways—Muroc is twenty-five miles long and for years the hard, dry lake surface served as a natural landing strip.

In its earlier days, Edwards was a broiled Antarctica—a bleak wasteland whose monotony was broken only by a few hangars and tarpaper shacks. Those who were shipped there by train got off at the town of Mojave, forty miles from Edwards, and took a bus the rest of the way.

Edwards, by the time I reported there, was no longer the primitive province of a handful of military and civilian test pilots, but a full-fledged military base with 10,000 personnel and paved streets named after pilots who had been killed in the line of duty at Edwards. Concrete ramps and runways had augmented the dry lake strips, and there were modern hangars, a well-stocked PX, and an officers' club.

Yet it still was the pits, as isolated as ever, with that constant hot wind from the Devil's own lungs—a stark and depressing contrast to what we had just left at West Point. We arrived there on a blistering July day, our first sight being a sign that read WELCOME TO EDWARDS AIR FORCE BASE. We drove for another fifty miles before the base itself came into view, and the only vegetation we saw was the grotesque Joshua trees with their ugly, gnarled branches and dagger-shaped, spiny leaves.

I had been assigned to what was officially called the USAF Experimental Flight Test Pilot School. Students were at the bottom of the housing barrel, and we were given a very tiny house—9 Kelly Court—as crummy and barren as the desert outside. For Susan in particular, it was another period of not knowing anyone and having to make new friends.

This is one of the most difficult elements of military society—every time you move, you're starting all over again, a kind of instant reincarnation. It has its good side in that you can become more mature and resilient, but it's not easy and it's especially tough on wives, even wives as resilient as Susan. I felt sorry for her, but the tug-of-war between a husband's sympathy and an officer's career ambition was an uneven contest—Edwards to me was a move up the ladder that had to be made.

In a sense, I was starting all over again, too. The test pilot school at Edwards was the most exclusive training facility in the Air Force, accepting the lowest percentage of applicants of any school. On the average, only twenty pilots were admitted to each of the two classes operated annually and they were the elite. If I had any temptation to feel smugly superior about my hard-won master's degree, it would have been an exercise in futile ego—most of my classmates had their own.

I met three pilots at the school who would become fellow astronauts in the Apollo program. Two were Annapolis graduates who had transferred to the Air Force—classmate Jim Irwin, who a decade later would be the eighth man to walk on the moon, and Tom Stafford, who was one of our instructors. The third, Mike Collins, was an Air Force fighter jock like myself. He was sharp-witted, amusingly perceptive in his appraisal of others, and easily the most talented writer of all the astronauts. He also was armed with a devastating sense of humor. He christened Stafford, who was chief of the school's Performance Section, "Old Mumbles"—an apt description of Tom's rather soft, pedantic delivery, which made us wish we had brought hearing aids to class.

Mike zeroed in quickly on my own personality traits. I was one of the earliest arrivals before classes began, a status that Collins duly noted in his fine autobiography, *Carrying the Fire*. He wrote: "First there was Frank Borman, greeting us all at the door like a politician with a close election coming up. Fresh from a teaching assignment . . . Frank was a tough competitor who flew well and who raced through the academic curriculum with slide rule practically smoking. . . . Aggressive, capable, makes decisions faster than anyone I have ever met—with amazingly good batting average, which would be even better if he slowed down a bit."

Mike was right about my sailing through the academic side of the flight test school—after Cal Tech, it was a breeze. The flying side contained a minor disappointment, for the basic training airplane was none other than the old T-28 Trojan I had flown at Williams almost a decade before. Not until later would the school get the high-performance training aircraft it really needed, although before the six-month course was over I had also flown F-86s, B-57 jet bombers, T-33s, and for final test work the supersonic Lockheed F-104 Starfighter, which had a top speed of more than 1,500 mph at 40,000 feet.

We were taught the basics of flight testing: how to put an airplane through the major parameters of performance, stability, and control characteristics. By the time I graduated, I ranked first academically, winning the British Empire Test Pilot School Award for scholastic excellence and the Hontz Award for best overall student. But the honor I would have prized most, first in flying, escaped me (I finished second) and it was my own fault.

I was taking my final T-28 check ride and went into the climb-out performance test, watching my instruments carefully.

Everything looked good except for my rate of climb. It was crawling up the scale as if I had an anchor tied to the tail. I checked the panel trying to figure out what was wrong. Engine temperature was fine, power output normal. I compared the altitude dial to the rate-of-climb indicator—maybe the latter was just out of whack and I was climbing faster than it showed.

No dice. Altitude and rate of climb correlated and now I was stuck with an apparently sick airplane. It couldn't be me—I was flying right by the numbers. My eyes swept over the instrument panel again and for the first time I noticed I had three green lights.

The landing gear was still down—I had forgotten to retract it on takeoff.

I wasn't just embarrassed—I was humiliated. Making it worse was the fact that I had more flying time than most of the guys in the class; I think Greg Neubeck, who had logged some three thousand hours in the T-33 alone, might have been the only one with more hours.

Despite that stupid mistake, my record still was good enough to get a shot at whatever I wanted for my next assignment at Edwards. Virtually the entire class was opting for the macho thing: fighter operations at Edwards. I was tempted, and I also considered returning to my old goal of going to an operational fighter squadron, but every time I pondered the future I kept thinking about the technical background I had acquired. And to me, technology was becoming synonymous with space. I had felt that way since *Sputnik 1*, and felt even stronger because of a later event.

In April 1961, Russian cosmonaut Yuri Alekseyevich Gagarin became the first man to circle the globe above the earth's atmosphere in a spacecraft. This achievement of manned orbital flight stunned the United States as much as *Sputnik 1* had; our own Mercury program had yet to put an astronaut in space, and the pressures to catch up were mounting. The Air Force itself felt the same pressures and it had a space program of its own, separate from NASA's, already in full swing.

This was the now almost-forgotten Dyna-Soar project, aimed at putting into space orbit a manned vehicle capable of reentering the earth's atmosphere under a pilot's control, much like a conventional airplane. It was also perceived as a means of attaining a rendezvous with a space station in permanent orbit. In a very real sense, Dyna-Soar was the forerunner of the space shuttle.

The Dyna-Soar vehicle designed by Boeing was called the X-20—forty-five feet long with tiny delta wings, twin vertical fins, and a completely flat belly. This last was actually the product of the "dynamic soaring" theory developed by a German rocket scientist named Saenger during World War II. Saenger believed that a spacecraft with a flat bottom could literally skip across the atmosphere's upper layer like a stone skipping over water. Boeing's X-20 would have done just that, first reaching orbital speed via a booster rocket and then slowing down just enough so that the craft's speed, combined with the atmosphere's thickness, would cause it to go into a skipping nose-up motion. With each subsequent upward skip, the speed would be reduced further until a safe reentry rate was reached and the powerless X-20 could glide to a pilot-controled landing.

The Dyna-Soar project cost $500 million and lasted six years, but never got beyond the construction of the vehicle mockup—no real X-20 was ever built. The major difficulty was an inability to design the right booster rocket soon enough. By the time the Titan II was developed, Defense Secretary Robert McNamara had soured on the whole idea as wasteful competition with NASA's own space program. In 1963, after emasculating Dyna-Soar to the level of a relatively minor experimental project by progressively reducing its funding, he finally canceled it.

Yet the Dyna-Soar was not a total failure or boondoggle. NASA itself learned a few things from the program's research that it later applied to the shuttle. And Dyna-Soar also focused a lot of research on the problem of protecting a space pilot from the enormous vehicle skin heat generated by reentry at near-orbital speeds. The X-20, while it was nothing but a very sophisticated high-altitude glider, would have been built out of new metal alloys, such as molybdenum, with a specially insulated cockpit.

While Dyna-Soar's demise made it clear that NASA was going to run the U.S. space show, it was equally obvious that the astronauts themselves would come largely from the military, which had the greatest number of men with test pilot backgrounds or experience in high-performance airplanes. And the Air Force wanted very badly to make sure it was adequately represented in this cadre.

As I approached graduation time, another option opened up. Edwards offered me an instructorship in the test pilot school, a proposition with considerable appeal. But it also was at this time that the Air Force decided to establish a test pilot graduate school at Edwards, whose primary mission was to create a readily available pool of test pilots well prepared to enter the astronaut training program that NASA had already formulated for the first seven Mercury astronauts.

The Air Force started with just a name for the program: the Aerospace Research Pilot School. It was a school with no faculty and no curriculum. The ultimate goal was to teach the basics of manned orbital flight in all its phases—in effect, a kind of postgraduate test pilot course to groom pilots for advancement into NASA. And what the Air Force offered me was the task of helping to set up the curriculum for such a school.

Five of us were picked. My four colleagues were:

- Tom McElmurry, an Air Force major with an aeronautical engineering background like myself and a keenly analytical mind.
- William Schweikhard, who was a civilian ground school instructor at the test pilot school and an excellent engineer; he's now a professor at the University of Kansas.
- James McDivitt, another fighter pilot with combat duty in Korea; deeply religious and very thorough.
- Robert "Buck" Buchanan, an Air Force colonel with broad experience in research and development.

Each of us was an engineer, McElmurry being the one with the most engineering experience. We formed a pretty good team, and by establishing a curriculum, we literally became the first ones to go through it. We began by taking a course in orbital mechanics at the University of Michigan's summer school.

We went to Wright-Patterson AFB in Dayton for rides on the pair of zero-G airplanes they had there, a modified KC-135 and C-131 (the military versions of the Boeing 707 and Convair 340 transports, respectively). The aircraft flew parabolic flight paths to create short periods of weightlessness, and it was like being in a huge roller coaster. Parabolic is nothing but a steep up-and-down motion that we endured for one or two hours, a nauseating experience. Zero G occurred between the end of each climb and the first stage of the subsequent dive, a period lasting not more than thirty seconds but sufficiently long to earn the planes the nickname Vomit Comets.

We even volunteered to be research subjects in a program involving the effects of G forces on the human body, and compared to this ordeal the Vomit Comets gave us a joyride. The research was being done at the Johnsville Naval Air Station near Philadelphia, where doctors were strapping their human guinea pigs into a huge centrifuge machine and exposing them to forces up to twelve times that of gravity—basically an extension of the experiments USAF Colonel John P. Stapp had conducted between 1946 and 1958 using rocket sleds. He was strapped into a rocket-propelled sled that accelerated up to 632 miles an hour and brought to a stop in 1.4 seconds—a deceleration force forty times the pressure of gravity.

The medical people at Johnsville were seeking ways to improve resistance to high G forces that cause pilot blackouts. Spacecraft are launched by rocket propulsion and such propulsion creates abnormally high G forces, which, in turn, produce severe breathing problems because of the pressure on the rib cage. The doctors had a theory that if you breathed pressurized oxygen when experiencing high G forces, it would have the effect of pressurizing the lungs and thus reducing the strain on the rib cage. They were just groping, which was fine as a medical experiment but unshirted hell on us guinea pigs.

They ran us through various G forces both with and without pressurized breathing, and while this horizontal version of an amuck Ferris wheel was spinning around, they had us performing manual dexterity exercises—simple stuff like putting pegs into the right holes.

First, 6 Gs under pressurized breathing for two minutes, and another two minutes' unpressurized breathing. Then 8 Gs . . . 10 Gs . . . 12 Gs. They held 12 Gs for a full minute with the pressurization and another sixty seconds without—the latter was like trying to breathe with an elephant sitting on your chest, and I couldn't have put a one-inch peg into a hole five feet wide.

When I staggered out of that damned contraption, I felt twenty years older and so did my four fellow volunteers. The stress on the human body was indescribable. McElmurry was sick for a month after his centrifuge ordeal. Looking back, I realize we had taken a tremendous risk because those doctors were exposing us to a flock of unknown health consequences. Yet we took the chance because volunteering was the only way we could get into a centrifuge program, which we knew should be part of astronaut training.

In setting up the curriculum, my field of responsibility was developing the flight training program and it was clear we couldn't establish the school without higher-performance airplanes. Edwards gave us the TF-102, a Convair product called the Delta Dagger, which did not have the performance our training required. Its service ceiling was only 54,000 feet and its maximum speed was 825 mph at 36,000 feet, not much more than a modest Mach 1, whereas we needed Mach 2 airplanes or better.

We later acquired a few F-104 Starfighters and I managed to

scrounge another hot bird, the F-106 Convair Delta Dart, which could hit 1,525 mph at 40,000 feet, just about the same performance as the Starfighter. We didn't win any popularity contests when we began lobbying to get F-104s from the fighter operations branch at Edwards. We used them as much for experimental flying as for training aircraft, because what we were doing amounted to experimental training.

I introduced into the curriculum a little number called the zoom program. We'd take an F-104 up to 40,000 feet, turn on the afterburner, and start climbing at Mach 2.2 with a pull-up force of between 2 and 3 Gs. The afterburner would blow out around 55,000 or 60,000 feet from lack of air. Between 65,000 and 70,000 feet, the air-starved engine had to be shut down to avoid overheating, and with the engine out there was no cockpit pressurization. So at this point we'd activate our pressure suits and coast up to 90,000.

Then we'd go into a powerless descent (where the aircraft is subject only to gravitational forces and the minimal resistance of the atmosphere) until we reached heavier air and could relight the engine. It was touchy and tricky stuff because few pilots had ever handled an F-104 with the engine out at 70,000 feet.

Operating at such altitudes required a pressure suit, an uncomfortably bulky, four-layer garment but still vastly improved over the first flight-approved suit introduced in 1934. In the typical four-layer job, the outer layer is a heat-resistant metallic fabric. Under this is a nylon net that acts as a restraint layer; it provides both mobility and protection against the suit's ballooning when it inflates. The third layer is a rubberized fabric that keeps the suit airtight, and the inner layer is made of a soft nylon for the pilot's comfort.

We also experimented with so-called very high drag landings, using a TF-102. This involved coming in with engine at idle, gear down, speed brakes extended, and missile bay open. You come down in one hell of a hurry, almost like a spent rocket; it's basically the same technique they've been using with the space shuttle. In the Edwards program, the purpose was to teach pilots how to manage the aircraft's energy, timing everything exactly right so they'd have just enough speed and lift to round out for the landing. First the steep dive, then pulling up and bleeding off energy slowly, and finally approaching the touchdown point with sufficient speed to avoid a stall. We didn't invent the technique at Edwards—high-drag landings had first been developed by a NASA test pilot named Drinkwater at Ames

AFB in California—but we developed it into a fine art.

The first landing I made in a TF-102 at Edwards as part of our high-drag exercises was exciting. I chopped the throttle, lowered the gear, activated the speed brakes, and opened the missile bay; that damned Dagger came down like an elevator with all cables snapped. Bill Schweikhard was riding with me that day and I'll bet it still gives him nightmares. We decided to scrub high-drag landings in the TF-102 from the training program as too risky, but we kept them in for the F-104.

I took an F-104 up one day to try one of my zoom procedures. I was doing Mach 2.2 at 40,000 feet when, without warning, the Starfighter shook with a teeth-rattling explosion.

I looked at the tailpipe temperature indicator, which showed a reading past the red line. The fire warning light was staring at me malevolently and I knew the engine had exploded. I shut it down instantly and radioed a Mayday. My first impulse was to bail out. The plane was vibrating so badly that I thought it was going to shake itself to pieces. I reached for the ejection handle, but fortunately glanced at my airspeed indicator before pulling it. I was still doing Mach 2 and one does not eject from an airplane at twice the speed of sound, not even an airplane threatening to come apart.

I thought, *I'd better stay with this mother for a while,* and so informed Edwards. I started gliding down, praying that the tail wasn't going to burn itself off or fail from the vibration. I finally saw Edwards below, with its lifesaving long runways, and half-hoped I might make it. But my airspeed now was down to 250 knots, the F-104 was still vibrating badly, and I knew I wasn't going to make any runway—the Starfighter is a heavy fighter, weighing more than 20,000 pounds loaded, its glide angle is steep, and my airspeed was deteriorating fast.

I should have bailed out right then and there, but I was too bloody stubborn. At this particular time we had only two F-104s and I was damned if I was going to lose 50 percent of our Starfighter fleet. So I did something I never should have done.

I restarted the engine just to see if I could get some thrust.

I still was too far away from the Edwards runway, but there was a dry lake bed ahead of my flight path. I figured all I needed was a couple more minutes of additional thrust for my crippled bird to make it to the dry lake, and radioed Edwards my intentions. Just two or three minutes of power to give me a few extra miles.

I really was betting against the house. When I restarted the engine, thrust returned, but so did the ominous fire warning light, and the vibration increased. I kept the big General Electric J79 engine running for three precious minutes that seemed like three hours. Then I shut it down.

I saw the fire trucks from nearby Edwards already moving into position along the dry lake bed and I dead-sticked in. As soon as we stopped rolling, I jumped out and ran like hell, expecting the plane to explode, but the fire trucks roared up and sprayed the red-hot engine. Only then did I go back and look at the damage. There was a huge hole on the side of the rear fuselage where the explosion had occurred, and it was a miracle the tail had stayed on.

I grabbed a ride back to Edwards in a jeep and later phoned Susan.

"You're going to hear about a problem and you may have seen the fire trucks go out," I told her. "It was me and I'm fine."

"What happened?"

"I just lost an engine and dead-sticked in."

The investigation board found that one of the fuel nozzles had come loose, directing fuel toward the external part of the engine— in a direction that saved my life, incidentally.

They gave me a flying safety award for bringing the plane back. With delicious irony, they also gave the award to another pilot for *not* restarting his engine under almost the same circumstances. He had bailed out instead, and the investigators found that if he had restarted his engine, he would have blown the plane into five million pieces.

By the time our first class reported, I had been promoted to major and was a faculty member again—a flying faculty member whose initial classroom was a T-33. I'd first take my students up for an eye-opening introductory ride; most pilots had never spun a jet before, and for that matter had never experienced engine failure or a dead-stick landing. My procedure was to do hammerhead stalls, go into a spin, and while in the spin shut down the engine. Then I'd make them go through spin recovery and prepare for a powerless landing.

One student balked. "I can't do it, Major," he moaned. "Let's go back and just say I spun it."

"No spin, no graduation," I told him. "Look, I'll demonstrate one again, but then you have to do two spins."

He managed to get through the ordeal, and by the time we landed, he was strutting. At the officers' club that night, I overheard him bragging what a great fighter pilot he was—Captain Courageous, no less.

The cocky, overconfident students bothered me as much as the nervous Nellies. I had a foreign pilot who was convinced he could fly an iron bathtub if it had an engine and wings. We took off in a TF-104 with him flying the airplane. As we broke ground and began climbing fast, the fire warning light came on.

The student ignored it, so I retarded the throttle to shut off the afterburner.

"Why did you do that?" he yelled. "I'm flying this airplane!"

"Okay, if that's the way you want it, put the afterburner back in."

He did, and the fire warning came on again, glowing an ominous red.

"We've got to bail out!" he shouted.

"Sit still!" I ordered. I took over and nursed the plane down to a landing, followed by an instructor-to-student lecture on proper reaction to an obvious emergency.

My students were sharp—one was Dave Scott, who later flew three space missions. The accident rate at Edwards was very low—both the test pilot school and our own aerospace school got superior pilots, and the Air Force itself had been steadily weaned away from its old macho attitude about training. The tigers still had fangs and claws, but the tigers were also being taught that being aggressive didn't mean you had to kill yourself trying.

There was agreement among us instructors that our F-104s didn't have the capability that was needed for training pilots to make the transition from atmospheric flight to space flight and back to atmospheric. What we wanted was a conventional jet with performance approaching that of the rocket-powered X-15, a very tall order. The X-15 was purely experimental and extremely expensive to fly, totally unacceptable for training.

Through the Air Force, we requested formal proposals from airframe manufacturers for such an aircraft, and we had the backing of the new commanding officer of the test pilot school, none other than Chuck Yeager. He took over shortly after we got our graduate school in operation. He spent an awful lot of time hunting and fishing but he was an excellent boss, completely supportive and very likable in his own gruff way. He also happened to be one pilot who lived up to his press clippings. I flew with him a number of times and he was great. Yeager's presence was a good thing for the school— he didn't like to get involved with the nitty-gritty details of running it and never interfered with us because he trusted us.

Eventually, Northrop came back with a proposal to modify its T-38 Talon, the first supersonic jet trainer ever built, into an all-rocket plane. It looked promising but also looked too expensive. So one night Tom McElmurry and I took over Susan's kitchen and drew up a plan to put an auxiliary rocket engine into the F-104. We figured you could to to Mach 2.2 using conventional power, pull up the nose, shut down the main engine, and then fire the rocket. This would shoot the F-104 up to 130,000 feet, well above the atmosphere. When you came back down to around 40,000 feet, you'd restart the engine. We sent this proposal to Lockheed, builder of the Starfighter, and drew an instant response.

Among the people Lockheed sent to Edwards to discuss our modification-idea presentation was a tall young representative named Russell Ray. Years later he would be one of my senior vice presidents at Eastern in charge of marketing. After he left Eastern to become president of Pacific Southwest Airlines, he told a mutual friend, "You know, the first time I met Borman at Edwards, I thought he was running the test pilot school. Frank just had an air of command about him, the kind of abrupt personality that told you instantly you'd better get to the point fast because he didn't want you to waste his time."

We needed Air Force approval for an aircraft meeting our needs. Without mentioning the F-104 specifically, we took our plan to Washington and got approval there, but the specs still had to run the technical obstacle course at Wright-Patterson with the Air Force engineering brass. We went over our ideas with about thirty guys there and got thirty different reasons why the design wouldn't work. They kept insisting it amounted to a brand-new airplane and refused to approve it.

We finally got it classified as a simple modification to an existing aircraft, which could be done at McClellan AFB in Sacramento, California. A contract was signed with Lockheed, which proceeded to convert three F-104s into part-rocket aircraft, including the installation of rocket reaction controls. We were going to be pushing these planes up to altitudes where normal stabilizers would be biting into virtually nothing, and to give us some kind of control stability in the almost nonexistent air of the upper atmosphere we needed reaction controls—tiny thrusters, literally miniature rockets. They had first been used on the X-2 rocket plane.

To aid us in preparing our pilots for this new kind of flying we also asked for a sophisticated flight simulator, one realistic enough to give them an idea of what they'd be facing up there before they exposed their inexperience to the real thing. Yeager backed us 100 percent in this, too. Chuck was no aeronautical engineer, but he happened to be a superb test pilot with a gut feeling for what we were trying to accomplish, and he gave us plenty of leeway.

He was absolutely fearless, with a streak of the daredevil in him, an admirable trait in a test pilot but also a trait that on one unhappy occasion undid all the work we had put into our F-104 rocket planes.

Yeager regarded every new airplane as a fresh challenge to his flying skills, and he couldn't resist a challenge. So one day he decided to take up one of our hybrid beasts and try for a new altitude record. He got up to 108,000 feet on his first attempt, but wasn't satisfied and tried it again later that day. This time something went wrong; he got into an uncontrollable spin and had to bail out. He not only lost the airplane but ruined its reputation.

The Air Force figured that if the world's greatest test pilot had nearly bought the farm in our bird, it must be inherently unsafe, and it was scrubbed from the Edwards training program. I was in astronaut training at the time, and when I heard the rocket version had been grounded I had to blame Yeager for it. I thought he'd pulled a showboat stunt with an airplane designed for a specific purpose, and setting altitude records wasn't on its agenda. What Chuck had done was wipe out the most cost-effective vehicle ever developed for preliminary space training.

Yeager later claimed that trying for an altitude record had been mostly an afterthought. He said his main purpose had been to determine at what altitude the aircraft's tendency to "pitch up" (the nose would rise sharply) could overcome the rocket thruster and cause a spin. He said he wanted to test this before students began flying the hybrid. He must have gotten his chronology mixed up, because students already were flying the modified F-104s before he tried for that record.

It took more than a year, but when we finally got our hybrid-powered airplanes and the fancy simulator, we had turned Edwards into a top-notch training facility for military pilots making the transition to new vistas of flight. Long before this was achieved, however, I already had been seduced by those same vistas. In the spring of 1961, NASA had asked the Air Force and Navy to submit the names of additional astronaut candidates for the upcoming Gemini and Apollo space programs. The seven original astronauts had completed training and were getting ready to launch their series of Mercury flights.

The minute NASA's request for applications became known, I knew I was at one of those crucial crossroads in my life when a decision had to be made about whether to change career direction.

I laid out my options to Susan.

"I can stay at Edwards doing an important job," I explained. "The space flight school we're building is going to be vital to the whole space program. Or I can try to get into that program myself, as an astronaut. It's a chance to help make history, but you have to understand it will involve unknown risks."

She said, "Look, Frank, you have to choose your own career and you'll succeed at it. I'll go along with whatever you decide."

In March of 1961, I submitted my application to NASA; and while waiting, I kept busy getting the new graduate school underway. There were two interruptions, the first being a special Air Force physical examination required of all astronaut applicants. After the tests were completed, we candidates were sent to Washington for a meeting with top Air Force brass, including the legendary General Curtis LeMay.

It was the first time I had met the cigar-smoking Air Force Chief of Staff, and this guy wore an air of command authority like it was part of his uniform. He was a corncob made out of steel—when he walked into the room where we were gathered, you could almost hear our spines stiffen.

If I had any doubts about derailing my Air Force career in favor of offering up my body and soul to NASA, or any feeling that I was letting the Air Force down, all concerns evaporated when LeMay spoke. His leathery, jowled face wore an expression that was closer to bristling defiance than anything else.

"There are a lot of people who'll say you're deserting the Air Force if you're accepted into NASA," he began in a rasping voice. "Well, gentlemen, I'm Chief of the Air Force and I want you to know I want you in this program. I want you to succeed in it, and that's your Air Force mission. I can't think of anything more important, so don't any of you feel like a deserter."

I think there were about eighty of us who survived the first cut, and the Air Force soon pruned this number by almost fifty. I was one of the survivors of the screening, a process that included sending us to a kind of "charm school" where we were taught how to handle press interviews and use the proper utensils at dinner parties. The instructors even impressed upon us the importance of wearing long socks, and they introduced us to an inordinate number of general officers so we wouldn't be overawed by any top brass.

All this was part of the Air Force's pre-astronaut training. There were no written or oral tests, either psychological or intelligence. The Air Force was going by each man's previous record and the impression he had made during charm school and on the brass he had met. The hardest part of the screening process was the initial Air Force medical examination, conducted at Brooks AFB in San Antonio. The physical lasted three days and I thought that damned infamous ear of mine was going to wash me right out of NASA's hair. Every time a doctor would look at it, he'd yell, "Boy, look at this ear!" and call over another physician to inspect it.

After I resumed my duties at Edwards, I got orders to report back to Brooks for a separate NASA physical. Inasmuch as I had passed the Air Force's medical gauntlet with no problems (except for my ear becoming a sideshow attraction), I figured NASA would be a piece of cake. It turned out to be more difficult than I expected. Mike Collins was in our little group of survivors and I also met the man who would be my partner on two space missions: Lieutenant Commander James Arthur Lovell, Jr., of the United States Navy. Also representing the Navy was Charles "Pete" Conrad. Jim and Pete were to become trusted comrades and good friends, but at that stage of our astronaut careers Mike and I were looking at all these Navy types as competitors.

We had to endure a battery of psychological tests, my first full encounter with the mysteries of psychiatry. There were the usual ink blot tests, which implanted in us the fear that if something looked like a tree, it was a definite indication that we were sexual deviates. One test was a lulu—listening to Morse code signals while simultaneously performing some manual dexterity task. It would have befuddled an intelligent octopus.

Several tests were used to measure physical endurance. We blew up enough balloons to launch a dirigible. We were put on tilt tables with our feet immersed in ice water—you'd think we were being trained for a South Pole expedition. We must have accumulated hundreds of miles walking on treadmills while hooked up to EKG machines.

In one test, ice water was poured into one ear, a shock that destroyed your equilibrium. And while you were still reeling from this unexpected invasion of a very sensitive organ, they put you on a chair and spun you at a high rate of speed. When the chair stopped, you were supposed to stand up and stay as motionless as possible. The idea was to see how fast you could recover your balance.

The psychological testing could be more difficult than the physical phases, largely because few of us really understood the logic behind such questions as "Who I am?" We had to write down twenty answers in order of personal importance.

We had a session with several of the Mercury astronauts. They asked questions testing our technical knowledge, which weren't nearly as bad as what the psychiatrists threw at us. The shrinks worked from hundreds of pages of data compiled in the countless questionnaires we had filled out—including the number of traffic tickets we had acquired since getting our driver's licenses. (Speeding was the most common offense.)

Pete Conrad's advice on handling interviews was "If you can't be good, be colorful," but not many of us could be both good *and* colorful as Pete was—he had a wonderful sense of humor that he erected as a facade over his exceptional ability. One of the most dreaded questions ostensibly was one of the simplest: "Why do you want to be an astronaut?"

The trouble was that nobody was sure what kind of answer NASA preferred. I suspect more than one applicant was tempted to get flippant and come back with "Well, I love to travel. . . ."

When they threw the question at me, I replied, "Because being an astronaut is an extension of what I've been doing in the Air Force. I'm teaching people how to fly in space and NASA is the only area in which I can practice what I've been teaching."

We were at Brooks for a week, the majority of the time being spent in the medical department. I was walking a treadmill on May 6, 1961, the day Alan Shepard, riding the *Freedom 7* capsule, became the first American to fly in space. They suspended all testing so we could watch the Mercury-Redstone rocket launched on a flight that lasted only fifteen minutes and twenty-two seconds, attaining a maximum height of slightly over 116 miles and a maximum speed of 5,180 mph. We all cheered as we watched this Navy lieutenant commander take America into space for the first time, then went back to our treadmills, hypodermic needles, and ink blots.

The final part of the physical was a series of gastrointestinal tests, which included a proctoscope exam. Mine revealed a polyp the size of a BB shot; they took it out and, although a biopsy showed it to be non-malignant, they insisted on my staying over for additional GI tests.

I got the usual barium enema, followed by a session with some kind of X-ray machine hooked up to a small screen. They laid me on one side and started looking at the feature presentation on the screen.

One doctor exclaimed, "My God, look at that!"

Another said in the tone of a hanging judge, "You've got a mass in your belly, Major—it's a tumor. Very serious. You'll have to go into surgery this afternoon."

"You're nuts!" I retorted. "There isn't a damned thing wrong with me."

The four internists clustered around the table clucked disapprovingly at this amateur diagnosis. "Take a look at what's on the screen," the principal voice of doom advised ominously.

I looked and broke into a cold sweat. Sure enough, there was a white mass in my intestines. They were still conferring over the telltale X ray when a radiologist, a Dr. Randall, happened to come in and immediately asked what all the fuss was about. A definite tumor, possibly malignant, he was told. He looked at the screen and shook his head.

"Turn him over," he ordered.

The did. The white mass disappeared. Randall stared unbelievingly at his colleagues, as if they were a quartet of medical students about to flunk out.

"You've been looking at a pool of barium," he murmured.

By the time I left Edwards, in the early fall of 1962, I had logged more than fifty-five hundred flying hours, forty-five hundred of them in jets. I thought I had a good chance for NASA approval. I knew the Air Force itself was pushing hard to get more of its pilots into the space program. Shepard was Navy; John Glenn, who successfully flew *Friendship 7* in Mercury's first round-the-world orbital trip, was a Marine lieutenant colonel; and Scott Carpenter, a Navy lieutenant, had duplicated Glenn's feat in *Aurora 7*. Of the first four Mercury missions, three were flown by Navy or Marine pilots. The only Air Force representative was Virgil "Gus" Grissom, whose *Liberty Bell 7* followed Shepard's flight and preceded Glenn's. Unfortunately, Grissom's capsule sank after its splashdown in the Atlantic.

The Air Force was slightly embarrassed, and its pride was further hurt when USAF Captain Donald "Deke" Slayton, who should have flown *Aurora 7* instead of Carpenter, developed a heart murmur that grounded him. He was appointed director of astronaut activities and it was Deke who ended my suspense by telling me I had been accepted.

This left me with one more task. I had to tell Chuck Yeager, so I marched jauntily into his office. "Colonel, I just received great news."

"What's your good news, Borman?"

"Deke Slayton called me and I've been accepted into the NASA program."

Yeager gave me a look that should have been reserved for someone who had just announced he was being audited by the IRS.

"Well, Borman," he growled, "you can kiss your goddamned Air Force career good-bye."

He apparently hadn't heard of LeMay's approval of Air Force officers going into the space program.

But in a way, Chuck Yeager was right.

PART TWO
1962–1970

6

CAPTAIN KIRK'S ANCESTORS

Not even NASA's own historical section knows exactly who decided to call America's space crew members "astronauts."

It probably came out of some committee meeting when the Mercury program was in the early planning stages, as almost simultaneously the Soviet Union tagged its own space explorers with the title "cosmonauts." Both words are derived from the name for the mythical searchers for the Golden Fleece, the Argonauts. The word "astronaut" first appeared in a French science fiction novel published in 1880.

On September 17, 1962, an Air Force pilot who as a boy had never read science fiction because it bored him became an astronaut.

There were nine of us assigned to the forthcoming Gemini and Apollo programs, missions aimed at achieving in gradual stages the ultimate goal of lunar landing. Mercury had been the first stage of this carefully orchestrated plan, and several of the Mercury astronauts would be carried over into the Gemini phase. The nine men constituting America's second group of astronauts included myself and, from the Navy, Lieutenant Charles Conrad, thirty-two; Lieutenant Commander James Lovell, thirty-four; and Lieutenant Commander John Young, thirty-two. From the Air Force, Captain James McDivitt, thirty-four; Captain Thomas Stafford, thirty; and Captain Edward White, thirty-two. From civilian test pilot ranks, Neil Armstrong, thirty-two, and Elliot See, thirty-five—both ex-Navy.

All were married and all of us had children. We each had an aeronautical engineering background and test pilot experience, but none of us was poured out of the same mold. Our personalities varied from the reserved ones like Armstrong to the more outgoing Lovell and Conrad. The most important thing we had in common was dedication; in that crucial quality, I've never known a finer group of men.

That also went for the two Mercury astronauts I got to know especially well, Deke Slayton and Wally Schirra. A lesser man than Deke could have become embittered by his terrible disappointment, but instead he was an enthusiastic team worker who might as well have been up there with us on every mission. And the extroverted Wally was just sheer fun. Schirra was one of the astronauts who honestly enjoyed the hoopla and attention; while I didn't share all his enthusiasm, I sure appreciated being treated so royally.

All of us in the Borman family knew our world had changed when we arrived in Houston—we were sudden celebrities. Fred was eleven and Edwin only nine; they had been uprooted and moved around from pillar to post all their young lives, so I don't think my being an astronaut really sank in until we got to Houston. Up to then, they had expected just another change of scenery, but suddenly they were caught up in all the publicity attached to the astronaut program. My own publicity baptism had already occurred shortly after I was accepted into NASA and flown to Houston with the other new astronauts for a news conference.

I had been told to take the family to the Shamrock Hilton as soon as we arrived. At the time, it was one of the plushest hotels in the United States, and as soon as we walked into the ornate lobby, I whispered to Susan, "My God, we can't afford to stay here." Then we learned we were being given a complimentary suite for as long as it took us to find more permanent quarters—a magnanimous gesture on the part of owner Eric Hilton, one of Conrad's sons.

I didn't get much chance to enjoy the unexpected luxury. We had just checked in when NASA advised us that all nine new astronauts would be flown to Cape Canaveral (it didn't become Cape Kennedy until November 1963, when President Johnson renamed it in honor of his predecessor) to watch Wally Schirra's flight aboard *Sigma 7* launched into orbit by an Atlas rocket on October 3, 1962.

This was Project Mercury's fifth mission and it was a textbook operation. Schirra completed six orbits in nine hours and fourteen minutes after launch. Not only were the orbital passes successful, but Wally also accomplished most of his assigned scientific experiments, including one that involved "drifting flight"—a test in which he shut down all the maneuvering systems to determine what effect random motion in a spacecraft would have on the pilot. Drifting flight meant fuel conservation, and when Schirra demonstrated that it presented no serious problems, he paved the way for longer flights.

This was the key element of the Mercury, Gemini, and Apollo projects—each succeeding mission was one more step toward the lunar landing goal. Every flight proved something new; every step was deliberately cautious, to reduce risk as much as possible. Patience, in fact, was synonymous with safety, for each mission operated within its established parameters. As the unknowns were progressively exposed and understood, the parameters were extended. Schirra's flight was typical of this philosophy. Before we could attempt long flights through fuel conservation, NASA had to know whether a pilot could handle drifting flight.

In 1962, the Manned Spacecraft Center in Houston wasn't a "center" at all—NASA's offices were spread all over the city. Where the huge Johnson Space Center now stands was nothing but a cow pasture; the site had been chosen but construction hadn't started. I wanted to settle down in a home near where I'd be working, as close to the future center as possible, and when we couldn't find any existing homes in the area we rented a house in Houston temporarily and decided to build. Susan and some of the other astronauts' wives went looking for lots and I signed my first home-building contract for a purchase price of $26,500.

I didn't really get to know my eight brother astronauts until we started training. We were to spend the next eight years together, and I'd sum up my impressions with this observation: They were all talented and highly individualistic, and I can't think of a single man who didn't perform his mission or missions in a superior manner. Their personalities varied, but on the job each was tough, realistic, and knowledgeable.

We were very much alike in physical characteristics, and this was because the cramped cockpit of the early space modules (spacecraft) dictated our size. Originally, NASA set a maximum height limit of five feet eleven inches; there was no official weight restriction, but the screeners would have looked askance at anyone weighing more than 180 pounds. For our bunch, NASA stretched the height limit to an even six feet. Stafford just made it, and although Ed White was listed at five-eleven I always thought he was as tall as Tom. None of us weighed more than 175, and McDivitt, who was almost a six-footer, was our beanpole at 155. Conrad at just under five-seven and 145 pounds was the shortest and lightest. I was sort of in the middle at five-ten and 163.

We had rapport that created a unique brand of friendship. All nine of us were extremely competitive, but I can't remember anyone playing politics or angling to get ahead of the rest. The only inter-service rivalry among four Air Force and five Navy or ex-Navy pilots was good-natured ribbing. Our service personalities evaporated almost to the vanishing point as we went through our metamorphosis into astronauts.

NASA recruited men, not saints, although our group was pretty straightlaced. I knew one married astronaut in another program who would chase anything in skirts—not that he had to do much chasing. Every Mercury, Gemini, and Apollo astronaut was faced with an inordinate amount of temptation. We were glamorous celebrities, often separated from our families for long periods of time, and there always were the groupies who regarded going to bed with an astronaut as the ultimate romantic accomplishment. At least one girl kept score of her conquests, like a fighter pilot recording kills.

The astronauts brought their own moral and ethical standards into a celebrity environment that had its own way of intensifying those standards. The pressures of temptation caused those few with somewhat flexible ethics to go overboard, but those same pressures had the opposite effect on the astronauts with strong moral and family commitments.

No one had trouble switching from a military career to the space program. I was fresh out of Edwards, where I had been doing essentially the same thing.

NASA began our training by assigning each of us a specialty, the mastery of a specific phase of space flight. Mine was booster rockets, and my first job was to learn everything there was to learn about the Titan II that would launch the two-man Gemini modules into orbit. We still had to be interchangeable of course; we all had to know something about everything in addition to our specialties, because every man had to be ready to assume someone else's duties if necessary.

My booster assignment was mostly to become an expert on the launch abort system and other safety systems that were being incorporated into the Gemini and Apollo boosters and spacecraft. It was in this capacity that I met and became friends with the legendary Wernher von Braun, easily the world's most renowned living rocket and aerospace expert. He was director of NASA's George C. Marshall Space Flight Center in Huntsville, Alabama, formerly the Army's Redstone Arsenal; although he had been the guiding force behind Germany's V-2 rockets, he was never a Nazi and was one of the German rocket scientists who emigrated to the United States after the war.

He was one of the most fascinating persons I ever met. He spoke perfect English with only a slight trace of accent, and his voice was rather high, almost melodic. The "von" in his name meant nothing—he was about as Prussian as Jimmy Stewart and just as likable. He also possessed unusual characteristics you seldom find together in one man.

First, he was an excellent engineer and scientist, and you couldn't fool him with a bunch of uninformed opinions or theories—von Braun knew details, he knew math, and he knew mechanics. But in addition to being a pragmatist he also was a visionary, an unusual combination. America's Robert Goddard and Germany's Wernher von Braun were the joint fathers of space travel in their zeal and dedication to that dream. Third, von Braun was a natural leader with the ability to choose equally dedicated and competent assistants and associates, Americans as well as Germans, and they all adored him. Finally, he was a natural-born salesman with the enthusiasm and persuasive skills of a pitchman. He *sold* the space program in such a way as to silence the cynics and reassure the pessimists.

I spent months working closely with von Braun's team mostly developing the emergency detection system (EDS) we'd have to use in the event of a launch abort. The eventual system was an excellent interface between man and machine—our EDS was designed to put the machine in command when man didn't have sufficient reaction time to cope with an abort emergency, but could be switched to the pilot when he had time for judgment and action.

I came into this crew safety program during its second phase, smack in the middle of a controversy. Several NASA engineers, as well as some of the astronauts, felt strongly that only the man should be pushing the buttons when everything hit the fan. That was the way the Mercury astronauts had operated and there was considerable support for continuing this philosophy.

A number of engineers were making a case for allowing the crew to pilot the booster into orbit in the event of a failure in the booster's guidance system. But after discussing this man-versus-machine debate with von Braun, and studying the EDS he wanted, I sided with what I thought was a more pragmatic solution—to put the crew into a secondary position when they clearly couldn't function in time.

I never had any feeling that von Braun was trying to cut man out of the loop entirely. There was no question in either of our minds that the crew could handle an emergency—provided they had enough time to react. If they didn't, we were convinced the crew needed a mechanical backup system. I took that stand much to the consternation of some of my friends in the astronaut program, including an able engineer named Warren North. North was a former pilot and, like so many pilots, he was never sold on the idea that any machine was superior to human judgment and skill.

Yet there was a significance to all these arguments. NASA in those days really *listened* to the astronauts' opinions, and so did the top scientists like von Braun. There may have been honest disagreements, but at least there was communication and exchange of ideas. When I saw the movie *The Right Stuff,* I was furious at the hatchet job on von Braun, with the implication that he and the other scientists didn't give a damn about astronauts' opinions.

NASA also sent me to the Martin Marietta plants in Denver and Baltimore where the Titans were being built. These were just two of many trips I took during the astronaut years; I was away from home two thirds of the time, causing separations from the family that were far longer than those I had subjected them to in the Air Force. As Fred and Edwin grew older, I spent as much time with them as I could, usually taking them hunting or fishing, but I was a part-time father, and it was Susan who bore most of the responsibility for raising our sons. My input was well meant and sincere, but it was also too sporadic for me to take much credit for how well they turned out.

After I became pretty well versed in boosters, I briefed the other eight on what I had learned. They followed the same procedure according to their own specialties. The preliminary training, before mission assignments were handed out, was fairly general and divided between the scholastic and the physical. We had about two hundred hours of classroom sessions on such subjects as astronomy, aerodynamics as it applied to spacecraft, rocket propulsion, communications (including space lingo, which literally was a new language), meteorology, atmospheric physics, guidance and navigation, flight mechanics (the mathematical aspects of trajectories and orbits), digital computers, and geology.

Some of it was valuable; some I judged to be a waste of time. They gave us about fifty hours of geology, which included trips to such fun places as the Grand Canyon and Meteor Crater in Arizona. The idea was to prepare those astronauts who would be assigned moon landings and subsequent exploration of the lunar surface, but fifty hours? I didn't think that much was necessary.

When Mike Collins went through this training a year later, he was especially critical of how some of the technical subjects were being taught, computers being his pet peeve. He argued that NASA was emphasizing how computers were made instead of teaching the astronauts how to use them as a vital part of space flight. Mike's point was well taken; it was like asking somebody the time and getting an hour's lecture on how to make a watch.

The most difficult part of the training was the huge volume of information we were supposed to absorb. It was coming at us out of a high-pressure firehose instead of a faucet. Fortunately we weren't being graded, or there might have been some undeserved washouts. Conversely, the physical training—which included a lot of jogging— wasn't that hard for men who were in pretty good shape to begin with. The overall curriculum had to be experimental in itself—both Gemini and Apollo involved a lot of unknown factors, so NASA was feeling its way in grooming us.

We went to Panama for an Air Force survival course, but compared to the one I had taken in Nevada, it was about as tough as a cooking class. We spent two days in classroom instruction and three days foraging (we ate lizards) and hiking through the Panama jungles. The greatest discomfort came from two of nature's most minuscule menaces, neither of which was very prevalent in the Sierra Nevada: chiggers and mosquitoes. If I had to come down in some wilderness, I'd far prefer mountain country to a jungle.

Throughout training, particularly in the later stages, the chief subject of conversation concerned which Gemini missions we'd be assigned to. Crew assignments were the responsibility of Deke Slayton, and he performed this task with unquestioned integrity. It was only natural for us to speculate on whether our specialties would be the main factors in Deke's crew choices, although there was no connection.

Three of the Mercury astronauts were carried over into Gemini— Gus Grissom, Gordon Cooper, and Wally Schirra, Grissom getting command of *Gemini 3* (the first manned Gemini flight), Cooper *Gemini 5,* and Schirra *Gemini 6.* (*Gemini 1* was an unmanned test of the Titan II, and *Gemini 2,* also unmanned, was used to confirm the integrity of the heat-resistant shields on the fully equipped module.) But Slayton gave the Mercury veterans a sort of veto power over the men selected to accompany them on the two-man Gemini missions. I found this out when Grissom called me one day.

"Look, I've got *Gemini 3* and you've been picked as my co-pilot," he told me.

"That's fine, Gus. I'm really pleased."

"Why don't you come over to my house and we'll talk."

I did, and we talked for about an hour. I haven't the slightest idea what went wrong, but he apparently wasn't too impressed with me. The next thing I knew, I had been replaced by John Young, who didn't try very hard to conceal his delight, for which I couldn't blame him.

But Slayton gave me another assignment: commander of the backup crew for *Gemini 4,* the second manned mission, with Jim Lovell as my co-pilot. McDivitt and White would be the primary crew and we all began mission training together. Visits to the factories where the major components of *Gemini 4* spacecraft were being built were first on the agenda, starting with McDonnell Douglas in St. Louis.

James "Old Mac" McDonnell himself, head of the huge firm, was our host at a welcoming cocktail party held at a beautiful country club on a weeknight shortly after we arrived. McDonnell was a hard-nosed, no-nonsense gentleman, a true giant in the aerospace industry, and while he was a genial host he did something unusual that night. At precisely 10 P.M., he ordered musicians to play "The Star-Spangled Banner," announcing to his guests, "These young men have work to do tomorrow, so the party's over." It was the first and only time I've ever seen a cocktail party terminated by the national anthem.

We also went out to Aerojet in Sacramento to witness the firing of a Gemini launch-vehicle engine cluster. The Titan II cluster had two barrels or rocket engines; one scenario for a catastrophic failure would be to have only one engine fire at launch time—this would impart such a violent yawing motion that the Titan would break up before the crew had a chance to get out.

We discussed the possibility of this happening with the Aerojet engineers, who kept assuring us it couldn't happen because of elaborate safeguards built into the system. Absolutely fail-safe, we were told.

So we went into a protective blockhouse to witness a first firing, waiting expectantly for the countdown to finish. *Five, four, three, two, one*—ignition!

But in only one engine.

There were an awful lot of chagrined, red faces in that blockhouse, but the engineers took their setback like men and I gained great respect for them, one in particular. His name was Al Feldman; later he became president of Frontier Airlines and then Continental. He was typical of the dedicated aerospace engineers working with NASA and all the astronauts in this era. At Aerojet that day, for example, we heard no alibis, no buck passing, no rationalization that it must have been a fluke. In effect the staff admitted, "We goofed and we'll go right back to the drawing board until we get it right."

This attitude applied not just to the engineers but also to the people on the assembly lines. We astronauts were the beneficiaries of stringent quality-control procedures that showed in the superb hardware we were able to take into space. We'd go through factories, day and night, and the workers would call out to us, "Don't worry, guys—we'll give you the best." And they did. Like the astronauts themselves, they had been infected with the mystique of early space exploration.

Yet it was more than a mystique. There was a can-do attitude, an espirit de corps forged out of sheer patriotism. We were racing the Russians, and the challenge to catch up and surpass them affected every man and woman even remotely associated with the space program, from NASA's top officials right down to the workers producing the tools. We lost this nationalistic fervor later and paid dearly for it—progress slowed, pride deteriorated, and brave lives were sacrificed. I wince when I compare the NASA of my time to the sloppy design work, bungled planning, and misguided emphasis on a public relations image that led to the *Challenger* disaster. We had a "zero defects" commitment from the aerospace industry entrusted with building Gemini and Apollo hardware. The *Challenger* crew took off on the wings of a launch vehicle known to be only marginally safe, and actually dangerous in the weather conditions prevailing that tragic day.

God knows our programs weren't perfect, and we learned this the hard way, but we were still groping, searching, experimenting. We— and I mean NASA as well as the contractors, technicians, engineers, and astronauts—didn't try to sweep our mistakes under rugs labeled "Image," "Public Relations," "Profits," and "Face." The astronauts of Mercury, Gemini, and Apollo worked for a NASA run by men of integrity and consummate ability. Its high standards started at the top and percolated right down through the ranks, and it had a leadership that *listened* to those who had to carry out its orders.

The NASA I knew was a unique government agency—a bureaucracy that contained relatively few bureaucrats—and this was due largely to its director, James E. Webb, who had headed NASA since 1961 when he succeeded T. Keith Glennan, the agency's first director. In my view, no finer public servant ever lived than Webb. This heavy-set, drawling native of North Carolina was something of a sleeper when President Kennedy put the space program in his hands; a lawyer by profession, he had sparse scientific background and not much more in aviation—he had served a brief stint as a Marine Corps pilot back in the 1930s.

But the infant NASA didn't need an Albert Einstein or a Charles Lindbergh. What it needed, and what it got in the person of Jim Webb, was a skilled administrator with guts, vision, motivation, and dedication—the same qualities he would expect, in turn, from those working under him.

Webb ran an agency that in many respects was a Washington anomaly. Its surprisingly meager supply of bureaucratic procrastination and inaction was its main feature and perhaps its greatest strength, and this was due largely to the fact that the heart and soul of the space program lay not in the nation's capital but in the field— at such places as the Manned Spacecraft Center in Houston, the launch complex at the cape, and the Space Flight Center in Huntsville.

NASA's partial decentralization of the decision-making process not only diminished Washington's influence but tended to eliminate interference with men who were not politicians or bureaucrats, but scientists and engineers. This didn't mean Jim Webb was a figurehead; on the contrary, he was a tough boss who simply understood that in an operation almost entirely technological, there had to be some measure of autonomy in the field. Not every top official could have accepted this fact of life, but it worked at NASA because one of Webb's greatest virtues was his lack of ego.

It also worked because of the caliber of his lieutenants. Webb was to the space program what General George Catlett Marshall had been to the Army in World War II. As Army Chief of Staff, Marshall had given his generals a great deal of latitude, trusting them to make the right field decisions while he fought their battles in Washington. Webb did much the same at NASA, leaving scientific decisions up to the technical experts while he fought their battles in Washington.

It would take scores of pages to list all the unselfish professionals behind every space mission during my eight years with NASA, but several of the most outstanding deserve special mention.

There was Robert Rowe Gilruth, the bald-headed director of the Manned Spacecraft Center, whose thin voice belied his unfailing equilibrium under pressure. Compassionate, calm, and competent—that was Bob Gilruth, a bear of a man with laughing eyes and a quiet, reserved manner that provided the program with stability and leadership. He had been a flight research engineer since 1937, when he joined the old National Advisory Committee on Aeronautics (NACA), NASA's forerunner, and later was chief of the pilotless aircraft research program at Langley Aeronautical Center in Virginia.

Almost every astronaut of that era respected Chris Kraft, our director of flight operations and another NACA and Langley veteran. He was a medium-sized guy with thinning hair, a ready smile, and a Virginia accent that made you want to start waving a Confederate flag. Kraft was absolutely unflappable in a crisis and he shared with Gilruth a determination never to let any man or woman in the program neglect what they considered to have as high a priority as the mission itself: the astronauts' safety.

Gilruth reported to Webb and Kraft reported to Gilruth, while Deke Slayton was in charge of flight crew operations. There also was an Office of Manned Space Flight in Washington, headed at the time I entered the program by George Mueller. Under Mueller was Lieutenant General Sam Phillips of the Air Force, whose cold-steel appearance masked a man of great compassion and brilliance; Sam was to head the Apollo program as its Washington director.

These men were typical of the brains and leadership behind each mission, willingly letting us grab the glory and the headlines while they grappled with the headaches and heartaches. I don't think the country has ever realized the debt it owed them. All I know is that when they began to leave NASA, the space agency began to slide downhill until the *Challenger* tragedy became almost inevitable.

While all of us griped about certain individual aspects of our training, we couldn't criticize its intense thoroughness. We were not only prepared but fine-tuned, honed, and brainwashed. The biggest drawback was that this ruthless but necessary regime turned our domestic lives into a shambles.

While training for Gemini and Apollo, I averaged 250 days a year away from home. Jim Lovell's family used to call him "the traveling salesman," and I was just as bad. In fact, while I was preparing for *Gemini 7*, I could find every switch, knob, and lever in the spacecraft blindfolded. But when I got home, I didn't know where Susan kept the water glasses.

We were never counseled on this difficult adjustment. It wasn't really NASA's fault, because the space agency itself wasn't prepared. And some of our adjustment problems were our own fault. Basically most of us still had the fighter pilot's macho hangups and would have regarded any psychological assistance as a form of weakness. So we expected our families to suppress their fears, look happy every time a camera was pointed in their direction, and perform like trained seals. And what made it worse was that too many people in NASA expected this of them, too.

Most of us, I think, tolerated the distractions foisted on us in the interests of public relations without honestly enjoying them. We had to admit we were news, yet there were times when I wished NASA had imitated the Soviets' policy when it came to publicizing the exploits of their space crews. The Russians didn't earn the title of cosmonaut until they had completed training, and as public figures they were anonymous until they had flown a mission. In contrast, we became astronauts from day one and were accorded a hero's status before we did anything to deserve it.

We lived the kind of fishbowl existence that demolished personal privacy, and this was a new and unexpected source of tension for our families. Wives and children alike were expected to be perpetually cheerful, brave, and understanding before the news media, even when they were depressed, scared, and afflicted with a loneliness that defied understanding.

The newsmen and newswomen assigned to cover the space program were a mixed breed. We met incompetent reporters, obnoxious reporters, and overaggressive reporters. We also met professionals who earned our trust and respect. My personal favorite was Dick Witkin of *The New York Times,* in my opinion the most objective, knowledgeable, and skilled of them all.

Another newsman I grew to like and admire was the late Jules Bergman, science reporter for ABC television. He was terribly aggressive, a trait that made him unpopular among some of his colleagues as well as the astronauts, and he was overly zealous in seeking the sensational side of any story. But if you told him the truth, it stuck.

Like Witkin, who was in a class by himself, Bergman was indefatigable in checking his facts and in seeking both sides of a story, which is more than I can say for some of their compatriots. Actually the famous (or infamous, depending on one's point of view) *Life* magazine contract with the Mercury, Gemini, and Apollo astronauts protected us to some extent from the invading press.

This was the controversial, much-criticized deal negotiated with *Life* and Field Enterprises giving those two organizations exclusive rights to the "personal stories" of the astronauts and their families. Jim Webb was strongly opposed to the contract and tried to block it, but, as I heard the story, he was overruled by President Kennedy himself after John Glenn convinced JFK it was a fair and logical arrangement.

All I know is that the sixteen thousand dollars a year we got out of the contract was a godsend. It enabled us to keep up the payments on the Houston house, allowed me to pay some exorbitant premiums for previously acquired life insurance, and elevated the Bormans to the economic status of a middle-class family. It sure as hell didn't make us rich. We were still on regular military pay, and as astronauts we couldn't buy additional life insurance because at the time our jobs were considered too risky.

Certainly there was some natural resentment about the whole deal. Test pilots like Yeager, who had really taken the first step into space by flying the X-15, got no financial reward, whereas the astronauts—including those who hadn't flown a space mission yet—were getting sixteen thousand dollars extra a year, plus all the adulation. But that sum was *all* we got; we weren't allowed to endorse anything, and I've always felt the contract was fair because it provided our families with a modicum of financial security in an exceptionally demanding environment.

The *Life* reporter assigned to the Bormans was a sensitive, perceptive lady named Georgeann Hamlin. Everyone called her Dody and she practically moved in with us and became a member of the family. Dody was one of the few newspeople who came anywhere close to understanding what the astronauts' wives and children were going through. Actually, the news coverage was rather sterilized, as if the news media itself was infected with the patriotic aura—almost everyone wanted the space program to be presented in the most favorable light possible. I know it took a damned fine reporter with unusual perceptiveness to win the confidence of Susan and the boys; neither Fred nor Edwin thought much of all the notoriety, although they coped with it well.

There were times when living in the space complex was like residing in a foreign country, where you tend to concentrate friendships solely among your fellow Americans. But we did manage to create some extensions to the outside community and we made some good friends in Houston. One family in particular was to play an important role in our lives—the Elkinses, all native Houstonians. Bill Elkins was a local lawyer who introduced us to his banker brother, Jim, and Jim's wife, Margaret. Jim was president of the First City National Bank.

Bill had a home on a nearby lake and we used to take the family fishing there. Some of the astronauts became almost totally isolated from the outside world, but the Elkinses saved us from that. We lived in a community called El Largo, which was almost exclusively populated by NASA people, including many of the astronauts' families. I tried my best to establish the closest thing to a normal family life that was possible under the circumstances; although we astronauts traveled almost constantly, I headed home every chance I got, and having airplanes at my disposal was a decided advantage even though it often meant flying back to Houston at two or three o'clock in the morning.

Maintaining even the slightest semblance of normal family ties during training was important to me. I knew that when the real thing came along, an actual space mission, those ties would be further strained.

And the real thing turned out to be *Gemini 7*.

7

COUNTDOWN
TO THE COUNTDOWN

"T minus five . . ."

The tinny voice of Capsule Communications (CapCom) cut through my earphones.

". . . four . . . three . . . two . . . one."

A heartbeat of a pause.

Then, *"Gemini 7,* you have ignition."

I heard a tiny rumble and felt the motion of lift-off. My eyes scanned the instrument panel, like a mentally guided searchlight probing for the first sign of trouble. And the first sign glared back at me—one dial was fluctuating, slowly at first glance, but then with increasing wildness. Something was wrong with the guidance system.

"CapCom, our pitch indicator is diverging."

"Roger, *Gemini 7.* We have a malfunction showing, too. Hang on for a while."

A logical suggestion. Probably a faulty instrument, I thought, and not a real emergency. Eject now and the whole mission goes down the drain. On the other hand, we were sitting on top of a 100-foot rocket loaded with 100,000 pounds of highly explosive fuel. . . .

Two heartbeats later, the pitch needle began spinning crazily and the entire instrument panel blurred out of focus.

Every light in the spacecraft went out.

"We're dead," I said to Jim Lovell. "I waited too long."

That scenario was played out in a *Gemini 7* spacecraft simulator and the amuck pitch indicator was one of about four hundred separate emergencies tossed at us during training. Simulators were easily the most important cog in the training process, but there was another, rather subtle factor involved: the hundreds and thousands of hours we had spent flying different types of airplanes, including high-performance models.

Nothing could have better prepared me for space flight than what I had experienced as a fighter pilot, instructor, and test pilot. And this is why we insisted on flying the T-33s and T-38s assigned to NASA, over voluminous objections from a few bureaucrats within NASA and the Office of Management and Budget. NASA thought we were taking unnecessary risks; OMB complained we were wasting money and should limit our flying to simulators, which didn't consume expensive fuel.

Bunk. Flying involves decision making and it's as much a part of a pilot as the airplane itself, or a spacecraft. You could put an ape into a space module and eventually teach him by rote to fly the damned thing, but you can't give him the background that comes from what you've gone through before. You can't teach him to make split-second decisions based more on instinct than on book-learned judgment—the kind of gut instinct that comes from having cheated death a few hundred times.

All through astronaut training, I kept thinking back to those occasions and realized *they* had been a part of my astronaut training, too.

Late one night, I was taking off in a NASA T-33 from Scott AFB, Illinois, bound for an important Gemini conference in Washington. Thunderstorms were all around, vicious and threatening. But there was no way I was going to miss that meeting, so I gunned down the runway and began climbing, right into the sharp teeth of a thunderhead.

At 5,000 feet, the engine died in a flameout caused by water ingestion—it was raining so hard I might as well have been in a submarine.

The book told me to turn back and land. Instinct told me otherwise—it wasn't my first flameout or my first thunderstorm. I hit the ignition switch, the engine restarted, and I made my meeting.

I learned that airplanes—and spacecraft—are designed and built to fly by the numbers. Those numbers can be critical, with a sliver-thin margin for error—so thin that an inexperienced pilot doesn't always believe them and panics. Once I took off from Luke in a heavy F-84 with the summer temperature above 100 degrees. I had calculated the length of the takeoff roll based on outside temperature, aircraft weight, wind, and engine performance. It was a 10,000-foot runway and the slide rule told me I'd use up 9,800 feet before I could get airborne. When I rotated and broke ground, that's all I left—a bare 200 feet of concrete ahead of me. A rookie might have looked at the same 200 feet, figured the numbers had to be wrong, and blown out three tires vainly trying to abort the takeoff.

The NASA of more recent years got the idea that you could put almost any highly intelligent person into a spacecraft and qualify him as an astronaut pilot. Wrong. We took into those simulators the accumulated knowledge, experience, and seat-of-the-pants instincts derived from flying aircraft that could be even more temperamental and treacherous than a spacecraft. We were veteran pilots before we became rookie astronauts, and that made the difference.

I never turned back from a mission unless I knew it was hopeless and stupid to continue. I always weighed the urge to quit against confidence in my ability and in the aircraft I was flying.

This was the philosophy I took into *Gemini 7* training.

"Gemini" itself is a Latin word meaning twins. Originally the program was to be called Project Mercury Mark II, but everyone at NASA thought this rather uninspiring. It was Alex Nagy of the Office of Manned Space Flight in Washington who suggested naming the second phase Project Gemini, after the mythological twin brothers Castor and Pollux, the patron gods of voyagers. Gemini is also the third constellation of the zodiac, which made the choice even more appropriate.

Project Gemini officially began on April 8, 1964, with the successful test launching of a Titan II rocket, and ten months later *Gemini 2* demonstrated the integrity of the heat shield in the reentry of an unmanned capsule similar to the ones we'd be flying. At this stage, we still were trailing the Soviet Union and Gemini itself was about a year behind NASA's own schedule, largely because it took time to cure the Titan II of severe "pogo stick" problems—longitudinal vibrations. The Russians launched their own multi-manned space flights in October of 1964, when we hadn't even gotten around to *Gemini 2* yet.

But on March 23, 1965—nine days after my thirty-seventh birthday—the United States really began catching up. That was the day *Gemini 3* was launched, our first test of a fully maneuverable spacecraft and the start of an accelerated program that was to culminate in beating the Soviet Union in the race to put a man on the moon.

It also was the day astronauts, in effect, stopped being mere passengers and became space pilots. I don't mean that to be disparaging of the Mercury astronauts. The chief difference between Mercury and Gemini was in the capsules. Our predecessors were put into primitive, unsophisticated vehicles over which they had virtually no control. If we in Gemini had the longer, more difficult missions, it was because we had the vehicles in which to accomplish those missions.

In terms of scientific complexity, however, Gemini was more of an extension of Mercury's progressively longer orbital goals than an entirely new program. Mercury taught us how to crawl, Gemini how to walk and run; in Apollo we would learn how to fly. What all three programs had in common was NASA's meticulous preparation, embracing everything from astronaut training to insistence on every component in every launch rocket and spacecraft meeting all performance and safety requirements. The fact that NASA not only allowed but invited the astronauts themselves to participate in this policy simply enhanced the chances for success. It was a policy that could be summed up in one sentence: "Don't take a single thing for granted."

Tough decisions had to be made prior to *Gemini 3*—decisions that definitely contributed to the program's falling behind schedule, but that NASA felt were essential to preventing failure or tragedy as far as was humanly possible. Time after time, contractors were sent back to the drawing board to correct any suspected or known deficiencies.

One of Gemini's goals was to rendezvous a spacecraft with an unmanned target vehicle, a preparatory step leading to the time when we could dock two capsules or dock a spacecraft with a future space station. The rocket chosen was the reliable Atlas-Agena—the Agena being a small target vehicle mounted on the nose of the Atlas—but modifying the Atlas to carry an Agena produced enough bugs to satisfy an entomologists' convention, and the bug eradication took time.

Then there was the paraglider controversy, an internal war among NASA's engineers over the safest way to land the Gemini astronauts and recover their spacecraft, which were at least twice the weight of the Mercury capsules. The paraglider concept, invented by Langley's Frances Rogallo, was something of a Rube Goldberg affair in which the spacecraft would sprout inflated wings after reentry and glide to a landing. Built into the system were ejection seats to be used in case there was trouble with the glider wings. The main purpose of the paraglider was to provide a means of landing a spacecraft on land instead of water.

North American got a contract to develop, test, and install a paraglider system, but people like Max Faget, head of NASA's engineering and development office, and Chris Kraft were adamantly opposed to the concept right from the start and fought hard to prevent its adoption. Faget argued in behalf of an improved large-parachute technology instead of spending time and money on a complicated and unproven concept. Chris, too, felt the paraglider system was too complicated to be totally reliable.

Faget and Kraft eventually won out, with NASA deciding to use huge new parachutes for the cushioning requirements. But they came damned close to losing their battle; NASA actually scheduled the paraglider system for installation on *Gemini 3*. When the test program developed a number of flaws, installation was rescheduled for the *Gemini 5* mission. But North American itself doomed the program after being named prime contractor to build the Apollo spacecraft; it froze the number of engineers assigned to the paraglider, which already was in trouble. Subsequent tests showed the system was what Faget and Kraft had feared—too unreliable. It actually worked perfectly only twice in tests. Maybe further development would have perfected it, but this would have been one more setback to NASA's well-bruised timetable.

And all along, NASA was not averse to accepting suggestions, criticism, and advice from the astronauts. One example: Long before *Gemini 3*, John Young went to Wright-Patterson AFB, where McDonnell Douglas had put a mockup of the Gemini capsule into the zero-G KC-135 airplane. John looked it over, returned to Houston, and told the brass the mockup "is just terrible," explaining that it wasn't realistic enough. A newer, more exact replica was built immediately.

Then McDivitt and White checked out the revised mockup and informed NASA it still wasn't satisfactory—the seats were so high, their helmets bumped the ceiling hatch. McDonnell Douglas decreased the padding thickness on the underside of the hatch and removed contour bumps on the seats themselves. A small matter, perhaps, but so very indicative of the way both NASA and the supporting manufacturers willingly cooperated with us.

While the *Gemini 4* primary and backup crews were training jointly for the mission, the four of us started an "Unresolved Problems List," with Ed White as our coordinator. We had too many facilities to visit and too much equipment that we had to understand and learn how to operate, so we decided that each man would concentrate on certain areas of the training and advise the rest when he encountered anything to worry about. It was an extension of NASA's "learn everything but specialize in something" curriculum—we still trained together, yet by individually zeroing in on specific problems we made it easier for those problems to get solved. When one was corrected, it was checked off on the list, and this allowed us to judge what overall progress was being accomplished. After we moved into crew quarters at Cape Kennedy a week before *Gemini 4*'s launch, we asked Alan Shepard (he was then chief of the astronaut office) to take over our little "committee's" duties. Deke Slayton agreed and the Unresolved Problems List procedure was not only applied to subsequent Gemini missions but carried over into the Apollo program.

On July 1, 1965, NASA announced that Frank Borman and James Lovell would be the commander and pilot, respectively, of *Gemini 7*, the project's longest mission, with Ed White and Mike Collins as the backup crew.

Five months of training and preparation lay ahead of us, but in truth Jim and I already had gone through what amounted to a dress rehearsal as *Gemini 4*'s alternate crew. The Gemini spacecraft, twice the size of the Mercury capsules and far more sophisticated, were identical in their exterior and internal dimensions; they varied only in the amount and complexity of equipment carried.

We lived in those spacecraft. We watched them being built and we flew their simulator replicas for hours upon hours. With spacecraft, of course, there was a far greater emphasis on system engineering and system involvement than with conventional aircraft. Yet the gradual development of a relationship between man and machine was the same, for one of the unique things about flying aircraft or flying in space is the wonderful, almost indescribable feeling created by being in perfect harmony with your machine. It's like the intimate awareness you achieve with a wife or child; you sense and anticipate moods, you can predict reactions and act accordingly. Your loved ones become extensions of yourself, part of you just as you're a part of them.

It's the same relationship a pilot would like to have with the machine he flies—when human brains, blood, and muscles seem to fuse with metal cables and fuel lines and aluminum to become a single entity. That was the case with the Gemini and even more complex Apollo capsules—they were extensions of us, totally predictable because we knew the systems and their responses so well.

You don't get this magic feeling with everything you fly. I had it with the sturdy, dependable T-33. I had it with the F-86 Sabrejet, the fighter that performed so well against Russian-made MiGs in the Korean War. The Sabrejet, like the T-33, was an honest airplane with no bad habits, easy to fly and reliable. At the other end of my yardstick was the F-84 (overweight and underpowered) and the F-104. I loved the F-104 for its performance and flew it for hundreds of hours. But it was like a dog I didn't quite trust. He may have been smiling and wagging his tail most of the time, but I never knew when the son of a bitch was going to turn around and bite me.

Not so with the spacecraft, and it was mostly the training that established this mysterious man-and-machine fusion. NASA put us through every conceivable flying procedure and technique, every possible failure mode and emergency situation. The modules became as familiar to each astronaut as a car he had been driving for ten years, so when Jim and I got the *Gemini 7* assignment, some of the training on our spacecraft was more of a refresher course than anything else—it was *Gemini 4* capsule training all over again.

Our training was in four phases: simulator training at Houston, several weeks following the construction of the spacecraft in St. Louis (the Ramada Inn at the St. Louis airport became our home away from home), classroom studies, and finally simulator flying at the Cape. Every mission's primary commander was responsible for training both his own pilot and the backup crew, and I had the complete, unquestioning cooperation of Lovell, White, and Collins.

For all but one Project Gemini flight, NASA abandoned its practice of giving each spacecraft an individual name, like *Friendship, Sigma,* and *Freedom,* although the practice was resumed for Apollo's lunar landing missions to differentiate the command and landing modules. Our capsules simply carried the mission number.

The single exception was *Gemini 3,* the Grissom-Young mission. With tongue in cheek, they named their capsule *Molly Brown* after the Broadway musical *The Unsinkable Molly Brown*—a lighthearted reference to Grissom's previous Mercury flight, when his capsule had sunk like the *Titanic.*

By the time Lovell and I were ready for our mission, we had already absorbed valuable information from the previous Gemini missions, starting with the Grissom-Young flight. *Gemini 3* had gone off perfectly, the lift-off so smooth that neither of the astronauts realized they were off the pad until they saw that the clock on the instrument panel had started running and they heard Capsule Communications advise them, "You're on your way, *Molly Brown.*"

Grissom and Young had three major areas to test: the capsule's maneuverability, the life support system's reliability, and the controlled reentry of the spacecraft after the orbital phase was concluded. They accomplished all three tests in what was a near-perfect mission. Even the lone hitch that developed in flight—a very minor one—had its positive side because it showed how the intense training had paid off.

Only a few minutes into the first orbit, the oxygen pressure gauge of the life support system displayed a sudden drop. It was one of those emergency situations thrown at us numerous times in the simulator, and Young calmly went through the prescribed procedures. He immediately checked other gauges, saw that he was getting abnormal readings on them, too, and deduced that the trouble had to be in the instrument power supply. John switched from primary to secondary power and all gauge readings returned to normal.

Only forty-five seconds elapsed from the time Young noticed the pressure drop to his analysis of the situation and corrective action. A rather inconsequential forty-five-second problem, yes, but proof of the quality of our training.

The maneuvering tests began as *Gemini 3* neared the end of the first orbit, Gus firing the forward and aft thrusters at precisely timed intervals to achieve a slight speed reduction. During the second orbit, he used the thrusters to move laterally, changing the orbital path. During the third orbit, the crew went through the fail-safe maneuver—firing the thrusters for two and a half minutes, which dropped *Gemini 3* down to its lowest altitude, or perigee, of forty-five miles. It was a critical test because the maneuver was intended to assure safe reentry even if the retro-rockets failed to fire after they began reentry.

The spacecraft had been in orbit for four and a half hours when the crew armed and then fired the four retro-rockets, slowing *Gemini 3* down for reentry. Grissom jettisoned the retro package and the capsule began its flaming plunge through the earth's atmosphere, positioned with the heat shields forward to protect the crew from reentry temperatures that reached 3,500 degrees Fahrenheit.

(Reentry heat is generated by the high-speed passage of the space capsule from the vacuum of space to the earth's increasingly denser atmosphere. The earliest method of protection was so-called heat sink—aerodynamically shaped slabs of metal that absorbed the heat without transmitting it to the occupants. Then scientists developed abalition cooling, in which the outer coating of the shields flaked off or burned away, carrying most of the heat with it. The older metal shields had the disadvantage of adding too much weight, but the abalitive shields were made of lightweight fiberglass bonded with a special phenolic resin. Further protection from reentry heat was provided by the blunt, dish-shaped nose of the capsule, first conceived by H. Julian Allen of NACA, whose studies showed that the blunt nose design absorbed less heat.)

Gemini 3 splashed down in the Atlantic near the recovery ship, the aircraft carrier *Intrepid,* but a bit farther away than Gus wanted. The astronauts weren't picked up for a half hour, and Young later commented wryly that the *Molly Brown* "was no boat." But aside from the landing being slightly off target, the mission was a total success except for a minor flap that was more funny than serious.

The irrepressible Wally Schirra had slipped a corned beef sandwich to John Young before the launch, and Young had smuggled it aboard the spacecraft. During the flight John shared this rare space delicacy with Grissom, and when they later confessed to their non-regulation diet, NASA officials were furious—one would think they had smuggled a chorus girl aboard. A few congressmen even issued statements denouncing the astronauts for imperiling their mission.

Personally, I thought it was a tempest in a teapot, although NASA did have a legitimate reason for being upset. Gus and John had been operating in an atmosphere of 100 percent oxygen and theoretically that illegal corned beef sandwich could have produced "outgassing" contamination. The other fear was that in a weightless environment, crumbs from the bread might have gotten into the instruments. At any rate, NASA issued strict orders that nothing was to be brought aboard a spacecraft without authorization.

Jim McDivitt and Ed White formed a perfect team for *Gemini 4*. They were more than fellow astronauts—they happened to be good friends who had known each other since college and gone through the Edwards test pilot school together. Originally NASA primarily intended their mission to be a much longer flight than *Gemini 3*'s three-orbit duration—seven days, with the emphasis on various defense, engineering, scientific, and medical tests. The Defense Department, for instance, wanted data on space radiation and navigation. Scientists asked for synoptic terrain and weather photographs, while NASA's medical department ordered a test of an in-flight exerciser, in-flight phonocardiograms, and a test to determine whether bone demineralization occurred during a space flight.

All this alone would have kept McDivitt and White busy, but on March 18, 1965—less than a week before *Gemini 3*—Soviet cosmonaut Aleksei Leonov left his spacecraft, *Voskhod 2,* while it was in orbit and became the first man to walk in space. The repercussions of that feat were felt immediately, with the news media once again complaining that the Russians were beating us to the punch.

NASA had been considering for some time the possibility of adding extravehicular activity (EVA) to *Gemini 4*'s mission, EVA being the terminology assigned to any activity performed by an astronaut while operating in the vacuum of space—i.e., walking in space. The general feeling was that we weren't quite ready for EVA at this stage of the program, but the Soviet walk in space changed that thinking in a hurry. One additional factor in revising NASA's previous reluctance was the unexpectedly successful demonstration of a jet gun, the "hand-held maneuvering unit," which was nothing but a small hand rocket capable of propelling an astronaut around in space. Also demonstrated was an oxygen umbilical cord, a life-sustaining safety tether developed by NASA technicians working with AiResearch.

So NASA decided to give a green light for EVA on *Gemini 4,* along with the so-called station-keeping test; the latter involved chasing the second-stage booster rocket after separation, and once the spacecraft caught up to its target it was supposed to stay briefly with the booster in a loose orbital formation. This was a substitution for a previously planned but discarded exercise using an ejected rendez-vous evaluation pod (REP), a pod equipped with a radar transponder, beacons, and flashing lights. The pod idea was scrubbed because of problems with the radar unit and NASA switched to the booster target plan. Martin Marietta hurriedly installed flashing lights on the second-stage rocket so McDivitt and White could see their chase target.

Another revision for *Gemini 4* had come from NASA's medical director, Dr. Charles Berry, who wanted NASA to reduce the duration from seven days to not more than four. The reduction was ordered more than a year before the mission began, but Berry's objection on medical grounds (he was worried about possible harmful physiological effects of seven days in space) wasn't the only reason. There had been a delay in development of a new power source to replace the batteries used on the Mercury capsules. This was the fuel cell, a device that converts chemical energy directly into electrical energy and increases the life of the power source manyfold. Fuel cells would be ready for *Gemini 5,* but *Gemini 4* had to rely on the shorter-lived batteries with four days judged as the maximum safe limit.

Naturally, Ed White's fifteen-minute walk in space overshadowed the rest of *Gemini 4*'s accomplishments, including the more than ninety-seven hours the mission lasted. When NASA first got around to admitting that EVA had been added to *Gemini 4*'s agenda, the initial announcement was a rather cautiously coy statement that Ed "would open the hatch and stick his head outside." His actual EVA, of course, was a full-fledged effort helped immeasurably by White's unusual strength.

The problem was simple: The hatch stuck, and when it finally got unstuck it was almost impossible to move. The cabin had been depressurized to allow the hatch to open, but this necessary step hadn't helped much. Ed overcame the first obstacle when he realized a spring had failed to compress. He and McDivitt tugged and prodded at a ratchet until the door suddenly unlatched. During training, we had found the hatch extremely difficult to push open under zero-G conditions, and White discovered it wasn't any easier in real space. But the barrel-chested, powerfully built astronaut managed to get it open and left the capsule for his historic walk, the gold-braided umbilical cord and maneuvering gun working perfectly. When he reentered the capsule, the hatch was as difficult to close as it had been to open. Making it even tougher were the awkward, rather primitive spacesuits White and McDivitt were wearing—performing any manual task with those bulky gloves was like trying to open a can with handcuffs on your wrists. I've often wondered if any of the rest of us could have pulled off what the exceptionally strong White did.

The space walk was preceded by the station-keeping attempt, and this was *Gemini 4*'s only major failure. Several times McDivitt tried to catch up to the elusive booster target but never could close the distance. Yet we learned a lot from his futile efforts, namely that we couldn't catch up to a target in space by moving faster toward it in a straight line, as we would on the ground. Every time Jim increased speed, the capsule would gain altitude and go into a higher orbit than the target. He finally gave up because fuel consumption was becoming a problem.

Gemini 4's experience taught us that to achieve rendezvous with a fast-moving target, the trick was to decrease speed slightly instead of increasing it. This would drop the spacecraft into a lower orbit than the target. Then when speed increased, the capsule would climb into the same orbit as the target. Once both vehicles were close enough for the station-keeping, minor variations in speed could close the distance.

McDivitt and White came down a few miles from the carrier *Wasp*. After recovery, Ed surprised everyone—especially Dr. Berry—by doing a little jig on the flight deck. The next day, White saw a few Marines and midshipmen having a tug-of-war and invited himself into the action. Quite a guy was Edward Higgins White II.

The *Gemini 4* crew had admitted to fatigue during their four-day flight and both put partial blame on those bulky spacesuits NASA had insisted that the astronauts wear every minute of the Gemini mission. They were necessary on the *Gemini 4* flight because the capsule had to be depressurized for White's EVA, and no one except a midget could put a spacesuit on and take it off in that cramped cockpit.

The primary crew for *Gemini 5* campaigned hard for flying their mission without the suits. Gordon Cooper and Pete Conrad pointed out that there would be no EVA on their flight, that they'd be flying around without helmets anyway in the pressurized capsule, and that if a catastrophic failure occurred—such as leaks or rupture—they wouldn't have time to put on their helmets and the pressure suits would be useless. But they lost the argument and the pressure suit requirement stayed in force. We agreed with Gordon and Pete, but it took *Gemini 5* to show NASA that its insistence was stupid, if well meant.

We didn't lose all the battles with NASA headquarters. McDivitt and White were sharply critical of NASA's order to conserve thruster fuel in case the thrusters had to be used to prevent premature orbit decay before the reentry phase, a task normally assigned to the retro-rockets. NASA simply wasn't sure of the latter's reliability and fail-safe reentry was a prime requisite. McDivitt and White, however, complained that the fuel conservation edict had limited both operations and experiments. They emphasized that the retros had worked perfectly after exposure to four days in space and there was no reason to question their reliability anymore. Washington surrendered to Houston, which thankfully was not an uncommon occurrence in those golden years.

Cooper and Conrad were up for seven days on the *Gemini 5* mission, which began on August 21, 1965. They successfully completed their seventeen assigned medical, technical, and scientific experiments, and Cooper did a beautiful job of simulating rendezvous maneuvers.

But they also had problems, particularly in the early stages of the flight, and these compounded the insidious march of fatigue in the week-long mission. *Gemini 5* was the initial test of the new fuel cells, which during the first orbit showed some abnormally low oxygen-pressure readings and caused much concern—Chris Kraft's Mission Control came close to terminating the flight. While the backup batteries, representative of NASA's fail-safe policy, were good for thirteen hours, Kraft wanted to make sure the flight wouldn't last so long that the spacecraft would lack sufficient power for reentry.

The oxygen pressure stabilized after the third orbit, the fuel cells were working normally, and Kraft gave *Gemini 5* permission to continue. But when Cooper and Conrad landed, they had lost more weight than expected (we all lost weight during a space mission) and were almost totally exhausted. Pete hadn't been affected quite as much as Gordon overall, but both were very tired guys. All medical readings returned to normal in two days, though Pete's recovery was somewhat faster than Gordon's. Both had lost considerable calcium, more than the *Gemini 4* crew.

Among their medical experiments was the first wearing of inflatable leg cuffs, pressurized automatically for two minutes out of every six to restrict blood flow. Conrad thought they helped and would be especially useful on longer flights. But they didn't solve the fatigue problem and both astronauts told NASA its spacesuit policy was asinine.

Gemini 6, a rendezvous mission involving an Agena target vehicle, was scheduled for late October 1965 and *Gemini 7,* my flight, would follow about a month later. It is a mathematical certainty that number 7 follows the number 6. Or so we thought.

Jim Lovell and I knew right from the start that ours would be a fourteen-day mission, the longest space flight to date, and we trained for it physically as well as technically and mentally.

A typical day started with being at work at the astronaut office by 7 A.M., and lunchtime was spent mostly jogging and lifting weights. Lovell and I usually ran two or three miles a day and after work we'd play handball; "after work" could mean several hours after normal quitting time. Then there was the travel. One week we'd be in St. Louis, where our spacecraft—at 8,076 pounds about 250 pounds heavier than previous Gemini capsules—was being built. The next week we'd be at the Cape flying the simulator (there was a duplicate in Houston), and the following week we might be at the David Clark Company in Worcester, Massachusetts, watching seamstresses working on the new spacesuits we'd be wearing.

It was a meat grinder of a schedule that required an extra effort to keep our family lives from disintegrating. When Jim and I came home, either from work or a trip, we centered our activities around our children. For Fred and Edwin, I tried to provide as normal a life as I could, supplementing what Susan consistently offered them when I was away.

Wally Schirra sold me a used fifteen-foot motorboat. I borrowed a book from the public library on how to water-ski, and the whole family got involved in the sport, but for Fred and Edwin the epitome of fun with Father was going duck hunting on Saturday mornings.

Jim Lovell was an outstanding partner. Like all the others in our group, he was bright and competent, but he had something else, too—a marvelous sense of humor, always a positive and cheerful outlook. Not once did he ever shirk a duty or a responsibility. I'll be forever grateful to Deke Slayton for having picked him as my pilot.

Jim and I weren't really social companions. Our respective wives did more socializing with each other than we did, and this was true of most of the astronaut teams—on weekends, they all usually went their own way. Lovell and I saw enough of each other during the week not to feel compelled to make it a seven-day relationship.

I was something of a loner, anyway. What mattered to me most was compatibility in the cockpit. With one exception, I regarded the other astronauts more as professional comrades than as truly intimate friends. The exception was Ed White.

The Whites lived catercorner from us, and Ed's and my off-duty hours were totally oriented toward our wives and children. We weren't the only good family men, of course, but being close neighbors in addition to our shared philosophy brought us close together. Yet Ed himself didn't limit his friendship to me—I don't know of any astronaut who was more genuinely liked and admired, although his devotion to physical conditioning drove those with more sedentary habits absolutely bonkers.

Ed used to jog at least three miles daily without even breathing hard, then would play two or three hours of handball or squash. This was anathema to guys like Schirra and Armstrong; Neil once commented, after watching White go through one of his conditioning regimes, that man had been allotted a finite number of heartbeats in a lifetime and there was no need to speed up the process.

NASA, with the willing aid of the news media, projected a single image of the astronauts that could have been derived from the Boy Scout oath. We were all loyal, brave, true, and so on—a kind of sterilized portrait that wasn't totally inaccurate as far as it went. The selection and training process did cast us in a single mold, but not every astronaut emerging from that mold matched NASA's image of perfection.

There were no weak sisters in our group—we had nine dedicated professionals. We differed in temperament, but those differences were cosmetic when it came to doing our jobs. Although prior to *Gemini 3* we had never flown with any of the Mercury astronauts, we were well briefed on their individual performances and got to know them well enough to form our opinions.

We all understood, although it was never an officially declared policy, that if you botched a mission you'd never be given a second chance. I never worried for one minute that this would happen to anyone in our bunch, and I felt that way about most of the Mercury astronauts including those who followed us into the Apollo program. But there were a few exceptions in the latter batch, and frankly I was surprised at some of the selections.

Not being assigned to a second mission didn't always mean an astronaut had been parked permanently in NASA's doghouse. A few simply didn't want to fly again for varying reasons, and one of them was John Glenn. I went for a ride with him one day in his convertible and he talked at length about his concern for American society and how he wanted to contribute to its betterment. I got the clear impression that he was using his lone, five-hour space flight as a platform from which to launch his personal crusade. The *Friendship 7* mission he flew had brought him fame; he intended to parlay that fame into a socially conscious political career and he made no bones about it. The members of the Kennedy family were his idols.

Buzz Aldrin was a separate case. I was worried about him even before he landed on the moon with Armstrong. I thought he had difficulty coping with life's simpler problems, despite his acknowledged intelligence and ability. Some of the other astronauts suspected that Buzz always resented the fact that Armstrong, not Aldrin, was the first man to set foot on the moon. Jealousy definitely was not a desired attribute in any astronaut—we had absolutely none in our second group, and I also cite the selfless example set by Mike Collins, who as the command module pilot on *Apollo 11* didn't receive as much public attention as two moon-walkers did but never complained, even privately.

Collins typified the real pros among the third astronaut group. I always thought he was underrated. After he retired from the space program, he became the first director of the majestic new National Air and Space Museum in Washington. He was assigned to the project almost from its conception and brought it in ahead of schedule and under budget—which in Washington was a historical achievement ranking slightly below the discovery of America. We would have welcomed him into our little nine-man Gemini fraternity—a closely knit bunch whose bull sessions, significantly, seldom if ever involved such topics as politics, religion, or sex. They might be favorite subjects for a typical group of males, but we weren't typical. We were too busy talking about missions.

I was the most impatient and outspoken of them all. I had a very simple code: If you can't do your job, get the hell out of the way so I can do mine. I had started being that way when I was at West Point and I never changed. I'll concede I wasn't the most popular astronaut for that very reason, but I didn't give a damn.

I actually resented the presence of the few weaker astronauts in

the program—I felt every man had to be well qualified in every respect, with no ifs, ands, or buts. Project Gemini's four major objectives demanded total astronaut excellence. They were:

1. Before astronauts could fly a lunar landing module from the com-
    mand module to the moon's surface and return to the command
    module, we had to prove it was possible for two spacecraft to
    rendezvous.
2. We had to demonstrate that astronauts could spend up to two
    weeks in space—*Apollo 11*'s mission was to last nine days, but
    when NASA was planning both Gemini and Apollo it figured two
    weeks was a state-of-the-art maximum.
3. We had to prove the feasibility of guided reentry in a maneuver-
    able spacecraft, because there was no other way to go to the
    moon and return.
4. We had to show that EVA was not only possible but reasonably
    safe, inasmuch as the moon landing astronauts would have to get
    out of the lunar module and walk on the surface.

Gemini 4 met two of these objectives—guided reentry and EVA.
Gemini 5 was part of the endurance test. *Gemini 6* was to confirm
rendezvous capability, and the astronauts assigned to this mission
were Wally Schirra as commander and Tom Stafford as pilot. Their
capsule was the last to be powered by batteries, for the mission was
to last only two days. The plan was to first launch an Atlas-Agena
combination, the slender Agena with its restartable engine then separating from the Atlas and becoming *Gemini 6*'s rendezvous target.
     October 25, 1965 . . .

The countdown for both the Atlas-Agena and *Gemini 6*'s Titan II
had begun simultaneously; the former was poised on Pad 14 and the
Schirra-Stafford rocket on Pad 19. The two astronauts climbed into
their spacecraft about 9:45 A.M., fifteen minutes before the scheduled launch of the Atlas-Agena.
     At 10 A.M., right on target, the push of a button sent the Atlas
soaring off the pad and in a few minutes the Agena separated from
the booster as planned. Except that it suddenly began to wobble, its
attitude control system fighting to maintain stability. A small secondary engine ignited and this fired the primary engine, which was
supposed to boost Agena into its assigned orbit. But the wobbling
increased so severely that the Agena came apart—one tracking sta-

tion informed Houston that the target vehicle was in at least five
pieces. Sadly, Chris Kraft scrubbed the mission.

I was in the outside viewing stands with Lovell, waiting for Schirra
and Stafford to finish their countdown, when we heard that something had gone wrong. We ran over to the Launch Control Center
to find out what had happened, and the gloom there was thick enough
to walk on. We were standing near two McDonnell Douglas officials, Walter Burke and John Yardley. Burke remarked to his companion, "Why couldn't we launch a Gemini as a target instead of an
Agena?"

The idea wasn't new—Martin Marietta some months before had
proposed a fast one-two launch of two Gemini spacecraft, but got
nowhere. As Burke and Yardley discussed Burke's suggestion, I joined
the conversation. On the back of an envelope, Burke drew a rough
sketch of an inflatable cone that could be attached to our *Gemini 7*
spacecraft and used to dock with *Gemini 6*.

"That's how it would work," Burke said to me, Yardley nodding
in agreement.

I shook my head. "No way, Walt. I don't like the idea of anything
nuzzling us that close—too much chance of damaging both capsules.
But I'd settle for just flying in close formation. That's all the rendezvous demonstration we'd need."

The sight of *Gemini 6*'s Titan II, ready and waiting on Pad 19
with no place to go, must have been a tempting one. NASA's first
reaction to the Agena failure was to consider switching spacecraft—
putting the *Gemini 7* capsule on *Gemini 6*'s booster and launching
our long-duration mission ahead of *Gemini 6*'s rendezvous flight.
The latter would have to wait for another Atlas-Agena to be delivered, thus pushing its launch back to the following February or March.

There was one major problem, however. No one was sure whether
the *Gemini 6* booster could put *Gemini 7*'s heavier spacecraft into
orbit; the Titan II being readied for our mission had more thrust.
And while the brains and the brass were hastily debating the pros
and cons of the switch, Burke's plan raised enough objections to
discourage a determined bulldog. Even the open-minded Bob Gilruth
and Chris Kraft were dubious at first. Gilruth didn't think the tracking network could handle two spacecraft simultaneously, and Kraft
considered the operational problems involved in a double launch almost insurmountable. So, at first, did Charlie Mathews, Gemini's
project director and a most capable one.

Kraft, whose first remark upon hearing the plan was "You're out of your minds—it can't be done," talked it over with his people. Then he briefed Deke Slayton, who asked Schirra and Stafford what they thought.

"It's a hell of an idea," Wally enthused.

Burke still wasn't home free, for one question remained to be answered: Inasmuch as both missions were to be launched from the same pad, would *Gemini 7*'s launch inflict so much pad damage that *Gemini 6* couldn't use it? There would be no answers until after we lifted off, but NASA's small army of pad technicians swore they'd have everything cleaned up in time for *Gemini 6*. Theirs was a can-do spirit so typical of those pioneering days.

The decision to combine *Gemini 6* and *Gemini 7* into a joint mission, with the latter serving as a target vehicle, came only three days after the Agena debacle, with Jim Webb giving the final green light in a memorandum to President Johnson. Johnson announced the double launch at a news conference on October 28, 1965.

Adding the rendezvous exercise to the agenda already being drawn up wasn't going to give us much time to ponder the affairs of the world at our leisure. This was one reason why we lobbied so hard for lighter, more comfortable spacesuits and against the policy of requiring astronauts to wear them throughout the mission.

I told the powers that be, "Look, you want us to stay up there for fourteen days and I don't think we can unless you give us lighter suits." I argued that since *Gemini 7* wouldn't have an EVA to perform, we needed a spacesuit designed specifically for a mission that was largely a test of human endurance. It should be a "soft" suit, I added, which would allow us to function during launch and reentry, and could be removed with relative ease so we could fly around in our underwear. NASA listened. I wasn't told, "Go away, dummy, we know what's best."

It was another example of NASA's accepting astronaut demands on some key issues. The new suit was developed at our request and just about to our specifications, one of them being that the suit could be removed in flight without requiring too much effort. The David Clark Company—which I suppose you could call the Brooks Brothers of the space program—did a good job for us. It designed a soft cloth hood to be used instead of the heavy fiberglass shell helmet, and a rather ingenious array of zippers replaced our old neck ring for fastening the hood to the torso portion of the suit. A regular pilot's helmet fitted under the inflatable hood.

The suit itself was ventilated for greater comfort and was designed to inflate only when the spacecraft lost cabin pressure—in that sense, it was mostly an emergency garment. It wouldn't work at all in an EVA, because once the suit was pressurized you could hardly move. Lovell and I tried it out and we looked like the Michelin boy in the tire ads. Actually we were less mobile than young Mr. Michelin— there were no joints in the arms or legs. After testing the new suits in evaluation and training sessions, Jim and I thought they were heavier than we'd hoped, although Clark had reduced the weight from the old suit's twenty-three and a half pounds to sixteen.

They really were a vast improvement, for there was no way we could have lasted two weeks in those old bulky inner tubes without physical harm. We would have been totally dehydrated, compounding the tendency of space flight to cause loss of weight.

Before the rendezvous was added, few if any astronauts wanted any part of *Gemini 7,* mostly because under its original major objective—duration—it was not considered a pilot's flight, and almost everyone regarded the medical experiments foisted on us as a pain in the butt.

I didn't feel that way and neither did Jim. We recognized that *Gemini 7* was the beginning of medicine's understanding of long space flights and their effects on the human body. The medical probing actually started before the flight. We spent one night in a Houston hospital having our brain waves measured, and these EEG readings would be compared to those recorded during the flight and immediately after our return.

The biggest nuisance was a calcium balance study. We had to keep a complete record of body intake and wastes for nine days before the flight, then continue this "diary" during the entire mission and for four days after we came back. The researchers put us on a regimented diet for the entire twenty-seven days; a nutritionist from the National Institutes of Health told us exactly what we could eat and how much—we had our meals weighed down to the gram. After the flight, our underwear would be checked to see what minerals had been lost through normal sweat. Nothing was sacred to the medics.

We had eight assigned experiments directly related to space medicine: cardiovascular conditioning, in-flight exercising, in-flight phonocardiograms, and analysis of body fluids, bone demineralization, calcium and nitrogen balance, in-flight sleep patterns, and human otolith function—this last to determine whether prolonged weightlessness had any effect on balance.

All these tests involved comparing data compiled preflight, in flight, and postflight, so in space we were going to be hooked up to more electrodes and other measuring devices than Frankenstein's monster.

When Susan and the boys came to Cape Kennedy for the *Gemini 7* launch, I was sporting the brand-new silver oak leaves of a lieutenant colonel. Yet to them it wasn't an Air Force officer and astronaut on top of a huge rocket, but a husband and father.

A manned mission launch is spectacular and awesome, a fiery, deafening roar of defiance against the unknown. But for an astronaut's family, it also can be a frightening experience that brings home the very fragility of man's dependence on machine. They just weren't prepared for the tension of the countdown and what followed—a majestic sight, yes, but a terrifying one in the eyes of three people whose minds were registering the unspoken words: "*What if . . .*"

Early in the space program, the only impact my job had on them had been in terms of media attention. The *Life* contract became almost a solace because it tended to keep away reporters who knew that Dody Hamlin and a few of her *Life* colleagues were the only ones with access to our home. But as the launch neared, the media pressure intensified and may have even contributed to the family's sense of dread at the launch itself. Reporters literally began parking on our front lawn, and it grew worse at launch time.

A battery of cameras was trained on their faces. Fred looked up at his mother and asked plaintively, "Mom, why didn't you tell us it would be so difficult?" They had seen previous launches on television, but no TV picture could capture the tension of the countdown and the thundering, earthshaking noise of a blast-off taking place in your presence.

I didn't sleep much the night before launch. I had a stabbing awareness, even sharper than I had ever felt in all my Air Force years, that I was in a very dangerous business. I didn't feel fear; I felt agonizing concern for the wife and sons I loved. I didn't want to be a heroic casualty in man's conquest of space and I was not oblivious to the hazards involved. I wanted to stay a living, breathing husband and father.

There's a dichotomy in all this, a kind of conflict of interest. On one hand, there's a sense of mission accomplishment that becomes a very self-centered thing; the mission has been pounded into your brain until it alone is in sharp focus, with everything else blurred.

But then there creeps into your thoughts the other image—the family that you know damned well could be left without husband or father, their dependency and their own world destroyed in a split second of disaster—and the mind changes its focus. The mission momentarily blurs and retreats, replaced by wife and children, standing out in your mind like a picture etched in Braille.

This inner turmoil was nothing new. Many a night I'd sat in the cockpit of a fighter, poised on a runway ready for takeoff, knowing that the weather ahead was terrible and that the flight was inviting trouble. The conflict was always there—Mission versus Family. Do I push the throttle forward or wait for better weather?

I always opted for the Mission. I had seen too many Air Force pilots put their families first—out of concern, not personal fear— and I never knew one who was truly happy after making that decision. I didn't regard them as cowards, either. The wrenching dilemma they faced I had experienced myself.

Yet there really was no decision to make, and maybe that's why I couldn't sleep. I knew that I had no options, that I *wanted* to go— my family *must* take second place in my priorities. So I did the obvious. . . .

I prayed. I've never been a religious person in the context of regular church attendance, but I have a genuine belief in God and I turned to Him, not to help me solve my conflict, but to help me understand it. I asked Him to keep me safe for my family's sake while I carried out the sacred obligations I felt so deeply as an American astronaut.

Being the person I am, that was all I could do. Once the countdown started, there was no time to pray or even think of Susan and the boys. I was too busy for anything else except the Mission. The rigid establishment of priorities applied to this stage of my life already had been made three years ago when I became an astronaut. It was a commitment now culminating at 2:30 P.M. on December 4, 1965, with the launch signal that sent a 4-ton spacecraft attached to a 200,000-pound rocket off Pad 19 and into history.

8

TWO WEEKS IN THE FRONT SEAT OF A VOLKSWAGEN

". . . seven . . . six . . . five . . . four . . . three . . . two . . . one . . ."

We tensed. After months of simulator make-believe, this one was for real.

"Ignition," Capsule Communications said calmly, two seconds later.

"Lift-off fourteen-thirty plus three."

Lovell said excitedly, "We're on our way, Frank!"

"Right!"

"Looking real good," CapCom announced.

"Roll initiate," I informed CapCom.

"Roger. Roll."

"Pitch initiate."

"Roger. Pitch."

Two minutes after lift-off, CapCom advised, "Guidance is looking real good here, *Gemini 7.*"

"Roger. Stage two . . ."

The mission clock showed we were two minutes and five seconds into the flight. We still had two weeks to go.

* * *

We had breakfasted that morning of December 4 with ten of our colleagues—Dick Gordon, Deke Slayton, Dave Scott, Young, Conrad, Armstrong, Grissom, Shepard, Schirra, and Stafford. We had tenderloin steak, eggs, toast, orange juice, and coffee, all a delight compared to what we were going to be eating for the next two weeks.

We left the crew quarters on Merritt Island after breakfast and were taken to the suit trailer at Launch Complex 16, where we each put on one of the new spacesuits and a pilot's helmet under the soft hood. From there we went to Pad 19.

All previous Gemini flights had been launched early in the morning; ours was midafternoon to better coordinate with the *Gemini 6* rendezvous scheduled for eight days later. Within minutes after our lift-off, a small army of technicians and cleaning crews swarmed over Pad 19, getting it ready for the rendezvous launch.

The incredible realism of the simulators had prepared us for the physical sensations of lift-off. We felt them building up as we accelerated, but there was no great physical discomfort. What the simulator hadn't taught us to expect was the noise. Even in our insulated cabin, about 120 feet above the Titan II's mighty engines belching smoke and flames, the sound was almost deafening.

We were parked in the bulbous nose of a spacecraft whose overall exterior dimensions measured eleven feet in length and slightly over seven feet in diameter at its base, which was the widest part. The vehicle was bell-shaped with the crew compartment at the top, like the nipple of a baby bottle. The rest of the spacecraft, representing 90 percent of its total size, consisted of three sections—reentry control, rendezvous and recovery equipment, and the adapter that housed the retrograde rockets.

The crew compartment was roughly the size of a Volkswagen Beetle's front seat, which meant we didn't have a hell of a lot of room for a fourteen-day trip involving twenty experiments and a midspace rendezvous.

Almost everything in the cabin was tiny, including its two windows. It was simultaneously a workroom, kitchen, bathroom, and bedroom—the only facilities of any size were the narrow but deep and long stowage compartments.

Room was so limited that Jim and I had spent hours figuring out where to stow everything—including the two paperback books we brought with us. Lovell's was Walter Edmonds's novel *Drums Along the Mohawk* and mine a little-known work of Mark Twain's,

Roughing It. I suppose the subjects we picked to read about in outer space—an eighteenth-century Indian war and a nineteenth-century trip—represented the ultimate in literary anomalies.

We never did get to read much—neither of us finished his book—but we had to get NASA's permission to bring the books aboard in the first place, listing them as part of the paraphernalia we were stowing away. This was the result of the famous "corned beef" incident that had occurred on the *Gemini 3* mission.

Because ours was the heaviest of all the Gemini spacecraft, the lift-off itself added tension to a moment always packed with tension anyway. The previous Gemini–Titan II launch vehicles had produced 430,000 pounds of thrust to achieve lift-off. That's an enormous amount of power from two engines; by comparison, the four engines of a Boeing 747 have a combined thrust of about 200,000 pounds. The *Gemini 7* launch vehicle had several thousand more pounds of thrust than the earlier Titans, but not until we cleared the pad and were climbing normally was anyone sure the extra power had been sufficient.

We performed our first experiment immediately after the spacecraft separated from the Titan II's second stage, which had boosted us into our initial planned orbital path with a 203-mile apogee and a 100-mile perigee—the highest orbit of all the Gemini missions to date and one reached only six minutes after lift-off. (On the fifth day, we changed to a more circular orbit to become *Gemini 6*'s target vehicle.) The experiment involved flying in formation with the second-stage rocket and was more a test of our maneuvering ability than anything else.

We didn't exactly resemble the Thunderbirds in precision flying, but we managed to stay in reasonable formation even though the target rocket was unstable and spinning. For that reason I didn't get too close, and besides we were using too much fuel trying to maintain station-keeping—chasing that tumbling rocket was like trying to collar a giant butterfly with a torn net. Lovell and I took turns maneuvering and taking pictures, but after fifteen minutes we'd had enough—I fired the thrusters and moved away, then we settled down for the rest of our long flight.

My own first impression of space was that it was just a higher altitude; flying our spacecraft was much like flying an airplane because I still had a horizon for reference. But later came the phenomenon of looking out of one window where everything was in bright sunlight, and then looking out of the opposite window and seeing nothing except the pitch-blackness of space. The deep ebony of that latter view was startling, and it first brought home the vastness of space itself.

Our second experiment also involved the second-stage rocket. We were supposed to keep tracing our bouncing target with infrared instruments after we broke off station-keeping, and in my conversations with CapCom I kept referring to it as a "bogey." This was misinterpreted as a report that we had seen an unidentified flying object or UFO. It was just a joke at first and I didn't think anything about it until *True,* the most misnamed magazine in journalistic history, subsequently published an article citing my "bogey" report as proof that we had been tracked by some mysterious interplanetary spacecraft. *True*'s deliberate distortion of a routine report has been perpetuated in several books on UFOs.

We began the first medical experiment by activating cardiovascular cuffs on Lovell's legs about a half hour into the flight; like tiny bellows, they pulsed in and out to restrict circulation. At 9:30 we ate our first meal in space, the usual astronaut fare of freeze-dried food that we mixed with water. Most of the guys thought Army C rations were a gourmet meal compared to what they had to eat on space missions. The meals were prepared in plastic packages and turned to a very unappetizing mush when we added water, but I didn't care. We drank water out of a new squirt gun tested by John Young on *Gemini 3.*

One problem was forcing ourselves to drink enough fluids. The controlled atmosphere in the pressurized spacecraft was the equivalent of a cabin altitude of 27,000 feet, which was somewhat dehydrating in itself. Adding the 100 percent oxygen we were breathing increased the dehydration to the point where our skins were flaking—our scalps, in fact, looked like two cases of terminal dandruff. Other than the uncomfortable cramped space, however, the only early physical discomfort was the effect of zero G on the blood. During weightlessness, the blood flow lacks the force of gravity and this tends to build up pressure in the head until the nose is plugged up. After a couple of days the blood flow adjusts to zero G, but for a while both of us complained of stuffy noses and irritated eyes until we got used to the cabin environment.

Yet weightlessness also was a physical blessing, the main factor enabling us to survive the grueling flight. It allowed us to float free from our seats (although not very far) while performing chores and experiments; it also helped circulation as the hours passed into days. The only times we would have welcomed full gravity were the occasions when we had to get into a stowage compartment for some item. While we were groping, loose objects would come out of the compartment and float around the cabin. Putting them back after grabbing what we were looking for was like trying to collar slippery goldfish in a tank.

The morning after launch, Elliot See (our first CapCom voice) read us a few football scores from Saturday's games and also relayed news that a United DC-8 and a TWA Constellation had collided over New York City.

"Looks like it's safer up here than down there," I remarked.

Lovell looked at me. "We're not down yet, buddy," he reminded me.

Sleeping was difficult. We had planned it so one of us would be awake while the other got some shut-eye, but this didn't work out very well. We were in such close proximity that the least movement by the man awake would disturb the other. (We changed this procedure during Apollo, the whole crew going to sleep at the same time. This was possible because Mission Control could keep a constant telemetry lock on us when we got away from the earth. During Gemini's earth orbital flights, there were periods when a telemetry lock was impossible.)

We urinated into a condom, which we'd put into a tiny bag and dump overboard through the quarter-inch vent. But we also had to take urine samples for that damned calcium test and a condom was an awfully small target. So at times we had urine floating all over the weightless spacecraft.

Feces went into a plastic bag shaped like a top hat turned upside down. After defecating, we'd put a chemical into the bag, seal it, and stow it in the waste material compartment. Space travel then, I'm afraid, was not for the fastidious or excessively modest. We were a pretty odorous pair when we got back.

We hadn't anticipated the excessive heat in the cabin. Our new spacesuits were too warm and the discomfort persisted even after I turned the cabin heat down to the lowest setting. This led to the continuation of a debate that had started before the launch and was to go on for nearly six days into the mission. The subject: When could we take off the suits?

The original decision, which Jim and I had agreed to, was to have us wear the suits at all times during the first two days only, while we continually checked the environmental system, after which we could take them off. But George Mueller in Washington vetoed this plan prior to launch, insisting that if one astronaut had his suit off, the other had to be wearing his. Furthermore, we both were to be suited during the launch, rendezvous, and reentry phases. Either astronaut, Mueller told Bob Gilruth, could take off his suit for periods of up to twenty-four hours.

Like so many well-meant plans, it looked reasonable on paper but proved impractical in actual operation. Nobody had figured on those new suits being so hot. Lovell was the first to take off his suit, forty-five hours into the mission, and was in the astronaut's version of hog heaven. I was miserable. The cabin temperature improved somewhat, but not sufficiently to overcome the discomfort of my suit.

I tried unzipping it to get more ventilation and took off the gloves. Still no major relief. Jim stayed suitless for his twenty-four hours and told me he'd like to keep it off during his second night of sleep, and this is where Mueller's dictate fell apart like an overcooked turkey. I let Lovell stay in his underwear for the second night and much longer out of sheer compassion—taller and heavier than I, he found it difficult to get in and out of the spacesuit; the process actually took him a full hour. I didn't have the heart to follow the twenty-four-hour exchange arrangement, so I took the only other course possible—I started campaigning to let both of us fly suitless.

We were one hundred hours into the flight when I asked a controller to advise Chris Kraft that I was thinking about taking my suit off. This started a debate that lasted several hours, and I finally told CapCom, "Listen, this request to take the suit off is not a big deal. I'm very comfortable [a small white lie]. I've got it unzipped and everything. So don't make out like it's an emergency, will you?"

"Okay. I think we understand it pretty well."

I had probably complained a little too much, because while awaiting the decision from the higher-ups, Houston began insisting that Lovell get dressed again so I could get undressed. We told the controllers we'd rather stay as we were until after the rendezvous. Houston argued that if we switched, the medical telemetry (we spent the entire two weeks hooked up to various measuring devices) could compare the bodily effects of being suited or suitless.

The cabin remained warmer than we wanted and we reported this to CapCom. This led to one of those medical discussions that kept wandering in and out of the mission communications. After one of our water intake reports, CapCom expressed concern.

CapCom: "We would like to ask first of all why—how is it that Jim is not taking in quite as much fluid as we think he ought to and wonder why. Does he have—first of all, is he thirsty?"

Lovell answered the question. "This is Lovell. Number one is I'm out of the suit and Frank's in it. I'm not sweating as much as he is."

"Does—do you notice in looking at him that his skin is moist?"

"I'll let him answer that."

I said, "During the ten days before when we ran the 1030 [calcium study] experiment, I drank almost twice as much water as Jim did, and I think it is probably natural for me to drink a little more. I'm pretty comfortable now. Our cabin temperature's gone down, my suit temperature's gone down, and we both feel we are in pretty good shape."

"Understand. Have you been sweating at all, Frank? *Gemini 7,* did you copy?"

"About sweating? I'd say yes, I'm perspiring a little."

This exchange took place fifteen hours after we'd passed the one-hundred-hour mark. Some thirty hours later, Kraft gave me a flat order: Take off the suit, while Lovell put his back on. We complied but the debate within NASA continued; even Wernher von Braun got into the act as one of the members of the Gemini Design Certification Board, which NASA actually polled on the issue.

Our chief ally was Bob Gilruth, who probably had the most influence with Mueller. But the final decision really rested with Dr. Chuck Berry, NASA's medical director in Houston, who was told by Mueller to prepare a medical evaluation based on the telemetry data already collected and fresh readings from both Lovell and me after we switched. Berry then reported that our blood pressures and pulses were more normal with the suits off, and the certification board added its opinion that the reasons for being unsuited definitely outweighed those for wearing the suits.

The debate was over—we'd wear the suits during the rendezvous and again during reentry, but go unsuited the rest of the mission. I'll tell you how much difference this made: The first time I took my rest period without the suit, I slept solidly for six hours and told Houston the next morning, "I feel like a million dollars!"

Throughout the pre-rendezvous period, we evaluated and reported on all spacecraft systems, conducted our assigned medical and technical experiments, exercised, slept, and occasionally joked. Of the 1,011 pages comprising NASA's official transcript of all voice communications, 750 pages cover the time between launch and the *Gemini* 6 rendezvous. Two examples follow, one to show the complexity of space jargon and the other a good sample of our regimented existence.

A CapCom report to *Gemini 7* on our orbital path: "*D-4/ D-7—113:57:37; Sequence 427; Mode X 03; pitch 4 degrees down, yaw 115 degrees left; passing right to left; closest approach at 113:58:00; record 30 seconds maximum.*"

One of our medical reports on food and water intake: "*Carnarvon Surgeon, Gemini 7. Here is the total water now: for the command pilot, 435 ounces. We both had Meal A, except the pilot did not eat any of the gingerbread squares, and the command pilot ate only two of them. The pilot has now had a total of 350 ounces of water and we've both had one urination since last report.*"

CapCom was our major link to home, manned by various shifts of fellow astronauts whose banter and understanding of what we were going through kept up our morale even when fatigue became a problem. They gave us welcome news reports at regular intervals, usually in the morning before we started our daily activities. Typical was this newscast from Elliot See: "There was a big demonstration in Moscow yesterday against U.S. policy in Vietnam. U.S. Steel indicates that it might build a new steel mill in Baytown. Tommy Nobis [a Texas linebacker] still hasn't made up his mind whether he wants to play for Houston or Atlanta. And finally, Johnny Unitas is out for the season. He suffered torn ligaments in their game against Chicago Sunday."

"Elliot," I broke in, "will you please tell Nobis to sign with Houston?"

"Roger. We'll tell him that a voice from outer space had that message." (The "voice from outer space" apparently didn't carry much weight because Nobis eventually signed with the Atlanta Falcons.)

Frequently they told us how our families were holding up and passed on messages from them. Lovell got one from Gene Cernan, one of our CapCom contacts, who reported that Lovell's twelve-year-old daughter had requested Houston to play a special song for him. Cernan added, "Request was made in the hopes that it might stimulate her daddy to have him home in a hurry."

In our earphones came the sound of "I Saw Mommy Kissing Santa Clause." Lovell broke up.

There was another welcome exchange on our seventh day in space. See was on the CapCom and informed Jim, "The Lovell family's all here this morning observing this pass. We'd like to tell you congratulations on your halfway mark. You're now heading downhill."

"Elliot," Lovell said, "would you say hello to them for me, please, and I'll thank you very much."

"You just did it yourself. I also see the Borman boys are here."

That really surprised me and all I could muster was an inadequate "Hi, boys!" (I talked to Susan during another pass over Houston, where the family had gone after the launch. She told me Edwin was worried I'd be too tired to take them fishing when we got back, as I promised. I kept that promise.)

A few minutes later, Lovell couldn't prevent his sense of humor from protruding through the usual maze of temperature data, photography, fuel cell readings, and medical reports. "Elliot, you can tell the Lovell family that our grass needs mowing."

See, who had children of his own, was especially decent about reassuring us that our families were well.

At such moments we felt closer to our loved ones, and yet, with a curious perversity, these fleeting contacts merely accentuated the separation. Traveling some 200 miles above the earth at more than 17,000 mph, with fatigue creeping up on us, we relished the occasional reassurances CapCom gave us. But they were also stabbing reminders of those we had left behind.

Boredom was almost as much a problem as fatigue. The boredom of the endless, repetitious medical and systems reports. The boredom of regimentation. The boredom of cramped confinement. It got to the point that, late in the flight, Lovell suddenly voiced the opinion that since legs were so useless in zero G, maybe future astronauts should be legless.

"It would be perfect," Jim expounded, "because you could use the space for something else."

Then there was the boredom of eating monotonous, tasteless food. Of necessity, freeze-dried meals (first introduced on *Gemini 3*) had to be compactly packaged, simple to prepare, and easy to digest, none of which lent itself to culinary excellence. The worst items were the beef and egg bites—terribly dry, leaving a bad taste in the mouth and a coating on the tongue. The desserts were too sweet and we would have preferred larger servings of fruit juices.

About halfway through the flight, we gave NASA a critique on dining in outer space. We recommended cooler, moist food instead of overly dry and concentrated menus. We did this with other aspects of the flight, too; it was inevitable that several pieces of hardware didn't work out as well as expected under the rigors of a two-week flight. The new spacesuit hoods restricted our vision more than we would have liked, and the otherwise well-designed helmets had inadequate air circulation, to the point of causing some discomfort.

There were a few other problems with various components, but nothing that impeded the mission. I fouled up one medical experiment myself. I accidentally knocked the electrode sensors recording sleep depth patterns off my head and couldn't get them back on, even with Lovell's help.

On day six, we ran into trouble with a stack in one of the two fuel cell sections and we never got it corrected. Five days later, another stack in the same section failed.

On the morning of the seventh day, the spacecraft began tumbling at a rate of 10 degrees per second. When we reported the oscillations to Houston, engineers deduced that the tumbling was caused by the water boiler exhaust. They advised us to bypass the radiator and then spin the capsule rapidly to throw the water off. It worked.

Considering the volume of medical, technological, and engineering experiments assigned to *Gemini 7,* our batting average was high— two major strikeouts (in-flight sleep analysis and an astronomical photography experiment) out of a total of twenty. Using a special space sextant, we made thirty-seven star-to-horizon measurements, six star-to-star, five planet- or star-to-moon, and eight star-to-zero, compiling data that would aid future space navigation techniques.

NASA wanted us to obtain spectral irradiance information about terrestrial features on celestial objects. We radiometrically measured twenty-nine out of thirty-two assigned objects. We also performed an experiment measuring proton and electron intensities outside the spacecraft and the dose we were receiving inside the capsule. An assignment only partially successful was a test of an optical communications system, in which we used a laser transmitter, a flashing beacon, and an instrument capable of interpreting coded optical signals from three tracking stations located in New Mexico, Hawaii, and the South Atlantic. Unfavorable cloud conditions interfered with all but four attempts.

In one respect, even occasional abnormalities were blessings in that they kept us alert and at least broke the monotony of the regimented routine. They weren't necessarily pleasant interludes, but they furnished a few interesting moments. And we enjoyed some unusual sights, such as the time we tracked the firing of a Polaris missile from the submarine *Benjamin Franklin*. CapCom gave us the coordinates, and while we were staring at thousands of square miles of empty ocean, all of a sudden out of the water popped the rocket, right on schedule. We photographed the firing.

Despite our velocity (we entered orbit at 17,593 mph), we had little sensation of speed—about the same as you'd feel in a jetliner—and unless we were looking at some point that gave us visual reference, we seemed to be motionless. We captured glimpses of breathtaking beauty, like the startling clearness of the clouds beneath us under a full moon—it was like staring into broad daylight.

Our first sunrise in space began as a tiny wedge that kept expanding, until we had the illusion that we were looking into a huge cave with red mouth, yellow roof, and blue outer rim. It was a light blue at first, then the cave seemed to explode in slow motion into a kaleidoscope of colors. The blue became a deeper shade, blending with bands of reddish orange and a mustard-yellow. For more than five minutes, Lovell and I watched the phenomenon, groping in vain to describe the awe we felt.

The *Gemini* 6 launch was scheduled for December 12 and the ground crews had performed a minor miracle. Only twenty-four hours after we left the earth, Schirra and Stafford's Titan II and spacecraft had been moved to Pad 19, erected, and mechanically mated. By the following day, all electrical connections between the launch vehicle and capsule were completed.

Launch time on the twelfth was scheduled for 9:54 A.M. and ignition was achieved at precisely that moment. Less than two seconds later, both Titan engines shut down even though the blockhouse had received a telemetric lift-off signal. Potential disaster was glaring right in *Gemini* 6's face. If the lift-off signal had been correct and the Titan had moved even a few feet off the pad, the engine shutdown would have sent 150 tons of volatile fuel smashing into the pad, consuming rocket and capsule alike in a deadly fireball.

All of Wally Schirra's training dictated immediate ejection the instant he got the lift-off signal and knew the engines had shut down. But in this emergency, his airman's instinct overrode his astronaut training. He hadn't felt lift-off, so in not much more time than it takes to blink an eye he made the decision to stay in the spacecraft. Ejection not only would have resulted in a serious mission delay, but might have injured both men. It was one hell of a gamble, but as I said, you don't buy that kind of instinct and judgment in a simulator; you acquire them during the years you've spent strapped into airplanes.

Gemini 6 was finally launched on December 15 at 8:37 A.M. and at lift-off was about 1,400 miles behind us. Schirra and Stafford, who didn't have any fuel consumption worries in a two-day mission, caught up to *Gemini 7* in a little over five hours, setting the stage for America's first major victory in what had become a race in space: a rendezvous between two manned spacecraft.

After achieving the requisite orbital path, Schirra and Stafford completed a height-adjusting maneuver over New Orleans; at that stage, we were 730 miles apart. During *Gemini 6*'s second orbit, they executed two more maneuvers—phasing and plane changing—which narrowed the distance to 430 miles. As they closed in, *Gemini 6* got a faint radar signal from *Gemini 7* and this increased to a solid lock-on with the two spacecraft now only 190 miles apart. Schirra maneuvered *Gemini 6* into a prescribed narrower orbital path and entered the same orbital plane as *Gemini 7*.

They went into the computerized rendezvous mode a few minutes later, narrowing the distance to sixty-two miles, at which point Stafford exclaimed, "My gosh, there's a real bright star out there—that must be Sirius."

It wasn't Sirius. It was *Gemini 7*. And our first glimpse of the other spacecraft was identical to Stafford's view of us—*Gemini 6* looked like a star rushing toward us. Both ships had docking lights of such high intensity that at close range they were almost blinding.

Gemini 6 closed to within 37 miles at 24 minutes past the 261st hour of our mission, flying slightly below us and moving up fast. There had been difficulties in radio communications between the two vehicles. I had just given CapCom some readouts on fuel stack currents and Houston, with tongue in cheek, inquired, "Where's Jim? Out to lunch?"

"Not exactly. But he's busy."

Lovell, grinning, broke in. "Right in the middle of a rendezvous."

"*Gemini 6*," I asked, "how do you read *Gemini 7* now?"

Back came Wally's voice. "Loud and clear, fellows. We're looking at you!"

Moments before rendezvous, CapCom—sounding like a worried parent sending two teen-agers off on a date in the family car—reminded us that fuel conservation was becoming critical.

"Your fuel cutoff for station-keeping is eleven percent," Elliot See warned. "Under no circumstances are you to use the reserve tank."

"I understand," I acknowledged.

We came into the full view of our sister spacecraft at a distance of only 1,000 yards, and it maneuvered to close within 130 feet. As the distance narrowed to the rendezvous point, Schirra and Stafford saw the twin stars Castor and Pollux plainly visible in the Gemini constellation. It was one of those coincidences so strangely appropriate, almost *too* coincidental, like a sign of approval from an unknown power.

At 2:33 P.M., December 15, *Gemini* 6 pulled abreast of *Gemini* 7—only 120 feet apart—and the first manned spacecraft rendezvous had been accomplished. In the Mission Control Center, cheers swept the huge room and a small American flag was attached to each console, while the smiling Gilruth and Kraft lit fat cigars as if they had just become new fathers.

"There just seems to be a little traffic up here," Stafford joked.

"Call a policeman," CapCom advised jubilantly.

We stayed in formation together for almost four complete orbits, flying at distances that ranged from 290 feet to as little as 1 foot apart. *Gemini* 6, which at rendezvous time still had more than 60 percent of its fuel left, did most of the maneuvering. At one point, Schirra held up a hand-lettered sign that we saw from *Gemini* 7. It read: BEAT ARMY.

Schirra, Stafford, and Lovell were Navy—I was outnumbered.

Both Wally and Tom were impressed with the maneuverability of their spacecraft. Control movements were so precise, as they later reported to NASA, it was obvious that nuzzling right up to a target vehicle and docking with it would not be a problem. And proving this was the chief reason for the rendezvous.

During the night of December 15, *Gemini* 6 stationed itself about ten miles away, motionless and still within our sight.

"We have company tonight," I remarked to one of the tracking stations.

The next morning, Lieutenant Commander Walter Marty Schirra, Jr., of the United States Navy demonstrated once again that humor belonged in space. He had sneaked another unapproved item aboard *Gemini* 6—and this time it was a harmonica.

The first indication came when Tom startled Mission Control by reporting a UFO sighting.

"This is *Gemini 6*," he radioed. "We have an object, looks like a satellite, going from north to south, up in a polar orbit. He's in a very low trajectory . . . looks like he may be going to reentry pretty soon. Stand by—it looks like he's trying to signal us."

The Mission Control personnel must have been trying to climb through their consoles at this news, but suddenly from outer space came the wheezing strains of "Jingle Bells" played on Wally's harmonica, with Stafford shaking a string of tiny bells in accompaniment.

Not long after adding "first music from space" to the mission's long list of achievements, Schirra decided it was time to leave. His final transmission to *Gemini 7:* "Really a good job, Frank and Jim. We'll see you on the beach."

Gemini 6 pulled away, almost like a fighter breaking formation.

Lovell and I envied the other crew. Rendezvous had occurred on the eleventh day of our mission. We still had almost three days to go and once more we were alone in space.

Those final three days were the longest of our lives. We were just about exhausted and the adrenaline that had pumped us up for the rendezvous had drained away.

Added to fatigue were the nagging fuel cell problems and another onslaught of tumbling. We had already lost one cell stack on day six, and on the twelfth day the other cell in the same section began failing. We tried to stop the tumbling, but two of our thrusters were acting up. Houston asked me to test one after I reported the spacecraft's persistent dancing antics.

"*Gemini 7*," CapCom inquired anxiously, "did you get a burst?"

"We get nothing, other than the solenoid clicking."

"Say again, *Seven*."

"We're venting. It looks like it's coming through the thruster without igniting."

"Okay, disregard. We'll stop the test at this time."

A few minutes later, CapCom's concern was reflected in this exchange:

CapCom: "We'd like another rundown on exactly how you lost the—or discovered the loss of attitude control. Also, we'd like a reading on your present rates [of tumbling]."

Gemini 7: "Roger, Elliot. When we woke up this morning, the first thing we were told to do was to monitor *Gemini 6*'s reentry, and when we unbuttoned to look out, we were drifting quite badly. We turned on the control and we didn't have any right yaw. Our rates have now built up so I imagine they're on the order of five to six degrees per second."

Chris Kraft had been listening to the exchange. Obviously sensing the fatigue in my voice, he took over CapCom.

"Frank, what do you think about controlling yaw with the maneuver thrusters?"

Just that calm voice of his was like a cold towel on my neck. "Well, Chris, I think we can control the rates [of tumbling] up here all right. I'm more concerned about this Delta-P light [indicating problems in the next-to-last fuel cell] than I am the rates." Chris knew why I was worried—this meant we were down to one last fuel cell that was working properly.

"Yes. So are we, Frank."

"It looks to me like this time, the cells are really on their way."

We were yawing again, and before Kraft could comment on the failing cells, I tried the maneuver thrusters.

"The maneuver thrusters work pretty well in yaw," I reported.

"Okay," Kraft said. "Why are you more concerned about the Delta-P light this time? Do you see something different about it?"

"No. Same way with those two stacks this morning. We could almost tell up here that those two stacks had had it before we kept playing with them."

Kraft's response was coated with reassurance. "Frank, the people down here feel fairly confident in Section One." (This was the remaining cell.)

"Okay. Good."

"We're watching it with you, Frank. We'll be recognizing it just as quick as you will."

"Okay."

That one-word acknowledgment was my way of telling Kraft that I wanted the mission to continue. For the rest of the flight, getting down safely was our only task. We had run out of experiments to perform, which probably was just as well because we were too tired even to take each other's pulse. Shortly after *Gemini 6* departed, Houston became concerned over a huge storm system of hurricane strength forming in the Pacific. This, combined with our tumbling reports and the continuing malfunction of the fuel cells generating electricity, caused Mission Control to seriously consider bringing us back early.

Chris Kraft's calmness had kept everything going. Tired as we were, we wanted to fly a perfect mission; a premature return would almost have been a humiliation. It took a hard-nosed man like Kraft to keep our nagging problems in perspective, weighing each in terms of our ultimate safety and then making the gut decision to let us stay up there. It's hard to admit, but if the choice had been up to me, I probably would have come down with two days still left to go. With the attitude control fuel almost gone and the energy fuel cells giving us constant trouble, I was damned near convinced that if we didn't abandon the flight we might not make it back. It was worry fed by fatigue, and the combination was debilitating.

We never told Mission Control we wanted to come down ahead of schedule, but at one stage during the final two days we actually prepared for reentry, stowing everything away in accordance with the reentry procedures. That's why I'm so indebted to Chris and the rest of the ground team—they knew we still had one good fuel cell capable of keeping us powered for the remaining allotted time, and their cool reassurances kept the mission going. I was simply so dead tired that I wasn't thinking straight.

Even with near exhaustion, Lovell retained his sense of humor. During one of the final news reports prior to reentry, CapCom included a report from Postmaster General Lawrence O'Brien that people were waiting too long to mail Christmas gifts.

"I have a stack of stuff up here," Lovell remarked, "but I can't find a post office."

On December 18, at 19 minutes after the 323rd hour of our mission, CapCom messaged: "*Gemini 7*, you ready to come home now?"

"Ready! Ready!" I almost shouted.

The reentry procedures were initiated and the adrenaline was flowing again. (The procedures included taking Dexedrine pills two hours before we fired the retro-rockets.) We both had our suits on as I flew the reentry, and although the simulator had prepared us for the reentry techniques, we were somewhat surprised by the actual experience. As the plunging spacecraft's velocity carried it into the atmosphere, the external heat built up until the cabin was flooded with bright light from the pyrotechnics spewing over the heat shields. It was like flying inside a neon tube, although we didn't feel any heat.

The crucial braking action of retro-fire was a tense moment, next to the launch itself the most apprehensive time of any manned flight. It wasn't like being in an airplane, where if something goes wrong you know you're going to come down with a reasonable chance of ejecting safely. But if the retro-rockets on a spacecraft don't function, you've bought a very unique type of farm. At this critical stage of our flight, we had twenty-four hours of oxygen left, ten hours of electrical power, and damned little water—and that's all we had between us and drifting like a dead derelict in space if the braking retros didn't work.

But they worked, the first one firing automatically and on time, followed in quick order by the remaining three. I flew the next reentry phase by engaging the computerized space flight director at around 280,000 feet. We were in a 35-degree left bank when I engaged the guidance system.

The needles came alive, fed by the incoming pulses of computer calculations. From now on it was precision flying dictated by precision instrumentation, not unlike using an instrument landing system (ILS) to bring an airplane down in the soup. For most of the reentry, I couldn't see outside and just followed what the dials were telling me. But this time, instead of the usual 10- to 15-degree banks required during an ILS approach, we were banking as much as 90 degrees in response to the guidance director's computations.

The computer-ordered direction turns were so sharp that I began to wonder if the guidance system was functioning properly—never in the simulator had we had so many abrupt and drastic course changes. The needles would call for a left bank and then suddenly tell me to come back 180 degrees. I kept one hand on the manual control switchover just in case; if the system was malfunctioning, we could burn up by obeying false signals. The urge to go manual was strong, yet I had to believe those needles. Instinct again. Trust in the machine again. Faith in my own ability again.

The needles settled down; the course changes became less massive and I breathed easier. I wanted to fly that reentry approach perfectly, putting *Gemini 7* down as close to our landing target as possible. I had bet Wally Schirra a couple of bucks we'd land closer to the recovery ship than he had.

Waiting for us in the Atlantic, just off Cape Kennedy, was our target: the 27,000-ton aircraft carrier *Wasp*, veteran of World War II and Korea and the namesake of her gallant predecessor sunk off Guadalcanal in 1942. At 50,000 feet we deployed the high-altitude drogue chute, which began oscillating wildly, causing the spacecraft to rock 20 degrees to each side. I stopped the gyrations by firing the reaction control rockets, which also allowed us to burn off no longer needed fuel—I didn't want to hit the water with any more explosive fuel than necessary.

The second chute opened at slightly under 11,000 feet, and at 9,000 feet the peppermint-striped main chute blossomed above the capsule, slowing us down to a descent rate of 30 feet per second. That was our impact speed and we hit the water with a jarring jolt.

I peered outside, trying to spot a helicopter. When I didn't see any welcoming committee yet, my first reaction was disappointment.

"Shoot!" I said to Lovell. "We must have missed it by more than Wally did." (I was wrong; Wally had come down 7 miles from the carrier and our touchdown was 6.4 miles away.)

Our more realistic concern was the effect on our equilibrium of returning to a one-G environment. The medical boys had predicted we might pass out, because two weeks of weightless confinement would cause a pooling of blood in the legs. They figured that as soon as we tried to stand up in one G, we'd probably faint. This was why Lovell had worn those pneumatic leg cuffs, which periodically would clamp down, preventing the pooling of blood in the legs and thus acting like gravity. I hadn't worn any cuffs—I was the guinea pig in this controlled experiment and was half-expected to pass out when returned to one G, while Lovell presumably remained conscious.

So there we were, sitting in the capsule waiting for the helicopter and frogmen to arrive from the *Wasp,* and also waiting for one of us to faint, mostly me.

"Jim, do you feel like passing out?" I asked.

"No."

"Neither do I."

So much for the leg cuff experiment.

Finally we heard the growls of a hovering helicopter, and pretty soon the hatch was opened from the outside, revealing the grinning face of a Navy frogman. He said something like "Welcome home." When we climbed out to be lifted into the chopper, returning to one G really socked us. The main muscles in our legs had deteriorated and we could hardly stand. No queasiness or dizziness, just a feeling that our legs had turned to spongy rubber.

We had traveled more than 5.1 million miles, completing 206 orbits and staying up for 330 hours, 35 minutes, and 31 seconds. *Gemini*

7 had set records for time in space, distance covered, and number of earth orbits, but these weren't as important as what Project Gemini had achieved in 1965 overall:

- The first rendezvous of two manned, maneuverable spacecraft
- The first controlled reentry to a predetermined landing point, accomplished by both *Gemini* 6 and 7
- The most manned flights in a single year by any nation (five)
- The most men in space in one year (ten)

The ground personnel added a record of their own: fastest turnaround time between launches from a single pad. The best previous time had been two months. After *Gemini* 7's launch, Pad 19 was ready in two days.

When Jim and I stuck our heads out of the capsule, setting records was the farthest thing from our minds. We were just glad to be back, thankful that we were safe, and proud that we had accomplished our mission. Lovell had a full beard and I looked like a skid row bum recovering from a week-long binge. But nobody cared about our personal grooming—as we climbed wearily from the helicopter onto the *Wasp*'s mammoth flight deck, some three thousand sailors roared their welcome.

(One of my most vivid memories of December 18, 1965, is of the awe I felt at the size of the carrier. Lovell had flown off carriers many times, but I had never been on one before; I had just flown more than 5 million miles but I couldn't help being impressed by the 872-foot flight deck—it seemed like an Edwards runway transplanted to the Atlantic Ocean.)

I can still get choked up remembering those cheers from three thousand throats—I think the noise helped keep us upright on our wobbly, weakened legs. It was two weeks before we could walk normally, and going up steps was actually painful.

The postflight medical tests remain mostly a blur. What stands out most in my memory is a letter someone handed me, the envelope simply addressed to "Lt. Col. Frank Borman," shortly after we reached the *Wasp*. I recognized Susan's handwriting, and when I finally got some privacy, I read the contents.

My dearest Frank—
I only wish I could be the one to open the left hatch. This note is the next best way to reach you as soon as possible. In our hearts

we have been together these past two weeks—every moment. Our two boys have been a great comfort and hearing your voice literally made it bearable. My love and my pride just can't be put into words—and knowing you're safe and on the way home, God has been so very good to me.

All my love—forever,
Susan

She had given the note to someone in Houston she knew was going to be on the *Wasp*. Enclosed were two smiling snapshots of her and the boys.

The crew of the *Wasp* treated us like visiting royalty. The mess even baked us a special cake, which helped make up for the ordeal of postmission medical tests that began even before we got our legs back. The greatest luxury, however, wasn't food—it was the first shower, when we washed away the pigpen residue of two weeks in space and had a chance to shave.

The Navy flew us off the carrier to Cape Kennedy, and from there we were taken to Houston for more medical tests and a major debriefing. We told NASA that our biggest problem, other than persistent trouble with the fuel cells, had been the tendency of the windows to fog up—apparently the epoxy around the windows would outgas and cause misting. We critiqued the equipment and saved our most fulsome praise for the maneuverability of the spacecraft, in which Schirra and Stafford concurred.

The various medical tests showed we had suffered no serious ill effects, after the results were analyzed by no fewer than twenty doctors. I had lost ten pounds during the mission, Lovell six and a half. Some of our experiments tended to disprove Soviet reports of several adverse physical effects on cosmonauts.

The next postmission chore was a Houston news conference with the crews of both *Gemini 6* and 7 present. One question concerned the Russians' claim that they, not the United States, had achieved the first space rendezvous.

On August 12, 1962, two Soviet spacecraft had come within three miles of each other, and *Pravda*, Russia's state newspaper, heralded this as the first rendezvous. In truth, however, those vehicles had met almost by accident—they were in different orbital planes and they couldn't maneuver, as Schirra and Stafford did, to stop relative motion between them; *Gemini 6* at times stayed motionless and side by side with *Gemini 7*. As Schirra put it at the press conference, "If anybody thinks they've pulled a rendezvous off at three miles, have fun! This is when we started doing our work. I don't think rendezvous is over until you are stopped—completely stopped—with no relative motion between the two vehicles, at a range of approximately one hundred twenty feet. That's rendezvous! From there on, it's station-keeping."

Two days after our return, Jim Webb awarded NASA's Exceptional Service Medal to each member of the *Gemini 6* and 7 crews. Among other honors handed out were Distinguished Service Medals to Deke Slayton for his work on the Mercury and Gemini projects and to Schirra for "his courage and judgment in the face of great personal danger"—an appropriate reference to his refusal to "abandon ship" during *Gemini 6*'s first launch attempt.

Even more welcome than medals was some time off to spend with our families. The next time I saw the trusty little spacecraft that had taken us to fame was several years later, displayed in Washington's new National Air and Space Museum. I read once that every time Charles Lindbergh visited his *Spirit of St. Louis* in the Smithsonian (it's now in the NASM), he couldn't believe he had flown the Atlantic in such a tiny airplane.

I felt the same way when I viewed *Gemini 7* for the first time since the mission. I couldn't imagine how I could have endured two weeks trapped in a metal container not much bigger than a phone booth.

Yet I also felt affection and gratitude. It was just another machine, an inanimate object created by man to serve man, but for those fourteen days it had been a living womb protecting two still-groping space infants from harm.

9

TRAGEDY

Death visited the astronauts for the first time on February 28, 1966.

Wally Schirra and I, along with our wives, were on a thirty-two-day goodwill tour of the Far East when we got the news that Elliot See and Charles Bassett had been killed in a plane crash. See, whose cheerful voice I had come to welcome during *Gemini 7,* was to have commanded *Gemini 9,* with Bassett as his pilot.

They were flying a T-38 to St. Louis, where McDonnell Douglas was building their spacecraft, and crashed while trying to land in foul weather. Even though we were deeply affected by the tragedy, we felt some relief that it hadn't happened during a space mission— and I don't mean that to sound heartless. We simply recognized that a major accident in space would have had devastating consequences for the whole program.

It almost happened just as we were completing our tour.

Gemini 8 was launched on March 16, 1966, with Neil Armstrong as commander and my old pupil at Edwards, Dave Scott, as pilot.

Their mission was another of NASA's logical, cautiously progressive steps building up to the Apollo project. It had two major objectives: actually docking with an Agena target vehicle, and an extended EVA exercise using the Air Force's new astronaut maneuvering unit (AMU). The first would demonstrate the feasibility of in-space docking, vital if the future lunar landing module was to return to the command module safely. The AMU, far more complex and efficient than the combination of oxygen tether and hand-held maneuvering gun used by Ed White, was a self-contained package—the type that would be necessary for walking on the moon's surface. A tiny rocket thruster unit strapped to the back and a built-in oxygen system were its principal features.

Armstrong and Scott attained the first objective with a textbook operation. Neil eased their spacecraft up to the Agena on the third orbit, maintained station-keeping at a distance of fifty feet for about a half hour, then maneuvered into docking position. The closing speed was only three inches per second. He radioed, "About two feet out," and seconds later he advised Flight Control, "We are docked! It's really a smoothie—no noticeable oscillations at all."

The cheers in Houston were as loud as the celebration that had greeted the *Gemini* 6 and 7 rendezvous. The docking was another U.S. first, and more important than the competitive aspect was the fact that the moon mission now appeared more possible than ever before. The yelling, handshakes, and backslapping in Mission Control had scarcely ended, however, when everything went sour in a hurry.

Jim Lovell, on duty at CapCom, only a few moments before had warned *Gemini* 8 that there was something wrong with the Agena's attitude controls. The target vehicle wasn't responding fully to ground signals, and Lovell told the crew, "If you run into trouble and the attitude control system in the Agena goes wild, just turn it off and take control with the spacecraft."

Forewarned, Scott began transmitting disconnect control signals to the Agena as soon as docking was completed. Then he dialed in a command to turn right. Both vehicles began an obedient turn, but Scott realized the response was abnormally fast, glanced at the instrument panel, and called out, "Neil, we're in a bank!"

It was a sharp bank that suddenly became an uncontrolled roll. Armstrong, believing the Agena was causing the trouble, immediately shut off the target vehicle's thrusters. The roll continued and, still convinced they were locked in the embrace of a runaway rocket, Neil ordered Dave to hit the undocking switch and back away. Freed from the Agena, they waited for the automatic maneuvering control system to take over and right the spacecraft.

But the roll continued, and now both astronauts knew there was something wrong with their own ship. They were rolling at a rate of one revolution per second. Following what they had been taught in simulator training, they turned off the maneuvering controls and shifted to the reentry hand control system, trying desperately to stop the wild spinning. There was no response, but they refused to panic. They tried the hand controls again and this time they worked. Armstrong steadied the spacecraft and, partially reprieved from disaster, they went to work on the next immediate task: finding out what had gone wrong.

Armstrong knew the problem had to be in the maneuvering system, a logical suspect because it hadn't stopped the roll. One by one, he tested each maneuvering thruster. The first seven were normal; number eight was stuck in an open position, like a jammed automobile accelerator pedal. Both men realized that what was supposed to be a four-day mission was over on the first day. *Gemini 8* had consumed too much reentry fuel in stopping the gyrations—the astronauts had to return immediately or risk coming down like an uncontrolled meteor.

Their splash-down site was originally supposed to be in the Atlantic off the Cape after the four days. But when everything hit the fan, the spacecraft was over the Pacific within range of the Hawaiian tracking station. Hawaii sent a "terminate mission" order that was superfluous—Neil had already decided to cut the flight short.

The astronauts nursed their crippled spacecraft to a safe landing about 620 miles east of Okinawa. There were a few more anxious moments because no rescue vessels were in sight, but Air Force planes from Japan and Okinawa spotted them and eventually they were taken aboard the secondary recovery ship, the destroyer *Leonard B. Mason*, which headed for Okinawa.

The Schirras and Bormans had just arrived in Hawaii for a four-day vacation break after the tiring goodwill tour through the Far East. But waiting for us were orders from Houston: Wally was to grab the first available air transportation to Okinawa, pick up Armstrong and Scott, and fly with them back to Hawaii. I was told to prepare for their arrival—especially arrangements for press coverage. I knew the newspeople would be on those astronauts like food-sensing sharks—they had damned near become the first U.S. casualties in space.

I informed NASA officials in Hawaii that the crew members were to be examined at the Army hospital in Honolulu before being subjected to a press conference. I was informed in turn that the news conference had a higher priority than medical checkups.

"If you send them to the hospital first," a NASA press officer insisted, "everyone will assume they're sick or hurt and that'll look bad."

I stood my ground and the local NASA flacks stood theirs. The debate continued via phone conversations between Honolulu and Houston until I got fed up and called Bob Gilruth myself.

"Bob, you told me I was in charge here. Do you trust my judgment?"

"Yes."

"Then tell those people out here I'm going to do exactly what I think is best for Neil and Dave. I'm keeping the press away from them until I know they're okay."

I don't suppose you can hear anyone smile, but the tone in Gilruth's next words convinced me he had to be grinning. "You do that, Frank" was all he said.

The astronauts were fine when they landed in Hawaii, but they were a little shaken. I put them in the hospital primarily to let them get some rest before facing the hungry media. It was to be expected that some of the coverage emphasized *Gemini 8*'s difficulties to the detriment of its significant achievement: the world's first space docking. This was the second consecutive U.S. triumph and it was obvious we had caught up with our Russian counterparts. An incredible amount of progress had been made since the days when our rockets were exploding on the pad while the Soviets were putting men into space.

My promotion to full colonel came automatically at the end of *Gemini 7*—at thirty-seven, I was the youngest bird colonel in the Air Force. West Point offered me a full professorship if I'd come back and teach on a more permanent basis, but I wasn't ready for that kind of sedate life. Susan wanted me to accept—our West Point years had been the happiest ones of our marriage.

Yet she understood. I wasn't in the space program for its fringe benefits—the postmission cheers and parades, the honors and the headlines. Tasting this heady experience just once would have been enough to satisfy a man's natural ego. I not only wanted to keep flying, I had to. Flying to me was living, as much a part of me as breathing.

The space program simply meant more flying—just a different kind. Beyond that was a far deeper motivation: Gemini was merely the first challenge. We had crept only a few yards down the pathway to the stars; we had pierced the dark mysteries of space with mere pinpoints of light.

Project Gemini wound down while NASA already was gearing up for Apollo. The remaining four missions showed a lot of work still had to be done before any Apollo moon flights. *Gemini 9,* with Stafford and Cernan as commander and pilot, experienced the most headaches, in what would become known as the "angry alligator" mission. They hoped to repeat *Gemini 8*'s successful docking experiment with another Agena target and then accomplish the EVA/AMU test that Scott had had to scrub on the previous flight.

After several delays, the crew finally shot into orbit on June 3 and caught the Agena during the second orbit, only to collide with one more unexpected hitch. This Agena's nose had clamshell doors that were supposed to open wide enough to permit the spacecraft to dock. When Stafford began the docking procedure, the doors opened only partially and stuck in that position.

"It looks like an angry alligator out here," Stafford told CapCom sadly.

Mission Control ordered him to abandon any docking efforts, but Tom did perform three close rendezvous maneuvers—including one that brought him within inches of the misbehaving target. On the mission's third day, Gene Cernan opened the hatch and ventured out into space. He was hooked to a 125-foot tether (we used to call it the snake); the 175-pound AMU backpack was attached to the outside of the spacecraft's adapter section. Gene was supposed to work his way back toward the adapter, don the AMU, and then test its maneuvering abilities. The whole experiment was scheduled to last two hours and forty-seven minutes, and Cernan accomplished the first phase: He retrieved a micrometeorite instrument from the module's hull and handed it to Stafford. Then he began the careful path back to the adapter.

Ed White's space walk hadn't lasted long enough to show what physical exertions would really be required for walks in space. The theory was that being weightless, an astronaut should be able to move around easily. Cernan found it just the opposite. His movements were not only painfully slow but extremely difficult, contrary to what he had experienced in a simulator. Every motion required

My first airplane—the one in which I soloed

The undefeated 1945 Tucson High varsity. I'm 58; number 67 is fullback Karl Eller, now chairman of Circle K.

The running quarterback—mostly because I couldn't pass

West Point cadet
Borman—my plebe year

Wedding day, 1950

The Borman family in the Air Force years. That's Edwin in
his mother's lap, Fred in mine.

One father, two sons,
and a football—ready for our
favorite sport

The rocket-powered F-104
I helped design at Edwards

"Don't you dare eat until grace is said." Taken before
Gemini 7.

I guess they really
wanted hamburgers.

Blast-off for *Gemini 7*.
No other words are necessary.

Rendezvous—and Navy
propaganda—in outer space.
Note the BEAT ARMY sign the
Gemini 6 crew displayed.

The ones we left behind. Left to right: astronaut wives
Marilyn Lovell, Jo Schirra, Fay Stafford, and Susan.

Welcome home! I'm being lifted into a helicopter after *Gemini 7*'s splashdown.

A great ad for a razor blade company: Jim Lovell and myself on the *Wasp*

On the way to the moon

Homecoming in Houston after *Gemini 7*. That's Edwin behind Susan.

Tight fit. This is inside the *Apollo 8* simulator, with me on the right and Lovell in the center.

One of the most famous pictures in photographic
history—taken after I grabbed the camera away from Bill Anders

tremendous effort; by the time he reached his AMU target he was almost exhausted and sweating so much that his helmet visor fogged up, seriously obstructing his vision. He also was having trouble communicating with Stafford, and Tom decided his partner had done all he could. With Mission Control's permission, he ordered Cernan back to the spacecraft about forty minutes short of the space walk's planned duration, and to forget about testing the AMU. *Gemini 9* completed the rest of its experiments successfully and proceeded to break our record by landing only two miles from the *Wasp* after spending seventy-two hours and twenty minutes in space.

Less than two months later, on July 18, *Gemini 10* lifted off on a mission that in several respects was the most complicated to date. There were two Agena targets this time—the first a docking target and the second a dead Agena that had been in space for four months. Mike Collins, John Young's pilot, was to take two space walks, one of which would feature the retrieving of another micrometeorite package attached to the lifeless Agena. Added to the docking objective was a tricky little number in which Young would dock with the other Agena and then use its rocket to propel both vehicles into a higher orbit.

The latter experiment not only worked but attained a record apogee of 474 miles. Mike's space walks were successful, too, although he experienced some of the same difficulties Cernan had encountered during *Gemini 9*—inability to move around with reasonable stability. After making one trip to the drifting Agena, he went back to his own spacecraft and got a refined version of White's old hand-held gun. This improved his maneuverability and he picked up the micrometeorite package as planned. He still had to use the tether, however, and every tug caused the *Gemini 10* spacecraft to change attitude, which activated a corrective thruster and burned fuel. Young advised Mission Control it was impossible to conserve fuel "with Mike out there bumping things." Collins was ordered back into the capsule fifteen minutes ahead of schedule. Counting his first walk in space—in which he'd taken photographs for almost an hour—he had been outside the spacecraft for nearly two hours. By now the fuel supply was down close to only 7 percent of capacity—the danger margin—and Young decided it was time to go home without completing most of the other fourteen planned experiments. To reduce weight and conserve fuel, they dumped the EVA equipment and every other inessential item—including, much to NASA's regret, several cameras. There was no reprimand, however; their lives were more important than even the most historic pictures. So critical was the fuel supply situation that when they changed orbit linked to Agena, they had to use the target vehicle's fuel instead of their own.

In some respects, *Gemini 11* was a mirror image of *Gemini 10*. With Pete Conrad as commander and Dick Gordon as pilot, the mission scored two more firsts: Conrad, doing a superb job of flying, achieved rendezvous with an Agena target during the first orbit, only an hour and eighteen minutes after lift-off: Gordon, on one of his two space walks, attached a tether between the spacecraft and the Agena to see whether a spinning maneuver by both vehicles would create an artificial gravity field. It did, although a weak one.

Both space walks added more confirmation to the evidence gathered by Cernan and Collins; like them, Gordon experienced severe fatigue and it was apparent that EVA still was a problem. But when *Gemini 11* splashed down in the Atlantic on September 15, 1966, after three days in space, it had two more achievements to brag about. Conrad had flown the first hands-off reentry; with arms folded, he merely monitored a computer guidance system that landed the spacecraft only 1.2 miles from the carrier *Guam.* I was glad I hadn't bet with either Stafford or Pete.

Gemini 12, the project's final mission, was launched on November 11 with my old partner Jim Lovell in his first command and Edwin "Buzz" Aldrin his pilot. Buzz may have been the most brilliant and also the most complex of all the astronauts. His flight with Lovell was his first trip in space, but he was no rookie in the space program; it was Aldrin who was largely responsible for the rendezvous and docking procedures that were such an important part of Gemini. After he left NASA in 1971 (*Apollo 11* was his last mission), he had trouble adjusting to a more mundane life and experienced emotional problems, including a bout with alcoholism. Later he wrote a book, *Return to Earth,* in which he painfully described what he had gone through following the glory years.

Originally he was supposed to test the still-virgin AMU during the *Gemini 12* mission, but NASA changed its mind and gave him a number of EVA chores using new portable handholds, foot restraints, and waist tethers. Aldrin wound up spending nearly five hours outside the spacecraft on two separate walks, and the new aids worked beautifully. Among his tasks was turning bolts with wrenches, detaching and then rejoining electrical connections, and cutting metal with special clippers—all of which demonstrated the feasibility of assembling or repairing structures in space.

At the end of the second space walk, he paused to wipe Lovell's window playfully.

"Hey," Jim suggested, "would you change the oil, too?"

Lovell himself flew an excellent mission despite a spate of mechanical problems, the major one being the failure of the rendezvous radar before docking. Lovell had to mate with the target using just his eyesight and a space sextant. *Gemini 12* also had fuel cell problems and malfunctioning thrusters, but Lovell kept the mission going for its full planned duration and splashed down near the *Wasp* ninety-four hours and thirty-four minutes after lift-off.

Project Gemini was over, with ten completed and generally successful manned flights in only eighteen months. It was a period in our space history that many Americans may have forgotten, replaced in their memories by the more glamorous moon shots of Apollo. Perhaps only those who participated in Gemini can understand its importance to the achievements of Apollo. And only the astronauts themselves can acknowledge our dependency on the mission planners and support teams—particularly those giants of integrity who were the Webbs, Gilruths, and Krafts.

Project Gemini cost about $1.2 billion. About half of that sum went for the spacecraft, mock-ups, simulators, and various support equipment, but it could be said that the entire amount was spent to maximize the safety of the astronauts during the far more difficult and complex Apollo flights into space, free of earth's gravity and toward a target nearly a quarter of a million miles away, where the slightest course miscalculation would be catastrophic.

To the NASA of those epochal years, "success" and "safety" were interchangeable words. Yet NASA also recognized the existence of two other interchangeable words: "mission" and "risk." To maximize safety merely meant reducing risk, without forgetting that some risk—even terrible risk—was unavoidable.

The NASA of later years seemed to forget or, worse, ignore the risk element when it turned the space shuttle program into a public relations exercise. To me, the idea of carrying congressmen, schoolteachers, and reporters on space shuttle flights is abysmally, almost stupidly wrong. Even after all we've learned from the space program, manned space flight remains dangerous and still largely experimental.

The *Challenger* itself was just that: an experimental vehicle pitifully vulnerable to the most hazardous phase of any mission—the launch. Every shuttle is parked on top of an extremely volatile rocket with a long history of imperfect reliability, and to expose innocent civilians, even if cursorily trained, to such potential danger represented some muddled and misguided thinking. The fact that the *Challenger*'s launch rocket was especially and even known to be flawed is beside the point—disaster also could have occurred with a supposedly perfect launch vehicle. Rockets can blow up and their guidance systems can go crazy; they are complex, temperamental machines that should work but sometimes don't.

I happen to think the whole shuttle program came too soon. We should have first expanded our efforts in the direction of a manned space station and let unmanned rockets launch satellites—it would have been far more cost-effective—but that's another matter for debate. My beef is with a NASA that complacently assumed the shuttle wasn't much more than a scientifically equipped airplane that could be flown almost routinely. The trouble is that launches are never routine and neither is flight above the earth's atmosphere. Space is for professionals, not passengers.

The seeds of the *Challenger* catastrophe were planted even before I left NASA. Sometime after *Apollo 8,* I thought I was going to become heavily involved with a space station project that never really got off the drawing board. Instead, NASA hired a group of consultants who convinced the agency it should concentrate on a space shuttle program, which would be the most cost-effective program yet devised. Hypnotized by the prospect of turning our expensive space efforts into a commercially viable venture, NASA sold the shuttle program to Congress on just such a basis. NASA's fatal mistake was to justify the shuttle vehicles as merely an exploitation of known technology. They were far from that—as a matter of fact, ships like the *Challenger* borrowed very little if anything from the entire Apollo program. They were experimental craft designed for research in areas Apollo hardly touched.

I told an interviewer this six months before the *Challenger*'s booster rocket blew up. I said NASA had sold Congress and the public on the erroneous notion that the shuttle was an operational vehicle; it was a hell of a long way from deserving that status. I added that taking civilians on space shuttle flights seemed to indicate that space travel already was a tourist attraction and that somebody was going to get hurt.

So I'm not playing Monday morning quarterback in this criticism. I made those comments at a time when NASA actually was asking the airlines to operate the shuttle program—American, United, and Pan Am did submit bids. I wouldn't let Eastern get involved, and for the sake of the airline industry I'm damned glad the other airlines eventually backed away, too.

Even in Gemini, where NASA consistently demonstrated an admirable commitment to safety, risk still couldn't be eliminated; there always was the unplanned incident, the unexpected malfunction, the uninvited emergency that popped up without warning. We almost lost *Gemini 8* and there wasn't a single mission in which something didn't go wrong. Every flight was an attempt to get answers to questions, but some questions remained unanswered.

As we found out on the black day of January 27, 1967.

Project Apollo was well under way, and I had been in the training process for months. During 1966, NASA had conducted three unmanned flights to test the gigantic Saturn launch rocket. There had been snags in the design of a lunar landing module, but work on the big three-man Apollo command spacecraft had progressed much faster. I had been spending a lot of time at the Draper Laboratories in Massachusetts learning about programming the Apollo autopilot, and another home away from home was the North American Aviation plant in California where the Apollo spacecraft were being built.

I had taken Susan and the boys to a small lake near Huntsville, Texas, where Jim and Margaret Elkins had a cottage. It was a weekend we all had looked forward to, me more than anyone else, because I knew the phone number was unlisted and there was no way anybody was going to interrupt two days of relaxation with family and friends.

We had just sat down to dinner Friday evening when Jim got up to answer a knock on the door. He returned a few seconds later.

"Frank, there's a Texas Ranger here who wants to see you."

I went to the front door where a tall young trooper was standing, an expression of apology on his face. Apparently someone knew we were friends with the Elkinses and had found out where their cottage was.

"Colonel Borman?"

"That's me."

"Sorry to disturb you, sir, but the Manned Space Center in Houston has been trying to reach you. There's been some kind of emergency and you're to phone them immediately."

I called Houston and was transferred to Deke Slayton, who gave me the bad news.

"Frank, we've had a bad fire on Pad Thirty-four and we've got three astronauts dead—Grissom, White, and one of the new boys, Roger Chaffee."

"What in God's name happened?"

"We don't know yet. We're organizing an investigation committee and you're on it. Get to the Cape as soon as possible."

"Deke, I'd like to stop off first at Ed White's house. Pat White and Susan are pretty close."

"Fine with me. I'll have an airplane available as soon as you're ready to leave."

When we got to the White home, some NASA officials had already bugged her about funeral plans. Bugged, hell—they had pressured her. Someone in Washington had decided all three astronauts were to be buried in Arlington National Cemetery and Pat was staging a tearful but losing battle. White's father had also been a West Pointer, and Ed had told Pat that if anything ever happened, he wanted to be buried at the academy.

"They told me there has to be only one ceremony," she sobbed.

I couldn't believe it. They were worrying about what would make it easier on them than on the victims' families. It was a typical bureaucratic reaction and I was angry.

"That's nonsense," I told Pat. "We're going to do exactly what you want and I'll take care of it."

I don't remember just who I called in Washington except that he was damned high up on the bureaucratic totem pole.

"Ed White's funeral will be at West Point like the family wants," I declared, "so you might as well go ahead and arrange things— that's the way it's going to be."

I went home, leaving Susan to help console Pat and the children. The Grissoms lived across the artificial lake decorating our development, but we didn't know them very well, and we hardly knew Roger and Martha Chaffee at all. Rog was thirty-two, a Navy lieutenant, pilot, and specialist in engineering reliability. He was a "third-generation" astronaut—a member of the third group to enter the program. I grabbed a few hours of fitful sleep, packed, and went out to the airport where Deke had commandeered a T-38 for me. I was lucky—I was escaping the trauma of tragedy and plunging into an investigative grind that left no time to grieve. But behind me was a wife who was almost as badly shaken as the widow she was trying to comfort.

Ed's death hit me hard, too. We had lost many friends before, but never had we lost someone so close, nor anyone in the space program who had been killed in a spacecraft. He might as well have been the brother I never had, a man of gentle strength and quiet humor.

Flying an airplane was the best antidote for sorrow; Susan didn't have that luxury. The normal route the astronauts flew from Houston to Cape Kennedy took us over land, bypassing the Gulf of Mexico even though cutting across the Gulf was much shorter. We were forbidden to take the overwater route because the NASA planes didn't carry life rafts, and air traffic control would have looked askance at anything except an overland flight plan. This time I was cleared straight across the Gulf with no questions asked. And throughout the flight, controllers would hear my NASA aircraft call sign and come back with something like "By the way, we were damned sorry to hear the news," or "Hang in there, NASA."

I pushed that T-38 hard, almost as if speed could outrace memories of Ed White. I landed at Patrick AFB around 9 A.M., checked into a Holiday Inn at Cocoa Beach, rented a car, and drove right to the Kennedy Space Center. The investigative wheels already were turning—I was told that Floyd Thompson, NASA's top man at the Langley facility, would head the committee and that Deke Slayton would be arriving that afternoon, along with Max Faget of NASA's engineering and development section. This was the nucleus of the group and we met that first night to begin the probe.

We knew what had happened; we had to find out why. At 1:19 P.M. on Friday, January 27, Grissom, White, and Chaffee had entered their spacecraft to conduct a pressurization test and simulated launch countdown. This particular module was AS-204 (AS for Apollo-Saturn). At the time, NASA was intending to designate each Apollo mission by the joint number assigned to the flight's launch and command vehicles. AS-204, the fourth spacecraft built, would carry these three astronauts on the first manned Apollo mission, commanded by Grissom, scheduled for exactly one month later. Subsequently, it would be known as Apollo 1.

The spacecraft itself was already mounted on top of a Saturn IB booster, 218 feet above Pad 34. With the crew going through a regular launch countdown procedure, the hatch was sealed and the cabin pressurized with 100 percent pure oxygen. Not long after the countdown began, Grissom reported smelling a peculiar odor in the spacecraft and the countdown was halted while technicians tried to trace the source.

They found nothing wrong, and the countdown resumed. It was interrupted again when radio transmissions became garbled and Gus, obviously irritated, asked Mission Control, "How do you expect to talk to me in space if you can't hear me five miles away?" Gus had been griping about *AS-204* on more than one previous occasion. One day he had picked a large lemon from a tree and hung it on the spacecraft—the gesture came uncomfortably close to being a premonition.

At 6:31 P.M., an almost casual announcement, believed to be Chaffee's voice: "Fire. I smell fire."

The next transmission was far from casual.

"Fire in the spacecraft!"

Followed by a scream. Then other voices, their words undecipherable but the tone unmistakable—first urgency, next panic.

The ground crews couldn't see inside the spacecraft, but a small television camera, trained on *AS-204*'s hatch window, caught the drama in sickening if indistinct detail—a fleeting image of legs and feet moving, followed by an obliterating flash of orange flame. Mission Control heard a sharp cry from one of the trapped astronauts—whether from pain or disbelief that the impossible was happening, only the doomed man knew.

Now ground crews could see for themselves. Only fourteen seconds after the laconic "I smell fire" report, the heat-tortured module erupted into a boiling ball of flames and black smoke. Technicians at first couldn't get to the hatch because of the heat, and almost six minutes went by before they somehow managed to open it. They were at least six minutes too late. Grissom, White, and Chaffee were dead—an Apollo spacecraft, the most intricate machine ever devised by man, had turned into a death chamber for three helpless astronauts. The direct cause: carbon monoxide asphyxiation.

I was no stranger to violent death and its aftermath, having occasionally been emotionally and professionally close to a victim or victims. But nothing I had witnessed in the past came close to what I saw at Cape Kennedy. The giant complex was in a mass state of shock.

I had gone out that morning to see *AS-204*. As the first one who entered it, I can't even begin to describe that chamber of horror. To me, the interior of a spacecraft had always provided a reassuring sight of gleaming instruments and spotless equipment, creating the illusion of total indestructibility. *AS-204* was a fire-blackened charnel house, a charred shell that wasn't even a recognizable facsimile of a spacecraft. It almost was a scene of mockery, as if that seared cabin were laughing at the effrontery of man in challenging the unknown.

I could only agree with what Jim Webb had said after the fire: "We've always known that something like this would happen sooner or later, [but] who would have thought the first tragedy would be on the ground?"

He was right—that's what made the Pad 34 disaster so hard to take. Three superbly trained pilots had died, trapped during a supposedly routine ground test that shouldn't have been any more dangerous than taking a bath. I don't think the grief would have been any less if they had perished in space, but at least it would have been more logical and half-expected. The fact that three had died in a motionless spacecraft parked safely on a launch pad was totally illogical, and this was what spawned guilt as well as grief.

It all led to an emotional state that not only was prevalent at the Cape but actually invaded the investigation team itself. The NASA community at Cape Kennedy was a family, closely knit socially, and virtually overnight it became a troubled family. There were an awful lot of commiseration parties and an awful lot of drinking.

I stayed away from the chest-beating, heavy-drinking social affairs, with one exception. Seeing the spacecraft itself affected me so deeply that the same night I went out with Deke and Max to a nightclub; getting drunk seemed like a good idea. First we drank several toasts to Gus, Ed, and Roger. After the floor show and numerous other drinks, it came to the dignified Faget that in addition to being a great scientist, in his youth he had also been something of a tumbler. He proceeded to demonstrate this athletic skill by standing on his hands. We closed the evening by throwing glasses against a wall—it was right out of a World War I movie. The only thing we left out was the bravado toast, "Here's to the next man to die," and we might as well have spoken that, too. It was a fighter pilots' farewell from Deke and me, and one that Max understood and joined.

But then, sorrow ended and work began. We spent four months of total immersion in the investigative process. Our chairman, Dr. Thompson, was a tower of calm strength and sage advice, one of the truly grand old men of aerodynamics, he lightened our grim task by telling us stories of his early research days, like the time he'd walked along the top of a blimp with a probe instrument, trying to find out where airflow was the most turbulent. We brought in every learned mind we could enlist—including a chemistry expert from Cornell, an explosives specialist from the Bureau of Mines, and technical people from North American and other aerospace firms. One of the latter was my old friend John Yardley of McDonnell Douglas, builder of the Gemini spacecraft.

Hour after hour, I'd sit in the charred cabin—for a long time, I was the only one allowed to enter. I went in first to catalogue and inspect the switches, trying to unearth some unknown flaw in the electrical system. Over and over again I examined the hatch, and finally concluded that if Ed White couldn't open it, nobody could have; its design had frustrated even the strongest of the astronauts.

I kept playing the communications tapes until I heard them in my dreams. Especially that one unidentified voice: "Fire in the spacecraft!" Especially the unidentified scream that followed. The only comfort derived from listening to the tapes was the knowledge that the agony hadn't lasted long; that death had come from noxious fumes before the flames reached them.

One basic flaw was apparent from the start—NASA had allowed the installation of too many hydrocarbon materials into the spacecraft interior, flammable nylon and Velcro, for example. While this may have been an acceptable hazard, it was based on the assumption that, even in a volatile environment of 100 percent oxygen, combustible materials were perfectly safe because there was no ignition source. This was wrong assumption number one—the murderous fire couldn't have started by itself, so there had been an ignition source.

Wrong assumption number two was more a matter of complacency than anything else, because it relied completely on the validity of the first assumption. The three men had been conducting a cabin pressurization test that was part of a normal countdown, which meant pressurizing the atmosphere within the spacecraft to 5.5 pounds per square inch—the same level employed in space. But they hadn't been in space; they'd been only a couple of hundred feet from the ground, with the outside atmospheric pressure 14.7 psi, and to achieve the required 5.5 psi environment inside the cabin they had to go up to 20.2 psi. That is an extremely dangerous environment, the equivalent of sitting on a live bomb, waiting for someone to light the fuse.

The "fuse" of course, was the mysterious ignition spark; fed by pure oxygen, it had exploded into a real fire, consuming the flammable materials inside the spacecraft and turning them into spewing faucets of toxic fumes. We never did determine definitely what had caused the spark, although we would have bet our combined bank accounts that it originated in a bundle of electrical wiring in front of Grissom's feet. It had to have been some kind of short circuit, because we did have evidence of a bright arc that appeared in this one area just before fire swept through the cabin.

Sometimes it was hard to stay emotionally detached from our task. It got to us in different ways. I began to get progressively angrier at what we gradually unearthed—sloppy planning and supervision on NASA's part and some shamefully inadequate design and test work by North American.

There's a time to mourn and a time to get back to the business of living—something that, tragically, too many people in and out of NASA couldn't accept, including a few of our own investigation associates. The more we probed for answers, the more depressed they got. They'd take downers to ease the pain of guilt and uppers so they could face the next day. The result was inevitable: They became relatively ineffective, and two became basket cases.

I don't want to mention their names; both were fine, dedicated men who simply succumbed to the pressures of the investigation, and both were weighed down by what they felt was their own guilt. Each was swallowing uppers and downers like harmless candy, and this addiction played a large part in their eventual breakdowns.

The first crack-up occurred without warning and right before our eyes. We were in Houston, having finished writing our three-thousand-page report, and were in Bob Gilruth's office discussing the status of Apollo in general and the need for major redesign of the moon spacecraft based on what our investigation had uncovered. One of the engineers (not a NASA man) got up, a glazed look on his face, and walked over to a blackboard in the room.

He began to draw what looked like one of those corporate organizational charts, with one large box at the top and lines leading down to smaller boxes.

"This is my organizational chart for heaven," he announced. "At the top is God, whom we'll call Big Daddy. . . ."

On he went, drawing the chart with a running commentary that became totally incoherent. We called an ambulance and his company flew him home in a straitjacket. After long psychiatric therapy, including shock treatments, he recovered his health. The other case, a NASA official, had an unhappier ending. Only about a week after the incident in Gilruth's office, he drove onto a Houston expressway and raced his car at speeds of more than 100 miles an hour until the engine caught fire. He climbed out and watched the vehicle burn. He explained later that he'd seen a metaphysical connection between the pad fire and the one that destroyed his automobile.

He should have been committed for treatment, but for some reason this wasn't done, and he paid the price. Years went by before I saw him again—he came into my office at Eastern, unshaven and with the telltale bloodshot eyes of a huge hangover. He announced it was his duty to save the country from the Russians and asked me to help him.

"I'd like to be secretary of the Air Force," he said in pitiful seriousness. "I know you've been close to Richard Nixon and I'd like you to call him and recommend me."

When he left, I couldn't help but think, *There's another victim of Pad 34.* But there were other victims. The most visibly and deeply affected were the engineers most closely associated with the spacecraft design, both within NASA and those of North American and other support companies. The man I felt sorriest for was Joe Shea, director of the Apollo program in Houston. A former top official at Raytheon and a brilliant, very intense scientist, he took it very hard, to the point of feeling depressing guilt.

Then there were the astronauts' wives. Pat White, who committed suicide a few years later, was the most extreme case of the pad fire's aftereffects, which swept from the Cape to Houston. Our wives began to look at the space program through eyes of fear. They couldn't turn to us for support; the risk we accepted as part of our jobs was something they had to cope with themselves. This shouldn't have happened and I have to fault NASA's medical department in Houston's Manned Spacecraft Center.

The department was run by Dr. Charles Berry, who relished being known as "the astronauts' doctor." I was not alone in believing he could have spent more time helping people who were under more stress than we were.

Berry also was a gossip—Mike Collins once called him "the biggest blabbermouth in the space program." The doctor angered me just before the *Apollo 11* moon mission. Astronauts Armstrong, Collins, and Aldrin were invited to a White House reception in their honor, but Berry told reporters they shouldn't be allowed to go because they might become contaminated. When the news media asked me to comment on this supposed menace, I snapped, "He should keep his big mouth shut!"

For years I have kept in my files a letter I received after my retort appeared in print. It is dated July 17, 1969, addressed to me with a copy to Major General James W. Humphreys, Jr., director of space medicine, NASA. It begins: "We couldn't possibly be more in accordance than we are with your comment concerning Doctor (and [we] use the word loosely) Charles Berry. . . . His selfish, dishonest effort to be in the public limelight has caused him to steal the research of others and publish same under his own name, make medical statements that we, as physicians, can't endorse, and, above all, represent a very important agency . . . in the go-off-their-rocker, half-shod, unprofessional, uninformed manner that he does."

I won't quote the entire letter, but it is signed by twenty-one doctors of the U.S. Air Force Medical Department.

Granted, Berry was not a psychiatrist. But he was the top NASA medical man in Houston and he had a capable psychiatric staff to call on. Our wives needed guidance and counseling, not uppers, downers, or drinks. I should know—Susan was one of them.

Maybe we astronauts, as husbands and fathers, were at least partially responsible, with our assumption that our families could somehow absorb our macho philosophy. Yet I doubt very much if the space program could have succeeded *without* that assumption, cruel as that sounds. We had too much to learn, too much to do, without domestic distractions. If blame has to be shared, I'd put part of it on the failure of the armed forces themselves to ever consider the stresses military wives must endure.

There has never been a concerted effort to prepare wives for those almost inevitable stresses. Teaching a young bride bits of military protocol, like leaving a calling card with the commanding officer when assigned to a new post, doesn't educate her to the true realities of military life. It doesn't prepare her to deal with danger, or with the ultimate danger: death. Counseling and guidance must be as much a part of the military wife's curriculum as combat education is part of her husband's.

If you must fault the astronauts themselves for ignoring all the signs of domestic tension—as I did, along with most of the others—remember that we all came out of the military; the space program was nothing but an extension of the disciplined concentration we had been taught to apply to our jobs. The Mission came first. If the Air Force, the Navy, and NASA insisted on our adhering to that philosophy, as well they should, they still somehow had to take up the slack we left dangling at home in the form of loneliness and fear, especially after the pad fire.

In our investigation of the tragic fire, the area of suspicion from the very beginning was the environmental control system. As the investigation progressed, all sorts of nuts came out of the woodwork with their own theories. There also were some serious allegations directed against North American Aviation, most of them coming from former employees with large axes to grind. They charged the company with criminal neglect and mismanagement, and we investigated each accusation thoroughly. We found that in every case we were getting input from people who simply had personal grievances against the company, with no evidence to back them up.

Yet we didn't need testimony from disgruntled employees to realize that North American's skirts were far from clean, and neither were NASA's. We became painfully aware that part of the trouble lay in the management of Project Apollo itself, and that put the onus on poor Joe Shea's doorstep. He was unquestionably an excellent scientist, but also a poor administrator who had simply let North American's design mistakes pile up like unnoticed garbage.

Our report was an impartial analysis of the fire and we listed a number of recommended changes in the design of Apollo's spacecraft. We didn't sweep a single mistake under the rug, and to this day I'm proud of the committee's honesty and integrity.

Congress, naturally, didn't wait for our investigation to conclude and our report to be written before some members began demanding that the House and Senate conduct their own probes. This is inevitable after every major disaster, when politicians see a golden opportunity to march on center stage while a tragedy is fresh in the public's mind. The congressional investigative hearings too often are premature, carelessly conducted, overplayed by news media catering to the headline hunters, and motivated too much by sheer politics. I have yet to see a congressional committee looking into air safety, for example, come up with anything that the real experts didn't already know.

But we were lucky, thanks to two lawmakers who were statesmen first and politicians second: Olin Teague of Texas, chairman of the House Committee on Science and Technology, and his Senate counterpart, Clinton Anderson of New Mexico. Both these men held off demands that Congress get into the act, insisting that everyone wait until after we finished our investigation and issued our report. They not only did us a favor but did the country one as well, for which I will always be personally grateful, as NASA selected me to testify when Teague and Anderson announced that their respective committees would hold hearings.

They were under pressure, too, not only from some of their own publicity-happy colleagues but from a segment of the media clamoring loudly for scapegoats and scalps, not to mention an end to the space program itself. There weren't enough guys like Witkin and the AP's veteran space reporter Vern Haugland, who could be sharply, sometimes embarrassingly critical, but always tried to be fair.

So, I think, did the American public, which mourned the astronauts and rightfully questioned the circumstances of the tragedy, but also acknowledged that danger and possible death were clauses in any space exploration contract. Less than two months after the pad fire, the Soviet Union revealed the death of cosmonaut Vladimir Komarov during the landing of *Soyuz 1,* a new Russian spacecraft. The lesson was clear: Risk plays no favorites and salutes no flag.

I looked forward to testifying on Capitol Hill with all the eager anticipation of a man going to a dentist and facing certain tooth extraction. The House appearance was first, and I met privately with Jim Webb in his office before going to the Hill. Once again, he gave me evidence of his inherent integrity.

"Frank," he said, "the American people need to understand what happened just as we now understand. You are not to try in any way to hold back facts or color your testimony in NASA's favor. Just tell them exactly what your investigation group found, no holds barred, even if it makes NASA look bad."

He had given me a remarkable and courageous set of instructions. The House hearing was scheduled for that evening and Webb rode over with me, accompanied by Shepard, McDivitt, Schirra, and Slayton. We were about to walk into the committee room when he took my arm.

"Remember, tell the whole truth," he said quietly.

I did exactly that.

"We are confident in our management, our engineering, and ourselves," I began. "I think the question is, are you confident in us?"

Then I went on to explain what we had learned from the investigation and assured the committee that NASA was fully committed to incorporating our recommendations into all Apollo spacecraft.

Testifying wasn't as bad as I expected, but it wasn't a carefree outing, either. I survived because I followed Webb's orders and no amount of hostile, uninformed interrogation rattled or confused me. Olin Teague was magnificent—sympathetic and understanding, yet also firm in his probing for the facts.

There were moments when I realized why so many people fear a congressional hearing and occasionally stumble in their testimony. Even the physical setup is intimidating—the witnesses sit facing a committee whose members are looking down at them from the vantage point of a raised dias, putting them at a psychological disadvantage before they open their mouths.

Surprisingly, I encountered hostility from a congressman I would have expected to display the most objectivity—Don Rumsfeld. A former Navy pilot, he had some caustic remarks to make about the space program and its apparent lack of concern for safety.

Rumsfeld, at least, had some technical knowledge behind his questions. There was one congressman from New York who gave an excellent impersonation of a ventriloquist's dummy—he had plenty of questions, but virtually all of them came out of the audience. Unfriendly members of the press would hand him slips of paper with their own questions written out, and he would dutifully ask them.

My testimony was straight to the point: I said, basically, that we in the space program had overlooked the obvious hazard of putting a 100 percent oxygen environment into a spacecraft pressurized to more than 20 psi.

Why couldn't the three astronauts have escaped? I explained that the Apollo command module had only a plug-type door—under pressurization, it sealed tight and couldn't be opened except from the outside. And I frankly admitted that we had found some serious flaws in the module's design, faults that had to be corrected before Apollo could proceed.

The next day, I repeated my testimony before Senator Anderson's committee in what was a rather perfunctory appearance—like Teague,

Anderson made it clear he had no intention of doing a hatchet job on NASA or Apollo; he and the other senators merely wanted assurances that we knew what had really happened on Pad 34 and had learned from the mistakes.

I returned to Cape Kennedy to clean up a few odds and ends from our investigation, expecting to resume my Apollo training. It came as no surprise to hear that Joe Shea had just resigned and that George Low, Bob Gilruth's deputy, had replaced him as Apollo director in Houston. Gilruth had already confided to me that Low was going to be his choice to succeed Shea. While the investigation was still in progress, Gilruth had stopped me in a corridor one day.

"You know, Frank," he said, "I'd like very much to have you run the Apollo program instead of Shea. But I also know you want to keep flying and that you don't have the administrative experience we need so badly right now. George Low is my choice to take over from Shea, but if you're really interested, I'll reconsider. How do you honestly feel about it?"

"I couldn't agree with you more," I assured him. "I have no desire to become a full-time program manager."

I couldn't help but feel very good about his even considering me, however. And almost as soon as I arrived at the Cape from Washington, Gilruth gave me further evidence of his faith in me. He was at the Cape, too, and asked me to see him in private. I thought it might involve my next astronaut assignment, but it was far more than that.

"We're establishing a spacecraft redefinition team that'll be based at the North American plant in Downey, California," he told me. "Would you consider leaving the astronaut group temporarily to head this team?"

I didn't hesitate for one second. "I'll not only consider it but I'll accept right now," I said.

"That fast?" He smiled.

"That fast, Bob. No Apollo astronaut is going to fly again anyway until we fix what's wrong with the spacecraft. And after four months of investigation, I think I know as well as anyone else what has to be done."

I did. What I didn't know was that redesigning the spacecraft was going to mean months of frustration, battles with my own astronaut comrades, and more loneliness for my family.

10

GETTING READY FOR APOLLO 8

Each aerospace company I worked with during my astronaut years seemed to have an individual personality that reflected the style of its management.

If you mentioned the men at Lockheed's plant in Sunnyvale, California, I pictured Gucci shoes, silk shirts, and high rollers at a Las Vegas craps table. Grumman's people were very conservative, even stodgy, but devoted to good quality. And North American was positively schizophrenic, populated by conscientious men who knew what they were doing and at least an equal number who didn't know their butts from third base.

There was a massive case of nerves at North American when I arrived at Downey. North American had just been taken over by Rockwell International and heads were already rolling. Rockwell had brought in Bill Bergen, who had helped design the Titan II, from Martin Marietta. Rockwell had given him carte blanche to clean house.

As soon as he got there, Bergen called a meeting of all managers and designers involved in the spacecraft program.

"We all know there's been a serious failure here," he began. "It was a failure that not only involved three brave lives but also this country's future. There's blame enough for everyone, but it's clear not everyone in this room was doing his job. So take a good look to your right and take another look to your left, because one of your neighbors is going to be gone tomorrow."

The first time we met, he told me, "I want you to know you have unlimited access to me at all times. If you run into problems, bring 'em straight to me. That's the way NASA wants it, Frank, and that's the way it's going to be."

Basically my job was to provide any technical input needed in the redesign work and to keep Houston advised of progress, or lack of same. But Bergen gave me a lot of free rein, even though my orders came from Houston. Right from the start, Bill and I agreed that quality had to be given the highest priority—we could redesign components and materials to our heart's content, but they wouldn't be worth a damn if production quality slipped. We asked for a zero-defects program and we got it.

I had been at North American only a few days when I found out that most of the plant workers were going across the street to a bar at break or lunchtime for a beer or two.

I couldn't believe it. These guys were working on highly sensitive and complex equipment, requiring absolute perfection, and here they were guzzling beer right in the middle of their workday. I went right to the leadership of their union, the International Association of Machinists and Aerospace Workers (IAM).

"I don't mind a cold brew myself," I told them, "but not while I'm working. This has got to stop or somebody's going to make a mistake that could involve an astronaut's life."

I received not one iota of static from the union leaders. They issued orders to their members: no drinking until you finish your shift. And in turn, they got very little if any static from the rank and file—those were the days when the unions were willing to put the cause of America's space program ahead of everything else.

Ironically, some of the static I did receive came from the astronauts themselves. We welcomed their suggestions, but we had also established a chain of command for offering them. If the astronauts had any ideas relating to the redesign work, they were to put them to NASA's Change Control Board in Houston, and the board would relay them to Downey. The board was headed by George Low, and occasionally he'd get some wild idea from an astronaut who'd pressure him to adopt it.

"George," I'd tell him, "you don't understand the problem—the suggestion makes no sense, so knock it off!"

Some astronauts began getting the idea that the board was nothing but a roadblock, so they'd try to get around it by coming out to Downey uninvited and doing a selling job on me. John Young flew in one day with some proposal I was sure wasn't going to work.

I said, "John, get back in your airplane and go back to Houston because you're not going to screw us up."

He wasn't happy and neither were my other compatriots after I put out an order that no astronaut could visit North American without my advance approval. They meant well, but their wish list was longer than a rich kid's letter to Santa Claus. If we had redesigned the spacecraft in accordance with everything they wanted, Neil Armstrong and Buzz Aldrin might not have landed on the moon for another five years.

One of the recommendations the investigation committee had made was provision of an emergency oxygen system for the spacecraft. If Grissom, White, and Chaffee had had this, they might have survived long enough for rescuers to reach them before the flames did. Former test pilot Scott Crossfield was in charge of safety engineering at North American and we clashed bitterly over what an effective emergency oxygen system was supposed to be.

What North American proposed to install was something that looked like an emergency system but actually wasn't worth a damn, because it didn't provide a foolproof means of preventing fumes from getting to the crew. I refused to approve it and thus made some enemies, including Crossfield.

North American also had the contract to build the second stage of the Saturn V launch vehicle, known as the S-2. It was Wernher von Braun's baby and when hitches developed—mostly insulation problems—he had his number two man, Dr. Eberhard Rees, spend a lot of time at North American. Stymied by my opposition to an inadequate emergency oxygen system on the spacecraft, Crossfield decided that the second-stage rocket itself was unsafe, and he declared that if North American ever tried to push it out of the factory he'd lie down in front of it.

Because he had been a famous test pilot, he made a well-publicized whistle-blower. I talked it over with a very frustrated Rees and finally called the NASA brass. "Crossfield has created an untenable situation," I fumed.

NASA agreed; North American was informed that it was impossible to work with Crossfield, and he eventually left the company. Crossfield knew damned well who his opponent was and he never forgave me.

A major priority was developing a hatch that opened outward; it wasn't simple, and by the time we achieved a satisfactory new door, we had added about 1,500 pounds to the weight of the spacecraft. This meant we had to reengineer the reentry parachute system to accommodate the extra poundage. The current chute was strong enough if fully open, but not strong enough to absorb the shock of opening.

The Northrop Corporation, which had designed the chute, had developed an excellent system. Because of the weight involved, it was necessary to open the chute in stages, gradually slowing the spacecraft's falling velocity. This was accomplished by two rows of explosive cords, called dereefers; detonation of the first row opened the chute partially, reducing velocity so that the second row could open the chute fully without tearing it apart.

With the added weight of that new door, however, it was obvious that two rows of dereefers weren't going to be enough. So we decided to install a third row. Northrop, worried that even this wasn't sufficient to prevent the chute from tearing itself apart, recommended a realistic test so we'd be sure, and most of NASA's own engineers agreed. Northrop proposed dropping the redesigned Apollo chute from a B-66 bomber, attached to a 13,000-pound load—the approximate weight of the command module during reentry.

The test was going to cost around $250,000, which wasn't in the budget, but I authorized it anyway. George Mueller, who was coming out to Downey every two weeks or so, arrived just after I gave the test a green light and raised hell.

"It doesn't need to be tested and you'll be wasting a quarter of a million dollars," he insisted.

"It's going to cost a hell of a lot more if you've got three astronauts depending on it and the damned thing doesn't work," I retorted.

Mueller reminded me that he was as much my boss as Jim Webb or Bob Gilruth. I reminded him that I was in charge of the team at Downey, and if he didn't like it, he could depart the premises. This was an obvious impasse, so I called Webb.

"I've got a problem and his name's Mueller," I told Webb. I ex-

plained why we had to test the new chute design and added, "Keep
him away from here so we can do our jobs."

Mueller left Downey and never came back. From then on, I dealt
with Sam Phillips, the Air Force general heading Project Apollo in
Washington—a straight shooter who hated red tape and procrastinating bureaucrats as much as I did. Sam and I got along fine and,
more important, I respected him. He was no desk-flying general—
he'd had two combat tours with the Eighth Air Force in World War
II and had flown every type of aircraft in the USAF arsenal from the
P-38 to modern jets. A man with sparse, graying hair and a stern
visage that gave one the impression he could bite through shoe leather,
Phillips was personable, with a fine sense of humor.

So we tested the new chute system and it worked. Maybe Mueller
was right in questioning the expenditure of $250,000 on something
that looked so good on paper, but nobody at Downey was willing
to cut any corners—not after what had happened on Pad 34. The
actual spacecraft that emerged from the redesign team's efforts out-
wardly was pretty much a twin of *AS-204,* but the visual resem-
blance didn't tell the whole story. Included in the major modifications
were:

- Rerouting and better shielding of all wiring.
- Elimination of all combustibles (this was extended even to the astronauts' spacesuits), replacing them with flameproof materials such
  as Beta cloth.
- Changing the cockpit's ground atmospheric pressurization from
  100 percent oxygen to 60 percent oxygen and 40 percent nitrogen,
  providing a less volatile environment on the launch pad; this new
  system also increased the oxygen content gradually after lift-off so
  that the crew would be breathing pure oxygen in space.

In designing the new hatch, we went beyond merely devising a
door that could be opened from the inside. We also made it easier
to open—in just three seconds compared to the nearly two minutes
it had taken to open *AS-204*'s.

One day when I was at North American, long before I got the
Apollo 8 assignment, I got into the Apollo simulator and tried out
the controls. I pulled back on the stick and the nose went down. I
pushed forward and the nose went up. Exactly the opposite from
flying an airplane. I called over the engineer in charge of the simulator.

"You've got the polarity reversed," I told him.

"It's not reversed, Colonel. It's the way it should be."

I just stared at him unbelievingly. Those controls negated all the training we had received as pilots and astronauts—no flying machine ever built goes down when you pull the stick back and up when you push forward. It works exactly the opposite.

I said, "Reverse it so I can fly the damned thing."

"But this is the way Apollo is going to fly," he insisted.

"Not with me or any other astronaut in it. Fix the goddamned thing or nobody'll fly it."

He reversed the controls, muttering something I gathered was a reflection on my parents' marital status. Just to make sure they stayed reversed, I called the people at Houston, told them what a dumb thing North American had done, and got an official order to keep the stick oriented properly.

Yet the spacecraft wasn't the only item subjected to drastic modifications and revisions throughout 1967 and part of 1968. NASA overhauled everything from crew assignments to the Apollo timetable itself. I spent a good part of a year at Downey. It was an especially traumatic time for Susan, and I thank God for the support our two sons gave her during the long months when I was neither a father nor a husband. I wasn't even there when she had to have a hysterectomy, a psychological trauma for every woman that I didn't even consider at the time. I admit I could have flown to Houston to be with her then—hell, I know now I *should* have been with her—but I was working seven days a week at this stage of the Downey assignment and "Apollo" was synonymous with "priority." I'd like to think I was more blind than callous, more fiercely dedicated than uncaring.

At its peak, from 1967 into the early seventies, some twenty thousand companies and more than three hundred fifty thousand persons were involved in Apollo's $25.5 billion mission to land men on the moon. In the end, this massive concentration of scientific and industrial efforts was to compress what normally would have taken two, three, or even four decades of technological progress into less than one. Only eight years and two months elapsed between President Kennedy's 1961 commitment to a lunar landing program and *Apollo 11*'s actual landing.

Considering the technical obstacles, not the least of which were the devastating effects of the pad fire, NASA's meeting Kennedy's

"before this decade is out" timetable was an incredible accomplishment. Just one word describes how it was done: commitment. I always felt I was part of that commitment, and I suppose if I had to
do it all over again, I would march to the same drum, wearing the
same blinders that kept me from seeing anything except the Mission
ahead.

For quite a while, I wasn't sure what particular mission I'd be
flying. Initially I was supposed to command the backup crew for
Apollo 7, which would be the first manned Apollo flight; the primary crew consisted of that old space veteran Wally Schirra, plus
rookies Donn Eisele and Walt Cunningham. *Apollo 7* would be an
earth orbital flight launched on a Saturn IB and carrying the command and service modules, but no lunar module—it was more of a
test for the command module than anything else.

But my involvement at Downey scrubbed me from the backup
assignment, and while I still was at Downey, I was assigned to *Apollo
8*—planned as another earth orbital flight, this time carrying the
command, service, and lunar modules and launched on the gigantic
Saturn V that would eventually be used on the moon flights. Mike
Collins and Bill Anders, another Naval Academy graduate who had
chosen the Air Force as his career, would be my crew. So after Downey, I resumed astronaut training, not overly enthusiastic about my
first Apollo assignment. Flying around the earth again didn't seem
very challenging, and like everyone else, I was hoping to get a moon
flight.

Under NASA's revised schedule, *Apollo 4, 5,* and *6* were all unmanned flights to test the hardware. *Apollo 4* was the most critical
and also most successful; it was the first test of the Saturn V linked
to the second-stage S-2, and it achieved a simulated lunar trajectory
that took its spacecraft 11,000 miles into outer space. It also exposed the heat shields to temperatures of more than 5,000 degrees
Fahrenheit, generated at a speed of 24,400 miles per hour—the velocity needed for a lunar return.

Apollo 7, the first manned Apollo mission, was also successful. It
was launched on October 11, 1968, and its main objective was to
check out the reliability of all systems on a long-duration flight. Schirra
and his crew orbited the earth for almost eleven days, far in excess
of the seven to nine days planned for the moon shot. Wally hosted
seven live television transmissions from the spacecraft, introducing
one of them with classic Schirra commentary.

"We're coming to you from the lovely Apollo room high atop everything," Schirra broadcast.

A "101 percent successful" mission, Houston labeled *Apollo 7*. So successful that, it has been written many times, NASA was encouraged to go for broke and change *Apollo 8* into a moon flight. It's true that Wally's flight proved we were prepared for a lunar mission sooner than anyone expected, but that wasn't the whole story. There was another reason, one involving none other than the Central Intelligence Agency.

It was early August 1968—the unmanned Apollo flights had already been accomplished, but *Apollo 7* was still about two months away. I was back at North American temporarily, doing some test work on a Sunday, when I got a call from Deke Slayton.

"Frank, get back to Houston right away. I have to talk to you."

"So talk to me now. I'm busy, Deke—the module's still got problems and . . ."

"I can't talk over the phone. Grab an airplane on the double."

I flew a T-38 to Houston and walked into Deke's office. I knew something was up when he asked me to close the door.

"We just got word from the CIA that the Russians are planning a lunar fly-by before the end of the year," he said. "We want to change *Apollo 8* from an earth orbital to a lunar orbital flight. I know that doesn't give us much time, so I have to ask you: Do you want to do it or not?"

"Yes," I said promptly.

I found out later that the Soviets were a hell of a lot closer to a manned lunar mission than we would have liked. Only about a month after I talked to Slayton, the Russians sent an unmanned spacecraft, *Zond 5*, into lunar orbit and returned it safely to earth. If *Apollo 7* hadn't been such a perfect flight, I'd hate to think what the effects would have been on our suddenly accelerated program. As it was, the lunar module was giving everyone fits and more than anything else was threatening to delay the timetable. *Apollo 7*, launched on a Saturn IB, had carried only the command and service modules. So would *Apollo 8*.

To accomplish a lunar orbital flight by the end of 1968 required some fast planning. I joined Chris Kraft and several other people in his office one afternoon. We began at 1 P.M. and by 5 P.M. we had hammered out the objectives and a flight plan for the mission. In only four hours, we agreed on what we were supposed to achieve, how long we'd stay in orbit around the moon, the individual crew assignments, and the general blueprint for the whole flight.

That cigar-smoking Kraft was a professional of consummate ability who wasn't afraid to make tough decisions. He was as hard-nosed as any fighter pilot I ever knew. Just as my performance in flying spacecraft was based on years of experience, Kraft's genius stemmed from his years of apprenticeship at NACA, learning aeronautical engineering from the ground up in that pioneering organization. He called every shot the way he saw it and, like me, he hated wasting time in indecisive debate.

Mike Collins developed a painful bone spur that required major surgery about this time. Deke and I discussed his dilemma and decided that Collins, who needed some time to recover from the operation, would miss too much training to make *Apollo 8*. Jim Lovell, from the mission's backup crew, was our choice to replace Mike, who was understandably upset.

But he was a good soldier and performed valiant service for us as a key participant in Mission Control throughout our flight. As for Lovell, I couldn't have had a better substitute; he was experienced, efficient, and about as compatible a crew member as I could wish.

We also lost, to everyone's regret, Jim Webb. He decided to retire and was succeeded by Dr. Thomas O. Paine, a reputable scientist in his own right. It was Paine who on November 12, 1968, made the announcement that must have jarred our friends in Moscow: "After a careful and thorough examination of all the systems and risks involved, we have concluded that we are now ready to fly the most advanced mission for *Apollo 8* launched in December—the orbit around the moon."

. . . *the risks involved.* . .

They were considerable but they were calculated. The biggest danger we faced was a simple one: There was little or no margin for error. What we were armed with basically were some excellent but as yet unproven theories about outer space travel, and the sobering knowledge that even if the theories worked, our vehicles—the launching rockets and the spacecraft itself—had to perform perfectly, under conditions no man and machine had ever faced before.

When we began planning the flight, there was no existing procedure for reentering the earth's atmosphere in a manned spacecraft traveling at a speed of nearly 25,000 mph on the way back from the moon. We had to devise one because unlike the Gemini flights, which had used retro-rockets to slow down, we couldn't carry reverse thrusters powerful enough to reduce Apollo's far greater velocity—7,000 mph faster than Gemini reentry.

So we had to depend on the friction of the atmosphere to provide the necessary breaking action, and this created a major problem of its own. In order to take advantage of that friction, it was imperative to make certain we didn't enter at such a steep angle that the tremendous G forces would destroy the spacecraft—it would be like hitting a brick wall. But if we entered at too shallow an angle, we wouldn't slow up enough and the spacecraft would be flung back into space, where we'd stay until we ran out of oxygen.

We had to establish a precise reentry corridor, a tunnel if you will. If we got below that corridor the angle was too steep, and if we got above it the angle was too shallow; it was certain death if we missed the tunnel. Once the procedure was established, we practiced it over and over again in simulators, recording every mistake we made, every situation we encountered in developing the technique.

A spacecraft doesn't have wings, but it still develops lift, like a rock skipping across water if it hits at the proper angle. The procedure for flying the Apollo command module wasn't much different from Gemini's—Apollo's was much bigger and heavier, yet almost as maneuverable. The vastly higher speed was the trickiest part. We learned how to come into the atmosphere backward, so the blunt rear end of the spacecraft would dig into the air. If we dug in too much, we'd reverse it by rolling 180 degrees so the lift was reversed.

All the Apollo crews literally lived with their spacecraft while they were being built. It was not only the best way to get acquainted with the vehicle, but damned if you didn't develop an affection for this six-ton hunk of metal as if it were a living creature; it was like watching your own child grow up.

Between training and playing midwife to our spacecraft, I didn't get to see my family much. From the time I began investigating the pad fire in January 1967 to the Apollo flight in December 1968, my chief contact with my family was through Ma Bell. That period of almost two years was hell on Susan, who developed some real fears about the moon mission; she became absolutely convinced I wasn't going to come back alive.

I wasn't that pessimistic but I damned well knew the risks, and from the very beginning I worked to increase the odds in our favor. I lost an argument against carrying a television camera aboard because of the extra weight. In retrospect, I wasn't very smart—it didn't add a dangerous amount of weight and the camera achieved the purpose for which it was intended: to give all Americans a real feeling for the mission and what it was accomplishing.

But I did win a debate over the time of our landing back on earth. The original trajectory called for a daytime landing, as in the Gemini missions. I fought for a night landing and for a very good reason. My choice of trajectory at that time of year would allow us to launch in the morning, orbit the moon no more than ten times—sufficient to do everything we wanted to do—and come home. I didn't want to spend any more time in lunar orbit than absolutely necessary, for any prolonging of the mission simply increased the chances of something going wrong. We didn't need the twelve or more orbits a day landing would have required.

Some NASA officials argued that in a night landing, the first time one had been tried, if the chute malfunctioned nobody could see what was happening.

"What the hell does that matter?" I asked. "If the chute works, great. If it doesn't work, we're all dead and it won't make any difference if nobody can see us."

Figuring out the right trajectory for a lunar round trip was one of our most difficult tasks, and without computers it couldn't have been done. If we ran into serious trouble on the way, we couldn't always just turn around and come back. At various times during the flight, we'd be subjected to the gravitational pulls of the earth, the moon, and even the sun. The computers told us, for example, that if we had to abort as we were nearing the moon, it would be safer to continue the flight, swing around the moon, and then fire up the gravity-escaping engine, the gravity pull acting like a slingshot. Every abort possibility was predicated on the fuel supply—the computers analyzed the fuel situation at each stage of the journey and determined the course of action we'd have to take.

So concerned was I about the mission's safety that I got unreasonable at times. In planning the trajectory, I insisted that Mission Control had to keep us on what amounted to an absolutely perfect path, never varying more than three feet per second. I was politely but firmly informed that achieving such perfection couldn't be performed by a computer being fed data from the Almighty himself.

Yet I felt I was justified in being conservative, in trying to maximize my crew's safety. Jerry Lederer, NASA's safety chief and the grand old man of all aviation safety, said it best a few days before we launched.

The mission, he pointed out, would "involve risks of great magnitude and probably risks that have not been foreseen. Apollo 8 has 5,600,000 parts and 1.5 million systems, sub-systems and assemblies. Even if all functioned with 99.9 percent reliability, we could expect 5,600 defects."

As we planned and trained and saw our *Apollo 8* vehicle evolve from blueprints into a real flying machine, I got to know my third crew member better. Rookie Bill Anders was thirty-five, slightly built, a devout Roman Catholic, and very serious-minded—almost intense about his work. I'm not sure he ever got used to my rather rough sense of humor or Lovell's freewheeling spirit. But Anders was one hell of a worker, a superb technician, and all in all a great guy. He was one of the third group of astronauts to enter the program and came to us fresh out of the Air Force Institute of Technology, where he had earned a master's degree in nuclear engineering, specializing in space radiation, reactor shielding, and radiation effects.

Anders was always friendly and cooperative, but he avoided the usual astronaut bull sessions. Some of the guys regarded him as a younger edition of Frank Borman in his single-minded concentration on work, his aversion to unnecessary conversation. In one respect, NASA threw him a curve when it switched *Apollo 8* from an earth orbital to a moon flight. Bill had been trained as a lunar module pilot, but the mission change eliminated the LM and he was forced to adapt quickly to different assignments.

The unflappable Lovell hadn't changed one bit from our *Gemini 7* days. He already had commanded a Gemini mission of his own, yet he never displayed a shred of resentment at being second banana on *Apollo 8*—he personified the team worker. Jim's hometown ties were stronger than those of most astronauts. He was raised in Milwaukee and the only way you could get his goat was to mention the Milwaukee Braves' decision to move their baseball franchise to Atlanta, or to criticize the Green Bay Packers.

We divided up our mission assignments while in training. Lovell would handle navigation, a subject on which he had become a true expert—he knew more about space navigation than Anders and I did combined. Bill would be the scientific crew member, monitoring all systems and also performing the photography duties that would be so important to the Apollo crew who actually landed on the moon;

one of our jobs was to pick out possible landing spots. I was the jack-of-all-trades.

There always was an element of conflict involved in mission planning. The scientists and engineers would have been happy if we could have stayed in lunar orbit longer than we planned; they wanted to gather as much data as possible and I didn't blame them. I wanted to stay as short a time as possible because we had an unproven piece of equipment. In the end, I think we all achieved what was necessary—NASA got an awful lot of valuable information and we came back alive. Frankly, I figured just making a few manned lunar orbits was accomplishment enough, not to mention the fact that we'd be showing the Russians our heels.

We had a manual backup in the event the primary inertial navigation system failed. The flight plan called for the inertial system to be shut down when it wasn't in use. During such moments as a burn or sighting, for example, it would be activated, and then shut off when the procedure was finished.

I didn't like the idea. Experience had taught me that when you have something running perfectly, particularly a mechanical or electrical device, it's best to leave it alone. So in preparing for the mission, I had written NASA a strong letter urging that on *Apollo 8* the system be left on at all times. NASA referred my letter to the Draper Laboratory at MIT, which had designed the system.

In due course, I received an answer from the Draper scientist who had developed *Apollo 8*'s system. He went on for two pages listing all the reasons why the system had to be turned off when not in use (mostly to conserve power) and insisted there'd be absolutely no problem if we operated it in the way it was intended to be operated. Then he added this postscript: "However, if I were going on this mission, I'd let it run the whole time, too."

That postscript was all I needed to convince NASA.

About six weeks before launch, I got a call from Julian Scheer, NASA's deputy administrator for public affairs.

"Look, Frank," he said, "we've determined that you'll be circling the moon on Christmas Eve and we've scheduled one of the television broadcasts from *Apollo 8* around that time. We figure more people will be listening to your voice than that of any man in history. So we want you to say something appropriate."

I asked the advice of several people, among them Si Bourgin, who had been one of our three escort officers during the post–*Gemini 7* tour of the Far East. I explained to Si what I needed, adding that

NASA had told me we were going to have an audience of about a billion people—which seemed to make Apollo's Christmas Eve remarks almost as important as our trajectory.

"I'm stumped, Si, and I'm too damned busy to go around researching in reference books. Can you help me?"

Bourgin went to an old friend, Joe Laitin, assistant to the Budget Bureau director and a former United Press International reporter. Laitin suggested that the Apollo crew read from Genesis.

I added Laitin's "script" to our flight plan, typing out the words on fireproof paper. We finally had something "appropriate" to say when the time came.

The *Apollo 8* crew and their wives were invited to the White House for dinner about two weeks before launch. It was the last time I saw Susan before the mission—she told me she didn't want to see the launch and would stay in Houston. NASA flew us up to Washington from the Cape and it was on this occasion that I first met my boyhood hero, Charles Lindbergh. He was there with his wife, Anne, and so was Wernher von Braun.

Talking to Lindbergh was the highlight of the evening. I may have been a famous astronaut about to fly into the history books, but that night I was just an awed hero-worshiper. His tiny wife was charming but quiet and shy.

President Johnson seemed terribly harassed and distressed because of the Vietnam bloodletting, which probably explained why he used the occasion to sound off against the press, particularly stories criticizing his daughter Luci for visiting her new Marine husband on duty in Vietnam.

"I don't know why they can't leave my family alone," he declared loudly. "Hell, all she wanted to do was go over there and shack up with her husband."

There were quite a few women at the table and I remember a couple of them almost dropped their forks. I was more surprised than anything else. While LBJ's table manners left something to be desired, he tried hard to be gracious and I felt sorry for this lame-duck president who would soon go out of office with that Vietnam albatross hung around his neck for all posterity to remember. The movie *The Right Stuff* was a Hollywood hatchet job on him, portraying Johnson as a loud-mouthed buffoon. He was rather crude but he was no buffoon—he gave me the impression of being a very tortured man.

While training at the Cape, we lived in the Holiday Inn at Cocoa

Beach, right next to the ocean and very pleasant. Holiday charged us the same amount we would have paid for bachelor officers' quarters. It was typical of how the lay public regarded the astronauts, as reflections of a national determination to prove the nation's greatness under pressure. At the Cape itself, the same attitude prevailed. To me it was a dimension that was lost in the NASA of later years; in the whole country, for that matter.

About three weeks before the scheduled launch, we had to move to the Cape, where our quarters were slightly more luxurious than Army barracks. The furniture was strictly GI—steel beds and steel desks. Lovell, Anders, and I each had a small room to ourselves, with a large living room that we shared. The rooms themselves amounted to mere cubicles and were just places to sleep.

The best thing about living at the Cape complex was the excellent cook assigned to us. He'd gotten his culinary experience working on tugboats, but as far as we were concerned, he was a cordon bleu chef.

The Lindberghs came down to the Cape before the launch and spent most of an afternoon with us. Lindy reportedly was at ease only when he was with fellow airmen, and after that afternoon I never doubted it. He had been gracious enough at the White House, but on this occasion he was almost garrulous.

We sat mesmerized by the stories he told about his own flight of four decades ago. He mentioned the time he'd met Robert Goddard, the father of U.S. space rocketry, about a year after the Paris flight. Goddard had shown him films of his primitive rocket tests and various rocket designs.

"He told me it was theoretically possible to design a multistage rocket capable of reaching the moon," Lindbergh recounted. "But even as he said this, he smiled and remarked that unfortunately it might cost as much as a million dollars."

We burst out laughing, Lindy laughing with us. (Actually, the direct costs of *Apollo 8* were about $24 million.)

He asked us how much fuel would be consumed at tomorrow's launch. After we gave him a ballpark figure, he began scribbling calculations on a piece of paper.

He finally looked up, a slight grin on his still handsome, boyish face. "In the first second of your flight tomorrow," he announced, "you'll burn ten times more fuel than I did all the way to Paris."

We flew the Link *Apollo 8* simulator day in and day out, learning how to cope with some eight hundred different emergency situations. We ran constant checks on our spacecraft and for exercise we mostly jogged. As launch time neared, each day got longer. At night, I used to go outside our spartan quarters and look up at that whitish silver object that was our target. The sky in southern Florida always seemed close, as if the world somehow had moved closer to the stars. But the moon . . .

It was so tempting. But still so far away. We were aiming at a target 239,000 miles away. We were going to be navigating between the earth, which revolves around the sun at 66,000 mph, and the moon, which circles the earth at 21,600 mph. Once Mission Control gave us the green light for trans-lunar injection (TLI)—the point at which we'd shift from earth orbit and head toward outer space—we'd lose all earth reference points and begin what amounted to a quarter-of-a-million-mile skeet shoot. We'd be aiming at an imaginary point, two and a half days away, 115 miles ahead of the speeding moon; in effect, we were leading our target, the intersection spot being just close enough to the moon to allow us to go into lunar orbit, yet not so close that we could be drawn too far into the moon's gravitational pull.

Navigation would have to be pinpoint—a mistake of only a few degrees could throw us off course by thousands of miles. Yet navigation didn't concern me as much as the mammoth three-stage Saturn on whose eleven engines *Apollo 8* must depend. This would be the first manned mission for the Saturn V. Boosters had remained my specialty in Apollo, just as they had been before my Gemini flight; I had a lot of faith in the monster that von Braun and his associates had created, but working with them so closely was a mixed blessing. I had gained respect for the Saturn's awesome power, and also for the potential danger that very power represented—tomorrow, we'd be sitting on top of 531,000 gallons of volatile kerosene and liquid oxygen, generating the equivalent energy of a small atomic bomb.

I went to church early the morning before launch. We went over our flight plan again and just lounged around, each of us with his own private thoughts. Anders showed up with a priest, a nice enough guy but for some reason he got on my nerves. I was getting edgy anyway and finally snapped testily at Bill, "Are you gonna take communion every thirty seconds before the flight?"

Anders looked hurt and I was sorry I had said it, but the good padre was a distraction I didn't need. I called Susan early that evening—we had been told wake-up call would be at 2:30 A.M. and were supposed to hit the sack right after dinner. I talked to the boys first and then to my wife, who sounded cheerful.

"Everything's going to be all right," I assured her. "I'll be perfectly safe."

"I know," she lied. Chris Kraft, in a rare moment of indiscretion, had told her *Apollo 8* was the riskiest mission to date.

My pre-Gemini insomnia was a good night's rest compared to the hours I lay awake that night of December 20. Those conflicting drives again, Mission versus Family. And somewhat perversely, as I lay awake on that steel bed staring up at the pastel ceiling, I also worried about our alternate mission. If we had to abort our primary objective, we were to spend ten days in earth orbit and come back—a mere rehash of *Gemini 7,* I fretted; a replay of *Apollo 7.*

We had a final medical checkup around 3 A.M. before eating a steak and eggs breakfast with Deke Slayton and several other astronauts. After breakfast, we climbed into our new spacesuits whose outer layer was made of Beta cloth—flame-resistant, woven glass filaments coated with a Teflon-like material to keep any minuscule glass particles from floating around in the cabin where they might be inhaled. The fireproof qualities of Beta cloth were superior even to those of the Nomex fabric we'd had on the Gemini suits.

And now it was time to show up for an invitation NASA had sent out.

YOU ARE CORDIALLY INVITED
TO ATTEND THE DEPARTURE OF UNITED STATES
SPACESHIP APOLLO 8 ON ITS VOYAGE AROUND THE MOON.
DEPARTING FROM LAUNCH COMPLEX 39,
KENNEDY SPACE CENTER, WITH THE
LAUNCH WINDOW COMMENCING AT SEVEN A.M.,
THE TWENTY-FIRST OF DECEMBER,
NINETEEN HUNDRED AND SIXTY-EIGHT.

11

APOLLO 8—"WHERE NO MAN HAS GONE BEFORE"

The closest any spectator could get was a bunker two miles from the gantry. We were in our assigned stations: I occupied the traditional left seat of a command pilot, Lovell was in the center, and Anders sat on the right. The seats themselves were more like old-fashioned high-back chairs; Lovell's could be folded out of the way, forming a narrow aisle providing access to the small alcove directly below the cockpit. The alcove housed our navigation system—sextant, telescope, inertial guidance unit, and computer.

Also in the alcove was the galley and a twelve-day supply of food, mostly freeze-dried but pleasantly varied. In keeping with the holiday season, NASA had provided us with such fare as a fruitcake, coated with a layer of gelatin to prevent crumbs from floating around the cabin. In general, the dieticians had cut down on sweets and high-calorie items because the *Apollo 7* crew had complained their food was too fattening.

I also was carrying in my gear a number of special "Snoopy the Astronaut" pins designed by cartoonist Charles Schulz. Snoopy had become the symbol of the Apollo program; the likeness of the ingratiating little beagle was on posters adorning the walls of hundreds of factories and NASA offices, some of them carrying the admonishing words: "It will not be one man going to the moon . . . it will be an entire nation." When we got back, I'd be handing out the silver pins to a few selected people who had made special contributions to the success of *Apollo 8*.

The command module that would be our home for six days measured nine feet in height and thirteen feet in diameter; in the overall dimensions of the cabin, *Apollo 8* was about three times the size of *Gemini 7*, although it fell considerably short of being a spacious living room—it was more like a large walk-in closet or pantry. At least we could move around, which to Lovell and me was a luxury.

Behind us was the service module, slightly larger than the command unit, containing our fuel cells for electrical power, the life support system, drinking water, and propellant tanks. Next came the service propulsion unit, including the engine that would take us in and out of lunar orbit and also provide the maneuvering power for course corrections. Attached to the service module and jutting below it was the powerful four-disk antenna we'd use to handle communications and television signals.

The third-stage S-4B rocket followed our service module, then the second-stage S-2, and finally the huge S-1C rocket; the S-2 and S-1C each had five engines, while the S-4B had one. Saturn V was a combination of the three stages.

Those five engines on the first stage alone generated 7.5 million pounds of thrust or the equivalent of 160 million horsepower—enough to equal the generating power of eighty-six Hoover Dams. Saturn V took five years to build and its sections were so huge that they had to be transported to the Cape by water on special barges; no railway car or truck could handle them. At lift-off, the first stage would be boosting 6.2 million pounds of weight off the pad alone.

The guys who washed the cavernous interior of the rocket before fueling had to be careful, because if a single thumbprint left enough grease to react with the liquid oxygen oxidizer, we could have had an explosion.

The countdown went smoothly. We dreaded any interruption because of the timing demanded by our launch window. The launch time—the predetermined time for lift-off based on the relative positions of the earth and the moon and synchronized to the precise second at which we would begin our escape from earth's gravity—was 7:51 A.M. EST.

(Every launch has a window; the earth is continually rotating, so if you don't lift off within the window's limited time frame, you can't achieve the desired trajectory. In the case of *Apollo 8*, the launch window actually determined our landing site in the Pacific.)

Lift-off was at 7:51 A.M., only six tenths of a second behind schedule. I heard the deep rumble of the first-stage engines, but they weren't loud, more like the distant thunder of a storm far over the horizon. I knew what was happening, but in the spacecraft I felt curiously detached, as if the Saturn V was moving but we weren't.

Then came the sensation of motion, very slow at first—so slow it was almost imperceptible. The clock that automatically began running at lift-off, and would record the mission's total elapsed time, had registered thirty-two seconds before I noticed it.

"The clock is running," I informed Mission Control, a bit belatedly.

The sensation of speed increased as we picked up momentum, and so did the noise generated by 3,000 tons of metal pushing through the atmosphere. But when we passed the speed of sound, everything grew quiet, as if we were in a powerless glider. The only sound was a humming noise that came from the electronic equipment in the cockpit. The ride was incredibly smooth; compared to *Apollo 8*, *Gemini 7* had traveled over a few hundred potholes.

Three pairs of eyes were on the display panel with its 24 instruments, 40 "event" indicators, 71 lights, and 566 switches, a befuddling array. But they were as familiar to us as the simple dials on an automobile dashboard. I kept my hands on the controls, alert to any malfunction, but the automatic controls were working perfectly.

Eleven minutes into the flight, the Saturn V's first and second stages had dropped away and fallen into the Atlantic as planned. Their job was finished and now it was up to the S-4B, the third-stage engine fueled by eighty tons of hydrogen, to take us into orbit. The simulators hadn't prepared us for the shock of losing the first two big stages. We were pushing 4 or 5 Gs and all of a sudden we were shoved forward and then back again when the third stage fired. We had already jettisoned the needlelike escape tower on the nose of our spacecraft—it would have been used if anything had gone wrong on the pad or in the early part of the flight, but in space was merely unwanted extra weight.

The S-4B was fired long enough to achieve an orbital speed of almost 17,500 mph—more than 25,000 feet a second—and put us into orbit 114 miles above the earth. Lovell unbuckled himself and, now weightless, worked his way back to the navigation area to take his first sightings with the sextant and scanning telescope.

He said he felt a little queasy, like he had a touch of seasickness, but he discovered that if he moved a little slower the nausea disappeared. We were wearing lightweight boots—they were more like slippers or booties, with soles made of adhesive that matched similar strips on the spacecraft floor, so maneuvering around wasn't that difficult.

Jim's telescope and sextant were attached to the side of the spacecraft and he used them to measure the angles between the earth's horizon and certain stars. Later, on the way to the moon, he'd determine the angles between those stars and the moon's horizon. The measurements told him where we were in space, our direction, and the spacecraft's speed.

Houston was receiving telemetry data from its worldwide network of tracking stations even as we began testing every major system in the command and service modules. Every reading, every check, every button pushed, and every figure that appeared on a computer screen were all aimed at the ultimate decision: when to go for trans-lunar injection—the second and final firing of the third-stage rocket, which would launch us toward the moon.

It wouldn't be our decision. The green light would be flashed in Houston, where three other men were the focal point of the data pouring into the computer banks—Chris Kraft, Flight Operations Director Bill Schneider, and Flight Director Cliff Charlesworth. Mostly it would be Kraft. Traveling more than 100 miles above earth, I could visualize him as if I were looking at Mission Control on a television screen—he'd be sitting behind some console, probably chomping on one of those foul cigars, digesting the telemetry data and our own reports in that computer-calm mind of his while he put Risk and Mission on his personal set of scales.

Orbiting brought back memories of *Gemini 7* and I couldn't help remembering how excited I'd been then and how routine space flight now seemed. CapCom broke into my reveries.

"*Apollo 8,* how does it feel up there?" Mike Collins inquired.

I looked out my window. We were over Africa.

"Very good, very good," I replied. "It looks just about the same way it did three years ago."

We were almost three hours into the mission when we completed a final systems check and informed Houston we were ready for TLI.

I glanced at my crew: Lovell, laconic as ever; Anders, doing a beautiful job of hiding his excitement—this was his first space flight.

02:50:31, read the mission clock.

"All right," CapCom's metallic voice said calmly. "You are to go for TLI."

"*Apollo 8,* roger," I responded.

02:50:37. We were over the Pacific.

The third-stage engine fired and we kept it burning for more than five minutes—232,000 pounds of thrust hurtling *Apollo 8* to a speed of 23,226 mph or 35,532 feet per second, the fastest man had ever traveled and sufficient to achieve the gravity-escaping trajectory that would take us to the moon. That speed was within 16 feet per second of what Houston had planned, although everyone would have been happy with a 50-foot-per-second variation.

We heard Kraft's voice. "You're on your way," he said with rare excitement. "You're *really* on your way!"

03:30:59.

Houston advised that the trajectory analysis was complete and we were on course. I turned a T-shaped handle, triggering explosive devices that blew the third-stage rocket away from the spacecraft, and once again we felt a bone-jarring shock.

Anders announced, "We have sep [separation] and looking good."

It wasn't looking quite as good as I wanted—the damned S-4B was uncomfortably close, its nose wandering within 500 feet of the spacecraft and getting no farther away than 1,000 feet. I fired our reaction control thrusters briefly to increase the distance, but the third stage seemed to be on a tether attached to our spacecraft.

"It looks like I might have to do a couple more small maneuvers to stay away from the front of this S-4B," I told Houston. "It sure is staying close. It's spewing out from all sides like a huge water sprinkler."

Lovell, who had floated back to the alcove for another navigation fix, reported with some amazement, "I see millions of stars!" He was trying to sight through my water sprinkler; the S-4B was throwing off a blizzard of fuel droplets so thick they looked like a snowstorm.

Houston finally let me try another short burn and we continued to climb, the third stage still with us but at a safer distance. Slightly less than five hours after lift-off we passed through the Van Allen radiation belt, and Anders transmitted our personal radiation dosimeter (PDR) readings. Even in the thickest part of the belt, they showed we were receiving about the same dosage we'd get from a chest X ray. So much for all the dire predictions some scientists had made about harmful, perhaps fatal, exposure to that belt.

By now we were 21,000 miles from earth, with speed dropping steadily. It was to take us two and a half days after TLI to reach the moon; at first glance this must seem like an inordinate amount of time in which to reach a target 239,000 miles away when our escape velocity was almost 25,000 mph. But escape velocity was only the speed necessary to overcome the earth's gravity in the initial stage, providing enough momentum to keep us going as the gravity pull lessened and our speed was reduced proportionately. About two thirds of the way to the moon, we'd come into the lunar gravity pull and begin accelerating again—until then, *Apollo 8* would literally be coasting on sheer momentum, as if hurled into space by a giant slingshot.

From 21,000 miles up, the view was spectacular. Reported Lovell, "Boy, it's really hard to describe what this earth looks like. I'm looking out my center window, the round window, and the window is bigger than the earth is right now. I can see most of South America all the way up to Central America, Yucatan, and the peninsula of Florida."

Anders and I were equally impressed. All of us had flown airplanes many times and seen airfields and buildings getting smaller as we climbed. But now it was the whole globe receding in size, dwindling until it became a disk. We were the first humans to see the world in its majestic totality, an intensely emotional experience for each of us. We said nothing to each other, but I was sure our thoughts were identical—of our families on that spinning globe. And maybe we shared another thought I had . . .

This must be what God sees.

Anders broke in to report a minor hitch—the center window had fogged up. We had five windows in *Apollo 8* and three of them proved vulnerable to the same outgassing effect that had plagued so many Gemini flights. Once again, the culprit was the sealing compound; the outgassing formed a deposit between the window's triple panes and obscured vision. I thought the damned problem had been licked—we had complained enough during Gemini—but this was one bug refusing to be eradicated. (On future Apollo flights, NASA solved outgassing by heat-curing the compound.)

My window was still unaffected and I spotted the third stage, about three miles away, starting to dump the rest of its fuel in a spectacu-

lar display. The reflection of sun rays on the ejected hydrogen produced great flashes of light that filled the sky. Its fuel supply spent,
the S-4B slowed down perceptibly and began moving toward the
east side of the moon. We were heading for the west side and would
be well out of its way. Eventually, lunar gravity would throw the
third stage into solar orbit.

Three hours after TLI, we were 26,000 miles from earth and speed
was down to less than 9,000 mph. We were using the passive ther-
mal control maneuver (PTC), which involved turning *Apollo 8* on
its long axis facing the sun and then doing a slow roll. It's known
as the "barbecue mode," and that's an apt description because a
PTC evens a spacecraft's exposure to heat.

At 60,000 miles out, we made our initial midcourse correction
using the service propulsion system for the first time. This was a
moment of tension—the SPS's single engine was now our only major
means of propulsion. Any trouble meant abort.

It fired perfectly, the burn lasting less than three seconds but enough
to achieve the desired correction and increase our speed slightly. We
happily reported the successful burn to Houston, and CapCom,
sounding like a stern mother sending her kid off to bed, told *Apollo
8*, "Okay . . . the flight plan shows commander should hit the sack."

Easier said than done. Unable to sleep, I asked for permission to
take a sleeping pill, but this didn't work either. Two hours later, I
was still awake and beginning to feel lousy. Lovell solicitously tried
to help.

"Houston, this is *Apollo 8*," he told CapCom. "We're going to
try to keep the conversation down here for a while so the commander can go to sleep."

He and Anders kept the conversation down, but unfortunately I
couldn't keep anything down. I became feverish and nauseated,
vomited twice and then got diarrhea. I didn't know why. All three
of us had been inoculated against the Hong Kong flu and at first I
suspected it was that sleeping pill—I seldom take pills of any kind.
Unhappily, I remembered spending two weeks in *Gemini 7* and never
getting sick. *Apollo 8* was only fourteen hours into its mission and
here was its commander feeling like a wet floor mop. It also may
well have been the weightless environment—Lovell had experienced
nausea earlier and was to feel queasy again later; Anders was affected briefly, too. The symptoms disappeared as we got accustomed
to weightless motion.

I finally managed to doze off, and about 6 A.M. earth time I told

Jim and Bill to get some sleep—they had been up for almost twenty-four hours. We were 100,000 miles from earth and I was feeling a little better. I told CapCom I thought I had a case of the twenty-four-hour flu, but I'm not sure this amateur diagnosis was right—quite a few astronauts and cosmonauts have been afflicted with what might be called space sickness.

Our sleeping arrangements worked out well. Unlike Gemini, where either Jim or I had had to stay awake because there were times when we were out of touch with the tracking stations, the *Apollo 8* crew could go to sleep at the same time. On the way to the moon and back, we were being tracked constantly and there was no need for one of us to stay awake.

Halfway to the moon, we staged the first of six television shows, using a camera weighing only four and a half pounds. We took turns panning around the cabin, catching Lovell in the act of injecting water into a bag of freeze-dried chocolate pudding and Anders demonstrating how a toothbrush floated in zero gravity. When we tried to show how the earth looked from our spacecraft, however, the camera's telephoto lens didn't work and the only image the small lens caught was that of a blurred ball of light.

"I certainly wish we could show you the earth," I disappointedly told CapCom. "It is a beautiful, beautiful view with predominantly blue background and just huge covers of white clouds—particularly one very strong vortex up near the terminator [the line that separates night from day]."

We did manage to get a great shot of Lovell's grinning face as he said happy birthday to his seventy-three-year-old mother, Blanche Lovell, in Edgewater, Florida. We all hammed it up a bit, but after we got back I heard that when CBS interrupted the pro football playoff game between the Vikings and Colts for our brief broadcast Sunday afternoon, the network had been swamped with protesting calls. Maybe we should have thrown a football around.

We tried again the next day, December 23, transmitting the TV signal to an 85-foot antenna dish in California, more than 200,000 miles away. This time the telephoto lens was functioning, and viewers not only got a glimpse of the earth from our vantage point but were treated to Lovell's accompanying commentary.

It wasn't as good a view as we had, certainly not sharp enough for anyone to share the somewhat sobering experience of not being able to see any of man's familiar works—cities, highways, the ships on earth's vast oceans, or jet contrails crossing its skies. There were more than 3 billion people down there, and no visual evidence they even existed. Lovell's narration spoke for the whole crew.

"We are maneuvering now for the TV," he reported. "Bill has got it set up in Frank's left rendezvous window and I'm over in Bill's spot looking out the right rendezvous window. The earth is now passing through my window. It's about as big as the end of my thumb. Waters are all sort of royal blue. Clouds, of course, are bright white. The reflection off the earth is much greater than the moon. The land areas are generally sort of darkish brown to light brown. What I keep imagining is, if I were a traveler from another planet, what would I think about the earth at this altitude. Whether I think it would be inhabited."

CapCom asked, "Don't see anybody waving, is that what you're saying?"

"I was just kind of curious if I would land on the blue part or the brown part," Jim mused.

I said dryly, "You better hope we land on the blue part."

The sense of humor Lovell had displayed on *Gemini 7* was just as prevalent on *Apollo 8*. At one point during the early part of the flight, Mike Collins sent us a couple of football scores and added, "Oh, I've got one more score when you're ready to copy. Ready to copy?"

"Go ahead," Lovell said.

"Roger. Navy, fourteen; Army, twenty-one."

We already knew that score—the game had been played several weeks before and Mike was using a very large needle.

"Would you like me to repeat that?" Collins asked.

"You're very garbled, Houston," Lovell came back. "I am unable to read and will call you back next year."

Houston kept us advised of how our families were doing, yet I still felt a strange sense of detachment up there, as if this nine-by-thirteen-foot box with only three inhabitants had suddenly become a tiny, self-contained world of its own, more familiar than the one we had left. As if our entire existence had been compressed into an environment of winking amber and red instrument lights, the filtered voice of CapCom, and the bizarre tools of a space flight—from plastic food bags squeezed like toothpaste tubes so we could eat, to the labyrinth of electronics, conduits, circuits, and tubing that kept alive the most complex vehicle ever created.

Even CapCom's newscasts seemed curiously remote. President-elect Nixon's youngest daughter, Julie, married David Eisenhower—Ike had to watch the ceremony on closed-circuit television from his hospital bed at Walter Reed. North Korea was about to release the crew of the USS *Pueblo*. Bob Hope was in Vietnam entertaining the troops. A haggard, dispirited Lyndon Johnson lit the national Christmas tree on the Ellipse behind the White House. All interesting, yet we were in another dimension where time meant only the moving numbers of the mission clock.

Shortly after the second telecast, we crossed the equigravisphere, the point at which earth and lunar gravitational pulls are the same—202,700 miles from earth and 38,900 miles from the moon. Our speed had dropped to slightly over 2,200 mph, but from now on we'd start accelerating, coasting downhill as the moon's gravity took over.

At no time were Lovell's navigational skills more essential than at this stage. He took a sighting with the telescope and sextant until he had a target star and a lunar landmark before him. He used *Apollo 8*'s superb navigation computer to calculate the angle between the two targets, fed in the spacecraft's relative position, and determined our final course into lunar orbit.

The ship's computer and the initial trajectory planned by Houston's computer banks laid out a path so precise that only two minor midcourse corrections were necessary over the 239,000-mile flight. One course change, in fact, was necessitated by our routine procedure of dumping urine bags through a small vent. The venting affected our speed just enough to alter the preorbital trajectory.

Apollo 8 swept toward the moon, accelerating steadily. At a distance of 24,000 miles, we fired the retrograde rockets for just under twelve seconds to slow us down. We were aiming at a minimum orbit of 69 miles above the lunar surface and without that slight speed reduction—1.4 feet per second—our perigee would have been 80 miles. We needed only that short burst to synchronize speed with trajectory.

Now we were six hours away from LOI—lunar orbit injection burn. Houston was checking telemetry data from *Apollo 8*'s systems and advised us, "Everything looks GO right now."

"Thank you," I replied. "We just completed day three, meal C, and we're each going to take a rest period."

"Okay, real fine," CapCom agreed. "Wanted to ask if you wouldn't try to get in some sack time before we go in. It's going to be a big day."

It surely would. On Tuesday, December 24, we expected to be in lunar orbit and observing the moon from less than seventy miles away.

We got in about six hours of badly needed sleep. Just as it had during *Gemini 7*, the early adrenaline had worn off and fatigue had set in. In a way, space travel reminded me of that ancient aviation adage: "Flying is hours of boredom punctuated by moments of sheer terror." There really are long period of boredom in space, a plethora of unexciting experiences such as housekeeping chores, eating simply because you have to eat, the repetitious reports, and the unpleasant intimacy of attending to bodily needs.

We all awoke refreshed and I surprised Houston by reporting that "as a matter of interest, we have yet to see the moon." I meant Anders and myself—Lovell had seen it occasionally through the telescope while navigating. But three of our five windows were fogged up, and when we were in one of our frequent barbecue modes, the front of the spacecraft was turned away from the moon.

CapCom apparently couldn't believe me.

"*Apollo 8*, what else are you seeing?"

Anders blurted, with great accuracy, "Nothing. It's like being on the inside of a submarine."

Our "submarine" was picking up speed. With LOI five minutes away, we were less than 500 miles from the moon and traveling 5,000 mph.

One minute to LOI.

"All systems GO," CapCom advised. "Safe journey, guys."

Anders acknowledged. "Thanks a lot, troops. See you on the other side."

Apollo 8 passed behind the moon, out of earth's sight and radio contact.

Thirty seconds to LOI. Speed, 5,700 mph.

The spacecraft was pointed backward, aft section first, so the engine's firing would slow us down.

Our eyes were on the DSKY, the display and keyboard of our computer.

GO/NO-GO? the computer asked.

I punched in the answer.

PROCEED.

The computer was now in control of the spacecraft, the mission's primary goal, and maybe the fate of its crew. It began the last countdown.

FIVE, FOUR, THREE, TWO, ONE . . .

At the count of one, my pulse rate was registering 130 beats per minute, double my normal rate and higher than either Lovell's or Anders's.

The engine fired—perfectly.

More than 20,000 pounds of thrust exploded into the vacuum of space, decelerating *Apollo 8* to less than 3,700 mph and sending it into an elliptical orbit that would be 69.5 miles above the moon at its lowest point and 190 miles at its highest.

The instruments told us the orbit was good, but we didn't need instruments. We had been told that if we looked down at a precise millisecond after LOI, we should be able to see the sun rising over the lunar horizon. And there it was—appearing at exactly the predetermined fraction of a second it was supposed to.

I was absolutely awestruck, not so much at what we had accomplished but at what had made the accomplishment possible. A machine produced by more than three hundred thousand Americans was circling the moon with three human beings aboard for the first time in history. And the enormity of this achievement was in direct proportion to the enormity of the consequences if the machine and its attendant computers hadn't worked perfectly. Too low an orbit would have plunged us into the moon. If our trajectory had been too high, we would have been flung into space, doomed to circle aimlessly until we ran out of oxygen.

Awe mixed with pride in the efforts of not merely three but thousands of Americans—that best describes my feelings as we entered orbit. *Apollo 8* swept around the moon thirty-six minutes after LOI. Lovell told an anxious Mission Control, "Go ahead, Houston. *Apollo 8.*"

We were back in radio contact and we could dimly hear the cheering nearly 240,000 miles away.

Lovell sighed and remarked, "Longest forty minutes of my life."

I felt the same way, but damned if I was going to admit it. "It's no time for congratulations yet," I reminded him. "Dig out the flight plan."

From then on, lunar orbit would become the busiest time of the flight. I was flying the spacecraft manually, firing our attitude-control thrusters constantly, because we had to keep our windows aligned to perform our tasks. Lovell had to make frequent navigation checks and verifications of lunar surface landmarks. Anders was just as busy; he had a photo plan and a flight plan to follow, plus numerous scientific observations to make.

Everyone wanted to look out whatever window was clear. Fogging remained a problem and the nine-inch-diameter circular hatch window, located directly over Jim's center couch, became badly iced when we dumped waste water. In a few minutes, however, nature provided us with its own defroster—the sun reflecting so brightly off the moon's surface that it melted the ice.

I didn't get to look out as much as the others; I was too busy flying the command module. But I'll never forget my first glimpse of the moon through the triangular eight-by-eleven window on my side. We had just completed the first turn that put us into orbit when I saw below us the hostile face of the moon. I felt as if *Apollo 8* had been transported into a world of science fiction, with incredible lighting and awesome, forlorn beauty—desolate beyond belief.

First things first. We discussed the LOI burn and the status of the cooling water evaporators. Then CapCom, unable to endure the suspense, finally asked the key question: *"Apollo 8, what does the ole moon look like?"*

"Okay, Houston," Lovell replied. "The moon is essentially gray, no color. Looks like plaster of Paris. Sort of grayish sand. Coming up now are old friends Messier and Pickering [craters named for scientists] that I looked at so much on earth. . . ."

One of our primary tasks was to locate possible sites for actual moon landings, and early in the first orbit Lovell reported seeing a triangular mountain that might serve as a landmark for a lunar module.

I still was thinking about the technological miracle that had taken place. "Houston," I said, "for your information we lost radio contact at the exact second you predicted. Or did you turn off the transmitters at that time?"

"Honest Injun, we didn't," CapCom joked.

"While these other guys are looking at the moon" I continued, "I want to make sure we have good SPS [service propulsion system]."

Houston dutifully took readings on the SPS, our means of getting back home safely. All data normal, but when I glanced at my companions, I could tell our equipment was holding up better than we were. Lovell, whose navigation duties required him to move around more than the rest of us, looked especially tired. I knew damned well I was tired—the stimulation of achieving a successful orbit and the effects of that rest period were wearing off. Houston knew what I meant when I messaged, rather wistfully, "The flight plan looks a lot fuller than it did in Florida."

During the second orbit, we transmitted earth's first televised pictures of the moon from seventy miles above the lunar surface, each of us providing his own commentary based on what he was seeing at a particular time.

Anders: "The color of the moon looks like a very whitish gray, like dirty beach sand with lots of footprints on it. Some of these craters look like pickaxes striking concrete, creating a lot of fine haze dust."

Lovell: "As a matter of interest, there's a lot of what appear to be small new craters that have these little white rays radiating from them. There's no trouble in picking out features that we learned on the map."

Borman: "The moon is very bright and not too distinct in this area."

On the third pass, we fired the service propulsion engine for just under ten seconds, changing the elliptical orbit to a circular one, as planned. By now I could see that Jim was really fatigued and I told him to get some rest while I took over navigation. Anders was looking increasingly tired, too, as well he might. He kept switching from one side of the spacecraft to the other, alternating between a movie camera and a number of different still cameras.

I happened to glance out one of the still-clear windows just at the moment the earth appeared over the lunar horizon. It was the most beautiful, heart-catching sight of my life, one that sent a torrent of nostalgia, of sheer homesickness, surging through me. It was the only thing in space that had any color to it. Everything else was either black or white, but not the earth. It was mostly a soft, peaceful blue, the continents outlined in a pinkish brown. And always the white clouds, like long streaks of cotton suspended above that immense globe.

I grabbed a camera and snapped the picture of that magnificent earthrise. It turned out to be the one the Postal Service used on a stamp, and few photographs have been more frequently reproduced.

Fatigue *was* becoming a problem. Lovell, exhausted, inadvertently punched a wrong number into the DSKY that erased part of the computer's memory. It restarted automatically and Houston, noticing the restart, inquired what had happened.

"Jim got screwed up on one of those programs," I reported. "He got kind of tired here and we got a restart and a couple of program alarms."

This rang alarm bells throughout Mission Control, Houston fearing the erased part might be the one controlling reentry. Fortunately a check showed it wasn't, but the incident worried me. We were only a few hours away from trans-earth injection (TEI), when the engine that had put us into lunar orbit would have to take us out and propel us back to earth. There still were some scientific experiments on our agenda, but I decided the crew's well-being was more important.

Apollo 8 had been in space for nearly eighty-two and a half hours when I advised Houston, "I'm going to scrub all the other experiments. We're a little bit tired [one of my finest understatements] and I want to use that last bit to really make sure we're right for TEI."

CapCom responded immediately. "Roger, I understand, Frank."

I told Lovell and Anders, "You guys get some sleep."

Five minutes later, a very familiar sound was heard in the cabin.

"Lovell's snoring already," I informed CapCom.

"Yeah, we can hear him down here."

On the ninth and next-to-last orbit, after Jim and Bill had gotten about five hours of sleep, we provided the final telecast from the moon, first summing up our individual impressions of what we had seen, as Anders panned the TV camera across the wasteland beneath us.

Borman: "The moon is a different thing to each of us. I know my own impression is that it's a vast, lonely, forbidding type of existence . . . a great expanse of nothing, that looks rather like clouds and clouds of pumice stone. It certainly would not be a very inviting place to live and work."

Lovell: "Frank, my thoughts are very similar. The vast loneliness of the moon up here is awe-inspiring, and it makes you realize just what you have back there on earth. The earth from here is a grand oasis in the big vastness of space."

Anders: "I think the thing that has impressed me most is the lunar sunrises and sunsets. The long shadows really bring out the relief."

Borman: "The sky is pitch-black and the moon is quite light. And the contrast between the sky and the moon is a vivid dark line."

Lovell: "Actually, I think the best way to describe this area is a vastness of black and white, absolutely no color."

I think the absence of color in space was etched more sharply in our minds than anything else, especially the colorless moon itself. That, plus the bleak, mottled lunar landscape. On one of our earlier passes over the so-called dark side of the moon, Anders had remarked, "The backside looks like a sand pile my kids have been playing in for a long time. It's all beat up, no definition. Just a lot of bumps and holes. The area we're over right now gives some hint of possible volcanic action."

There was one more impression we wanted to transmit: our feeling of closeness to the Creator of all things. This was Christmas Eve, December 24, 1968, and I handed Jim and Bill their lines from the Holy Scriptures.

Anders spoke first. "For all the people back on earth, the crew of *Apollo 8* has a message that we would like to send to you."

He cleared his throat, then began reading the opening words of the book of Genesis.

" 'In the beginning God created the heaven and the earth. And the earth was without form, and void; and darkness was upon the face of the deep. And the Spirit of God moved upon the face of the waters. And God said, Let there be light: and there was light. And God saw the light, that it was good: and God divided the light from the darkness.' "

Lovell was next, as the camera continued to pan the tortured lunar surface.

" 'And God called the light Day, and the darkness he called Night. And the evening and the morning were the first day. And God said, Let there be a firmament in the midst of the waters, and let it divide the waters from the waters. And God made the firmament, and divided the waters which were under the firmanent from the waters which were above the firmament: and it was so. And God called the firmament Heaven. And the evening and the morning were the second day.' "

I was last.

" 'And God said, Let the waters under the heaven be gathered together unto one place, and let the dry land appear: and it was so. And God called the dry land Earth, and the gathering together of the waters he called Seas: and God saw that it was good.' "

I added a postscript just before *Apollo 8* disappeared again behind the moon.

"And from the crew of Apollo, we close with a good night, good luck, a merry Christmas and God bless all of you—all of you on the good earth."

I can't speak for Jim and Bill's thoughts at the moment. I know I was thinking of my family. Never had they seemed so close. Nor so far away. But Lovell said to me, "I don't know who your two friends were [Bourgin and Laitin], but they sure hit the target."

During the tenth and final orbit, we made preparations for TEI and the most critical phase of our long journey. No time for banter or sentimental pangs now. Nothing but guidance equations, fuel supply checks, life support system checks, fresh computer input data. All important, but the most vital component was the big SPS engine, the reliability of its one hundred moving parts holding our lives hostage. If it ignored the DSKY's command to fire, or if it failed during approximately the same four-minute burn as LOI, we were doomed to stay in lunar orbit until we were as lifeless as the moon itself.

Apollo 8 had been in orbit for twenty hours as the countdown for TEI began. Each circumvention had taken about two hours, compared to ninety minutes for an earth orbit; despite the greater distance covered by the latter, the moon's weaker gravity allowed a far lower speed. But weak as it was, it still had to be overcome and we could feel the tension when I punched PROCEED into the DSKY.

There was a thump and a welcome surge as the engine fired, the burn lasting just under four minutes. The spacecraft, accelerating fast, sped out from behind the hidden side of the moon.

89:28:47, read the mission clock. The time on earth was 1:20 A.M. EST, Christmas morning.

"Please be informed there is a Santa Claus," Lovell dryly informed an anxious Mission Control, and the flight controllers broke into cheers.

We were on our way home.

Our first Christmas greeting came from Deke Slayton later that morning, *Apollo 8* already placed perfectly in its assigned trajectory toward earth.

"Good morning, Deke here," came his friendly voice. "I just would like to wish you all a very merry Christmas on behalf of everyone in the Control Center, and I'm sure everyone around the world. None of us ever expected a better Christmas than this one."

I replied, "Thank everyone on the ground for us. It's pretty clear we wouldn't be anywhere if we didn't have them doing it or helping us out here."

Our Christmas dinner in space was something special. The Whirlpool Corporation, which prepared astronaut meals, had devised for *Apollo 8* a new kind of turkey dinner. The meat was the same as canned turkey except that ours was prepared in a tinfoil package, cooked and packed in a thick gravy. The gravy was so thick it stayed in our spoons even during weightlessness.

Our dinner packages were marked with "Merry Christmas" labels, and the women in the Whirlpool mailing room had gone to the trouble of wrapping them with green ribbons made of fireproof plastic. It was the best meal of the trip, a lot better than what those on duty in Mission Control were eating—bologna sandwiches.

At a distance of 110,000 miles from earth, we staged the final telecast, with Anders speaking for the crew: "I think I must have the feeling that the travelers in the old sailing ships used to have, going on a long voyage away from home. And now that we're headed back, I have the feeling of being proud of the trip but still happy to be going home."

Feeling pretty chipper, we hammed it up some more. We gave viewers a guided tour of the spacecraft as I pointed out details of the instrument panel, and another spectacular look at earth from outer space. Lovell was filmed doing exercises with two elastic cords attached to the cabin wall and Bill demonstrated the preparation of a zero-gravity meal.

Most of the return voyage was spent stowing away cameras, film, used food bags, and other items no longer needed. We also managed to catch up on sleep. CapCom advised that messages of congratulations were coming in from all over the world, although London's International Flat Earth Society had announced that the entire *Apollo 8* flight was an elaborate hoax.

It was, indeed, a happy crew, the adrenaline again flowing like a flash flood. Lovell was wondering whether his wife, Marilyn, had received the mink coat he'd asked Neiman-Marcus to deliver on Christmas morning. (She had.) Anders was carrying his Christmas present to his wife, Valerie: a gold pin shaped like an 8 with a moonstone crescent. My gifts to the family were already under our Christmas tree in Houston, to be opened when I got home.

Apollo 8 had broken out of lunar orbit traveling at about 5,500 mph. The speed had begun increasing markedly after the spacecraft crossed the equigravisphere for the second time, earth's gravity pulling us as if we were attached to an invisible rope 200,000 miles long. Before reentry, I looked for our celestial landmark—the constellation Orion—and positioned the spacecraft to enter the earth's atmosphere with the blunt or rear end first, letting the ionizing air hit us where the heat shields were the thickest. If we had tried to come down nose first, we would have been burned to a crisp.

At a point about eighty miles over China, we fired the explosive bolts that severed the command module from the service module. In effect, we were now nothing but a big gumdrop racing to enter the atmosphere on sheer momentum, with no major source of propulsion left.

Jim and I had been kidding Anders, who had never flown a reentry before, to expect the ride of his life. Actually, we *all* got the ride of our lives—reentry on *Gemini 7* at 17,000 mph hadn't prepared us for *Apollo 8*'s plunge into the atmosphere at nearly 25,000 mph. We were flying upside down as well as pointing backward; deceleration forces were building up to nearly 7 Gs and they stayed there for six minutes.

The air, so disturbed that it was forming a red-hot plasma over the spacecraft, was generating some 5,000 degrees Fahrenheit on the shields. The glow was so bright that a Pan Am 747 pilot radioed he had seen us reenter, leaving a white incandescent trail 100 miles long. Inside the spacecraft we didn't feel the heat, but I had the same sensation experienced during *Gemini 7*'s reentry, that of being in a neon tube.

The spacecraft's maneuverability throughout the flight and particularly during reentry positioning was surprisingly agile. Flying the Apollo command module has been compared to steering an aircraft carrier with an outboard motor, but I didn't find it that sluggish, although I wouldn't have wanted to try a dogfight in it.

We were flying on autopilot, and from now on it was up to our inertial navigation system to get us the rest of the way, through that narrow corridor at precisely the right angle.

We had left the system on throughout the flight with a negligible drain on power, and already it was guiding us smoothly into the corridor. We had one malfunction warning that almost caused me to switch to manual control, but Houston was showing us to be on a perfect path. I sensed it was a false warning, and left the system alone.

Our landing target was the aircraft carrier *Yorktown,* waiting for us in the Pacific about 1,000 miles southwest of Hawaii. The *Yorktown* had us in radar contact shortly before the drogue chutes opened at about 24,000 feet. Both jolts were slight, but when the main chute opened it felt as if the spacecraft had just been hit by a giant fist.

Landing in the predawn darkness, we couldn't tell at first whether the main chute had deployed properly. The *Yorktown* crew knew before we did—they spotted the flashing strobe light mounted on the chute. We hit harder than anyone expected and a wave of water came surging through the spacecraft, from where we had no idea. I figured a check valve might have been forced open, although NASA engineers later theorized the water was condensation that had gathered on the environmental control system.

The landing impact was so jarring, I didn't move fast enough to pull a switch that fired an explosive cord, releasing the parachutes. Momentarily stunned, I hit the switch too late and the still-attached chutes pulled the spacecraft over, nose down in the water.

So there we were, the three most famous men in the world at this moment, hanging ignominiously head down by our belts like a trio of harnessed monkeys. I hit another switch, one that inflated some large balloonlike bags on the module's nose, and these pulled the spacecraft upright. We were less than three miles from the *Yorktown.*

It was still dark and we knew there'd be no recovery action until after dawn; the Navy didn't want to endanger frogmen by dropping them at night. But we were in radio contact with the rescue helicopters circling overhead and one pilot inquired, "Hey, *Apollo 8,* is the moon made of Limburger cheese?"

"No," Anders shot back, "it's made of American cheese."

We didn't have to be in the water very long to realize that our spacecraft was a lousy boat. Not only were we bobbing around in four-foot waves, but because the module's center of gravity was not in its actual center, we began rotating like a slowly spinning top. After flying a half-million miles through space, I proceeded to get seasick and throw up. Fortunately, by this time we had our helmets off.

We stayed in the water for an hour and a half. At dawn, the choppers dropped their frogmen. They fastened a flotation collar to the spacecraft and opened the hatch. And I think that may have been the best moment of the mission—to feel the fresh sea air of blessed earth on my face, realizing the mission was over and successful, knowing I was going to see Susan and the boys soon.

There was an electric razor waiting for me on the helicopter, something I had requested before the launch. It seemed NASA had spent some five thousand dollars trying unsuccessfully to develop an electric razor for *Apollo 8* that would catch all the loose bristles so the weightless particles wouldn't clog the instruments. Apprised of that rare scientific failure, I had asked that a conventional electric razor be available when we were picked up.

When we landed on the flight deck, the ship's band was playing and we saw the flag waving in the early morning breeze. If it's possible to reach a high that surpasses that day, it sure won't come in my lifetime.

The cheers from the crew massed on the deck really moved me. These guys were far from home and loved ones at Christmastime, too, but no one seemed to mind. They were cheering more than three men; they were cheering in pride for their country. The dissension and trauma of Vietnam had made 1968 an unhappy year, but you couldn't tell it on the *Yorktown* that morning of December 27.

We slept in the admiral's quarters the first night, between clean sheets for the first time in six nights, after dining on lobster tails with Captain John Fifield, the *Yorktown*'s commander. Friday we had a prime roast beef candlelight dinner with the ship's officers, and for breakfast on Sunday we ate steak and eggs with the carrier's chief petty officers. We were in culinary heaven.

While the carrier headed toward Hawaii we went through the expected medical examinations, but they weren't anything like what Lovell and I had endured after *Gemini 7*, essentially a medical mission. We were tired, but neither Jim nor I was as fatigued as we had been following *Gemini*. Except for some rather stiff legs, we felt great.

We flew off the *Yorktown*, received a roaring welcome when we landed in Hawaii, and boarded a noisy, cold Air Force C-141 for a nonstop flight to Houston and a reunion with our families. The whole space center turned out to greet us, and later we had a chance to read some of the congratulatory messages, including a cable from ten Soviet cosmonauts praising the *Apollo 8* crew for "the precision of your joint work and your courage." Another congratulatory message came from the just released crew of the *Pueblo*.

There also was a telegram from someone I didn't know, just an ordinary citizen. He wired: "To the crew of *Apollo 8*. Thank you. You saved 1968."

It was a mission accomplished. And above all, we showed what American determination, coordinated effort, and selfless cooperation could achieve. The whole Apollo program made a lot of scientists look foolish, starting with those who had pronounced the Van Allen radiation belt an insurmountable barrier to space flight. I've long since refused to take the word of any scientist as gospel.

Thomas Gold, a professor of astronomy, had earned himself quite a few headlines before Project Apollo by predicting that a moon landing would be disastrous. He said the moon was covered with a thick layer of dust that not only would make vision a problem but would act like quicksand if an astronaut tried to walk on the lunar surface.

Unfortunately, there exist in the academic and scientific community self-appointed experts with axes to grind, and those axes are coated with phony glibness that glides smoothly over any data or evidence that might refute their claims. Thanks to the news media, especially television, they never seem to lose their credibility even after they've been proved wrong; *Apollo 11* should have discredited Gold permanently, but it didn't.

Looking back on my final space mission almost twenty years ago, I can't help feeling a little sadness—maybe a little anger, too. Project Apollo marked the apogee of America's space program; we have let the Russians catch up and even surpass us in many critical areas. They have more powerful rockets, they have a small space station in orbit, they're reported to be seriously considering a manned flight to Mars, and they're even contracting to launch some of our own commercial satellites. We're still playing with the space shuttle; only recently has NASA established higher priorities, including a space station and a Mars expedition.

And the NASA of Mercury, Gemini, and Apollo is gone. When you lose men like Webb, Gilruth, von Braun, and Kraft, and their successors are merely good but far from great men, you end up with a real problem unless significant changes are made in the way checks and balances are distributed throughout the organization. This wasn't done and we're paying the piper. I honestly wonder whether the NASA of today is capable of conducting a project of Apollo's magnitude.

There would be nine more Apollo missions, *Apollo 11* being the most spectacular. I treasure this telegram I received after Armstrong and Aldrin landed on the moon: "Congratulations and thanks for *Apollo 11*. Today's success is yours."

It was signed "Olin E. Teague, Member of Congress."

12

OF KINGS AND QUEENS, POPES AND PRESIDENTS

Long before the moon mission, I had told NASA that *Apollo 8* would be my last flight.

It was a decision reached after a long talk with Susan, although the decision was strictly mine; as she always had, she left the choice up to me. I was being practical. I was only forty years old, but after *Apollo 8* I'd have just eighteen more months to go before accumulating the twenty years I needed for full retirement benefits from the Air Force. And I knew it would be time to start looking around for another kind of career.

I was willing to stay in NASA for that year and a half because my Air Force commission was still active. But, I informed NASA, when *Apollo 8* was over I would prefer some kind of administrative job.

There had been some discussion about turning our crew around and letting us fly *Apollo 11* to a lunar landing, the logic being that *Apollo 8* had been an excellent dress rehearsal for the biggest mission of them all, one that could be handled best by an experienced crew. But that assumption was wrong. We hadn't had much preparation on the lunar module—we didn't even have one on *Apollo 8*—and frankly I didn't think there was enough time to train us. NASA had scheduled only two more flights before *Apollo 11,* so I thought it was best to tell everyone up front that *Apollo 8* was my final mission even before we flew.

So NASA broke up our crew. Lovell was assigned to *Apollo 13* as commander, Anders to the backup crew for *Apollo 11.* It turned out that *Apollo 8* was Bill's last space flight, too—after Armstrong's mission, Anders resigned from NASA and the Air Force to become executive secretary of the National Aeronautics and Space Council and went on to one of the most successful careers of all the astronauts, including posts as chairman of the Nuclear Regulatory Commission and U.S. ambassador to Norway.

We spent our last times together during the few weeks following *Apollo 8.* I couldn't count the invitations we got for civic parades in our honor—Anders even got one from Hong Kong, where he'd been born; his father had been in the Navy and serving there at the time. The big one we all accepted was the traditional tickertape parade down Broadway in New York.

The city had changed all the Broadway street signs to APOLLO WAY, painted in orange and black. It was an extremely cold day and we were actually shivering as we waved to the hundreds of thousands lining the parade route. Riding with us was Mayor John Lindsay, who told me later he'd heard one spectator yell, "Hey, guys, the next time you go, take Lindsay with you!"

We were feted at the United Nations and New York Governor Nelson Rockefeller gave us a dinner that night at the Waldorf-Astoria, where he presented each of us with a magnificent Steuben sculpture, "Mountains of the Moon."

We had another parade in Chicago witnessed by more than a million people, but for me, the most exciting one was riding down Pennsylvania Avenue in Washington from the White House to Capitol Hill, where I was to address a joint session of Congress. The parade had been preceded by a ceremony at which President Johnson gave the crew NASA's top award, the Distinguished Service Medal. Nine NASA officials received the same medal, and we were glad to see that the honored men included von Braun, Gilruth, Kraft, Phillips, and Rocco Petrone, our launch operations chief.

The president, who had only a few more days before he left office, looked tired. He had come down with the Hong Kong flu while we were circling the moon, but he was most gracious and we managed to give him at least one laugh after the medals were passed out.

"Mr. President," I said, "Jim Lovell has a picture of your Texas ranch we think you'd like to have."

LBJ looked pleased, then broke out laughing. What Lovell handed him was the color shot I had taken of the earthrise—he couldn't have found his ranch with a microscope.

I was surprised to find I wasn't afflicted with stage fright or even much nervousness when I spoke to Congress. I was damned proud, however, and not a little excited. With Susan and the boys looking on from the visitors' gallery, I was speaking from a podium where men far greater than I had once stood—legendary heroes like Lindbergh and world leaders like Churchill and Franklin Roosevelt. Me, the high school quarterback who couldn't complete a forward pass . . . the scared, homesick West Point plebe of Beast Barracks days . . . the fighter pilot who wasn't allowed to fly.

I guess I wasn't nervous because I felt I had something important to say, and I hope that what I lacked in oratorical style was offset by earnestness. Cognizant that a new administration was coming to power and that it was rumored to be lukewarm toward the space program, I said that "exploration really is the essence of the human spirit," and added, "To pause, to falter, to turn our back on the quest for knowledge, is to perish."

I raised a few eyebrows when I said I hoped that in a few years we'd have an international community of exploration and research on the moon, much in the way many nations have jointly explored the Antarctic. I described our voyage in limited detail and mentioned the crew's reading from the book of Genesis on Christmas Eve.

"One of the things that was truly historic," I joked, "was that we got that good Roman Catholic Bill Anders to read from the King James Version of the Bible."

Then I looked down at the Supreme Court justices, all nine of them present; they had just ruled against reading the Bible in public schools.

"But now that I see those gentlemen in the front row," I remarked, "I'm not sure we should have read from the Bible at all."

The whole chamber rocked with laughter and applause.

I concluded by quoting from poet Archibald MacLeish, whose own impression of *Apollo 8* was far more eloquent than any words I could have composed: "To see the earth as it truly is, small and blue and beautiful in that eternal silence where it floats, is to see ourselves as riders on the earth together, brothers on the bright loveliness in the eternal cold—brothers who know now they are truly brothers."

While the crew was enjoying all the attention, scientists were analyzing the thousands of photographs taken from *Apollo 8*. Their most important conclusion: The flat Sea of Tranquility, which lies on the eastern side of the moon as seen from the earth, was safe and adequate for a lunar landing.

Naturally we had an enormous number of news conferences, mostly involving questions about our flight and how it related to the forthcoming *Apollo 11* mission. The Bible reading came up frequently, and at one press conference I noted that a Soviet cosmonaut orbiting the earth had reported back rather sarcastically, "I don't see God in the heavens."

"I can't comment on what he didn't see," I said, "but I saw evidence that God lives. I had a chance to see the lunar surface, a vast, lonely, forbidding, and expansive nothing, and at the same time compare it to the creation of the earth with its oceans and continents and, eventually, man. Reading from Genesis gave us a new meaning, a new grasp of the miracle of creation."

I also emphasized the freedom of expression enjoyed by the *Apollo 8* crew, and compared this to an incident that had occurred during our moon flight. The Soviet Union had launched an earth-orbiting spacecraft and its commander was broadcasting via live Soviet television on what was going on.

"Dear Soviet people," he began, "I am reporting from the spaceship from the working place of its commander." He went on to explain how he had withstood the strains of launching and adjustment to weightlessness, and then turned to more technical matters.

"I shall now tell you something about the construction of the spacecraft," he started to say. At this point ground control cut him off with a curt "Thank you very much."

In one interview, I deplored the "apple pie" image of the astronauts, an image that seemed to imply we had all been cloned from a monolithic block with identical motives, identical reactions, and identical ways of life.

"I don't think you could find a more diverse people," I told the reporter. I believed that then and I still believe it today. The one thing we had in common, outside of our military flying background, was dedication to the space program. Significantly, I think, once we left NASA we drifted apart.

Susan began filling several scrapbooks with clippings on the various activities that followed *Apollo 8*. I was browsing through them recently and came across a story that still fascinates me. It was an Associated Press feature pointing out the amazing similarities between *Apollo 8* and a novel about a moon flight written in 1865.

The novel was Jules Verne's *From the Earth to the Moon*. Verne's story began with a launching site near Tampa, Florida, only 100 miles from today's Cape Kennedy, and that was just the first of several almost unbelievable coincidences.

Both his imaginary moon rocket and *Apollo 8* flew to the moon and back in December, and both landed in the Pacific.

Verne's projectile escaped the earth's gravity at a speed of 25,000 mph; so did *Apollo 8*.

Verne's crew included a Frenchman named Andan—not quite Anders, but close enough to qualify as another coincidence.

His spacecraft was a cast-iron tube lined with aluminum, 12 feet high with a base of 54 square feet and weighing 12,230 pounds. Those were roughly the dimensions of our command module, which incidentally weighed 12,392 pounds and had an aluminum-alloy inner structure.

Verne's crew never landed on the moon, probably because in 1865 he couldn't figure out a way to have them land and then take off again. So his astronauts simply went around the moon and came back—the same mission we flew. Writing at a time when even the airplane hadn't been invented yet, this father of all science fiction proved to be a better prognosticator than scientists like Thomas Gold.

Some NASA officials, in fact, were worried that the negativism expressed by certain members of the scientific and academic communities might have rubbed off on the incoming Nixon administration. There had been hints in the press that the President-elect wasn't gung-ho about the space program, so there were sighs of relief among the NASA brass when it was announced that Susan and I had been invited to Richard Nixon's inauguration. We were somewhat surprised when we got to our assigned seats and found we were right behind the swearing-in podium. This was the first sign that Nixon was not only genuinely interested in space, but seemed to have embraced me personally as the space program's symbolic representative.

That in itself wasn't surprising. Every new administration wants to focus on a fresh beginning. In this case it also wanted to draw attention away from the Vietnam mess; the space program was a logical place to start, and I was the "available astronaut," so to speak. What did surprise me was the extent to which Richard Nixon accepted me.

Of all the presidents I have known, I was closest to Nixon. When the Watergate scandal broke and he finally had to admit his guilt, no one was more disappointed or disillusioned than I. I even felt betrayed. Yet I continue to admire the man. In many respects, he was an excellent president with great accomplishments to his credit, not the least of which was improving our relations with China. When it came to foreign affairs, Nixon was superb.

I liked him, I honestly did. To me, he always was kind and considerate. I know he was terribly shy, even ill at ease with people he didn't know, and when it came to making small talk he was a disaster. But we never had to engage in small talk; at every meeting I had with him, we always discussed important matters in a one-on-one relationship. He listened. He took advice—and sometimes it was advice that he either didn't want to hear or that was contrary to what his advisers had told him.

I'm sure that he trusted me personally and he trusted my judgment in areas in which he knew I had some knowledge. Bill Safire, at one time the chief presidential speechwriter and a trusted aide in his own right, had his own theory as to why Nixon welcomed the counsel of a man totally outside politics. In his book *Before the Fall,* Safire wrote: "Borman was the kind of well-organized, highly motivated, intelligent serviceman Nixon admired, the product of a mission the President identified with."

All I know is that rapport between us was established almost immediately, with the President suggesting that Susan and I go on a tour of Europe—"mostly goodwill," he told me, "but also to check on the space programs of our NATO allies."

I accepted and with considerable temerity asked if we could take our boys along.

"Of course," Nixon said.

We got the usual diplomatic and protocol briefings from the State Department, and on a cold February morning in 1969, we left Andrews Air Force Base for London, the first stop on a three-week trip that was also to take us to France, Germany, Italy, the Netherlands, Belgium, Spain, and Portugal. Our chief escorts—I suppose you could call them chaperons—were our old friend Si Bourgin and Nicholas Ruwe, the new Republican man in the State Department's Office of

Protocol; Nick turned out to be a good friend and a great help.

We flew in unaccustomed style. The President had given us the use of Air Force Two, the backup plane for the primary presidential jet. It was an older 707 and not as luxuriously furnished as Air Force One, but it was no flying freight car, either.

We knew that meeting royalty was on the agenda and Susan, like any wife, worried about doing, saying, and wearing the "proper" things. We had expected to stay in a British hotel but instead were put into the London Hilton, and damned if we didn't eat at Trader Vic's the first night. This was the U.S. Embassy's idea; throughout the trip, the various American embassies pretty much controlled our activities, decided whom we were supposed to meet, and kept us to our schedule. I think Fred and Edwin actually had a better time than Susan and I did—they were old enough to go off on their own and occasionally they did.

We went to Buckingham Palace on our second evening in England. I took identical gifts to each head of state in the countries we visited: a beautiful, extremely detailed model of the Saturn V including the command and service modules, and a framed color reproduction of the famous earthrise photograph, both gift wrapped. The reaction the model got in Buckingham Palace wasn't what I expected.

After being presented to Queen Elizabeth and Prince Philip, we accompanied them to their private quarters, where I handed them the gifts. Princess Anne was there and also Princes Andrew and Edward, then two very small boys who began clamoring to open the wrappings. They tore them off like two kids at Christmastime, and when they saw the Saturn model, they immediately appropriated it.

They proceeded to take it apart, which the Queen thought was very clever of them. I ended up helping them put it back together again, which seemed to disarm our hosts. Princess Anne, a teen-ager then, hit it off with our boys and the three of them were probably the most relaxed people in that palatial room. Prince Charles was away.

Susan and the Queen sat together on a loveseat and talked, while I had an interesting conversation with Philip, a pleasant and erudite man who asked me many questions about *Apollo 8*. He was surprisingly well versed in space matters; at one time he had visited NASA's facilities and had actually flown a command module simulator. We stood off in one corner and conversed informally while servants served cocktails. As we were leaving, one of the Queen's ladies-in-waiting whispered to Susan, "You know, ma'am, the older children are far better disciplined."

I spoke to the Royal Aeronautical Society and showed an *Apollo 8* film NASA had put together—this was repeated in each country, and so was the inevitable news conference. I used the press meeting in London to praise the British-made fuel cells we had used on *Apollo 8*. Admittedly, this was a little diplomatic buttering-up gesture, the kind that made the State Department happy, but I didn't mind. Those fuel cells *were* excellent and I was trying to get across the point that peaceful exploration of space could be an international effort.

Reporters posed about the same questions everywhere. What was the moon like? What was our most anxious moment? How did we navigate? Why did I get sick? What caused the *Apollo 1* pad fire? Were we afraid of being hit by meteorites?

There were frequent questions about the Soviet space program, and one reporter brought up something that had occurred during *Apollo 8's* flight, when we were only two days out. The Soviet Union had offered to rescue us if we got into trouble, and this newsman asked me what I thought about the offer.

"Very generous," I replied. But I went on to explain that *Apollo 8* had no docking equipment; the crew had no EVA gear, so we couldn't have left the spacecraft; and the Russians would have had to have a booster standing by on proper countdown for interception. Even if all these handicaps could have been overcome somehow, I added, "we still would have needed a Russian-English dictionary." I refrained from saying what I really thought; that the Soviet offer was a phony, made solely for publicity.

Another reporter wanted to know what a meeting between astronauts and cosmonauts would be like. "Like a pilots' bull session," I replied. "Great deeds and heroic lies."

Inevitably, European reporters sought my views on the technological gap between their countries and mine. Knowing how easy it is to bruise national pride, my answer was phrased very carefully.

"First," I pointed out, "we worked from the accumulated knowledge of centuries, most of it coming from Europe. From what I have seen of Europe's technology, *Apollo 8* could have been built here, assigning certain parts to certain countries or companies." (This was the gist of my report to President Nixon when we returned: that Europe was far behind us in space technology, but could catch up if efforts were pooled.)

Another frequently asked question: Why should any nation spend so much on space exploration when there is so much misery to overcome on earth?

My response: "The spur to technology provided by the space program is far more vital in the long run than any short-term relief of misery by the same expenditures in other areas. And I hope space exploration will bind peoples of the world together, so we will all begin to look on ourselves as earthlings, rather than Germans or Dutch or Americans."

There were many highlights of the three-week tour, but if I had to pick out one, it would have to be my meeting with General Charles de Gaulle. I say "my" meeting because Susan wasn't invited. De Gaulle was the only head of state on the entire trip who drew the line at including women.

Sargent Shriver, U.S. ambassador to France at the time, accompanied me into de Gaulle's office. There were only two other people in the big room—a French interpreter and the President of France himself, who was sitting behind a large, ornate desk when we entered. I don't think I've ever seen a more commanding figure, because of his austere personality as much as his height.

I had been told that the interpreter was necessary because de Gaulle spoke little if any English. It was apparent he had been well briefed on *Apollo 8* because, through the interpreter, he asked many technical questions about the flight. I got the impression he really wasn't that interested in the technical details, but wanted me to know he cared enough about meeting me to have been briefed so thoroughly.

For example, he'd ask something like "At eighty hours into your mission you experienced window fogging; did that cause you a lot of trouble?"

His side of the conversation was entirely in French. His final question, again asked in French and translated by the interpreter, was a lulu.

"Now my dear Colonel," he began, "you were three men on a very lonely, dangerous mission with obviously much anxiety and opportunities for distress. How did you manage to keep order? How did you manage to keep serenity on the flight?"

"Mr. President," I said, "there were three men but only one commander—*me*."

The interpreter started to translate my answer into French, but de Gaulle laughed and held up his hand before the interpreter could get two words out.

"Don't bother," he said in perfect English. *"That* I can understand."

As we were leaving, de Gaulle picked up a beautiful silver cigar case with his signature engraved on it, and handed it to me. Outside his office, one of his aides came running up.

"Did he give you the case?" he asked.

"Why do you want to know?" Shriver inquired.

"If the President doesn't like an interview, you don't get the case."

De Gaulle and I must have hit it off, and I still have that case. It was one of many generous gifts we received, but because of the circumstances I especially treasure it, even if I don't smoke cigars.

In Rome, we were granted an audience with Pope Paul VI. We were in Brussels when we got word that the Pope would see us during our visit to Italy, but we were also informed that everyone would have to be dressed in black for the audience. I happened to have a black suit with me, but Susan was planning to wear the most expensive outfit in her wardrobe, a handsome gray suit, and the boys had navy-blue suits. So we had to shop for new black clothes for the three of them.

It was impossible to resent this unexpected invasion of our finances, however, when we arrived at the stately Vatican and were ushered into the chambers where the College of Cardinals had convened to watch the *Apollo 8* film. I spoke to them from the very spot where in 1614 Galileo, the Italian astronomer, had been tried and found guilty of heresy for supporting Copernicus's theory that the earth revolved around the sun and not the opposite.

We were supposed to have a fifteen-minute audience with Paul VI after the film ended, but we stayed almost an hour. The Pope was small, almost tiny, and very delicate. The little red shoes he wore fascinated our boys more than anything else. He apologized for his English language imperfections, but actually he was surprisingly fluent.

He read a statement he had written himself, praising me for reading from Genesis during the flight and expressing his appreciation for bringing God into our mission.

"For that particular moment of time," he said softly, "the world was at peace."

Following the audience, the papal secretary of state escorted us to the summer Vatican for a private dinner with His Holiness. There the Pope presented us with a pair of magnificent Bibles, four medals depicting him that he had blessed, and a piece of stone the size of a half-dollar—part of the original Vatican wall. All in all, an inspiring and gratifying experience for a couple of avowed Episcopalians.

I had to turn down one gift during the trip; the French wanted to give me a sports car but I felt I had to decline, much to the boys' disappointment. What I did get in France was sick. I still was under the weather when we got to Holland and met Queen Juliana and her husband, the Queen in particular being one of the nicest people we met on the whole trip. She was the prototype of somebody's grandmother in appearance and solicitous manners, but she was one sharp lady.

Whatever was ailing me—flu or food poisoning, I was never sure—really clobbered me when we got to Belgium. While we were making the rounds, our guides had to stop the car periodically so I could get out and throw up. When I got back in, they'd hook me up to an IV to keep me going. But I was feeling better by the time we had a private dinner with King Baudouin and Queen Fabiola of Belgium, a very relaxing affair in which we were treated more like family than visiting celebrities.

Of all the royal personages we met, they were the closest to our own ages and easily the most relaxed and friendly. They were childless but had taken their fourteen-year-old nephew under their wing and were training him to take Baudouin's place someday. After dinner, I showed them the movie in a small private theater at the palace and they did something that really impressed us. They invited the entire household staff and their children in to see the film, and it was touching to see the King's obvious affection toward the kids—he knew every child by name and had something special to say to each one.

Fred and Edwin had their eyes opened in Germany, where they witnessed firsthand the stark differences between communism and a free society. The family was dining at the Berlin Hilton one night, with only members of our party present; it was one of the few evenings we had to ourselves. From the dining room, we could see not only the lights of West Berlin but the darkness of East Germany beyond the Berlin Wall. The contrast was so startling that even the boys commented on it—on our side, a vibrant, happy and prosperous people; on the other, a stifling, oppressive blackness. Fred and Edwin were missing school on this tour, but they learned a few lessons schools don't teach.

As soon as we arrived back in Washington, I was informed that

Dwight Eisenhower wanted to see the *Apollo 8* crew at Walter Reed Army Medical Center. Anders wasn't available but Jim Lovell and I went to the hospital, where we were warned not to stay longer than ten minutes—the former President was very ill and, in fact, would die only about a month later.

Ike was in bed, hooked up to an EKG machine, and he actually apologized for not being able to get up. He asked voluminous questions about the flight, and I told him all about the European trip— he grinned when I recounted my meeting with de Gaulle, who was not one of Eisenhower's favorite people. Every few minutes, a doctor or nurse would come in and suggest that we'd better leave.

"Get out!" Ike would order. "We're enjoying ourselves."

Jim and I stayed the whole afternoon, completely forgetting as we talked that he was a dying man. It was one of the most moving experiences of our lives.

We returned to Houston and NASA assigned me to a new task force monitoring contracts for construction of a long-term space station. But the agency suddenly switched signals and sent me to Washington on another assignment: acting as NASA's liaison with the White House for the upcoming lunar landing mission—*Apollo 11*.

Why a liaison man? Because this mission was obviously going to be one of the most epochal events in history if it succeeded, and by the same token an unparalleled catastrophe if the crew didn't survive. Potential triumph or potential tragedy would be at stake, and there was considerable concern as to how either should be handled. NASA wanted an experienced astronaut on hand as a public relations adviser. Public relations wasn't my cup of tea, but NASA apparently figured I had qualities far more important: common sense and good judgment.

So I reported to Peter Flanigan of the White House staff. He gave me a small office and in a short time I got to know all the so-called Nixon gang. The best of the lot was Bill Safire, a man of considerable charm, wit, intelligence, and also integrity—a rare commodity in that group, whose chief virtue was unyielding if misguided loyalty toward the President. There weren't many laughs around the White House during the Nixon era, and Safire was a breath of fresh air while he was there.

I remember one meeting I had with Dwight Chapin, Flanigan, and Safire shortly before *Apollo 11* took off; we were discussing such items as whether the crew should have a Bible with them and the wording on the plaque that Armstrong and Aldrin were to place on the moon. I relayed the information that the astronauts wanted the plaque to say they had "set foot" on the moon instead of "landed," because it was possible an unmanned Russian moon shot might have already put something on the lunar surface.

Safire was looking over NASA's proposed timetable for the mission and frowned.

"In the timetable here," he inquired, "who's this girl you're throwing out of the capsule?"

"Girl? What girl?"

"The line says, 'Egress for EVA.' "

"That means Armstrong leaves the capsule for extravehicular activity," I explained, unable to suppress a grin.

"Oh" was all this erudite master of the English language could muster. He was one of the few people around who could laugh at himself; most of the others were almost grim in their zeal to build a wall of unquestioning loyalty around Nixon, who was inherently suspicious to begin with. The anomaly of our relationship was that he respected me for always telling him the truth, and I think he respected Safire for the same reason.

The White House felt, with justification, that *Apollo 11* if successful would be an effective antidote for the nation's growing disenchantment with Vietnam. Yet disenchantment and its twin, disillusionment, were one thing; the outright rebellions exploding on campuses throughout the country were another.

Because my White House job wouldn't be full time until the time for *Apollo 11* grew closer, NASA asked me to tour a number of colleges and universities, explaining the space program and its importance to students. For the most part, the tour was a disaster and left me feeling just as bitter toward the students as they did toward the war.

I expected to encounter negativism on the part of many students and I sure got plenty, particularly at the eastern schools. What I didn't expect was the uncertainty, the absolute ineffectiveness, of the university faculty and administrators in dealing with sheer anarchy. The students at least had immaturity (and in some cases misplaced idealism) as an excuse for their behavior; their mentors were nothing but helpless nerds, naïve beyond belief, possessing no idea of how to cope with the vandalism and drug abuse sweeping their own campuses, and apparently lacking any basic beliefs themselves in what this country was all about. They just shrugged their shoulders and marched to the drums of permissiveness and surrender to the very ones to whom they were supposed to be teaching those beliefs. It was mass abdication of responsibility.

Professors and administrators alike seemed to have a collective feeling of guilt. And into their dangerously complacent world came a guy with no guilt feelings whatsoever, someone who wanted to espouse not only the space program but what he perceived as the fundamental values of American society. I wasn't trying to preach sermons and for the most part I tried to stick to space in general and *Apollo 8* in particular. At some schools, I wasn't even allowed to complete my remarks because of the booing and deliberately staged distractions. This wasn't honest dissent from young idealists; it was mob rule by adolescent ruffians. At Columbia, for example, I had hardly begun talking when the audience started throwing marshmallows at me. Then several students dressed in gorilla costumes climbed onto the stage. At one school in Boston, I had to arrive and depart in a helicopter because of the mob of students protesting the appearance of a military man on campus.

Not every campus was a wasteland of radical hostility. West Point, as might be expected, was hospitable, and so was Notre Dame, where Father Theodore Hesburgh had everything under control, to put it mildly. He told me that while he was concerned about the wisdom of the Vietnam War, he still was proud of America's inherent decency and values. Most of the southern and southwestern schools were great; at least they listened.

Then there was Cornell.

Susan went with me on this visit and she was looking forward to it—our host was none other than Carl Sagan. Although I was actually escorted into the lecture hall by an armed policeman, the talk itself went off peacefully enough. I talked about the space program and then answered questions. Most were along the lines of "How can you spend all this money going to the moon when there are so many poor, so many economic inequities, so much poverty?"

I tried to explain that the space program was a natural extension of the human mind, that it was something our society could not afford to abandon because the future—the students' future—depended on our keeping up with advanced technology. I got a very cool reception; in fact it was almost icy. I gathered from the questions that these kids wanted an agrarian society, and frankly, they were not only naïve but hopelessly unrealistic.

After the talk, Sagan invited us to his home "to meet some of the members of the Students for a Democratic Society," he explained, adding that he was their faculty adviser. We accepted, and all evening long they sneered at and ripped into everything about the United States—and Sagan orchestrated the entire attack. They insisted on quizzing me on Vietnam, and I admit I wasn't prepared to debate them.

We sat on the living room floor and with Sagan egging them on, they confronted us with specific charges. "Did you know that on such and such a date American troops massacred innocent civilians?"

"Look," I insisted, "our society with all its faults has produced the greatest amount of freedom for individuals and the greatest amount of material wealth of any nation in the world. I don't deny its faults but I don't forget its virtues, as you seem to be doing. How can it be all bad?"

Admittedly, this was not much of a rebuttal against specific allegations of American atrocities in Vietnam. What infuriated me more than anything else was Sagan's supporting them all night long. To me, the entire evening was a superficial, pseudo-intellectual attack on a country I loved, and I was angrier at him than I was at the kids; they looked up to him and he kept encouraging them.

Our parting that night was cool, to say the least. I'll never forget or forgive him for that unpleasant evening at Cornell. It's an ironic twist that Sagan has used all the self-promoting gimmicks of public relations and television to set himself up as a kind of scientific guru. Now he enjoys the fruits of the same society whose materialism he so viciously attacked.

I did get something constructive out of the Cornell experience, however. I was distressed at my inability to counter accusations and allegations of American atrocities with exact dates and details. So I made a point of obtaining from the State Department briefings and papers on Vietnam. I wanted to talk about space, not an unpopular war, yet I ended up becoming almost an apologist for the military-industrial complex in the eyes of my radical-minded audiences who didn't want to hear about space.

With the campus tour behind me, I went back to my White House duties as the time neared for *Apollo 11*'s scheduled mid-July launch. *Apollo 9* (March 3–12), an earth-orbital mission flown mostly to test the lunar module, and *Apollo 10* (May 18–26), which duplicated *Apollo 8*'s moon trip with the addition of a lunar module launch and docking, both had been successful.

I had expected to stay in Washington until *Apollo 11* was over. But in January I had received an invitation to attend the annual dinner of the Alfalfa Club in Washington—an invitation with some interesting consequences. A fellow guest there was Soviet Ambassador Anatoly Dobrynin, who turned out to be more than casually cordial. He asked me and my family to visit the Soviet Union.

I informed the President and then National Security Council Chairman Henry Kissinger of Dobrynin's surprise invitation. Both urged me to accept. This was at least one area in which I found Richard Nixon to be totally sincere and absolutely dedicated: his desire to improve relations with the Communist world on a live-and-let-live basis. In one word—détente.

Nixon, in fact, was already intrigued with the suggestion of many scientists that the United States and Russia cooperate in a joint space mission, and when the question of my going to the Soviet Union came up, he immediately perceived it as the opening wedge for such a mission. He asked me to sound out the Soviets on the possibility. As far as the President was concerned, this would be the most important aspect of my visit.

While I was getting ready for the Russian trip, NASA sent to the White House its own ideas on what the President should say on television to the astronauts when they landed on the moon. The gist of those remarks was that the current administration was responsible for *Apollo 11*'s success and most of the technological achievements that preceded the flight. The statement was pure politics, an exercise in self-congratulations, and when the President asked my opinion I wrote him a memo saying, "I think what NASA is suggesting is terrible and I don't think you should say it."

The next thing I knew, he called me into the Oval Office, invited me to sit down, and asked abruptly, "Okay, Frank, just why don't you like what NASA wants me to say?"

I was too mad even to try being diplomatic. "Look, Mr. President, you really don't have anything to do with *Apollo 11*. You're just the fortunate or unfortunate recipient of this mission, depending on whether it succeeds or fails. If it fails, you'll get tarred with it, and if it succeeds, you'll get *some* of the credit. But for you to say what NASA is suggesting—that in effect you were the father of the space program—is just plain wrong. What you really should say is something very simple and nonpartisan, a few words of congratulations, and then get off the air."

He thanked me, a noncommittal reaction, but in the end he followed my advice completely; he even vetoed, at my urging, the playing of "The Star-Spangled Banner" following his brief remarks in a telephone call to the astronauts on the moon. I pointed out to the President, in another memo, that playing the national anthem "would force the crew to stand at attention for some two and a half minutes," and added, "This time, plus the time allocated to unveiling the plaque, would add up to a significant portion of the time on the lunar surface which is nonproductive from a scientific or exploration standpoint."

He sent the memo back to me with two words scrawled at the top in his handwriting: *I agree.*

After the mission was over, Drew Pearson wrote a column headlined NIXONIZING THE MOON, claiming that the President himself had wanted to take all the credit for *Apollo 11* and turn the dramatic landing into a political show with Nixon, not the astronauts, as the star. I saw the article in *The Washington Post* and phoned Pearson, who later ran a retraction—one of the few times in his career, I believe, that he did.

Nixon's actual remarks when Armstrong and Aldrin landed on the moon, written by Safire and me, went: "Neil and Buzz, I am talking to you from the Oval Office at the White House and this certainly has to be the most historic telephone call ever made. Because of what you have done, the heavens have become part of man's world. As you talk to us from the Sea of Tranquility, it inspires us to redouble our efforts to bring peace and tranquility to Earth."

No great literature, but appropriate, brief, and achieving our purpose of not upstaging the mission or the *Apollo 11* crew itself. I didn't get any static from anyone in the White House, either. As a matter of fact, I might as well admit I got along exceptionally well with one of the chief "villains" of Watergate: Bob Haldeman. I liked him very much—he was always pleasant to me and invariably cooperative, certainly not the Prussian ogre others felt him to be. Flanigan was a decent, friendly guy, too. I never got to know Ehrlichman very well, but in general I had cordial relations with the people most closely associated with the Watergate scandal, which made my disillusionment even more traumatic.

I can't say the same for Vice President Spiro Agnew. I even had the temerity to write to Nixon when he was running for re-election and suggest that he get another vice presidential candidate. I was with Eastern at the time, but I had also been named to second Nixon's nomination at the 1972 Republican National Convention and felt I had a right to air my opinion of Agnew. Nixon's reply was in effect a friendly but firm "thank you but no thank you."

Yet he *did* trust me. After I returned from the Soviet Union, the President invited me to accompany him when he flew out to the *Apollo 11* recovery ship, the carrier *Hornet,* where he was to greet the triumphant astronauts. Also aboard Air Force One was Kissinger, a fascinating person and the most self-confident man I ever met. It wasn't conceit but a composed, unruffled air of assurance that could turn an ordinary conversation into an educational discourse. Kissinger didn't argue; he lectured.

From the *Hornet,* Kissinger and the President were to go into a series of meetings with the leaders of Far Eastern nations, and much of their time on the flight was spent discussing these forthcoming conferences. But Nixon also found time to chat with me privately during the flight to Johnson Island, from which helicopters would take us to the carrier.

We talked about his values and his concern for the nation's future in a world of constant confrontation between the two superpowers. To me, he came off as a sensitive, caring man, terribly aware of what a nuclear war would mean. He brought up the difficulty of obtaining good people for public service and surprised me by suggesting that I might be able to help.

"You've been with NASA a number of years, Frank," he observed. "I'd be very much interested in your assessment of the key figures you've gotten to know well—astronauts, managers, administrators and so forth—and whether there are people in the agency who could make potential contributions to departments and fields other than NASA. I'd appreciate a memorandum on this when I get back."

I had one ready for him—nine pages of thumbnail appraisals covering top NASA officials and sixteen astronauts. My ratings included the highest praise for Paine, Phillips, Low, and Kraft. I emphasized that I hadn't discussed the possibility of non-NASA assignments with any of the individuals I rated. And I cautioned the President that "personal ambitions and goals might influence their effectiveness in fields other than manned space flight." This was particularly true of the sixteen astronauts mentioned in the memorandum—I knew many of them had their eyes fixed on the private sector when their careers as astronauts ended, and this made it tough to judge them in terms of future government employment.

With one exception, I gave all the astronauts good to excellent ratings, although not necessarily as prospective bureaucrats. I judged three of them as having potentially promising political futures. One was Jim Lovell, the second was Tom Stafford, and the third was John Glenn. Of Glenn I said, "Very sensitive, not too bright, extremely concerned about the future of the country and is certain that any Kennedy has the right answer. I'm convinced he will run for the Senate in Ohio and he'll be a very effective campaigner and probably a good Democratic senator. Recommendation: Get an attractive Republican candidate from Ohio."

The other astronaut whose future I hit right on the nose was Wally Schirra, who had retired from NASA and the Navy after *Apollo 7*. "Very competent," my memorandum said. "Seems most interested at this time in succeeding in private business, making a lot of money, and hunting and fishing. No great inclination toward political life. Recommendation: Leave in the private sector and recruit him as a major contributor after he's made his million." I don't know if Wally made that million, but I'd sure like to have his residuals from television commercials.

Later I also submitted a lengthy report on my Russian visit and a separate memo to Kissinger on the prospects for future international cooperation in space exploration (see Chapter 13). But the mission to the Soviet Union actually paid off while *Apollo 11* still was on its way to the moon.

I had just returned to the White House from the trip when the Russians launched an unmanned lunar probe. NASA, fearing a possible midspace orbital collision, went into orbit itself and my phone started ringing. Chris Kraft, for example, asked bluntly, "What the hell's going on?"

"The best thing to do is just ask 'em," I told Kraft. So over the famed Hot Line, I sent a message signed by me to the head of the USSR Academy of Sciences and requested the exact orbital parameters of the Russian probe. Within hours I received this unprecedented cable:

Reference your inquiry on flight of Soviet automatic probe Luna 15. Inform you that on July 12 at 1300 hours Moscow time the probe was placed in selenocentric orbit with the following preliminary values of its elements: Period of revolution two hours and 30 seconds, eccentricity of orbit two, 04; argument of precentre position 60 degrees, declination to lunar equator plane 127 degrees, longitude of the ascending mode counted from lunar zero meridian 280 degrees. It is supposed that in this orbit probe Luna 15 will remain for two days. In case of further change in the orbit of this probe you will receive additional information. The orbit of probe Luna 15 does not intersect the trajectory of Apollo 11 spacecraft announced by you in flight program.

M. KELDYSCH

The message was heartwarming evidence of the trip's success. Never before had the Soviets provided such detailed information on one of their own space missions. Apparently I had won some friends in the country Winston Churchill once described as "a riddle wrapped in a mystery inside an enigma."

13

INSIDE THE ENIGMA

"Dad, this place reminds me of black-and-white television—everything's in different shades of gray."

That was my sixteen-year-old Edwin's reaction to our first glimpse of Moscow, and he gave a very apt description. Everything was drab, from the cars to the clothes people wore: Moscow seemed to reflect the grimness of the forbidding Kremlin itself, as if the entire city had absorbed its colorless, oppressive atmosphere.

But in the next two weeks, we were to discover that judging Russia solely by its capital was unfair. Besides, this was 1969, and on two subsequent visits to the Soviet Union we found Moscow itself had changed somewhat for the better—"brighter" is the only word I can use. Even in 1969 we were in major cities like Leningrad where the mood of the people and their surroundings were relatively cheerful.

We flew to Russia via Pan Am and arrived on July 2, 1969, at Moscow's Sheremetyevo Airport, almost eighteen hours late because of mechanical problems. Not a promising beginning, but our hosts took the delay with good grace—they were probably glad it was an American jetliner that was responsible. In fact, I learned later that our plane was supposed to unload at Gate 13 and had been shifted to Gate 12 instead, the controller explaining, "This plane has had enough trouble already."

The welcoming delegation included three veteran cosmonauts: Gherman Titov, Kostantin Feoktistov, and Georgi Beregovoi. Also greeting us was the chief of Soviet cosmonauts, Colonel General Nikolai Kamanin, as well as Victor Gorshov, the vice president of the Union of Soviet Societies for Friendship and Cultural Relations with Foreign Countries—the organization that had tendered our official invitation.

The dual purpose of the trip—goodwill and space cooperation—was uppermost in my mind when I responded to the airport reception.

"I expect this visit to the Soviet Union to promote the further investigation of outer space and the establishment of friendly cooperation between the United Stated and Soviet Union," I told the large crowd. For the next two weeks, I was to repeat this theme in virtually every speech and toast I made—and there were to be an awful lot of speeches and toasts.

Other Soviet officials were at the airport, but I had eyes mostly for my space counterparts. I won't say instant friendships were born, yet there was a feeling of kinship on my part and, I think, on theirs. They each had typical broad Russian features, rather pudgy, but a pudginess containing a hint of steel underneath, and for some reason they seemed a little older than I expected—Feoktistov in particular, with his receding hairline and scholarly-looking glasses.

Titov, a short stocky man with an ingratiating grin and a decided sense of humor, was the Soviet version of Jim Lovell; he turned out to be one of our favorites, although both of us got off on the wrong foot thanks mainly to my habit of saying what was on my mind. With Feoktistov and Beregovoi nodding enthusiastically, Titov exclaimed, "Colonel Borman, if there's anything you'd like to do, any place you want to visit, just tell us."

"Our country is yours," Feoktistov chimed in.

I said, "Well, there are two things I'd like to see. First, your supersonic transport, the TU-144, and then we'd like to visit your launch site."

They looked at me crestfallen, as if I had just asked to inspect the entire Soviet air defense system. They hemmed and hawed and Titov finally said, "We're sorry, but those two requests are not possible to fulfill."

This was my first exposure to the Soviets' propensity for secrecy, their almost paranoid fear of outsiders. Over the next two weeks, however, I got the distinct impression the cosmonauts themselves were just following orders and would have shown us a great deal if it were up to them, and that included the launch site. As it was, we were allowed almost unlimited freedom in our contacts with these fraternity brothers in space. We were guests in Titov's home and had several freewheeling bull sessions, all without the ominous presence of a government official to inhibit the conversations. But there were other times when it was made clear that our tour status as honored guests wasn't exactly a blank check.

On one leg of the trip, for example, we were supposed to take off for some Russian city early in the afternoon, according to the itinerary our embassy had provided. The Russians kept delaying the departure until well past sundown, and when we finally left it was dark. It didn't take a genius to figure out why—they didn't want us flying over a certain area in the daytime. They may have trusted an American astronaut, but not an astronaut who also was a U.S. Air Force colonel.

We saw very little of Moscow that first day—just enough to give Edwin that gloomy impression—for we were flown to Leningrad, a truly beautiful city, the same afternoon. There I laid a wreath on the "Motherland" monument honoring the thousands of women, children, and soldiers who died defending the city during its World War II siege by the Nazis.

It would take thousands of words to recount the details of all the sightseeing we did in Leningrad and elsewhere—old palaces, cathedrals, museums, historic warships, scientific centers, schools, and so on *ad infinitum*. Leningrad was typical of the Russians' deep respect for history—even though they like to rewrite it occasionally. Yet what fascinated us the most was the people, not places. For often we found common ground to share, intense curiosity about Americans and our beliefs, and even a sense of humor.

On our first night in Leningrad, we were at a reception given by the city's mayor, Alexander Sizov. He was telling me that the Leningrad soccer team's previous season had been a disaster, but added proudly, "We're building a covered stadium so our soccer players can practice all year round."

"Don't pin too much hope on that," I remarked. "After a covered stadium was built in Houston, our baseball team began to play worse than ever."

I doubt whether anyone in that crowded room knew anything about baseball, but my translated quip brought laughter. Susan, apparently figuring we might start discussing sports all night long, tugged my arm.

"May I say something?"

"Sure," I said "but don't forget we have only one more day in Leningrad left."

She gave me one of her "watch out, buster" looks and took the floor.

"I've long wanted to meet Soviet people and tell them that they are fully responsible for my becoming an astronaut's wife," she began, alluding to the competitive challenges of the two space programs which had motivated her husband to become an astronaut, and added, "The Russian cosmonauts' wives, my sisters, know only too well what this means. I propose a toast to the wives of spacemen, who share the equally heavy burden of anxieties and honors."

There was loud applause. Titov and Feoktistov, who had accompanied us to Leningrad and stayed with us the entire two weeks, wore smiles almost the width of their broad shoulders.

I should mention at this point that we had one hell of an interpreter assigned us by the government—a tall, red-haired young lady named Anna, whom the boys called Big Red. By the time we left Russia, Anna and Susan were like sorority sisters, exchanging confidences and talking for hours. They became so close that Susan was worried their relationship might get Anna into trouble; what apparently had started as a routine assignment for the interpreter, a historian by profession, had developed into a sincere friendship. At some formal dinners other interpreters were used, but Anna was with us the whole trip.

The reaction to Susan's toast was indicative of another thing we had in common with the Russians: our mutual realization that space exploration involves risk and sometimes sacrifice. Sizov mentioned the Pad 34 fire and said the Soviet people shared our grief at the tragedy.

"And we shared yours when Vladimir Komarov and Yuri Gagarin died," I said. This led to another toast—I think the Russians would offer a toast if you commented on the weather—to space exploration without sacrifices. Incidentally, I made a point throughout our trip of acknowledging Soviet accomplishments in space, and frequently I noted that we had learned much from their successes.

From Leningrad we returned to Moscow on the famed *Red Ar-*

row, the Soviets' crack express train. It was surprisingly plush for a proletarian railroad, looking much like the old Burlington *Zephyr* of my boyhood days.

We arrived back in the capital on July 4, an occasion on which every Russian we met offered congratulations, and began another round of sightseeing and receptions that lasted two days. Susan found the time to get her hair done, and when she returned to our hotel (I don't want to sound ungrateful, but in 1969 any Holiday Inn would have put a first-class Russian hotel to shame) I asked her what it was like.

"It's all self-service," she explained. "You stand in line for a shampoo, wait your turn, and then wash your hair yourself. Next you go to another line and wait your turn in front of the mirrors so you can set your hair and roll it. Then you wait in another line to use the dryers, which you operate yourself."

(When we returned to Russia about two years later, there was a very westernized beauty salon in a vastly improved hotel, complete with stylists!)

It was in Moscow that I first saw real evidence that many Russians, even the military and certainly the cosmonauts, have an inherent respect and even affection for Americans. Considering the anti-American propaganda with which they were indoctrinated and to which they were constantly exposed, I found this remarkable.

We were at a formal dinner, a very swank state reception awash with braid and medals. Titov had gone to get me a drink and I was standing alone when up to me came a Soviet Air Force general who introduced himself in broken but understandable English.

"Colonel Borman," he said, "I know our two countries are not on the best of terms. But I, for one, remember how you helped us defeat Hitler. You see, I flew your P-39s against the Nazis, planes that you gave us. So I want you to have these."

He unpinned his pilot's wings from his ribboned uniform, handed them to me and walked away. I still have those wings, in a display case next to the wings I earned in my Air Force and astronaut years. No incident on our trip touched me more. There is, indeed, a brotherhood of airmen that no propaganda—ours or the other side's—can totally destroy.

I found other reasons for hope on our next stop—Star City, where the cosmonauts live. Here we were Titov's personal guests and we couldn't have asked for a pleasanter host or, I might add, a better friend. The Titovs' own apartment became a kind of central meeting place where we got to know a number of cosmonauts and their wives. The latter were intrigued by the behavior of our boys; they told Susan their own teen-agers had become spoiled by all the notoriety accorded their fathers and were becoming difficult to raise. The modesty and easy yet respectful informality of our sons did us proud.

The cosmonauts were living very well in their own version of the Houston Space Center. By Russian standards, their apartments were luxurious, relatively small but modern and well furnished. They had color televisions, hi-fi equipment, and even their own automobiles, a privilege not common to ordinary citizens; most of them, in fact, drove sports cars. They were obviously considered a very special class, and while they lacked some of the material possessions we take for granted, their standard of living was far above that of the average Russian.

The highlight of our stay in Star City was a party Titov threw for us one of the nights we were there. I don't know how many cosmonauts came but there were a flock of them, including Aleksei Leonov, who was the first man to walk in space. He was a talented artist, and at one point during this evening of fellowship he took a napkin, began drawing something, and handed it to Susan.

He had drawn a dove of peace hovering over the lunar surface, with the words APOLLO 8 printed on the dove.

Everyone called me Frank, and I used their first names as far as I was able to remember them—Titov and I already were on a first-name basis. Inevitably, we got into a discussion of the differences between our two systems of government. We didn't convert each other, but at least we did more debating than arguing and there were a few unguarded moments when I sensed their frustrations and doubts about the rigid Soviet bureaucracy.

These friendly if sometimes intense discussions continued with various cosmonauts for the duration of the visit. Titov and Feoktistov were the ones most frequently involved, but we also talked with other cosmonauts and their wives who might be aboard on a long flight to some Russian city. We even played a game on these flights we called Capitalist Versus Communist, each side getting fifteen to thirty minutes to state its case.

Titov was hesitant the first time we proposed it. He was somewhat on the spot, being our official host and representing all the cosmonauts; he didn't want a goodwill mission turned into a nonstop debating society, and he said as much.

"Gherman," I told him, "we won't be debating or arguing. We're going to do a selling job on one another, so we won't let it get into a situation where we might start arguing. I can't think of a better way to get to know each other. I can't make a capitalist out of you and you can't make a communist out of me, but at least it's a starting point for friendship. Because, Gherman, the only way we're going to end up as true friends is by trying to understand each other. My understanding what you believe in and your understanding what I believe in."

Capitalist Versus Communist turned out to be fun. The cosmonauts ate it up and so did the wives. Yet it was that earlier evening with my Soviet counterparts in Titov's apartment that had really broken the ice and established the foundations of what became a natural give-and-take relationship. Toward the end of the party, Gherman gave me, on behalf of all the cosmonauts, what is now one of my most prized possessions: a splendid double-barreled shotgun. In turn, I presented him with the watch I had on *Apollo 8*, to be placed in the Soviet space museum.

Star City was a self-sufficient complex just outside of Moscow, serving not only as the cosmonauts' domicile but also their training center. We were the first Americans allowed to see it and the layout impressed me—with some reluctance because I was halfway hoping not to be impressed. The facilities included a medical clinic, school, shops, administrative buildings, and the equivalent of an officers' club, where the vodka flowed freely in our honor.

From what I could gather, their training was at least as rigorous as ours, and in the early years of their space program, when no one knew what to expect, it had probably been even tougher. I heard that their training in those days had included such pleasures as exposure to intense heat for up to twenty-four hours while wearing spacesuits, and two weeks in total isolation. When Thomas Canby, senior editor of *National Geographic,* visited Star City in 1986, he was told some trainees had died from stress in those days.

Death, as well as space, was another common ground on which we could meet. The cosmonauts wanted to know all about the Pad 34 fire and I answered as openly and honestly as possible. They, in turn, talked about their two late comrades, Gagarin and Komarov, and their fatal flights. Gagarin in particular had become almost a deity in Russian eyes; the cosmonauts' club had a big color portrait of him, dressed in a spacesuit, hanging on one wall and it seemed to dominate the huge room.

I never did find out if the Soviets have had more space accidents than they're willing to admit. Somehow I doubt it, even though they apparently regard any major accident as an affront to national pride. Crashes of Russian airliners go unreported for months if they're reported at all, unless foreigners happened to have been aboard. The Soviet penchant for secrecy may be extended to space tragedies, but I saw no evidence of it in my conversations with the cosmonauts.

The cosmonauts' wives were as gracious to Susan as their husbands were to me. Those wives all were well educated—several were doctors or lawyers—and all of them worked. Susan visited the child day-care center in Star City, her guides bursting with pride at what they showed her. The center was staffed by attendants in starched white uniforms and the whole place was so clean you could eat off the floor—"It was like walking into a laboratory," Susan related.

She saw tiny tots eating at tables spread with Irish linen, and being taught impeccable table manners. The impression Susan got was of a sterile, regimented environment that was almost frightening. She was asked what she thought of the day-care center.

"I don't like this," she said bluntly. "It's not the kind of environment in which we'd want to raise our children. I hope it never happens to us."

They actually appreciated her honesty and were fascinated by her rejection of what they considered so perfect. Significantly, their reaction was typical of what we encountered all over Russia: people seemed to admire our openness and frankness, even though they seldom agreed with what we were saying. Or maybe they were more surprised than appreciative—candor in the Soviet Union is a rare commodity, and one must remember that the Russians have been taught that Americans are devious and untrustworthy. I like to think our visit may have planted a few seeds of doubt about that.

I would have enjoyed spending more than our allotted two days in Star City but the itinerary was too crowded. What Star City did was whet my appetite for visiting the Soviet launch site some 500 miles from Moscow. This wasn't to be, but almost as a compensating gesture our hosts flew us to Simferopol in the Crimea, sixty miles from Yalta, and from there on a side trip via helicopter to inspect one of their tracking stations.

Flying over Russia is a good way to grasp the country's vastness— the Soviet Union has eleven time zones and I think we hit every one. We welcomed the long flights, however; they gave us the opportunity to chat freely, especially with Titov and Feoktistov, with whom I kept harping on the subject that was my principal mission: to encourage the possibility of a joint U.S.-Soviet space flight. I didn't expect any immediate agreement and I got none—in fact, they were cool toward the idea at first—but they became more interested and even receptive without committing themselves. *Those* seeds were really planted.

Big Red, our chief interpreter, was with us on our flight to Simferopol and a little incident gave us an insight into what it's like to live in a police state. What led up to it was her rapidly developing friendship with Susan. Anna was an atheist but curious about Susan's deep religious beliefs. They already had become quite adept at finding places where they knew they wouldn't be overheard (or bugged).

Anna had a habit of writing down "Susan's Sayings" in a little notebook—pertinent thoughts that intrigued her. During a conversation on atheism, she seized on Susan's remark that God would not deny His children regardless of what they thought of Him. Susan watched her write and shook her head.

"Anna," she warned, "I don't think that's a very good idea."

"Oh, but I want to study this tonight. I love the way you say and phrase things."

"Yes, but you're making me nervous. It's all well and good for me to be saying these things, because you're never going to be held accountable for anything I do. But you *will* be held accountable for anything *you* do, and I don't want you to get into trouble."

Anna scoffed at this idea, but when we flew to Simferopol and deplaned, she left that damned notebook on her seat. She realized her mistake as we were walking toward the terminal and the blood actually drained from her face. She ran back to the plane like an Olympic sprinter and fortunately retrieved it, both she and Susan breathing sighs of relief. I've seldom seen anyone so scared.

While I was inspecting the tracking station, Susan and the boys went by bus to Yalta, where I rejoined them the next day. Yalta in the summer is to Russia what Miami Beach in the winter is to the United States—a resort center, and a very picturesque one, too. It was, of course, the site of the historic 1945 summit meeting of Roosevelt, Churchill, and Stalin, and our hosts took pains to point out that one of the city's principal streets is named Franklin D. Roosevelt.

We went by hydrofoil boat to Artek, where the Young Pioneers—the Soviet version of Boy and Girl Scouts—have their largest camp. I love boats and that trip was something—a noisy but smooth ride at fifty miles per hour over the water. The Young Pioneers were something, too. There were five thousand kids in the camp, all healthy looking, bright, and happy. Yet I got the same impression that Susan had at the Star City day-care center. They seemed so damned regimented, as if their carefully controlled environment was turning them into an army of young robots. They laughed and played games like American youngsters; they also marched like miniature West Pointers, and somehow the sight was depressing.

On the way back to Yalta, we stopped at Massandra, the Crimea's wine-making center. It came as a complete surprise to us that while vodka is the Russians' national drink, they are far prouder of their wines. Massandra has been making wine since 1775 and claims its products are as good as anything the French can offer. I'm no wine connoisseur, but what I tasted was excellent, especially one called the Black Doctor, which had the kick of moonshine.

Of course, we were shown and given their best, and that applied to the food we ate and the hotels where we stayed. By Russian standards, we got deluxe treatment that wouldn't be rated deluxe anywhere else. We always were served fresh fruits and vegetables and plenty of meat, although a Soviet steak is a rather sorry thing—Russian cuts of beef are only distant relatives of what we're used to. We were guaranteed potatoes at every meal, and when the two weeks ended I couldn't look a potato in the face.

First-class Russian hotels are extremely clean, but spartan, with old-fashioned furniture—comfortable, massive, and generally ugly. Lighting was so poor it was hard to read in our rooms, and this was so typical of the contradictions we found in Soviet society—the Russians seemed to have one foot back in the nineteenth century and the other in modern times.

From Yalta we took a six-hour flight to Novosibirsk, a city whose chief attraction is Science Town, a scientific center of the Siberian branch of the USSR Academy of Sciences and located on the fringes of the magnificent Ural Mountains. As we taxied in, I noticed a squadron of MiG-17 fighters parked off to one side. I mentioned them to Titov, who nodded proudly.

"They're a pretty good airplane," he commented.

We got off the plane and were greeted by a Russian general commanding the Novosibirsk air defense area. He handed Susan some flowers and announced, "Colonel and Mrs. Borman—the city is all yours. If you want something, all you have to do is ask."

I said, "Thank you, General. I'd like to start off with a ride in one of those MiGs."

His complexion took on the color of the Soviet flag.

"There aren't any MiGs here," he snapped. "What MiGs are you talking about?"

I pointed to his apparently invisible squadron. "Those MiGs over there."

"Those aren't MiGs!" he insisted loudly.

I caught Titov's eye and he gave me an almost imperceptible shrug, as if to say, "What did you expect?"

That night, we attended a dinner hosted by one of the top generals in the Soviet Air Force. I had been told that this particular officer was slightly tougher than petrified wood—he was known, in fact, as the Russian Curtis LeMay, a compliment I'm sure would have pleased LeMay.

We sat at a U-shaped table so large it almost filled the entire room, which wasn't small to begin with. I was parked at the head of the U, next to the general, with officers of the lowest rank at the extreme ends. The toasting started early in the evening and went on forever, partly in brandy but mostly in vodka. I noticed that the grim-faced general, who looked as if he'd rather be starting World War III, drank either plain water or a very pale white wine.

By the time my turn came for a toast, I was feeling no pain. I rose, glass of vodka in hand and praying the military interpreter I had for this occasion could translate my remarks in terms everyone could understand.

"I want all you people to recognize something I already know," I said, glancing down at the dour general. "General so-and-so is not only a bomber pilot but a candy-assed bomber pilot at that."

The interpreter apparently knew damned well what "candy-assed" meant because the expression on his face was that of a man being tortured. Manfully he translated what I had said and, amid shocked silence, waited miserably for me to continue.

I went on, "I could tell he's a bomber pilot because while all of us fighter pilots have been drinking vodka, he's been drinking wine."

I guess 90 percent of the men at that table must have been fighter pilots, because a roar of laughter swept the room.

The general said nothing. He just filled a large water glass up to the brim with vodka, and poured more vodka into my glass. We linked arms and chug-a-lugged the entire contents, to the accompaniment of cheers and applause. I had a terrible hangover the next morning, but it was worth it.

We had arrived in Novosibirsk after going full speed for a week, both of us drinking too much and not getting enough sleep—I think we drank more during those two weeks than at any other time in our lives. The very next day, Susan became ill.

We were staying at a beautiful *dacha,* or cabin, and when we awoke that morning she could hardly function. Completely exhausted and out of gas, she told me, "You'll have to go without me today—I'm going to stay in bed because I think I'm coming down with something."

She said she felt sick to her stomach and ached all over. Then she began crying out of sheer frustration and fear—we were thousands of miles from home, we knew absolutely nothing about the quality of Russian medicine, and she thought she was ruining our trip. The sight of tears was all I needed. I got hold of our hosts and told them my wife needed a doctor.

They sent two. Both were women, weighing about 200 pounds and built like Chicago Bears linebackers. They wore traditional white medical coats, but in those outfits they resembled a pair of weight lifters dressed up as physicians on Halloween. My heart sank and the only comforting thought I had was that at least Soviet doctors made house calls.

Neither spoke English and their bedside manners fell somewhere between bored and brusque. They took Susan's blood pressure and temperature, exchanged a few mysterious words between them, put her shoes on, and half-lifted her out of bed. Supporting Susan between them, they walked out of the cabin and headed for some nearby woods on foot, one of them carrying a large, thick blanket. That was the last I saw of my wife for several hours, but from what she told me later, I can accurately recount what happened in those woods.

They marched Susan to the edge of a fast-running stream. Communicating mostly by gestures, they voiced the idea that she must get undressed, and helped her disrobe. They then picked her up and plopped her down, in a sitting position, right in the icy water. Strangely, Susan wasn't really frightened—by the tone of their voices, she sensed they knew what they were doing. They kept patting her reassuringly and finally both women took off their own shoes and sat down in the water with her.

After a few minutes of the cold bath, they helped her out of the water, motioned her to lie down under a tree, and covered her with the warm blanket. She fell sound asleep, awoke about twenty minutes later, and felt wonderful. They took her back to our cabin and put her to bed, where she slept the rest of the day. This was all she needed to finish the remainder of the trip completely refreshed. Neither of us ever discussed this unusual treatment with any American doctor, but those two Soviet physicians certainly had made a perfect diagnosis. There was nothing wrong with Susan other than exhaustion brought on by eighteen-hour days, too much drinking, and the tension of being in a strange country on her best behavior. Their prescription was perfect, too—no pills, no drugs, just that icy bath in a running mountain stream and sleep.

With Susan in good (also very large) hands, I went off to visit Science Town, an enormous complex with twenty separate research institutes and also the Soviet Far East's largest computer center. The later fascinated me in its very backwardness—the Soviets were years behind us in computer science, and the equipment I saw on their spacecraft simulators was at about the same stage as what we had used in the Mercury program. But then, maybe they deliberately avoided showing me their most modern hardware. If their current space program is any indication, they may have caught up in sophistication.

We returned to Moscow for another round of receptions, speeches, dinners, and sightseeing, but the most significant and far-reaching event was a private session I had with Dr. Mstislav Keldysch, president of the USSR Academy of Sciences. This is when I made a formal plea for the Soviets' joining us in space exploration, emphasizing the symbolic as well as the scientific advantages of a joint mission. No Soviet official would commit himself to anything without Kremlin approval, but Keldysch was encouraging, as I reported to Nixon and Kissinger later.

On our last morning in Moscow, I had breakfast with Titov and Feoktistov at our hotel.

"Have you enjoyed your visit?" Titov asked—almost anxiously, I thought.

"It was a wonderful experience, Gherman, and I believe we've made some friends. It was important for us to talk."

Both nodded thoughtfully but said nothing.

I continued, "But everywhere I've gone, I get apologies for not showing me things I really wanted to see. It's the system, they explain—I even heard that from you two."

"Frank, I think we've shown you just about everything we have to offer," Titov said defensively.

"No, you haven't, Gherman. When we first arrived, you said the country was mine and I could visit anywhere I wanted. I said there were two things I especially wanted to see: the TU-144 and your launch site. Either would have been a good first step. You probably thought I had forgotten about this, but I haven't. Now we're leaving tomorrow morning and those two very simple requests have not been fulfilled."

They had the good grace to look embarrassed and mumbled a half-baked apology. But later that morning, they came to our room wearing the secretive looks of two kids plotting some prank.

"We have inquired about taking you to the launch site," Feoktistov said, "and it is still out of the question. But we've planned a little surprise for you at dinner tonight."

We were picked up at 6 P.M. in a big limousine and drove for what seemed like several hours. We finally arrived at an airfield and parked in front of a huge hangar. As we stepped out of the car, the hangar doors rolled open.

Inside was the TU-144, gleaming in its white paint. Dinner tables had been set up under the giant wings. The fabled Andrei Tupolev, Russia's senior aircraft designer, was there with his son—the latter had designed the Soviet SST. So I got my tour of the TU-144 with the Tupolevs themselves as guides. The elder Tupolev, well into his eighties, was rather feeble, but it was an honor to meet him. He was responsible for designing more than a hundred different types of Russian planes, yet before World War II he had been declared an enemy of the state and served five years in prison.

That subject, of course, wasn't brought up during the course of the most pleasant evening we had in the Soviet Union. I was an airman among comrades, united by the common experience and love of flight. To pilots, there are no such things as national boundaries; they are only artificial lines on maps. So it was one great way to end our visit.

The final item on the agenda was a news conference at the airport just before we boarded a Pan Am 707. Both American and Soviet reporters were present and most of the questions were concerned with *Apollo 8* and the forthcoming *Apollo 11* mission. By and large, the Russian journalists we met during our visit shied away from political questions, which suited me fine. My emphasis was always on space cooperation, the theme that we are all the earth's children who must try to live together peacefully in one world.

I would like to say there's a great difference between the Russian people and their government. I can't, simply because we weren't there long enough to determine whether it's true, and I have contempt for those who claim instant expertise on the basis of a few days spent in a foreign country. Unfortunately, it was hard for us to know what people were really thinking, and that included the cosmonauts—the secrecy of their society is the most depressing thing about it.

As soon as I got back, I reported to President Nixon personally and he questioned me thoroughly about the trip. I had to tell him I hadn't gathered much technical information on the Soviets' space program, other than what I had been shown in their spacecraft simulators and computer center. But I did urge him to invite some cosmonauts to the United States with no holds barred—I recommended that they be shown everything they wanted to see of NASA's operations. And I also reported I thought the Soviets would be receptive to a joint space mission. I told Kissinger the same thing in a more specific memorandum that suggested joint tracking of space probes; complete advance publication of the trajectories and missions of all scientific probes, manned and unmanned; an international conference to set priorities and assign missions for unmanned exploration of planets; and a joint meeting of cosmonauts and astronauts and associated training personnel.

I also proposed to Kissinger that we invite selected astronauts, scientists, and engineers from the European community and Japan to participate in NASA's future space programs. This was never done to the extent I envisioned, but that memo bore its most important fruits on July 17, 1975.

At 11:09 A.M. EST of that day, an Apollo spacecraft docked in orbit with a Soviet Soyuz spacecraft. Three hours later, Apollo Commander Tom Stafford was shaking hands with Soyuz Commander Aleksei Leonov in the tunnel linking the two modules. Leonov's drawing of the peace dove on the napkin he had given us that night in Titov's apartment had turned out to be prophetic.

The midspace meeting was preceded by months of joint planning, including exchange visits between the cosmonauts and astronauts—the Russians going to Houston and the Americans to Star City. Sadly, it was the only joint mission to date; further cooperation dissolved under the usual hostility and suspicions that have existed between the two superpowers since the end of World War II.

Yet Apollo-Soyuz was still a lone shining moment of friendship in the long, grim years of the cold war—a harbinger of how things *could* be and *must* be on the blue sphere that is one world for all. Which is why I am so proud of a mission I never flew.

14

ANYONE INTERESTED IN HIRING AN EX-ASTRONAUT?

I got involved with *Apollo 13,* the third lunar landing mission, when it was only a few thousand miles from the moon and I was only a few months away from ending my NASA and Air Force careers.

The flight was launched on April 11, 1970. Jim Lovell was commanding, with Jack Swigert and Fred Haise as his crew. It was Haise's first space flight, but he had been training with Lovell for two years. Toward the end of the mission's second day, Lovell cheerfully informed Houston, "This is the crew of *Apollo 13* wishing everybody there a nice evening, and we're just about to close out our inspection of *Aquarius* [the lunar module] and get back for a pleasant evening in *Odyssey* [the command module]. Good night."

Nine minutes later, the number two oxygen tank in the service module blew up, in a blast so violent that it also ruptured the number one tank. *Apollo 13* at that point was 200,000 miles from earth, with the spacecraft's normal supply of electricity, light, and water gone and the oxygen supply drained to the critical stage.

The three astronauts made it back by using the lunar module as a kind of lifeboat—it had its own electrical and oxygen supply, and with a tense Mission Control relaying suggestions and advice, the crew managed to hook up the LM's electrical and oxygen systems to the command module. It took them almost two hours to complete the intricate task, which also involved using the LM's engine as their primary source of power. If that tank had blown up while the lunar module was on the moon, no one would have survived. As it was, the LM was designed to last only forty-five hours in flight, and they had to stretch this to ninety hours in order to get back.

A miracle occurred 200,000 miles in space that night, and it was wrought not only by the crew's bravery and calmness but by Houston's skillful plotting of an emergency return trajectory, plus the instructions it gave on conservation of electricity. This was a team effort if there ever was one, and another tribute to astronaut training.

Right in the middle of all the tension, NASA was notified that Vice President Agnew was coming to Houston, implying to the press that as head of the National Space Council he was going to take charge of the rescue efforts. Bob Gilruth was furious—Agnew's interference was the last thing NASA needed or deserved.

Gilruth summoned me to his office. "Is there anything you can do to keep the Vice President away from here?" he pleaded. "He's just going to distract everybody in the middle of a first-class jam."

"I'll try," I promised, and promptly phoned Bob Haldeman, explaining exactly why Agnew's presence in Houston would be about as welcome as a Martian invasion.

"I'll take care of him," Haldeman snapped.

Agnew was in Iowa and his plane was actually at the end of the runway awaiting takeoff clearance when Haldeman got through to the airport and ordered the vice president to stay out of Houston.

The modicum of clout I possessed around the White House stemmed mostly from the respect Richard Nixon consistently demonstrated toward all the astronauts. Not even Kennedy, whose vision had launched our space program, felt as deeply as Nixon that we were something special—not as individuals so much as for what we represented.

The day after *Apollo 13* ran into serious trouble, Nixon canceled all appointments and stayed in front of a television set in his private quarters. His concern was genuine—he seemed to regard us almost as family. Hugh Sidey, *Time*'s veteran White House correspondent, once observed that whenever Nixon was in the presence of any astronaut or astronauts, "the color comes to his face and the bounce to his step." Sidey and other reporters called it his "moonwalk," and Sidey better than anyone may have grasped the reason behind Nixon's affection for us.

"They are the sons he never had, the all-star teammates he never knew," Sidey wrote in *Life*. "They are the distillers of what Nixon considers to be the best in this country. . . . In his single-minded manner, he seems to be trying to assess and grasp the spirit of the astronauts, almost as if he wanted to bottle it and merchandise it from one end of the country to the other. Nixon has brooded about the nation which ceases to explore, turns in on itself and becomes spiritless."

I have to buy Sidey's analysis. Nixon obviously liked having me around, and as the time drew near for me to leave NASA, through Haldeman he offered me a job on the White House staff.

I was interested but cautious.

"What would I be doing?"

"It would be a position of responsibility," Haldeman said evasively.

"That's fine, Bob, but what kind of position?"

"You'd be at the senior staff level, in a policy-making role."

He refused to elaborate further and I suspect that neither he nor Nixon knew exactly what they had in mind for me except to keep me around. I talked it over with Susan, who liked the President and really admired Pat Nixon. But she confessed to having a nervous feeling about Haldeman, whose standing at the White House would inevitably make him my boss.

"I don't think you should accept," Susan declared. I agreed and politely informed Haldeman I wasn't interested. Yet Nixon wanted an "in-house astronaut" so badly that Haldeman subsequently repeated the offer several times, only to get the same answer.

Politics disillusioned me anyway. Nixon had wanted to give the *Apollo 11* crew a dinner when they got out of two weeks of isolation after their mission. The plan was to hold the affair at the Century Plaza in Los Angeles and the President had mentioned inviting a number of dignitaries who had played some role in the space program. The name of former Vice President Hubert Humphrey was brought up—he had been chairman of the National Space Council under Lyndon Johnson. The hard-liners on the White House staff blew their gaskets.

Flanigan asked me what I thought.

"Go ahead and invite him," I advised. "You'll look good by making it a nonpartisan event."

The dinner itself went off beautifully, and when it was over, Susan and I decided to call on Humphrey. So we went to his suite, where he had a waiter, a bartender, and enough food and beverages to supply a regiment. During the entire night, I think only three people showed up—Susan, myself, and Pete Conrad. Humphrey shrugged off the embarrassment, but I could tell he was hurt.

Through most of 1969 and half of 1970, I was officially field director of the Space Station Task Force, a job at which I spent relatively little time—even then, NASA was shifting its priorities to the space shuttle concept as the major post-Apollo space project. My base continued to be Houston, but I never knew what the White House or NASA might throw at me.

One assignment was being the official host for a small group of visiting cosmonauts—some of the seeds I had planted in Russia were sprouting. Susan and I met their Aeroflot flight in New York and were pleased to find that the group included two cosmonauts we already knew well: Feoktistov, who was acting as the delegation's interpreter, and Beregovoi, who was accompanied by his wife, Lydia, and their teen-age son, Victor. They had wanted to bring their daughter but couldn't get Kremlin permission.

The Air Force had put a twin-engine Convair 580 turboprop at the visitors' disposal and we flew directly from JFK Airport to Washington. No one in the party had ever been to the United States before and I had a blank check from the White House and NASA to give them red carpet treatment.

Victor, who was about the same age as my son Fred, took out a camera right after takeoff and started to snap a picture of Manhattan flashing below our wings.

"No!" his father shouted. "No!"

I interceded immediately. "Take pictures of whatever you want, Victor. And that applies to all of you for the rest of your stay."

Beregovoi looked surprised and I knew then they were in for a culture shock. Their stay in Washington was relatively brief, with time allotted mostly to a White House reception. From the capital we took them to Houston, landing at Ellington Air Force Base, where I caught Beregovoi looking wide-eyed at some parked T-38 jets assigned to NASA. After we deplaned, he was still sneaking glances at the trim little aircraft.

"Come on," I offered, "let's go take a look at 'em."

He hesitated. Here he was, a Soviet Air Force general, and he couldn't believe he was being given a chance to inspect U.S. military planes. They were merely trainers of course, not top-line fighters, but I intended the gesture to be symbolic and it was.

Beregovoi suddenly smiled, and nodded vigorously. We walked around the T-38s for a few minutes.

"If you'd like to take a ride, Georgi," I suggested, "it can be arranged."

Amazement and delight swept over his broad features. He said cautiously, "I'd love to, Frank, but first I think I should get permission from the Soviet Embassy."

To my knowledge, I don't think he ever got a chance to fly any U.S. airplane, but at least he knew my offer was sincere. Of all the cosmonauts I met, Beregovoi had the most clout; at this writing, in fact, he heads the USSR cosmonaut program as Kamanin's replacement. Susan and I went out of our way to befriend him and his wife.

My boys made friends with Victor Beregovoi, who went shopping along with everyone else, and Russians let loose in American stores and supermarkets are a sight to remember. The variety of choices seemed to impress them more than anything else, and these were privileged Soviet citizens. It was an incredible experience for Lydia Beregovoi to be given a selection of twenty different brands of soap. Victor came away from Houston with a supply of jeans and Beatles records. We did get the impression there were certain things they had been warned not to buy, although I was never able to identify specific items. Whey they left Houston, other astronauts took over as their guides for the rest of the U.S. tour. They were shown everything they wanted to see; they turned down an invitation to visit Cape Kennedy, apparently out of honest embarrassment that I hadn't been given the same opportunity.

As busy as various assignments kept me, I couldn't help thinking about what my future would be when I left the space program. My dilemma was simple: I didn't really know what I wanted to do.

I almost decided to go to work for the famous Ross Perot, the Texas multimillionaire, whom I met thanks to a phone call one day from Bob Haldeman.

This was in the spring of 1969; the Vietnam War was in full swing, and the Nixon administration was becoming increasingly concerned over reports that American POWs were being subjected to unspeakably harsh treatment, even deliberate torture. Nixon was hoping to work out some kind of prisoner exchange deal, one that might be arranged by getting the Soviet Union and other Iron Curtain countries to put some pressure on North Vietnam.

My name came up in White House discussions on the POW problem. The thinking was that to put pressure on Hanoi, pressure first had to be put on Moscow, and not through conventional diplomatic channels. What Nixon and his staff were considering was a campaign to muster worldwide denunciation of the way American POWs were being treated, a campaign instituted not by the administration itself but by prominent Americans unconnected with politics.

This was the background to the call I received in Houston from Haldeman. He explained the President's desire to start focusing world attention on the POW situation and told me I should meet with Perot, who was greatly interested in the plight of POWs.

"Sure," I said, and then completely forgot about the conversation until a few nights later when an unexpected visitor showed up at our house; Perot himself, a short, middle-aged man with rather large ears and a burr haircut. Frankly, he looked about as imposing as a Fuller Brush salesman. We invited him to share some hamburgers with us, and for the rest of the evening we talked about the POWs.

We also discussed a plan Perot had for regularly televised "town hall" meetings, which would present both sides of significant issues facing the country. His idea was to have the viewing audience vote by telephone on each issue after the debate; he even envisioned an eventual arrangement by which the audience could vote by pressing an electronic ballot attached to the television set.

He asked me what I thought of the plan. I said it sounded fascinating and would be an incredible means of education and of measuring public opinion.

"I'm glad you like it," he said. "I want us to develop this thing together. And when you leave the Air Force, I think you should go to work for me."

"I'd be very interested," I assured him.

He looked at me thoughtfully and half-smiled. "If you go to work for me, Frank, I want you to be financially independent so you can concentrate on the town hall project and not have to worry about your family's future."

"Easier said than done," I joked. The project was still in a very preliminary, formative stage when I left for Russia. On my return, I found out that Perot had invested $500,000 in my name. I was stunned and called him almost in a state of panic.

"I can't take that money, Ross," I protested.

"You have to take it. You should accumulate wealth so you'll be financially independent when the town hall idea gets rolling."

We took it to the three major networks, but all were adamant in insisting they had to control the programming completely, and Perot wouldn't agree.

So our baby died in infancy. Perot offered me a job with his electronics firm, but I turned him down because I wasn't enamored of the computer field, and I gave back the half-million dollars. We've remained friends over the years.

I did begin thinking, rather vaguely at first, about an airline career even before *Apollo 8*. A couple of months before the mission, I received a call from Floyd Hall, chief executive officer and board chairman of Eastern Airlines, inviting me to serve on the company's Advisory Council—a group, he told me, made up of outside technical and financial experts. There would be no compensation except for pass privileges on Eastern. My friend Jim Elkins, an Eastern director, had recommended me to Hall.

"I don't know a damn thing about the airline business," I pointed out. "I doubt if I could contribute anything."

Hall said, "I think you're wrong. Commercial aviation may have a lot to learn from the space program."

That interested me, so I accepted subject to NASA's approval.

NASA said no. I still had *Apollo 8* ahead of me and possible future missions, and NASA quite properly considered Hall's request an unnecessary distraction.

But Floyd Hall was a very persistent guy. He contacted me again via letter in January of 1969, and this time he suggested hiring me as a special consultant.

"Specifically," he wrote, "I'd suggest that we establish a relationship where, working directly with me, you could assist us in planning and general management of the rapidly advancing technology that is so characteristic of our industry. We would ask you to confer with our senior management and technical people about four times a year, and each conference should not last more than five days. I know that NASA must have first call on your time and we can keep our schedules flexible to meet your requirements.

"Eastern would, of course, reimburse you for expenses incurred in your activities with us. Also, we would pay you a consulting fee at a rate to be agreed upon between us for each project, based on the nature of your participation and the subject under consideration. I believe you would find the airline industry and Eastern Airlines, particularly, most interesting and challenging. . . ."

I was really intrigued and discussed Hall's offer with several NASA officials. After the bureaucratic wheels finally stopped spinning, I ended up with one foot inside the door of an airline.

The compensation Hall and I agreed on was a flat five-thousand-dollar consulting fee plus expenses, and I worked for that money. I attended a number of meetings of a technical committee Hall had established, headed by former Air Force general Bernard "Benny" Schriever, who was also an Eastern director. My introduction to the airline industry was somewhat on the esoteric side, our discussions mostly involving future technology that might be applied to air carrier operations, including new types of commercial planes such as the supersonic transport. On the latter subject, I imparted the skimpy knowledge I had gained from inspecting the Soviet TU-144. I told the committee that when I'd returned from Russia, several Pan Am officials had met the flight and quizzed me on the Soviet SST.

"I informed Pan Am," I related, "that the TU-144 appeared to be economically unfeasible and that I had heard the Soviets were having serious technical problems with it." (In 1973, a TU-144 making a demonstration flight at the Paris Air Show came apart in the air and crashed, a disaster resulting in the permanent withdrawal of the Soviet SST from passenger service.)

As my departure from NASA neared, job offers began appearing—one of them from the Air Force, offering to put me in charge of its own manned spacecraft program, a project still very much in the planning stage. I loved the Air Force and I wanted badly to try my hand at management; besides, the post probably would have called for promotion to brigadier general. Yet I decided against accepting, for a number of reasons.

I knew that because of my involvement with NASA, I hadn't really filled in all the Air Force squares. I had never been in the command structure, I hadn't gone to any command or staff school, I hadn't seen duty in Vietnam, and, most important, I couldn't see any future for a separate Air Force manned space program. There was room for only one, and that was NASA's.

Najeeb Halaby, president of Pan Am and former FAA administrator, suggested I go to work for his airline. Swearingen Aircraft of San Antonio asked if I'd be interested in running that company. Several other aerospace firms made inquiries as to my availability, and I got an offer to join American General Life Insurance Company at a tempting salary.

Too many of these "join us" invitations gave me the feeling I'd be a dancing bear, living off my astronaut fame for the rest of my life. It was a hazard all astronauts faced and one I personally discussed with *Apollo 11*'s crew members before their mission. Susan and I had invited them and their wives to dinner. It was a fun evening, but one mixed with sober admonitions on what they could expect if the mission succeeded.

"Your lives are going to change," I told them. "You have to know now what it's going to be like—all the ticker-tape parades, meeting celebrities and heads of state. You have to make sure it all doesn't go to your head. Your whole family will be affected and they have to understand, too. It happened to us after *Apollo 8* and we didn't even land on the moon."

Neil Armstrong and Mike Collins listened very soberly; they grasped what I was saying, but Buzz Aldrin did not. He thought I was telling them that they were going to make a lot of money out of the moon mission. In the book he wrote later, describing his postflight difficulties, he accused me of misleading the *Apollo 11* crew. Armstrong and Collins heard the same words and judged them as cautionary, not encouragement to get rich.

All I tried to do was urge them to keep the right perspective amid the inevitable adulation—they were going to be swamped with tempting offers to cash in on their popularity by using their names. It takes perspective to realize it's the celebrity they want, not his ability. Big bucks can be tantalizing, but when they involve exploitation, those fat paychecks might mean sacrifice of principles; you become afraid to give up a job you really hate.

But that wasn't the case with my most ardent suitor, Floyd Hall. He wooed me not with promises of fat salaries but with the challenge the dynamic airline industry had to offer.

His proselytizing methods reflected his own personality—smooth, with a touch of deft subtlety. While I was still with NASA he invited me to be his guest at the annual gathering of the Conquistadores del Cielo (Conquerers of the Sky), an exclusive aviation club founded by TWA's Jack Frye in 1939. Originally membership was limited to airline executives, but later was expanded to include officials in air-craft-manufacturing firms and other related fields. So on that occasion I met a Who's Who of U.S. commercial aviation; it was all part of Hall's recruiting campaign, and I had to admit he was really whetting my appetite. I wasn't awed in the presence of these industry giants, but I was impressed by one in particular: big Bob Six of Continental.

A few weeks before I left NASA, Floyd's courtship reached the proposal stage. He offered to make me vice president for Operations at a salary of sixty thousand dollars a year to start. Then he threw in the clincher.

He said, "Look, if you make a success of this, your age is just about right. I'll be stepping down one of these days and Sam Higginbottom [Eastern's president] will move up to chairman. When that happens, you'll become president."

President of what was then the nation's fourth-largest airline! I didn't care that it also was a sick airline, torn by internal feuding. I had talked over Eastern's situation with Jim Elkins and he'd warned me that the company was in trouble. Yet he also urged me to grab any acceptable offer Hall made.

The starting salary he mentioned was about half of what others had offered, but not for jobs that would test my ability to the extent Eastern promised. Floyd offered me a three-year contract but I refused; I wanted to prove myself first. The salary itself was still a vast improvement over the twenty thousand dollars a year I was making at NASA plus the fifteen thousand dollar annual stipend from the *Life* contract that was coming to an end. Nor did I have to worry about expensive college educations for my sons—Fred would be entering West Point in the summer of 1970 and Edwin, a high school senior, planned to follow his brother there when he graduated.

So on July 1, 1970, I joined Eastern Airlines. I hadn't been in Miami a month when the White House sent me on a worldwide tour to meet with heads of state and seek their support in getting Hanoi to improve POW conditions. The plan Bob Haldeman had talked about earlier, when he asked me to meet Perot, was finally being put into action.

I informed Floyd Hall of the mission, conceding that it was pretty poor timing to go charging off on a diplomatic mission when I was trying to adjust to airline life.

"By all means go," Hall said immediately, which was typical of him. Of all the airline officials I have known, Floyd Hall had the greatest sense of corporate responsibility to public service. Higginbottom, however, wasn't happy about my going.

Before leaving, I was briefed by both the State Department and CIA Director Richard Helms, the latter providing some classified and frightening details on what the POWs were going through. Organized barbarism was what it amounted to, and I wished the college kids who thought only Americans committed atrocities could have heard what Helms told me. By the time I left, accompanied by an Air Force colonel who served as a kind of aide, the mission had become a personal crusade.

The trip turned out to be Mission Impossible, and I received a bitter lesson in international politics, particularly in countries regarded as America's friends. Of all the nations I visited, democracies and Iron Curtain countries alike, only two expressed total support: Britain and West Germany.

Socialist Sweden is supposedly one of the world's most progressive nations. The late prime minister Olof Palme used our meeting to launch into a lecture on the evils of American capitalism, which he said had led to the Vietnam War. Never mind what was happening to thousands of young men whose only crime was fighting for their country. Palme was utterly hostile and hypocritical. When I reported the negative results to the U.S. ambassador, Brud Holland, he nodded in complete understanding. Holland, a black former All-American football player at Cornell, told me, "Never in all my days in the U.S. have I encountered such racial rejection and discrimination as I have in this so-called enlightened society of Sweden."

In Russia, the red carpet of 1969 was now the icy sidewalk of 1970. All I heard was *nyet*. Nothing could be done, America was the aggressor, and so on *ad nauseam*.

Then there was India. Ambassador Kenneth Keating took me to see Prime Minister Indira Gandhi, who graciously served us a delicious tea. This was followed by the most militant anti-American speech I ever heard, a vitriolic tongue-lashing that left me shaking. I tried to counter her outrageous statements without becoming abusive, but I had to call on every iota of self-restraint.

When Keating and I left the room, my blood pressure was in orbit.

"Mr. Ambassador," I said between gritted teeth, "that's the worst reception I've had on this trip. If the rest of her country thinks the way she does, I don't envy you your job."

Keating grimaced. "That's nothing. Today is the first time I've been able to see her in so long I can't remember when the last time was. If it hadn't been for you, I couldn't have gotten in the door."

Despite all the negativism I encountered, the news media were my allies—their coverage of a well-meaning mission achieved what I was unable to accomplish on the diplomatic level: world awareness of POW mistreatment. When I returned, Nixon arranged for me to speak to a joint session of Congress, and that's what I told the lawmakers. I hadn't achieved anything except publicity, which, in the long run, might make a difference.

Maybe it did. A few years later, when a number of POWs were released, several took the trouble to call and thank me for my efforts. One was a former POW named John McCain—the same John McCain who is now a U.S. senator from Arizona. But at the time, I felt I had failed. I came back exhausted, not a little disillusioned, and the only bright spot was that at long last I could really start my airline career.

The airline I had joined had been ailing since the dawn of the jet age in 1958. Up to then, it had earned an enviable reputation for operating efficiency and an unenviable reputation for the poorest passenger service in the entire industry. It was a carrier molded in the image of the benevolent despot who had run Eastern since 1935: Edward Vernon Rickenbacker—Captain Eddie.

He typified the old breed of airline pioneers, so dominant in personality and methods that their companies became mirror images of the men themselves. Thus did Eastern become a company whose planes ran on time with almost excessive punctuality—Rickenbacker thought nothing of scheduling a 3 A.M. departure time because he hated to see any aircraft sitting idle on the ground. That it was an inconvenient time for travelers didn't bother him one bit, which reflected Captain Eddie's cavalier attitude toward his passengers.

He thought serving free meals on planes was a waste of money. For years he balked at hiring female flight attendants, arguing that they didn't stay on the job long enough to warrant the expense of training them. Passenger complaints were treated in accordance with Rickenbacker's airline philosophy: Eastern's sole job was to fly from Point A to Point B as frequently and safely as possible—let the other airlines do the pampering.

So indifferent was Eastern's attitude toward passengers, it became the only carrier whose service prompted the formation of an anti-airline club. It was known as WHEAL, for We Hate Eastern Airlines. Yet far more destructive to Eastern's welfare was Captain Eddie's attitude toward the technology of the jet revolution. He mistrusted the jets to such an extent that after ordering six DC-8s, he allowed arch-rival Delta to take over their delivery positions with the excuse that those early models were underpowered. This delayed the airline's entrance into the jet age by almost a year, a period in which Delta took the jetliners Rickenbacker didn't want and used them to clobber Eastern on competitive routes; Delta's dominance over Eastern, in fact, dated back to the assumption of those delivery positions.

Supposedly, the decision had been made by a majority vote of the executive staff. Captain Eddie had passed out slips of paper on which each vice president was to write "Wait" or "Don't wait," and hand them back to Rickenbacker for the tally. He examined the ballots and announced that the majority had voted to wait. After the meeting, the vice presidents got to talking among themselves and discovered that only one man had sided with Rickenbacker.

During the explosive postwar expansion of the industry, Eastern's predominantly north-south route system remained stagnant; the airline couldn't beg, borrow, or steal a decent new route. The drought was blamed largely on Captain Eddie's avowed dislike for all politicians, Democrats being his favorite target. He hated Franklin Roosevelt, had contempt for Harry Truman, and openly backed Senator Robert Taft against Dwight Eisenhower—it was no wonder he was persona non grata at the politically appointed Civil Aeronautics Board, which was handing out route awards.

The irascible old lion who had molded Eastern into the nation's fourth-largest carrier was not without supporters. Within Eastern itself, especially among older employees who had never known any other leader, he was a beloved father figure. He was capable of great acts of individual kindness; his gruff manner hid a large, generous heart and he regarded the airline as his family. Ironically, the deep affection in which he was held contributed to Eastern's dizzying skid—the same employees who worshiped him aped his indifferent attitude toward passengers, resulting in surly service to the public.

Malcom MacIntyre became Eastern's president in 1959, Rickenbacker retaining his post as chairman of the board. MacIntyre, a capable disciple of American's C. R. Smith, didn't have a chance.

Captain Eddie began by looking over his shoulder and wound up openly interfering, while Eastern continued to go downhill.

Rickenbacker, a man with old-fashioned values and a giant-sized sense of integrity, was simply a nineteenth-century American trying vainly to cope with twentieth-century problems. Eastern's directors finally dethroned him after too many years of red ink and a soiled public image. They also fired MacIntyre.

The new head of Eastern was Floyd Hall, a former TWA captain who had demonstrated unexpected marketing skills after being promoted into TWA's management ranks. Hall was passenger oriented and under his guidance TWA blossomed into an airline known for superb service.

Floyd turned Eastern around brilliantly, with major improvements in passenger service and refurbished aircraft that also sported a brand-new exterior color scheme, the blue "flying hockey stick" motif that at this writing still adorns Eastern's fleet. In a relatively short time he eradicated Eastern's image as an indifferent airline, and he accomplished this on what amounted to a shoestring budget. The president of WHEAL showed up in Hall's office one day and tore up the organization's charter.

Hall formed one of the most brilliant executive teams in the industry. It was populated mostly by men roughly his own age, with his own ambition and his own drive. But in building that team, he unwittingly invited conflict and feuds among officers as strong-willed as he himself. As Hall's reforms took effect and the airline began to prosper, the team fractured into a collection of all-stars, men of great talent but also men seeking their own destinies—each jealous of his prerogatives, each fighting for his own policies and programs. When Floyd hired me, the team was already disintegrating.

And this was the atmosphere into which I entered.

PART THREE

1970–1988

15

THE NEW KID ON THE BLOCK

Sam Higginbottom assigned me my first mission at Eastern.

He called me into his office right after I returned from taking a thirteen-week course in modern management practices at the Harvard School of Business. Going back to school was Floyd Hall's idea, part of his orchestrated plan to prepare me for bigger and better things.

It was an interesting course, but it hadn't prepared me for the hot potato Sam threw at me. Contract negotiations between the company and the pilots' union were stalled and the pilots were staging slowdowns, such as deliberately delaying flights by complaining of dirt on cockpit windshields.

"You've got labor relation experts for that stuff," I protested. "The only time I've ever dealt with a union was telling the workers at North American they couldn't drink beer during lunch breaks."

"Our negotiators can't get to first base with the pilots," Sam insisted. "You're a fresh new voice they might listen to, so go settle the mess. Those slowdowns are killing us."

I went in and settled the mess, but not in the way Higginbottom wanted. I was naïve and inexperienced in a highly specialized field, and I also was overoptimistic. These were *pilots* I'd be dealing with,

I reasoned. Fellow birdmen. Devoted, mature professionals as concerned with Eastern's welfare as any fighter pilot would be with his squadron's.

I learned quickly that many airline pilots were a different breed from the airmen I had known in the military and NASA. Love of flying was a common denominator, but their motivation was entirely different. To military airmen and astronauts, missions came first and material rewards ran a poor second, while most airline pilots simply reversed those priorities.

In the end, I basically agreed to extend the pilots' 1968 contract, adding a few minor improvements that the union happily accepted. What I didn't realize were the implications of that 1968 agreement. It had saddled Eastern with the lowest pilot utilization in the industry, and extending it couldn't have come at a worse time.

The airline was in the process of taking deliveries on new DC-9s and 727-200s, stretched models, which put many pilots back into transitional training for the new aircraft. This, combined with generous work rules under the new contract, left Eastern so short of crews that we had to cancel trips right in the middle of the peak winter season.

Higginbottom was furious. He wasn't angry enough to fire me (although I heard he actually considered it), but he did propose reducing my incentive compensation—a bonus arrangement vice presidents were entitled to receive based on performance. Then he changed his mind and simply gave me a "below average" performance rating, which Floyd Hall rejected as unfair.

Hall pointed out it wasn't my fault that the new planes were being delivered at a particularly inopportune time considering pilot availability, or that Higginbottom had put me on the spot by having a greenhorn negotiate a difficult labor contract. Sam relented and changed my rating to "satisfactory," which restored the full incentive bonus. (One of my first acts when I became president was to abolish the bonus; rewarding executives on the basis of largely subjective appraisals by fellow officers is a lousy system of compensation.)

The disagreement Higginbottom and Hall had over my vice presidential debut was no big deal. Yet it reflected an animosity between the two men that had been developing since Sam became president. Although corporate headquarters was in New York, he began building a potent empire of his own in Miami.

I wasn't blind. The friction was obvious and I had no intention of getting involved, nor did I intend to let my inexperience expose me to any further criticism. I decided to wait, learn, and listen—to find out what was wrong with this airline before making waves outside my own department.

My first impressions of Eastern were dismal. Coming from the military and NASA, I was expecting a more austere environment; what I found was a plush and structured operation, full of committees and policy groups that met once a month apparently only to argue over whether Miami or New York was right about something. The new General Offices building typified Eastern's proclivity for spending a lot of money on unessential trappings—to me Building 16 looked like the Taj Mahal to begin with, but after it had been occupied for some time, it was given a complete redecorating job.

Eastern's management style was a long way from what I was used to at NASA, where the guy who had all the information and knowledge was directly involved in staff meetings, answering questions fast. At Eastern, the man who knew all the answers had to sift his expertise through three levels of management. Eastern seemed unable to make decisions rapidly.

As soon as I joined the airline, I told every person working under me that this wasn't the way I was going to run Operations. This caused some natural resentment—I was the new kid on the block, telling them I was going to do a lot of things differently.

I didn't give a damn. I had no way of knowing then whether Eastern's stratified structure was symptomatic of the whole industry or just peculiar to this company, but I respected men like Bob Six and I couldn't believe he or anyone else would run an airline the way Eastern was being run.

Things were being done that defied common sense. The airline spent $200,000 on options for two Concordes, British-French supersonic transports that at supersonic speeds had an optimum cruising altitude of 60,000 feet. We had no transcontinental or transatlantic routes at the time, so if we flew a Concorde between New York and Miami—Eastern's only prime long-haul route—by the time it climbed to 60,000 feet it'd be ready to start the descent.

Then there were the executive perks, like a private Lockheed JetStar that top officials used when they had to travel on company business. I commented to another officer, "We already have two hundred and fifty jets—what the hell do we need it for?"

He explained Eastern had acquired the executive jet at a rock-bottom price, a gesture of thanks from Lockheed after the airline had chosen the L-1011 widebody jetliner over the DC-10.

"We think it can pay for itself by chartering it out," he continued. "We have charter contracts for Southern Bell and the Robins drug company."

"Do we use our crews?"

"Sure, our pilots fly it."

I wondered how you could make a charter operation profitable if the pilots were being paid on our union's wage scales. Or how expensive it must be trying to maintain one airplane of a single type. It seemed crazy, and I began noticing that every time senior officers had to go somewhere, they'd take the JetStar—it wasn't available for many charter flights.

I used it a few times myself—it *was* convenient, especially if you had business in a city Eastern didn't serve—but I filed that JetStar in the back of my mind as one of the dispensable toys I'd like to get rid of someday. Snickering employees were calling the plane "the Wings of Sam," an unflattering takeoff of Eastern's "Wings of Man" advertising slogan.

I even went along with other ostentatious perks, like the fancy company rental cars Eastern offered all its officers, which contributed to the employees' image of executive fat cats. I used one myself. If I had fought perks openly, I would have been history. I didn't have any clout and I would have ruffled every feather in Building 16. But when the time came to set policy from a position of strength, I decided, those cars were going to disappear from the premises.

Like all other airlines, Eastern had an annual projected profit plan—an advance blueprint of how we were supposed to make money in the forthcoming year. I attended meeting after meeting and heard Floyd, Sam, and most of my fellow vice presidents reach the invariable conclusion that in order to make money, we had to cut the payroll. And the target of that strategy was always the service part of the airline—baggage handlers, agents, reservations personnel, and so on.

This made even less sense than ordering two supersonic transports. These profit plans could only be fulfilled by degrading the product we were trying to sell. Cutting costs was one thing; cutting them in the airline's most vulnerable area was asinine. Furloughing reservations agents was a good example. It simply added to the workload of others, increased the time it took to answer the phones, and irked potential passengers so that we lost business.

I came into the job full of idealism and naïveté. I thought both management and the work force would have the same fervor I had: to produce the best product possible, improve profitability, and subjugate short-term gains to long-term security. The unions sure as hell didn't have that fervor, and to my surprise neither did senior management. What most of the officers failed to realize, especially Hall and Higginbottom, was the incongruity of furloughing or firing hundreds of employees while supporting executive cars and a private jet. This had to affect morale and cause resentment. I remember the behind-the-back glares Sam got when he'd drive his Rolls-Royce into the ramp area.

I spent a lot of time during my first year traveling around the system, getting the feel of the airline. I talked to hundreds of employees, many times during middle-of-the-night shifts, and I always came away with a great deal of admiration. Eastern's men and women were tough and hardbitten, especially in the northeast region, but they were basically solid pros who took pride in their work. I tried my damnedest to make them realize they were meeting not with an astronaut "celebrity," but with a guy genuinely interested in their jobs and their opinions of the airline. Once I got my message across, they opened up.

I enjoyed meeting Eastern's pilots, my experience at the bargaining table notwithstanding. They, too, were a collection of pros, intensely proud of Eastern's safety record. As individuals, they were my kind of people. As union members, however, they were a different breed of cat. On an early flight I took on Eastern, before I became a company negotiator, the pilots' slowdown was in force. We had just pulled away from the gate when the captain announced, "We have to change runways, so there will be a forty-five-minute delay."

To me, this was the equivalent of stealing from the company. He had deliberately delayed the flight by canceling his takeoff clearance and getting assigned to another runway, which was not only unprofessional but childish and petty. After we landed, I introduced myself to the captain and blew my stack.

"That runway change was phony and you know it," I said angrily. "You guys are defeating your own purpose. Delays get passengers mad, and when we lose passengers it's eventually going to hurt the pilots."

"You don't understand our position, Colonel," he said calmly. "These delays get the company's attention."

Yet the pilot wasn't any more shortsighted than some members of senior management. If union greed was anathema to me, so was company complacency. A healthy, prosperous, well-run carrier has little to fear from labor. Eastern was light-years away from being healthy, prosperous, and well run.

Sam Higginbottom told me once, in sheer frustration, "Frank, this company is almost impossible to manage."

He was right. What both he and Floyd refused to admit was the reason. They had allowed Eastern to become a fractured airline, run with hopeless inefficiency by two constantly battling factions. Hall had his own staff and headquarters in New York; Sam had his own staff and headquarters in Miami. They even had separate public relations men who loved to leak stories to the press that were derogatory to the other clique.

Floyd Hall personified Class. He was an intellectual at heart and looked the part of an erudite modern executive—always impeccably dressed, with a dapper little mustache that reminded me of Adolphe Menjou's. But there was a vein of toughness beneath the sartorial perfection, a kind of mailed fist inside the velvet glove. Basically, he was a troubleshooter who relished challenge. But having met that challenge, he tended to climb into a corporate ivory tower, concentrating on esoteric projects far removed from day-by-day concerns.

Eastern for years had centered operating headquarters in Miami but kept corporate headquarters in New York. Floyd loved sophisticated New York with its theaters, opera, museums, and financial institutions. This two-headed airline worked for a while, but when Hall hired strong-minded Sam Higginbottom as president and chief operating officer, the two heads began growling at each other. Sam had his own ideas on how Eastern should be run and he thought some of Floyd's actions questionable—such as spending a half-million dollars to have Eastern serve as a Metropolitan Opera sponsor.

They began feuding over everything, from scheduling to aircraft purchases. Each accused the other of being a spendthrift, and the tragic truth was that both were right. It was Higginbottom who insisted on operating the JetStar. It was Hall who insisted on maintaining a fleet of limousines to carry VIP passengers to and from the

New York area airports. And while they were fighting over who was wasting the most money, Eastern was the loser.

I was far closer to Hall than to Higginbottom, even though I was based in Miami, and I had tremendous admiration and affection for Floyd. Soon after I came to Eastern, however, he started downhill himself—there were marital problems compounded by ill health. It was apparent he wasn't the Floyd Hall whose enthusiasm and dreams for Eastern had prompted me to choose an airline career.

The competing empires in New York and Miami created pockets of dissension throughout the management core. Almost every officer had his own orbit; every faction had its own leader. There was absolutely no management cohesion and this magnified what was clearly one of the airline's major problems: the hold the unions had achieved on the company's finances.

For a while I got along reasonably well with Sam, who was having a difficult time with Floyd. Something would finally be decided at those interminable committee meetings, Higginbottom would report the decision to Hall, and Hall would decide something else. All I knew was that we were doing a hell of a lot of things with no cost justification.

After six months, Floyd promoted me to senior vice president for the operations group, and the word "senior" carried some authority. Not as much as I'd have as president, but sufficient within my own department to start stepping on a few tender toes. I caused enough waves around Building 16 to generate an oft-repeated comment: "What's old Moonman gonna do next?"

I had flight operations reporting to me, as well as engineering and maintenance. The contract I had helped negotiate with the pilots was saturated with unproductive work rules, and within the boundaries of that agreement I tried to improve crew scheduling methods, ending up with a once-a-week meeting at which we managed to achieve some limited progress—that damned contract was a straitjacket.

Scott Crossfield, my old foe at North American, was now working for Eastern and I ran afoul of him when I began looking at some of Floyd's futuristic projects. One of them was Crossfield's baby. Eastern had an expensive contract with the British firm of Decca to develop a so-called area navigation system that Hall believed could be adopted to the airline's famed Shuttle in the Washington–New York–Boston corridor. The theory was that the Decca system would free the shuttle from conventional air traffic control, combining area navigation with STOL (short takeoff and landing) aircraft.

On paper it looked great. Hall and Crossfield envisioned the shuttle being operated with a fleet of STOL planes taking off and landing at downtown terminals, not only reducing traffic congestion at the regular airports but saving valuable time. The first problem, however, was that no manufacturer had produced a satisfactory STOL aircraft, and another was that there were no suitable midtown airfields. This failed to deter Crossfield, who urged that the Decca area navigation system be installed on Eastern's conventional shuttle planes.

"We'd save enough for the system to pay for itself," he argued.

"Fine," I said. "Let's test it for six weeks and see if you're right."

The six-week test showed that the time saved was infinitesimal, and I canceled the whole area navigation project. Decca was angry and Hall wasn't exactly happy—Crossfield had mesmerized him with the system's imaginary potential. Then I derailed another of Scott's pets: involvement in NASA's space shuttle. He actually had a couple of people monitoring the shuttle program and reporting to him on its progress. I reassigned Crossfield's two space cadets to work on airline engineering matters and that left Scott without a job.

I can't recall a single instance of Floyd remonstrating or overruling me in any major action I took as a senior vice president. Maybe he was too busy quarreling with Higginbottom, but a more logical explanation is that he had lost touch with the realities of what was happening to the airline. Part of this was due to his being in New York, and I was convinced he had reached the point where he was simply enjoying the trappings of power. I doubt whether he even realized how much he had changed. He never varied from the image I always had of him—a class act and a gentleman—but he progressed further and further into left field.

The core of Eastern's growing financial mess was easy to spot: Labor costs, the major controllable costs the company had, represented 40 percent of overall expenditures and the company had allowed the unions to manipulate the airline into becoming the highest-cost carrier in the industry. Items like fuel, landing fees, facility rentals, and so forth didn't differ among the airlines. But labor costs varied from contract to contract, and every succeeding contract carried a higher price tag than the previous one.

In the regulated airline industry, the common practice was to pass these increased costs on to the public in the form of boosted fares. I perceived this as a vicious circle, at best a temporary expedient that had to hurt in the long run. And higher fares didn't solve Eastern's problems; it was impossible to raise fares enough to offset the unproductive work rules dictated by expensive union contracts—like forcing the company to put three mechanics on a job that required only one, or union refusal to let a mechanic cross over to another area of maintenance even though he was perfectly capable of performing the other task.

Even as I steadily absorbed the reasons for Eastern's weaknesses, I bided my time when it came to making waves of major storm variety. I knew the game was going to be won or lost on how we could motivate the work force, but even as a senior vice president I couldn't do much from my limited power base. I was suspect among a lot of the top brass anyway, some of whom thought Floyd had hired a figurehead astronaut whose main job was to hand out free cuff links bearing the airline logo to visiting VIPs. Floyd didn't think that way, of course, but for a while I believe Sam did and he resented me. Admittedly he was in a tough position—I was supposed to be Hall's boy, yet I was reporting to Higginbottom.

The "Moonman" epithet was symbolic of how some regarded me. Yet a number of officers knew I had accomplished more at NASA than flying around in space. I had been a troubleshooter and a good project manager with a reputation for getting things done. Overall, my astronaut background was more of a plus than a minus.

So for three years, I carefully walked a tightrope between the Hall and Higginbottom factions. Emotionally, I gravitated toward Floyd, but I wanted no part of the destructive internecine warfare going on. It was an uncomfortable and discouraging situation—watching the airline's decline without being able to help forestall it was emotionally draining.

Only to Susan did I confide my frustration; around Building 16, I kept my feelings and opinions to myself, and my actions were confined to my own department. The only "Borman faction" in Miami consisted of me and my secretary, a tiny super-efficient blonde named Toni Zahn, who had worked for me in the astronauts' Houston office.

Only Susan—and perhaps Toni to a lesser extent—knew how discouraged I was becoming. But on the night of December 29, 1972, I learned something about Eastern Airlines and its people that gave me new hope.

* * *

Flight 401, a Lockheed L-1011 TriStar, was on final approach to Miami International after an uneventful trip from New York. As the big aircraft descended, the crew noticed the nose gear indicator showed that the wheels were not down and locked. Suspecting that the indicator light might be faulty, the captain decided to check the gear visually.

He put the plane on autopilot, in level flight holding at 2,000 feet, and sent the flight engineer and a maintenance technician riding deadhead in the cockpit into the forward electronics bay where the gear could be seen. As both pilots peered into the bay to see how the flight engineer and technician were progressing, the co-pilot inadvertently pressed against the control yoke with enough force to disconnect the autopilot. Neither realized that the L-1011 had gone into a gentle descent.

In Miami Approach Control, a controller watched the tiny blip representing Flight 401 move slowly across his green radar screen and his eyes narrowed. Next to the blip suddenly appeared the letters "CST," meaning coast or sea level.

The controller, thinking the plane might have landed, asked 401 if it needed emergency equipment—the captain had reported possible landing gear trouble before Approach Control told the flight to hold at 2,000 feet until the nature of the apparent malfunction was determined.

There was no reply.

The blip disappeared.

"Eastern 401," radioed the alarmed controller, "I've lost you on the radar. . . . What's your altitude now, Eastern 401?"

Silence.

Flight 401 had flown into an Everglades swamp.

It was after midnight when I got the call. I had already gone to bed and when the phone rang, I had a sense of dread—it was axiomatic in the airline industry that phone calls to an executive in the middle of the night usually meant disaster.

"Colonel," the voice said, "this is System Control. I think we've lost one."

I snapped wide awake. "We've what?"

"We had an L-1011 go off the radar screen on final approach. We think it's down in the Everglades."

"I'll be right over."

By the time I arrived at the System Control Center, it was clear that Flight 401 was down, but no one knew exactly where. The only known fact was that the plane had crashed in a virtually inaccessible part of the Everglades and no rescue crews had reached the site yet— the authorities were still mobilizing Coast Guard helicopters and all other available emergency units.

I hadn't planned to go to the scene, but as we waited in vain for some word of possible survivors, my impatience finally reached the breaking point. "Charter a helicopter," I told the System Control director. "Maybe we can find that plane."

I boarded a two-seat chopper at Eastern's ramp area and we flew toward the Everglades, following the tentative bearings System Control had obtained from the Miami tower. It was pitch-black, but we saw a couple of Coast Guard copters just ahead of us, growling their way toward a few dim lights barely visible on the ground.

"Where the hell can we land?" I asked my pilot. "There's nothing but swamp down there."

"Let's see if we can find anything solid," he suggested. He turned on his landing lights and spotted a small hummock, just large enough to squat on. It was about 150 yards from the crash site, and when I stepped out of the chopper I was up to my chest in swamp water and saw grass. I heard cries for help and started wading toward the voices.

A few rescue helicopters were arriving amid a scene of mass confusion and horror. All I could do at first was try to comfort the survivors—and thank God there *were* survivors. Many were sobbing, some were holding up well, and a lot of them were in shock. The dead and dying were all around.

I stumbled on a heavyset man trapped in a tangle of twisted metal. "Help me, help me," he moaned.

I tried to move the wreckage away from his pinned body, but it wouldn't budge. Someone came over to help, but we still couldn't free him and he died right before our eyes. I crawled into what remained of the once luxurious cabin and found more survivors, one of them a woman who kept screaming, "I've lost my baby!" I mumbled some meaningless words of reassurance, put my arms around her, and futilely looked around for the baby. I talked gently to other stricken victims and left the plane to see what else I could do.

The smell of kerosene mixed with swamp odors was sickening. Why the plane hadn't burned was a mystery—apparently the impact into water at a relatively gentle angle had prevented the fuel from exploding. By now, additional choppers were hovering overhead and it was obvious we needed some semblance of control to keep them from running into each other in the dark. By using flashlights, I organized a makeshift system of ground control, motioning the copters when and where to land. There was almost no solid ground on which they could put down, and we stood near the few available hummocks signaling them with the flashlights.

I spent the rest of the night assisting people into helicopters, the seriously injured going first. When I was satisfied that there were enough rescue personnel on the scene, I finally left on one of the last choppers. With me were two flight attendants from the crash—I had watched them work with the survivors and I was immensely proud of them. Also aboard was the stricken woman who had lost her baby. We flew straight to a hospital where the flight attendants and the grieving woman could be examined, and I returned to Building 16.

There was only one shower in the whole place—in the plush office Hall used when he was in Miami. I took a shower, put my filthy, soaked clothes back on, and drove home, my brain clogged with memories of that terrible night. I can find no words to describe adequately the carnage of a major airline accident. I had seen crashes before and death was no stranger, but this one was different. It involved my own airline and one of our own planes filled with trusting passengers.

The next day, Eastern's people had to face the handling of victims and their families. Humaneness guided every action. We dispatched various officials to hospitals where they handed out cash for the incidental expenses of survivors and their families. Later, we gave every survivor an additional five hundred dollars along with a formal notification that the money was "a pure gratuity and not a release, a settlement of any claim, or a set-off against any final settlement."

I assigned Frank Sharp, our veteran vice president for passenger service, to coordinate our efforts to help ease the pain and grief that are the tragic residue of every fatal accident. An injured Japanese woman, whose husband had been killed, spoke no English and had neither friends nor relatives in the United States—the couple had been vacationing. We located one of our flight attendants who spoke Japanese and the widow gave her the names and addresses of her mother and brother. We arranged for their air transportation from

Tokyo to Los Angeles, where the same flight attendant met them and accompanied them to Miami. The mother stayed in the attendant's home until the widow was ready to leave the hospital.

The Miami morgue was so understaffed that it couldn't handle all the work of victim identification. Eastern paid for additional morgue workers and I sent some of our people to help. We even summoned the president of a barbers' college to one of the hospitals so one survivor could get his beard trimmed. When other barbers refused to make hospital calls, one of our own officers—Madison Kelly—personally shaved an injured victim.

Humaneness included stationing airline representatives at every hospital to make telephone calls, shop for clothing, and perform countless other chores of simple kindness. We weren't trying to forestall lawsuits—hell, we knew lawyers would be coming out of the woodwork—we were trying to show human decency and understanding toward innocent victims.

Personally, I felt our settlements, both voluntary and those resulting from litigation, were fair. Legal niceties aside, however, people had been killed or injured in an Eastern aircraft (of the 163 passengers and 13 crew members aboard Flight 401, 93 passengers and 5 crew were fatally injured), and I swore I'd do everything possible to keep that nightmare of December 29 from happening again.

I was grateful for a letter I received from Higginbottom a few days after the crash. "Please accept my warmest personal thanks for your magnificent contributions to the bereaved families and to this company during the trying days following the accident," he wrote. "You have earned the respect and gratitude of our passengers and their families, as well as your fellow employees."

My fellow employees had earned my own respect and gratitude; they were magnificent and gave me my first real glimpse of an airline's spirit in the worst kind of crisis. For the first time I felt encouraged and believed that this airline, even riddled with inept management and uncaring unions, deserved to be saved.

"You know," I told Susan as if I had just made a miraculous discovery, "this airline has some great people." Out of tragedy had come a deep love for Eastern, not as an inanimate corporation, but as a living entity made up of a gallant, spirited army of human beings.

The Everglades crash, the first fatal accident involving a jumbo jet, was the last thing an embattled Sam Higginbottom needed in an airline steadily coming apart at the seams.

The big Lockheed L-1011 TriStar was one of his major headaches even without the accident. This great bird was nothing but a turkey in its initial months of service. Eastern was the first carrier to introduce the new jet in late fall of 1972, having ordered thirty-seven of them two years before I came to the airline at a cost of $800 million—the largest financial investment for aircraft in the airline's history.

I went out to the Lockheed factory in Burbank before we took delivery of the first aircraft and test-flew one. It was hard to judge the plane on the basis of a single brief flight, but I was impressed. Its handling qualities were excellent. It was also a very sophisticated airplane, with complicated electronics systems, a few steps ahead of either the 747 or the DC-10. When it came to landing an L-1011 in bad weather, you couldn't have asked for a better plane.

When we put it into service, however, our new bird proceeded to lay king-sized eggs; the L-1011 went far beyond normal phase-in troubles. The chief villain was its Rolls-Royce RB-211 engine, so unreliable that we suffered a nightmare of delayed and canceled L-1011 flights.

It was easy to spot a major source of what became an epidemic of engine failures. Rolls-Royce was using turbine blades made out of forged metal, and the blades simply couldn't stand up to the enormous heat generated by a jet engine's combustion—hot enough to melt lead in a fraction of a second. Pratt & Whitney as well as General Electric used casting instead of forging, a far newer technology for manufacturing the crucial blades, but for a long time we couldn't convince Rolls-Royce that forged blades were absolutely wrong.

We finally had to set up a highly specialized L-1011 maintenance program, mostly involving frequent blade inspection, but engine reliability continued to plague our TriStar fleet until Rolls finally admitted that forged blades were a mistake. The British swallowed their pride, asked Pratt & Whitney to help them develop a casting technique, and eventually our engines were modified. But this took time; throughout 1973, Eastern's L-1011s were a collection of flying deficits.

Higginbottom, the plane's biggest proponent, took the blame for its poor performance. As far as I was concerned, it was largely a bum rap. At the time Eastern had bought the TriStar, the whole industry was stampeding in a rush to acquire widebody jets. The thirty seven-aircraft order turned out to be excessive, but not in the context of the jumbo fever that swept the airlines in the late 1960s and early seventies.

Nor could Sam or anyone else have foreseen the L-1011's operational problems. On paper it was a superb aircraft, equal to the competing DC-10 in most areas and even superior in a few. And the whole L-1011 experience gave me an insight into one of the most difficult and risky areas of airline management: aircraft selection.

An average of four to five years elapses between the signing of a contract for a new type of airliner and putting it into service. In that period, traffic projections made at the time of purchase can fall far short of predictions, and the carrier winds up with an overcapacity fleet. Unexpected technical problems can hurt public confidence. And in some instances airplanes that look great on paper turn out to be lemons.

I didn't regard the TriStar as the worst aircraft in our fleet. I awarded that dubious honor to the Boeing 727-QC—the QC standing for "Quick Change." It was a standard 727 designed for fast conversion into an all-cargo aircraft, and in theory it was a wonderful idea. You could fly the plane all day in passenger service, strip out the seats in less than two hours, and operate it all night long carrying freight.

Eastern had forty-six standard 727s—designated 727-100s—and twenty-five QCs, these sixty-one aircraft constituting approximately one fourth of our entire fleet. However, in order to carry cargo the QC had to be built stronger than the standard 727, and the additional weight boosted its operating costs to unacceptable levels. Air freight wasn't that lucrative to begin with, and even with low fuel prices the QC was only marginally profitable when flying passengers.

Every time I looked at a report on the QC's operating costs, I wondered why we had bought this unprofitable, overweight hybrid. One night in late August, 1973, I flew up to La Guardia Airport in New York, where a 727-QC was scheduled for a midnight passenger-to-cargo transformation. I wanted to witness the process firsthand, hoping to find some justification for its use.

The conversion was about half-finished when an agent came up. "Colonel, System Control's been trying to reach you. Your wife's been taken ill."

I called home and my son Fred, on leave from West Point, answered. "Dad," he said in a voice he obviously was trying to keep calm, "Mother's in the hospital. Can you get back here fast?"

"As fast as I can," I promised.

I raced over to Operations and with sinking heart discovered we had no scheduled flights leaving for Miami at that late hour. I was about to check on other airlines when one of our dispatchers ended my frustration.

"Colonel," he said sympathetically, "we've got an L-1011 being ferried to Miami empty. She's ready to go and you'd be home in less than three hours."

Two hours and forty minutes, to be exact, during which time I sat in the cockpit jumpseat wondering what had happened to Susan.

Dr. Julio Serano, Eastern's chief medical officer, met me at Coral Gables Hospital, where she had been taken. He told me bluntly, "She has had a nervous breakdown. She is very sick and needs help."

Susan was under heavy sedation and I wasn't allowed to see her until the following morning. I stood by her bed and took her hand. She looked up at me.

"This has been going on for a long time," she murmured. "Frank, I want to get better. I'll do whatever it takes."

16

SUSAN

When Susan married me, she also married a man who may have been the most competitive brand-new second lieutenant in the whole United States Air Force.

I was someone driven not by materialistic demons but by an intense sense of duty. This, Susan quickly learned, was the central, unyielding force that overrode everything else in me.

She was not, by a long shot, the most competitive wife in the USAF. Yet she acquired as if by osmosis my single-minded philosophy of duty, honor, and achievement. She absorbed my intensity day by day, and directed this new, determined energy only toward matters that concerned me and my career. I was the focus and nothing else counted. We both knew that.

I never had to tell her, in so many words, "I'm going to succeed and as my wife you're going to help me succeed." I didn't have to. She accepted the idea—more than accepted it. Early in our marriage, someone gave her a copy of *The Army Wife*, the bible for anyone who marries into the military. She pored over that book. She swallowed it whole—every sentence, every paragraph, every page, every "suggestion" which became a command. A command about wearing her party manners at all times. Participating in officers' wives' activities. Keeping her children neat and well behaved. Deferring to the spouses of officers senior to her husband, even though in her heart she might consider some of them a collection of Lucretia Borgias.

Susan absorbed it all as holy scripture. In 1950, it *was* holy scripture to a young Air Force bride as dedicated to her husband as she was. She didn't resent the imposed discipline, the regimentation, the negation of self. In fact, she enjoyed it because it made her a part of my career. When there were separations and setbacks, uprootings and evaporation of important friendships, she did as I did—accepted it all as par for the course. She rode every punch because to do otherwise might have hurt me.

It was excellent preparation for becoming the wife of an astronaut, for she took this disciplined behavior into the space program. At first it was exciting. One day she was only one of a thousand wives at Edwards Air Force Base, and the next she was a member of a very small, elite group of women: the astronauts' wives.

She simply continued playing her Air Force role—the perfect military wife who never complained, kept any fears to herself, raised two fine boys of whom I was inordinately proud, and subordinated everything to my career advancement. My priorities were hers.

During the Air Force years, Susan bought my "it always happens to the other guy" philosophy. The trouble was that it kept happening to the other guy all too often. At bases like Nellis and Moody, we seemed to be going to some pilot's funeral at least once a week. And every death chipped away at the protective veneer she had erected around herself to keep away the dreadful realization that Frank Borman could be "the other guy."

She would not accept the possibility of my dying. At thirteen, she had lost her father in a nightmare of illogical unreality, and she sure wasn't going to lose the husband who subconsciously had taken his place. In a masterpiece of self-delusion, she went marching blithely in the other direction. She sent me off on every mission with the Air Force smile on her face.

It wasn't too difficult for her to be the archetype of an Air Force wife. She was something of a loner anyway, and she relied on our boys for all her emotional security. We were very, very lucky to have those two guys—they were born good, and I'm not being naïve. Susan once told me that she and our sons grew up together.

Like almost every Air Force family, we were nomadic, with no real roots except within the family itself. Fred and Edwin took my flying and frequent absences in stride—all their friends were in the same boat and what would have been an abnormal way of life to other kids was completely normal to them.

Whatever stress Susan felt, she repressed. She had been brought up by a mother who sacrificed much for her children, kept her troubles to herself and always smiled. Susan did the same and neither Fred nor Edwin ever suspected anything was wrong, even during the astronaut years when their mother, unknown to me, found her confidence eroding.

In fact, they showed stress before she did, starting with *Gemini* 7 when they were present at the launch. Their ages had a lot to do with it. Fred was twelve and Edwin eleven when it suddenly dawned on them, at the moment of the thundering, fiery lift-off, that they might very well lose their father. Susan knew what was happening. Without any warning or preparation, they were undergoing a combination of fear and unaccustomed celebrity, which were connected; if it was their father's turn to die, this was something they would have to share with the public.

The boys never discussed their fears with me. They took their repression cues from Susan, I'm afraid, just as they took their public behavior cues from me—they, too, accepted my 100 percent commitment to Duty, Honor, Country.

I knew there had to be some fears and I tried to allay them. I told Susan just before the *Gemini* 7 launch, "I'd give anything in the world to give you the confidence I have."

But, I realized later, this was a vain hope. Every vestige of confidence disintegrated when that gantry rolled away and they saw that naked rocket standing there poised for blast-off, a proud yet fearful sight. When the countdown reached eight, Fred grabbed his mother's hand, a tiny gesture of mutual reassurance.

"Come on, Mom," he said, "you know everything's gonna be okay."

So my family kept their anxieties to themselves. That was the expected form. Nobody in the astronaut community discussed anything with anybody. The astronauts' families went through that whole nine years of the Gemini and Apollo programs with smiles pasted on their faces, and too often they were phony smiles. That's the way NASA wanted it; that's the way we husbands wanted it. You *will* do your part even if it means wearing a fixed smile, a cosmetic paint job hiding inner pain.

The astronauts' wives, I realized much too late, didn't even share their true feelings. They played it cool with each other. The fierce if friendly competition among their husbands—about who was going to be assigned to command or go on what mission—spilled over onto our wives. They kept their own counsel, never complained or explained, no matter how they really felt. They faithfully followed a large book of unwritten rules, the first commandment being: You'd better be the healthiest, best-adjusted woman in the world, with no complaints whatsoever.

Keeping an awful lot to themselves took its toll physically, emotionally, and mentally. It was hard enough to maintain the Perfect Wife image for the benefit of their husbands and NASA, but the difficulty was compounded by the public relations requirements of their goldfish bowl existence. They were the astronauts' wives, spouses of men already or about to become famous, yet they also were fairly average women plunked down smack in the middle of worldwide attention. Each one was expected to appear to the public as the Perfect Wife married to the Perfect Husband who was a Perfect Astronaut in a Perfect American Family raising Perfect Children. But how they were supposed to accomplish this was totally ignored.

All anyone seemed to care about was the required result; the means were left to them. So they went along like programmed robots. Tragically—and it *was* tragic—our wives didn't understand that they had been assigned Mission Impossible. Although no one really wanted to be categorized as perfect, they had no deep comprehension of what this blind obedience was doing to them—the price they'd have to pay.

It was the Pad 34 fire that cracked Susan's armor. By then, Fred and Edwin were in high school with their own lives. Susan and I had become exceptionally close to the Whites. When Ed was killed and everyone was supposed to keep a stiff upper lip, Pat and Susan broke down to each other and realized they had been building their own emotional prisons.

In fact, that's when a lot of the wives began to grasp the impossibility, the futility of trying to maintain that stereotyped image. I know now that Ed's death brought it home to Susan. There was something very special about him. He really was the astronaut's astronaut, a handsome and powerfully built man who actually seemed indestructible. He and I were very much alike in our devotion to our families. When Ed died, it hit Susan—for the first time with that much strength—that I wasn't immortal, either. The space program, she suddenly realized, *was* dangerous and she was just as vulnerable as Pat White. For weeks after the funeral, Pat kept saying in a dazed voice like an incessant drumbeat, "Who am I, Susan? Who am I? I've lost everything. It's all gone."

And hearing her reach out so desperately for comfort, Susan thought, *My God, this could be me.*

We buried eight astronauts in three years: the three killed in the pad fire, four who died in plane crashes, and one in an automobile accident. After the fire, the tensions between husbands and wives increased, and to meet this mass emotional crisis Dr. Chuck Berry and his staff began handing out the tranquilizers. But the boundaries had been breached; the divorces started, right and left.

Susan was not immune to what was happening all around her. But she stayed away from pills and she never contemplated the divorce route—she loved me and the children too much to break up the family that way. Yet the pressures on her rose and rose. Some escape valve had to be found and hers was alcohol. Liquor became her crutch, a refuge of temporary forgetfulness, a means of coping with the absolute conviction that I wasn't coming back from *Apollo 8.*

One night during the mission, she was alone in our kitchen, her mind churning. In a kind of weird rationality, she thought, *If they don't get the* Apollo 8 *crew back safely, the press will really have a field day. Three dead astronauts circling the moon . . . They'll stage a big funeral in absentia, but I'll be damned if they're going to tell me how to run it.*

Goaded by what she perceived as the certainty of my impending death, she got out some paper and began writing feverishly. At that moment, Edwin walked into the kitchen.

"Mom, what are you writing?"

She said very calmly, "Your father's memorial service. He might not come back."

Our teen-age son, wise beyond his years, gently took the pen from her hand. "Just remember, Mom," he said softly, "Dad gets to choose the way he goes—you and I don't have that privilege."

Only then did Susan realize that our sons were facing the possibility of their father's death with their own brand of quiet courage, a kind of inner strength that Susan feared she lacked.

When Pat White committed suicide in 1984, both Susan and I felt very strongly that if Ed had been killed in Vietnam, say, or in any other way but that pad fire, Pat could have lived with her loss and would still be alive today. She was the last victim of Pad 34. She might even have survived if the space program had been what I first perceived it to be—merely the logical extension of the Edwards flight test program, with the astronauts regarded more as test pilots than as demigods whose families were required to conform to their exalted status.

Few people, if any, understood what our wives were going through, and I include the astronauts among those wearing blinders. Dody Hamlin of *Life* magazine came close to recognizing the unique strains on their morale and security, yet I doubt whether even she grasped the enormity of what was happening to them.

The one person who understood the astronauts' wives best was Dee O'Hara, the chief nurse at NASA's medical center in Houston. She was the sole individual in whom they could have confided, but unfortunately few if any of them ever did—that in itself would have been regarded as a sign of weakness. Nor, I suppose, would it have done much good. No nurse, not even a head nurse, was likely to win a confrontation with the medical brass by telling them they were doing a lousy job with the astronauts' wives. But Dee knew about them—believe me, she did.

Meanwhile Susan drank, that crutch being absolutely essential to maintain the grin-and-bear-it personality she had so carefully constructed. No matter what she was feeling—loneliness, insecurity, or sheer terror—I could count on the fingers of one hand the number of times she shed tears in front of me. I never suspected drinking had become a problem. Hell, everyone drank, including me. But for her, alcohol was anesthesia against the pain of stress.

Why did she never say anything to me? Because at that stage of our lives, it wouldn't have done a damned bit of good. This was Frank Borman she was married to, a man determined to complete whatever the Mission happened to be. I would have been upset if she had confided what was eating away at her. I would have tried to be sympathetic in my hard-nosed way, but I would have told her as nicely as I could, "Just pull yourself together, Susan. I'm going to be fine and you must stop worrying." I actually expected her to be strong, and considering the Academy Award performance she was putting on, I suppose it was a logical assumption on my part.

As a matter of fact, if I sensed she might be wavering, I'd really give her the Duty, Honor, Country spiel. It happened just before

Apollo 8 when I told Susan I had given a producer permission to have a television crew in our home, filming the family's reactions to the mission's progress for a documentary. She didn't want them there and told me so. I overruled her in no uncertain terms. I said I was sorry but it was good for the space program and this was the way it was going to be.

End protest. This was the way it was going to be. But not until weeks after her breakdown was I given any insight into her true feelings. She began telling herself, *I'm not big enough to handle all this. . . . I'm not sophisticated enough to carry it off. . . . Everyone may think I am, but I'm not, really. . . . I may appear that way, but why doesn't somebody see beyond how I look when I'm playacting and see how terrified and lonely I am?*

She was crying for help, but it was a cry I didn't hear. Once, at Edwards, she went through a shaky time when I was flying F-104s. She knew we were using obsolete pressure suits and this was one of the rare times she couldn't hide her concern. But when she mentioned it to me, I said something that at the time went over her head.

"Look, Susan," I remarked, "there's more to life than just living."

It was a simple equation for me. I was willing to give my life because the exciting and worthwhile challenges of my job outweighed the dangers. And I expected my family to understand and accept this uncompromising commitment. An adequate, satisfactory answer to her fears, I thought.

I was wrong. Once Susan became convinced she had to keep hiding her fears from me, she was licked. Gradually, she began to blame herself. She decided, wrongly, her problems were her own fault. She felt she wasn't up to what I expected. So she went inside her self-created prison and locked the doors.

I didn't grasp any of this until long after her breakdown. She did a beautiful job of hiding everything from me. She drank in solitude, possessing enough willpower never to appear intoxicated either in public or when she was with me. My frequent absences made her masquerade even easier, especially when I was in Downey redesigning the Apollo spacecraft. I was gone almost the entire year and ours was mostly a telephone relationship.

The few times I managed to fly home, they were usually overnight visits that didn't even seem real. Susan and the boys tried hard to make them perfect, maybe too hard in the sense that they didn't discuss family problems because they thought such problems would have appeared petty compared to what I was going through. It was no wonder I didn't suspect anything was wrong.

Most of the wives began leveling with one another after the fire, although this newborn honesty didn't help Susan much. She and Pat White talked a lot. Fay Stafford was a good friend and so was Barbara Young. Yet Susan remained pretty much a loner.

When Susan and I went to Russia after *Apollo 8,* she was surprised to find the wives of the cosmonauts shared the same fears and frustrations as their American counterparts. Thanks to our wonderful interpreter, Anna, Susan had several lengthy conversations with these fine women. They, too, were uncomfortable with their fame and they were especially concerned with its effect on many of their older children, who were giving their parents problems because they enjoyed the attention.

Susan couldn't keep suppressing her insecurity forever and not have something snap inside. Often she'd get physically ill from the internal pressures building up. She had no self-confidence and appearing in public became torture because she could never be herself. Experiences that should have been exciting and memorable turned into ordeals.

The post–*Apollo 8* European trip and the visit to the Soviet Union were typically ambivalent events for her. They were wonderful, but for Susan they also were filled with stress that totally escaped me, absorbed as I was in the purpose of those goodwill missions. I didn't know she was constantly asking herself questions. Had she said the right thing? Were her gloves clean? Did she have a run in her stocking when she met royalty? Was her dress appropriate for the occasion? Had she done me proud? She never felt relaxed and to this day regrets missing so much on those two trips because her insecurity kept shoving pleasure aside.

Insomnia became a problem during the astronaut years and continued after I left NASA. Yet she didn't dare take sleeping pills. I told Susan once, "No pills around this house. If you can't sleep, go outside and walk until you're tired and sleepy."

Susan had been rather proud that she was one of the few astronaut wives who wasn't swallowing Valium as if it were aspirin. But she continued to drink and alcohol became an antidote for insomnia, too. She was still able to fool me because once I joined Eastern I was away often and saw relatively little of her. The airline was now my latest mission; I was traveling as much as ever and working just as hard. I knew I was going to be Eastern's president and I was training myself for the post with the same intensity that had marked my astronaut career.

So when I was home, Susan was the same as always; she had been the Perfect Air Force Wife, the Perfect Astronaut's Wife, and now she was skillfully playing the part of the Perfect Airline Executive's Wife. Eventually, though, her facade crumbled. As she confided to me after the nightmare was over, she reached the crisis stage when both Fred and Edwin were at West Point. Her mind had reached the unassailable conclusion that neither son really needed her anymore. This reasoning progressed to the next logical conclusion: I didn't need her anymore, either. She had two sons on their way to successful military careers and a husband who was soon going to head one of the world's largest airlines. The rest of us had our lives in order and Susan, her self-esteem eroded, considered herself excess baggage.

So all this self-recrimination and drinking led to a nervous breakdown. Susan later remembered virtually nothing about being hospitalized briefly in Miami. But she did remember that she'd been angry with me, with her father for dying when she was so young, and with the whole damned world. And that was the attitude she had when she was admitted to the Institute for Living in Hartford, Connecticut, a privately run rehabilitation facility for substance abusers.

The senior psychiatrist at the Institute was Dr. Richard Brown, a compassionate, brilliant man in his sixties who became Susan's new father, her guru, her whole world. If men like Webb, Gilruth, and Kraft were giants to me, Dr. Brown was her own personal giant.

He was about my height but more slightly built, and the calmest person we ever met. Very gentle and exceptionally soft-spoken, he exuded a kind of inner peace that commanded instant trust. He was about to retire from active practice, but he took Susan on as a personal favor to me.

The Institute for Living looked for all the world like a typical New England college campus, needing only a few students carrying books around the tree-studded grounds to complete the picture. The ivy-covered buildings were of that classic English architecture that ages so gracefully. Although it took Susan awhile to appreciate it, the whole atmosphere was one of serenity, and it went with Dr. Brown's personality as if he had created the surroundings himself.

It took six weeks just to get my wife back into decent physical shape. Like almost every person exposed for the first time to institutionalized treatment, she thought she'd been cured right then and there. Six weeks of being pumped full of vitamins and healthy food, all in a protected environment of loving care and totally severed from the world that had given her so much trouble.

She wanted to go home, but decided to stay after Dr. Brown warned her that if she didn't get to the bottom of her illness, she'd be back every six weeks for the rest of her life. It was a tough decision that took great courage—Brown told me, in fact, "You'd better start praying that she stays here."

And I told Susan, "I want you to come out of there a whole human being and I don't care how long it takes."

Thus began three months of intensive therapy—an eternity for both of us, yet shorter than what Dr. Brown himself anticipated; when she had first been admitted, he'd thought she might have to stay a year. Susan's relatively fast response to treatment and counseling was typical of her own fortitude.

In the end, she understood herself. She not only had her frailties exposed but knew how to cope with them. And she understood her loved ones better as well. The painful experience helped me, too—I had many long talks with Dr. Brown, as part of a cleansing process through which Susan and I both came out of the ordeal better persons and more in love than ever.

When it became apparent that the therapy was taking hold, I was allowed to visit her. We took long walks together through the Institute's magnificent grounds, holding hands like two college sweethearts. And we talked. I felt tremendous guilt, but I faced it with honesty. I promised to be more understanding and I agreed it was absolutely essential that we communicate better from then on.

At the time, Susan didn't know that Dr. Brown also was constantly advising and counseling me. He made me realize that I was involved; I had been part of her illness and I had to be part of the cure. The first eighteen months after she left the Institute were crucial to her complete recovery and I tried to help her through this period, away from the controlled supervision of a hospital, when it would have been so easy for her to slip back.

A friend told Susan recently, "If Frank had married anyone else but you, someone who wouldn't have bought all that Duty, Honor, Country stuff, he couldn't have achieved what he did."

Susan smiled. "He would have gone through at least two divorces, but he still would have been a great test pilot, a famous astronaut, and a prominent chief executive of an airline."

No, it was Susan Borman, not Frank Borman, who had to change. Dr. Brown taught her that. I softened, yes. I communicated more. I let her share my career and my problems to some extent, but I also encouraged her to find her own direction. And the day she stopped drinking, so did I.

Susan established some goals and priorities of her own, yet without affecting the devotion and support she always had given me. She is stronger now than she's ever been; the difference is that she's doing it for *us,* not just for me.

Almost as soon as I became president of Eastern, I instituted a rehabilitation and counseling program for employees with alcohol and drug problems. It was one of the best in the industry and she was proud of me. No prouder than I was of her, however. I never wanted to sweep what had happened to her under a rug. I bragged about her recovery before friends to the point of embarrassing her. To me as well as to her, it was a victory we had won together.

She's not afraid anymore, but if she were, I know what I'd say: "What can I do to help you grow out of those fears? Let's examine them. If it's something you don't want me to do, I won't do it."

I thank God she sought and got the help she needed when she did. If ever there was a time in my life when I, in turn, needed the support of a strong, healthy, and understanding mate, it would be during the momentous, turbulent years at Eastern.

17

"I'LL DO MY BEST"

Call it soul-searching, introspection, or self-analysis, I don't care which—all I know is that I did a hell of a lot of thinking during the long weeks of Susan's confinement.

I've never been one to dwell on the past. Mistakes are something you learn from, not worry about. But this time I *had* to think about my involvement in her breakdown, about the twenty years of what I'd glibly assumed had been as happy a marriage for her as for me. It was difficult to admit that I had to share the responsibility for what had happened. I knew damned well I always had put Mission and Job ahead of my family. Yet it was equally difficult to admit that it couldn't have been any other way.

I was a man forged by the West Point experience, with Duty, Honor, Country branded on brain and soul until it achieved the status of lifeblood itself. I was a husband and father who had established irrevocable priorities that defied compromise. And now I was looking at the price tag and asking myself whether any mission was worth what I had inflicted upon my wife. My guilt was chasm-wide and just as deep.

While she was running her obstacle course at the Institute, I buried myself in work, traveling constantly, and when I wasn't on the road I was virtually living at the office. But keeping busy was no antidote for guilt and grief. There still were too many hours in which to think, and a hundred memories of Susan's loyalty kept flooding my mind. Sometimes even the little things hurt, insignificant in the broad picture of a marriage but painful recollections to me of how Susan had always subordinated herself to what I wanted.

I thought about that time I'd built a five-and-a-half-foot gas-powered model airplane while we were stationed at Williams AFB. It was a thing of beauty, and I put a timer on it so the tiny engine would cut off after a few minutes and allow the plane to glide to earth near the launching point. The first time I launched it, the timer didn't work and the plane flew out of sight. I tramped around the Arizona desert for hours without finding it and finally came home in a black mood—weeks of work destroyed because of that damned two-dollar timer.

Susan didn't say a word, but after I left for work the next day she got into the car and drove from ranch to ranch asking if anyone had seen my model airplane. She was pregnant with our first son at the time and the ranchers thought she was crazy. She never did find it, yet just trying was an act of love.

It was painful to remember little incidents like that. And painful recalling more important events. Shortly before she was hospitalized, Lockheed had asked me to accompany a small engineering and sales team to China; the Chinese were interested in acquiring some U.S.-built transport planes for their national airline and Lockheed was trying to sell them the L-1011, of which Eastern was a major user.

Susan went with me, but at our first stop in Singapore she became ill with a bad case of the flu. So what did her mission-oriented husband do? I left her in Singapore, went to China with the Lockheed group, and met Susan in Tokyo on the way home. There had been too many such instances of my work obsession.

When I was finally allowed to see her at the Institute, I had the first of many sessions with Dr. Brown and mentioned such examples as this and the time I skipped spending Thanksgiving with my family just to fly an officer to Washington for a date.

"That's why I feel so culpable," I told him. "I've always put the Mission and flying first. And now I feel terrible guilt. I'm still the same guy I was in the Air Force and NASA. I even work weekends at Eastern, trying to catch up and learn the business."

I paused, suddenly remembering something else. "You know, I took Susan's picture with me on *Apollo 8,* the same one I had with me on *Gemini 7.* Neither time did I even look at it. I just didn't want to get distracted from what I was doing."

"Not much of a distraction," Brown commented.

"Maybe, but it would have been for me. It would have represented the conflict I've wrestled with all my married life—Mission versus Family. Looking at her picture would have reminded me of the conflict and I didn't want to be reminded. Not during any mission or any flight."

At every session I had with him, the question of that conflict came up. Once, a little discouraged at Susan's slow early progress, I became desperate.

"If I've been putting too much pressure on her," I blurted, "I'll quit Eastern. I'll do whatever it takes to help her get well."

He smiled. "Frank, you'd be crazy. Working hard is simply your lifestyle and quitting Eastern won't help Susan. You just pushed her too hard, beyond her limits, but she's going to be all right. Stop feeling guilty, forget your sorrow, and go back to the airline. Work harder than ever if you want to. But make certain the demands you place on Susan are explained—that the job really justifies the time you spend away from her. When we get Susan all straightened out, everything will fall into place."

"I'll try," I promised.

"I hope so. She needs the same kind of support she's always given you." Then he hesitated, his eyes twinkling. "I'm curious about something, Frank. More than once you've brought up this conflict of weighing the importance of a mission against your responsibilities to your family. Tell me, have you been asking yourself lately if the missions were worth it?"

"Many times."

"And what was your answer?"

"They were."

He chuckled. "I would have been surprised if your answer was no."

While Susan still was at the Institute, our son Fred had to undergo major surgery for a tumor on his upper spinal cord. With Dr. Brown's permission, I picked her up in Hartford and we spent several anxious days at Walter Reed hospital in Washington until his surgeon finally told us he'd recover. It was another terrible ordeal for Susan, but she came through like a trooper.

* * *

I took Susan back to Hartford and returned to the floundering airline. Every weekend, however, I'd fly to Hartford to spend time with her—taking long walks, always talking and planning and *communicating*. In effect, we renewed our marriage vows—only I tossed in an extra vow of my own, namely never to let it happen to her again. I didn't stop working hard, but I began to set aside time for her.

Then I managed to strike a blow on her behalf. I was invited to address the annual convention of military flight surgeons, an audience composed of doctors from every branch of service.

"Boy, you're letting the fox into the chicken coop," I warned the convention official who asked me to speak.

I spoke off the cuff, but I remember the gist of my remarks very well. "I want to tell you something," I said. "This doesn't go just for my wife and my family but for every military wife and child whose problems and feelings you've been ignoring since time immemorial. This whole country has ignored them for too damned long. We talk glibly about the sacrifices the military men make, but how about their families? What have you doctors ever done for the lonely wives of SAC crews? For the wives of astronauts? For the wives of submariners who are alone while their husbands are under some ice pack for six months?

"I'll tell you what you've done, absolutely nothing. They need support, understanding, counseling, help. We train our military personnel to do their jobs, fly their missions, perform their duty. But we don't help their families to cope with the hardships and stresses of being married to the military."

I don't know how much good that speech did in terms of specific reforms. At best, I probably didn't accomplish much more than get people thinking, make them aware that their responsibilities as flight surgeons didn't stop with the men.

Susan's illness did more than remind me of my own failings. As tough as it was on her—and on me, to a far lesser extent—we were lucky. She recovered fully and our marriage not only survived but became stronger. Such a happy ending is not the usual case, however—broken homes are a far more common way of military life. I'm not the only guy who has let duty override everything else. Our real sin is the assumption that the family members back home can handle their lives, an inevitable but dangerous assumption. Support for the families must come from somewhere else, in the form of orientation, preparation, and aid if needed—a kind of basic training for military wives, you might call it.

And maybe for the wives of airline executives, too. For I was about to take over Eastern's destiny.

Sam Higginbottom resigned in a letter submitted to the directors on October 1, 1973.

Sam jumped without being pushed; he'd known his days were numbered since several of the most influential directors, in the spring of '73, had bluntly told Floyd Hall he had to spend more time in Miami and work things out with Higginbottom—which, freely translated, meant they wanted Hall to start running the airline.

Floyd balked at first. The strange thing about their relationship was that Hall honestly liked and respected Sam. He correctly suspected that Higginbottom would perceive his presence in the Miami bastion as interference and lack of confidence; immediately Sam threatened to resign. Floyd urged him to stay and Higginbottom said, "I'll give it until October."

It was an impossible situation. The lid blew off in September when *Business Week,* the *Miami Herald,* and *The Wall Street Journal* all published articles on Eastern's declining fortunes, each tagging Higginbottom as the villain and implying he was about to be ousted.

Sam hit the ceiling. He accused Jonathan Rinehart, Eastern's vice president for Public Relations, of planting the damaging stories—and when he accused Rinehart, he was accusing Hall. It was no secret around the airline that Rinehart was Floyd's boy and intensely loyal to him.

Almost simultaneously with this donnybrook came a decision by Hall and the senior vice president for Marketing, Tom McFadden, to hire hundreds of additional reservationists, ticket agents, and ramp personnel. At the time, Eastern was compiling losses that by the end of the year would amount to more than $50 million, a staggering figure for that day.

Sam's letter of resignation angrily criticized "the hiring and spending policies practiced in recent months and still being practiced," adding that taking on additional manpower would "not significantly contribute to a higher quality product."

He reminded the board that Eastern had too many historic handicaps: one of the highest break-even load factors in the industry, too

Susan during the flight of *Apollo 8*

I was the one who had the electric razor. On the *Yorktown* after *Apollo 8*.

Receiving congratulations from President Johnson while aboard *Yorktown*. Lovell and Anders still haven't shaved.

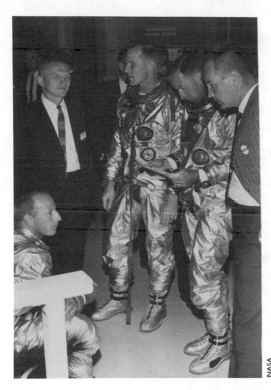

Left to right: Me, Ed White, and Lovell; *lower left:* Pete Conrad. Taken during a briefing at North American shortly before White's death.

NASA

With President Nixon during my White House liaison days

The Bormans meet Pope Paul. We treasure the fifteenth-century Bible he gave me.

A fellow bird lover—Senator Barry Goldwater—and one of the few pictures I have of myself in Air Force uniform after I made colonel

We visit the Soviet Space Center.

Testifying before a Senate subcommittee on airline
deregulation in 1977

Senator Goldwater tries to squeeze into a "deregulation
seat." That's Senator Howard Cannon about to try it, too.

Taken during my happier days at Eastern. I'm meeting
Newark-based mechanics after VEP went into effect.

"Now, if you'll just shave a little off the price . . ."
Meeting with Boeing officials in Seattle as we negotiate
the 757 contract.

Charlie Bryan in action at a shareholders' meeting after
the airline was sold

With Frank Lorenzo at a news conference following his
purchase of Eastern

Family portrait—with
our sons and their wives
and children

Grandfather Frank et al.

The Frank Bormans today

many years of low to medium profits, an enormous debt structure, and a very competitive, essentially short-haul route system that ran primarily north-south and relied too much on Florida vacation traffic. All true, but when I saw his letter, I wondered why he hadn't in-cluded among those "historic handicaps" Eastern's unrealistic and unproductive labor contracts.

So Floyd Hall assumed full command. He purchased a condo-minium in Miami and then moved the majority of his New York corporate staff down there, resulting in even worse friction. The 1973–1974 period became known as the carpetbagger era, and the label fit perfectly. Rinehart, as soon as he arrived in Miami, held a PR staff meeting and informed his underlings, "The only criterion is loyalty"—meaning, obviously, loyalty to Hall.

As a matter of fact, Floyd insisted on putting public relations un-der McFadden's marketing division, robbing it of its independence and fanning the discord. I stayed out of the feuding and bickering and continued, within my still limited sphere of authority, to clean my own house.

One of our top men in flight operations was a veteran pilot and something of a legend around Eastern. Everyone loved him to the extent of forgiving and forgetting his chief weakness: the bottle. I tried reasoning with him, lecturing, scolding, and eventually threat-ening. He refused treatment and continued his heavy drinking to the detriment of his performance. I had to force him to take early retire-ment—"It's either that or I'll have to fire you," I told him.

We had another inept official in charge of Facilities. The facilities department at a major airline, which includes all ground equipment and buildings, is a multimillion-dollar operation and this guy had let it get completely out of control. We had ordered some badly needed jetways for our JFK terminal. At a staff meeting, I asked when they were going to be delivered and was blandly informed the manufac-turer was running eighteen months behind schedule.

"Well, when *can* we get the jetways?"

"I don't know," the vice president for Facilities said. "I haven't been keeping track of them."

Disgusted, I flew out to St. Louis where the jetways were being built—or were supposed to be. I asked a company official to show me one and he couldn't find any—these people were so disorganized, they hadn't even begun construction. So I canceled the contract and ordered some new jetways from a different firm.

As soon as I got back to Miami, I fired the vice president for Facilities and began looking around for a replacement. There was no one in his department capable of running the whole show, and in desperation I called a former West Point classmate, Colonel Jack Hurst, who was working for the Army Chief of Staff in the Pentagon. He had been in the Corps of Engineers and had built more airfields than I could count.

I explained what an airline facilities operation was all about and added, "Jack, if you know anyone who's about to retire, who's looking for a job, and who's damned good, let me know."

"I'll see what I can do," Hurst promised.

He phoned back several days later. "Frank, I've got someone for you."

"Great! Who?"

"Me."

I hired him immediately and was never sorry. He did a superb job. His military background was a plus, not a minus; no one is tougher, more demanding, or more capable of cutting red tape than a good Army engineer. Naturally, I heard some secondhand criticism that I was apparently going to staff the airline with nothing but West Point graduates. This was plain baloney—during my entire tenure at Eastern, Hurst was the only prior acquaintance, military or otherwise, I ever hired.

False stories about me began appearing as soon as I joined the airline. A report that I insisted on being addressed as "Colonel Borman" was just one item of bunk. So was a published story that after I became president I issued orders for everyone in Building 16 to wear white shirts to work. Even my no-drinking-during-working-hours edict came in for some flack, the implication being that I was acting like a military martinet.

This order didn't come out of any West Point or Air Force manual. Anyone who has two or three martinis during lunch is incapable of performing his best, particularly if he's coming close to airplanes. I also demanded punctuality and I looked with disfavor on two-hour lunches. If insistence on a full day's work for a full day's pay is being a martinet, so be it. To me it was just common sense. Some of the stories printed about me came from the news media's apparent built-in aversion to anyone with military experience and background, especially service academy graduates.

I was tough because I had to be. I saw too much wasted motion,

deadwood, defeatism, and permissive acceptance of bad practices—
more than once I was told, "Hell, Colonel, we've always done it this
way." Even the airline's known weaknesses seemed to spawn tired
resignation instead of determination to correct them.

Floyd, who was now president and chief operating officer as well
as board chairman and chief executive officer, had the authority to
turn things around but not the will the job required. He was tired,
ailing, emotionally distraught, and a pale replica of the forceful leader
he had once been. He made a few ineffective economy moves, such
as chopping off some six hundred heads in the marketing division.
He even, although reluctantly, fired Jonathan Rinehart, who stayed
in Miami just long enough to revise the public relations pecking order—putting his New York staffers in positions that outranked the
Miami contingent.

But Rinehart made a fatal mistake. He alienated an influential director who happened to like Higginbottom and was furious at the
way Jonathan had handled the resignation announcement. The director couldn't save Sam's job, but he coldly ordered Hall to fire
Rinehart. The old Floyd Hall would have told the director to get
lost.

His selection to replace Rinehart was typical of his deteriorated
judgment in personnel. Hall's choice was Lefty Lethridge, a likable
and immensely popular veteran of the Rickenbacker era—capable
but totally inexperienced in the highly specialized field of public relations. There were officers Floyd should have fired or forced into
early retirement, but he didn't have the stomach for a major executive purge. He had hired some good people, among them Russ Ray,
my old friend from Lockheed and the F-104 days, but there were
too few of them and some he had placed in the wrong jobs. Ray,
for example, was given the title of vice president for Consumer Affairs, but his duties were vague.

There were several officers who were quite willing to stab Floyd
in the back, and one of them actually tried. When Hall was admitted
to a hospital for major surgery in the spring of 1975, rumors spread
that he had terminal cancer and would never return to work. One
of our senior vice presidents flew to New York and asked a head-
hunting firm to recommend him for Eastern's presidency, telling them,
"Hall is dying."

It was around this time that the board elected a new director,
hard-nosed Walter Hitesman, former president of *Reader's Digest*.

At the board's suggestion, Hall made him a senior vice president in the marketing division, but the job was a cover for his real task—something Hall wasn't even aware of. Hitesman actually was a troubleshooter representing Laurance Rockefeller, the airline's majority stockholder, and his assignment was to find out what was wrong with Eastern.

He was more investigator than spy; it didn't take a genius to figure out why Hitesman spent very little time learning about marketing and a hell of a lot of time quizzing virtually every ranking management man in Building 16. I should know—he questioned me for about two hours on why I thought Eastern was in such a deep hole. And I told him, without trying to make Hall the scapegoat.

"The truth is," I said, "Higginbottom's departure didn't end the New York–Miami factionalism. It's still a polarized company. The guys from New York have the attitude that anyone from Miami is just hired help, that New York has all the brains and should do all the thinking. Miami's where the real action is and that's where corporate headquarters should be."

I was leading with my chin with that last remark—Laurance Rockefeller was a New Yorker and so was Harper Woodward, the board's most powerful member; both were totally devoted to Eastern's welfare. But I didn't care if I was stepping on some toes and Hitesman obviously was listening carefully.

"There's too much rancor among the executives," I continued. "Say what you want about the military, but at least it's built on teamwork and cooperation. Around here it's as if management's style is to pit people against each other to see who survives. Eastern reminds me of a company being run with all the latest Harvard Business School techniques. It may work for an ITT, but it doesn't work for an airline. I'm not against scientific management per se, but almost from the day I arrived here I got the feeling Eastern was being managed by men who opened a business school textbook and followed every pedantic rule page by page. We also have the classic evidence of a decaying corporation—executive deadwood, men kept on because they tend to protect one another."

Hitesman stayed around just long enough to gather all the facts, figures, and opinions he needed for a confidential report to the board. While its contents were never made public, the gist of it was that poor Floyd was no longer an effective leader. It also was a verdict Hall himself agreed with, at least partially. Every time I saw him, he looked more exhausted and discouraged than before.

Even as the directors digested Hitesman's scathing report, the airline plunged deeper into a morass of deficits. To be honest, I couldn't wait to get my hands on the controls—1975 was turning into a disaster and would end with a loss of nearly $89 million. Shortly after Sam left, I had been named executive vice president, but Floyd was still running the show and I began to perceive my future as a race between my becoming president and the airline's crashing into bankruptcy. During the fifteen years between 1960 and 1975, Eastern's accumulated net was *minus* $114 million.

Early in May, the board's executive committee, composed of directors Woodward, Jim Elkins, and Ros Gilpatrick, began huddling at 10 Rockefeller Plaza, where Eastern maintained its corporate headquarters. They had been there for several days when Floyd asked me to come to New York. I had a small office in the building, so I checked in there first and then went to Floyd's office.

I had just begun conversing with him when the three directors strode in. I thought they looked a little grim.

"Frank," Elkins said, "we'd appreciate it if you'd go to your own office and wait there a few minutes."

I complied. The few minutes passed like a few hours. Then the executive committee came in and Elkins put out his hand.

"Congratulations," he said simply. "We're recommending to the full board that you be elected president and chief operating officer."

Maybe the occasion called for a modest acceptance speech, but all I could say was "Thank you—I'll do my best."

I called Susan immediately and then my sons. Yet when the euphoria subsided, I began to have misgivings. I was formally named president on May 27, 1975, but the directors allowed Hall to remain as chairman and chief executive officer. All I could see ahead was more friction and more polarization—a division of authority inherent in the appointment of one man as chief executive officer and another as chief operating officer. The only difference from the days of Hall-versus-Higginbottom factions would be the substitution of Hall-versus-Borman factions.

It was never made clear to me how long the directors intended to maintain this two-headed arrangement. Floyd honestly thought it was for two years, at which time he would have reached his sixty-fifth birthday and would retire. This was his understanding after a meeting with the board's compensation committee, and for some reason he got the idea that I had made him a similar promise.

I was in no position to make him any such promise. All I had with the executive committee was a tacit agreement that Hall was eventually going to have to bow out, but there was no timetable or deadline. I had nothing against this fine man who had been so loyal and generous to me.

But the friction began almost immediately. Some officers were reporting only to him and others directly to me. One disagreement arose because Floyd had always insisted that our customer service people at major airports wear business suits. Rare was the passenger who could identify them instantly as a source of aid—their only distinguishing mark was our small ID tag. So I put them into bright red jackets as colorful as the ones Delta customer service agents were wearing, and Hall hit the ceiling—he hated Delta with a passion and he chewed me out for copying our bitterest rival.

I had already ordered the jackets and he didn't reverse my decision this time, but there were other occasions when I'd issue an order and he'd override it. We clashed most frequently on personnel; I'd go into his office and announce, "I'm going to fire so-and-so."

"No, you won't," he'd say. "He's a good man who has some problems." I began to get the idea that Floyd was a pushover for every sob story in the airline—it was part of his inherent decency and compassion, but the executive deadwood was piled up like kindling.

We worked together in a kind of armed truce, our mutual respect putting an uneasy lid on open conflict. Then one day I received a call from a prominent airline consultant with an ear for industry gossip that acted like radar.

"Frank, did you know your boss is hiring Charlie Bucks away from Continental?"

Bucks was Continental's vice president of Marketing and rumored to be Bob Six's choice as his successor. It also was an industry rumor that Bucks was tired of waiting around for Six to step down.

"I don't know anything about it," I admitted. "What do you suppose it means?"

"Well, Hall made Bucks an offer—to come in as executive vice president and then battle it out with you to see who replaces Floyd when he retires."

I went charging into Hall's office and confronted him with the Bucks story. He had the grace to be embarrassed and tried to hedge with "Well, I've been thinking about it." But I couldn't get him to give me a flat denial, and I blew up.

"If you hire him," I said, "I have to resign. You have to make the choice now, Floyd, if you want me to stay with Eastern. I'm still young enough to find a career elsewhere. What's it going to be?"

He looked miserable. "I want you to stay," he mumbled. I don't know what he told Bucks, who never did join us.

By mid-December, Eastern was winding up the worst financial year in its history to date, and once again I was summoned to New York. On December 16, 1975, I was elected president and chief executive officer. Floyd congratulated me, but the handshakes were followed by a private meeting.

"I'd like to stay on as chairman," he said.

"Fine, but only for a limited period. You have to leave before the end of next year."

"The board's given me two more years," he insisted.

"Then I'll have to tell the directors it won't work. They'll have to decide."

In the end, the board backed me up and Floyd stayed on as chairman for only a few more months. Gentleman and class act to the end, he put up no real fight. I think as deeply as he was hurt, he knew it was best for Eastern, and he accepted the decision like a champion.

He had intelligence, imagination, integrity, and great courage. If it had not been for health and personal problems and his fixation on New York as the airline's only logical power base, he might well have gone out a winner. If he had one other flaw, it was his disdain for "getting his hands dirty"—in other words, Floyd didn't like to grapple with the mundane, day-to-day operating problems of an airline, preferring to think loftily of futuristic technology that would solve all problems.

I shared his respect for technology, but not his illusions. As I assumed full command, I was thinking of the future, too—but not in the way anyone expected.

18

THE NEW BROOM

The new president and chief executive officer of Eastern Airlines drove to work in a somewhat decrepit 1969 Chevrolet convertible that my father had found for me on a used-car lot in Phoenix.

Parked in front of Building 16 amid vice presidential Cadillacs, Lincolns, a couple of Mercedes-Benzes, and a Porsche, it looked like a weed growing in a field of orchids; it caused more raised eyebrows than if I had shown up daily wearing tennis shorts and a T-shirt.

Some officers actually resented the car. They never said it to my face, but they felt I was putting on an act, driving a car that seemed more appropriate for a ship cleaner or apprentice mechanic—a kind of phony "Look at me, I'm being very democratic." The truth is, I simply loved that little car. I did finally agree with a few brave and honest subordinates who told me as diplomatically as possible the Chevy looked like it had gone through the Battle of the Bulge; eventually I gave it a fresh paint job and a new top. And when it eventually succumbed to old age, I replaced it with a pickup truck—I love pickups even more than convertibles.

I didn't need any phony gestures to show the people of Eastern what kind of leader they were getting. I was too busy making real gestures. Airline employees expect platitudes from any change in command—the standard "Let's all get to work and turn this company around," along with the usual guff about economizing, teamwork, and sacrifice.

That's what the people of Eastern expected, and I didn't blame them. I had kept a relatively low profile for five years; to most of them I was an unknown quantity, and they had every right to be cynical. They had heard it all before. They figured, as usual, they'd be doing all the economizing and sacrificing while the brass hats continued drawing their usual perks.

Within the first twelve months, I fired, forced into early retirement, or demanded the resignation of twenty-four vice presidents.

I sold the JetStar and informed the executive echelons that from then on they'd travel on our regular flights.

I reduced the limousine fleet and its drivers to a single car and driver in each of three cities—New York, Washington, and Mexico City.

I canceled the leased company automobiles and eliminated the practice of having the company pay officers' membership dues in private clubs.

I transferred all major executive functions to Miami, leaving 10 Rockefeller Plaza staffed only with people whose jobs required them to work there.

The hardest part was the head-chopping. Only a sadist would get pleasure out of firing anybody and I hated having to tell employees they were finished. I didn't believe in the cold-blooded "pink slip" routine, either—when I had to let officers go, I told them face-to-face. And I heard enough sad stories to fill a season of soap operas and saw enough tears to float a battleship. I had one vice president sobbing on his knees as he pleaded for another chance.

The pruning wasn't unilateral. Many times I sought the advice of officers I respected before I made a final decision. One person I consulted frequently was Charlie Simons, senior vice president for Finance, which was something of a contradiction because I never quite trusted Charlie himself.

He had one of the best financial minds in the business and the balancing act he had performed during the Hall-Higginbottom feud would have done credit to a tightrope walker. He managed to stay in power without taking sides—he was a skilled corporate infighter who protected his flanks, and a conniver at times. But offsetting this was his unquestioned intelligence, his long and exceptionally able years of service, and his astute judgment of personnel based on that experience.

I knew I had a cobra in my pocket, and the only way to keep a cobra from biting you is to keep feeding it. If you understand Charlie, you could work with him—he was that good at his job. And I confess a certain admiration for him; he was the most typical corporate animal I ever knew, yet likable and cooperative. In his own way, once he knew who was flying the airplane, he was loyal.

It was especially hard to tell an officer I liked as a person that he was finished, and there was no easy way to do it. Not when I knew the man had a family and financial responsibilities. The corporate world at the executive level can be cold-blooded and heartless.

I tried to make these unpleasant occasions as brief and painless as possible, and while I succeeded in making them brief, I doubt whether any were painless. Usually I'd tell the departing officer that Eastern was more important than any individual—the "whole is greater than the sum of its parts" axiom. But I'd be kidding myself if I expected anyone being fired to accept this rationalization. More than once the temptation to be lenient challenged my judgment, and when that happened I relied on the same rationale I had given the victim: My responsibility was not to a man but to the airline.

I had two role models from whom I learned much without trying to ape them. One was Don Nyrop of Northwest and the other was Bob Six. The only thing they had in common was corncob toughness—in all other respects they were as wide apart as the North and South poles. Nyrop hated the limelight, his distaste for publicity reflected in Northwest's having the smallest PR department of any major carrier—smaller, in fact, than some carriers half its size. Don couldn't have cared less—public relations didn't generate revenues. No more efficiency-conscious, cost-conscious airline chief ever lived. When Northwest built its new General Offices in Minneapolis, Nyrop insisted that the building be windowless for two reasons: to save energy and so employees wouldn't waste time looking outside. He once had the stall doors removed from the rest rooms to prevent lingering.

He took more strikes than anyone in the industry and was generally regarded as the most anti-labor CEO of them all. Yet as I grew to know him better, I began to wonder if he was truly as anti-labor as his record showed. Nyrop's airline was one of the few that emerged from the deregulation chaos as strong as ever, and it was Don who laid the groundwork for this strength. He ran a tight, pencil-counting operation that was lean and efficient, one that gave his employees job security when most of the embattled airlines were laying off people by the thousands. In that sense, he was pro-labor, a truth too many union leaders couldn't grasp.

I admired Six for different reasons. Brash, flamboyant, and as colorful as a rainbow, he personified the essence of competitiveness. I don't think there's another man in aviation history who could have taken a tiny carrier like Continental and successfully pitted it against the giants. He put Continental into the already hotly contested Chicago–Los Angeles market as the fourth carrier, clobbered American, United, and TWA, and actually forced TWA out of the market. He did it with *service*.

Only one other carrier in the United States matched Continental in employee pride and that was non-unionized Delta. Good airline service is based on pride—pride in your job, in your company, and in yourself. And pride itself is based on motivation. That was Six's secret—he could have motivated a stone statue. Continental was as strongly unionized as any carrier, but it didn't seem to make much difference—somehow this John Wayne of the airline industry created employee loyalty toward the company as strong as loyalty toward any union, and from loyalty stemmed productivity.

When I took over Eastern, employee productivity was the lowest in the industry and morale was below sea level. But I wasn't daunted by the fact that Eastern was four times the size of Continental and that esprit de corps is supposed to be easier to achieve in a small, close-knit company than in an impersonal corporate goliath. Size notwithstanding, people are people; I thought Eastern's work force could be reached and motivated, if given a leadership that tried to be honest with them.

Admittedly, some of my first moves—such as selling the JetStar and eliminating certain executive perks—were more symbolic than examples of major economizing. I was trying to get across a message: This airline was going down a one-way street with everyone marching in the same direction, management and workers alike, and anyone doing an about-face was going to get stepped on.

I wasn't happy with what the unions had foisted on Eastern, totally heedless of the company's precarious financial condition, but the infection within the unions was no worse than the infection within management. The difference was that in management I could change things drastically and quickly, either by mandate or by getting new players. I knew with the unions, however, it was going to require a much longer and more difficult process before I could get them to understand what Don Nyrop had taught me. In the long run high operating costs are self-defeating and destructive to labor as well as the company.

I never thought I could bring Eastern back to health with two or three dramatic reforms; it had too many ailments, not just a few. As of the day I assumed command, we were $1 billion in debt. We had a fleet that was woefully fuel-inefficient and mostly obsolete—our best plane, the L-1011, was simply too big for most of our routes and we had too many of these goliaths.

There were big decisions to make but there also were small ones, and they could add up to visible results. At a staff meeting one day, I brought up the matter of ground equipment. I had a report showing that the average age of our ground vehicles, such as tractors, was twelve years and we were spending a fortune trying to keep them repaired.

"What would a new tractor cost?" I inquired of a maintenance official.

He gave me an approximate figure and I looked at the repair costs for one of our most ancient tractors over the past year. They were three times what we'd have to pay for a new machine.

That was the way Eastern had been doing things for years. Its policy was to go the cheapest short-term route without figuring the long-term costs. It applied to virtually every area of technical purchases. At one staff meeting, someone questioned the wisdom of buying a replacement engine larger and more powerful than the original power plant.

I shook my head. "I'd rather buy an engine that's too big, derate the thing, and have it run, than buy a smaller engine that doesn't work."

The stiffest and loudest opposition I encountered came from those who took a dim view of my making Miami instead of New York the center of Eastern's world.

One protested, "You can never get a good financial man to move from New York because he has to deal with all the financial institutions."

"Bull," I snapped. "How the hell can you run an organization when half of it is in one place and half in another? I realize people in New York don't want to move, but you have to subordinate personal desires."

I hadn't been in office very long when Charlie Simons informed me our lending institutions were about to call in about $75 million in short-term loans.

"We don't have the dough," Simons said sorrowfully. "We need an extension—buy some time until we get our act together."

"How long an extension?"

"We could use four years. But dammit, Frank, we'd be lucky if they gave us one year. We'll have to work up some kind of presentation with ideas for reducing our expenses. Show 'em we're potentially a viable company."

"Okay," I agreed. "Let's figure out that presentation and you can set up an appointment with the lenders as soon as we're ready."

A few days later, we met with the lenders and laid out our plans for Eastern's future—the usual fancy charts, graphs, and figures, which to these ice-hearted gentlemen, we hoped, would form an optimistic picture. Simons was good, damned good.

The lenders seemed impressed and, better than that, even friendly and sympathetic.

"An excellent presentation," one said beaming after we finished. "I must compliment you both on a quality job."

They conferred among themselves for a few minutes and then announced they were turning us down for a four-year extension. Or any extension.

It was a crushing blow. Simons and I talked about it on the way back to Miami that night, in full agreement that the cost savings we had projected in our presentation were inadequate—the lenders obviously thought we were using shovels in a situation calling for bulldozers.

"We need something big," I mused. "A single major step that would save enough money to convince those guys we mean business, that we're good credit risks because this airline does have a future."

By the time we landed, we had an idea that was more of an answer to our prayers. It was the only thing we could do to give Eastern some breathing room until the lenders were persuaded there was a real chance for a comeback.

"What we're proposing," I told an executive staff meeting the next morning, "is a voluntary wage freeze affecting every man and woman in this company, from top to bottom, until we get straightened out to the satisfaction of our lenders."

"You'll never sell it to the unions," someone predicted.

"The hell I won't. I'll sell it by telling everyone the truth. Eastern's going under if we don't do something drastic. I'll tell 'em their jobs are on the line and they'd damned well better believe it."

Another officer murmured, "It'll be anathema to labor. They'll never buy it."

"Yes, they will. Because for the first time in this airline's history, we're going to have a profit-sharing plan. We have to promise employees that if they'll go along with a wage freeze, when we do start making money they'll have a chance to participate in profits."

When it came time to sell employees on the freeze, I emphasized that we'd have to shoulder a double burden: We were already carrying a heavy debt and we were going to have to increase that debt even more in order to modernize our antiquated fleet. That was the only way, I pointed out, we could assure a secure future.

Over the next few weeks, I hit almost every city on our system. I cajoled, pleaded, argued, and demanded. I courted not merely the rank and file but their union leaders on both the local and national levels. I won the early support of the Air Line Pilots Association's then president, J. J. O'Donnell, and that of the Eastern pilots' Master Executive Council—MEC Chairman Otto Schick and Captain Chuck Dyer in particular. Of all the unions I had to deal with, ALPA was the most open-minded, and I was so impressed with Schick that I later talked him into becoming a management negotiator.

The local leaders of the International Association of Machinists and Aerospace Workers (IAM), Jim Cates and Steve Hyrtzay, were tough but they were willing to listen and eventually came around. The flight attendants were represented by the Transport Workers Union and I established a good relationship with Ernie Mitchell, the TWU national vice president. But the head of the TWU local was Bernice "Bernie" Dolan, whose attitude toward management was totally negative; if I had offered to double flight attendant salaries I think she would have denounced it as either inadequate or an attempt to break the union. She finally gave in—not without a push from Mitchell, I suspect.

So we got our wage freeze, thus putting a lid on costs even as revenues were climbing. And given solid evidence of a major accomplishment instead of optimistic projections, the impressed lenders agreed on a four-year extension of the short-term notes—as well they might. In 1976, Eastern netted $45.2 million, up to then the highest single-year profit in the company's history and a $134 million turnaround from 1975.

I had won unprecedented cooperation from labor and now it was time to do something further about the ineffective, atrophied management structure that had eroded morale and spread the plague of cynicism throughout the ranks. Five years as a vice president, most of the time cloistered in my own department, hadn't made me an expert on corporate organization—or, in this instance, corporate reorganization. What I felt was needed was an objective professional outside appraisal of management weaknesses.

The man I picked for this task was R. Dixon Speas, probably the most respected management consultant in the industry.

"Dix," I told him, "I want you to start with maintenance and engineering. Find out where we're inefficient. What jobs should be eliminated or consolidated. Who's not doing their job. Which ones are in the wrong jobs. I don't care whose toes are stepped on or whose feelings are hurt—if you have to point the finger at me, go ahead and point."

Early in 1977, Speas turned in a relatively modest report on maintenance and engineering. I liked its honesty and directness, the way it exposed specific areas of inefficiency. So I ordered him to extend his study to the entire airline and the results confirmed what I already knew or suspected: Eastern was abysmally top-heavy in management. A few examples will suffice:

- Management had become so stratified that there were dozens of people blocking the lines of communication between station personnel—the men and women on the firing line—and the brass in Miami. Inquiries, information, and decisions became lost in the clogged channels that separated the field from Miami.
- In one department, we had sixty people assigned to a job that at Delta required only twenty.
- We had brought in computer science people to initiate needed programs, but once those programs were well under way they stayed there, either doing virtually nothing or in many cases creating unnecessary work to justify their existence.
- Eastern had scores of regional vice presidents, directors, and man-

agers who formed a calcified, obstructive labyrinth of indecision; without clear guidance from Miami, local managers had to make decisions on their own and then accept all the blame if anything went wrong.

The Speas report worried me. I'd known we had a ship with a leaking, barnacle-rusted hull, but I hadn't realized how many leaks we'd sprung and how thick those barnacles were. A lot of people were going to be fired, shifted around, or demoted. Many, by virtue of seniority, had been moved into posts for which they were unqualified, or were performing functions that were no longer necessary. The blame belonged mostly to the top brass who had let this happen, but this didn't change the need for major reforms.

Middle management is the strength—or the weakness—of every large corporation. Middle management is composed of the corporals and sergeants of an American business institution. You can have a genius running a company or the greatest strategist in military history commanding an army, but decisions, orders, and policies have to be implemented at lower levels, where incompetence and inaction can be hidden for years.

I had heard about or personally witnessed previous attempts to prune management deadwood and produce greater efficiency. At the first hint of management dismissals, the wailing and moaning would echo through the antiseptic corridors of Building 16 and the brass would cave in. When the dust settled, virtually no one had been let go. This had been true of Captain Eddie's regime, MacIntyre's, and Floyd Hall's, too. Rickenbacker hated to fire veterans and Floyd hated to fire anybody—the hallmark of a decent man whose genuine concern for individuals often seemed to supersede his concern for the company.

The reorganization suggested by the Speas critique wasn't accomplished overnight; it actually took place throughout 1977 and was preceded by a carefully orchestrated campaign to prepare employees for what was coming.

When the smoke cleared, Eastern had a total of thirty-eight vice presidents compared to the sixty-nine when I became president. Our revised vice presidential corps actually was smaller than that of Western Airlines, a carrier one-fourth Eastern's size. Middle-management ranks were thinned by more than eight hundred persons, and scores of survivors found themselves in jobs that involved salary cuts. The overall payroll savings amounted to nearly $9 million annually.

Figures and statistics can't tell the whole story. What we ended up with was a leaner, hungrier management corps, one of the finest in the industry. As I told a staff meeting, "When we're finished, I don't want very many people between me and the baggage handler." And that's what we got. Under the reorganization plan, a sales manager in Houston, for example, found himself reporting directly to his regional vice president, who was in turn reporting directly to a senior vice president in Miami. That meant the man in Houston was only one position removed from the top man in his department and only two positions away from Frank Borman.

In some circles, the reshuffle and its adverse impact on hundreds of people gave me the reputation of being a cold-blooded computer with black ink for blood. It wasn't the first time I had been accused of being tough and unfeeling—some of my fellow astronauts had felt that way, too. But I had been given a task to perform, goals to meet, and problems to overcome. My philosophy at Eastern was identical to the one I had been expressing all my life: If you don't like what I'm doing, just get the hell out of my way because it has to be done.

I had one thing going for me: The middle-management purge occurred after I had been running Eastern for two years, and I had the airline solidly behind me. People knew where I stood and how I operated. Moreover, the average employee no longer had to compare the sacrifices he was expected to make against a backdrop of all the "rank hath its privileges" manifestations. I was an unpretentious man with a relatively simple lifestyle, someone with empathy for a guy who didn't work in a comfortable office.

During holidays, it was the custom to have volunteers from Building 16 go out to Miami International Airport and help with the traffic crush. The secretaries and office clerks loaded baggage, staffed the information desks, and helped with the passenger flow around the ticket counters.

At a regular executive staff meeting one morning, I mentioned the tradition. "I think it's great for employee morale," I added. "So great that we should expand this little volunteer army to include top management."

A few of our more portly vice presidents suddenly wore looks of apprehension.

"Yes, sir," I continued, "the day after New Year's I want to see every guy in this room go out there and help. I'll be working at the airport myself."

I turned to Marv Amos, the dapper senior vice president for Personnel. "Marv, you'll coordinate all the volunteer scheduling. There will be no exceptions."

I could hardly keep a straight face—they all resembled colonels who had just been told to clean the enlisted men's latrine. The only happy face I saw was that of Bob Christian, vice president for Public Relations. He was obviously envisioning the publicity aspects of my pronouncement—a whole platoon of well-tailored top officers suddenly exposed to the nitty-gritty of airline life. But I ruined his day, too.

"Bob, I don't want any photographers out there. This isn't a damned publicity stunt and I especially don't want the press to know we're showing up."

The day before the event, Don Bedwell of the *Miami Herald* phoned Jim Ashlock, Christian's assistant, to inquire if the annual tradition was going to be observed.

"Anything unusual about tomorrow's activities?" Bedwell asked.

"Oh, you can say we're expecting a lot of volunteers."

"Anybody else—just the usual volunteers?"

Among the virtues Ashlock possessed, perhaps to an excessive extent, was an inability to tell a lie.

"Well, there could be some officers there," he said cautiously.

"How high?"

Ashlock gulped. "Pretty high."

"How high is high?" Bedwell pressed.

Ashlock sighed. "About as high as you can get."

"Thanks, Jim," said the delighted reporter. "That's all I wanted to know."

I could cheerfully have strangled Ashlock when the media turned out in force, but I was too busy checking up on my army of vice presidents.

Most were having fun, but a few looked about as out of place as bankers at a stevedores' convention. I found the ticket counters and information desks fully manned, so I went outside to the baggage area and discovered that three vice presidents hadn't arrived.

"I've got three no-shows in baggage," I yelled at Ashlock. "Where the hell is Marv Amos?"

"I think he's still in his office."

I called our vice president in charge of volunteer scheduling. "Get more bodies out here, Marv, and that includes you!"

Amos sauntered into the Eastern terminal lobby around 10 A.M., casually looked around, and informed Ashlock, "Everything seems under control—I'll go out and see Frank before I go back to the office. I'm expecting an important phone call."

I never did find out whether he got the phone call. The minute he stepped into the baggage area, I snarled, "Get to work!" He was still loading baggage with me at 4:30 P.M. He finally glanced in my direction and I overheard him whisper wearily to Ashlock, "Is the son of bitch ever gonna quit?"

I finally did—at 6 P.M. I had worked straight through the shift, without a lunch break, stopping only to sign a few autographs and also refuse several tips. But I never had so much fun in my life.

I never did get around to chewing out Ashlock for tipping off the press. Frankly, it was kind of hard to get mad at Jim. He was a six-foot-six beanpole from Texas whose "aw shucks" country-boy drawl and folksy mannerisms camouflaged one of the sharpest minds I ever encountered. If he had one flaw, it was his infatuation with the telephone.

Much to my disappointment and even alarm, at first I found a great reluctance among officers to voice their views at staff meetings. They had a tendency to sit back and wait for me to air my opinion before they spoke. It was a throwback to the Rickenbacker era when nobody dared speak until they knew how the captain felt. It took awhile for everyone, especially the older officers, to realize I welcomed openness and frankness.

I believed in the adage "The customer is always right," but with reservations, for you never know what a passenger will try to pull in order to extort money from an airline with a threatened or actual lawsuit. One example came up when I was flying nonstop from Chicago to Miami one night. We were about forty miles northwest of Atlanta when a man got out of his seat, walked by me, and collapsed just before reaching the lavatory. I helped a flight attendant administer oxygen while the captain obtained an emergency clearance into Atlanta. An ambulance met the plane and took him to a hospital—he was hardly moving when they took him off.

Toni Zahn, who tried to screen my calls, got one she couldn't handle two days after the Atlanta emergency landing.

"It's some doctor in Miami Beach, Colonel. He's screaming that if he doesn't talk to you personally it'll be too bad for Eastern."

I picked up the phone. "Yes, Doctor, what can I do for you?"

"I'll tell you what *I'm* going to do!" he shouted. "I'm going to sue Eastern for every cent it's worth!"

"Calm down, Doctor, and tell me what's wrong."

"I was on a flight from Chicago to Miami the night before last and I fell asleep. Your incompetent crew mistook my napping for passing out, and when I woke up, I was in a strange Atlanta hospital. You'll be hearing from my lawyer and . . ."

"Hold it, Doctor," I interrupted. "You're talking to the wrong person. I was on the same flight and I was the guy who held an oxygen mask to your face while we made an emergency descent into Atlanta. Go ahead and sue, you son of a bitch. If you sue, we'll countersue—that emergency landing cost us a lot of money."

There was silence for a moment. "You were on the same flight?" he asked in a subdued voice.

"I sure as hell was."

He hung up. I checked with the Atlanta hospital and found the doctor had had an epileptic seizure. He had also hidden his epilepsy from Florida medical authorities. He was trying to stick Eastern with a phony lawsuit or a fat out-of-court settlement; the airlines are among the most vulnerable targets for sleazy lawyers with greedy clients.

The far happier side of our passenger service was its steady improvement. As employee morale blossomed, so did performance. We went from dead last in the Civil Aeronautics Board's passenger complaint ratings to second best in the industry—only Delta had fewer complaints per hundred thousand boardings. During the next ten years we never ranked lower than third among the majors. You could actually see and even feel the new pride developing, growing, and taking hold in the way our people looked and worked.

When I first took over, I brought up the poor CAB ratings at a staff meeting. Some of our marketing people scoffed at our cellar standing.

"The complaint list doesn't really count," they assured me. "Only the kooks and the weirdos bitch to the CAB."

I shook my head. "Maybe it doesn't count for anything, and maybe it's not an accurate barometer, but I won't stand for Eastern being at the bottom of *any* list. I want us to be at or near the top. So don't anyone alibi that it doesn't really matter. If something's wrong, we're gonna fix it."

We sent a lot of our public contact people to "charm school" classes based on a syllabus we obtained from the best source available: Disney World. The Disney organization has a reputation for running a superb employee-training program and we weren't ashamed to utilize its format. As a matter of fact, I always thought it was foolish false pride not to adopt ideas and programs just because somebody else had dreamed them up first.

Like Floyd Hall, a lot of Eastern veterans considered it heresy when we openly and deliberately used Delta, our bitterest rival, as the major prototype of our reorganization plan. I didn't give a hoot— Delta was one hell of an example to follow, successful and efficiently run with passenger loyalty almost as high as that of its employees. That outfit had to be doing things right. Part of the Speas report spotlighted Delta's *modus operandi,* including specific comparisons with similar functions at Eastern, and throughout the reorganization I didn't mind pointing out the differences.

"Delta has thirty-nine dispatchers and we have forty-eight," I'd tell our executives. "So let's us get down to thirty-two—Delta's almost the same size as Eastern.

Marv Amos was the one who worked most closely with Speas and engineered the major part of reshaping our management structure, doing a superb job. We economized where we had to, but we weren't cutting corners if economizing was going to affect service or safety. The best example I can cite is that in trimming all the fat and getting rid of all the deadwood, we still went after the best new talent we could find for middle management.

While I didn't pack the upper management ranks with ex–military brass, I wasn't averse to recruiting younger officers and noncoms who had demonstrated leadership qualities in the armed forces. We hired from non-airline service industries, too, and ran special management training courses for those with no previous airline experience. There were the expected gripes that I was operating a retirement home for ex-soldiers, and we were also accused of hiring token numbers of minority group members, which was bunk. The word I passed around Building 16 was simple: We want anyone who can do the job and it doesn't matter if the person is white, black, yellow, or red, male or female.

We ended up with two black vice presidents: Jim Plinton and Ed Green. They achieved that status because they were good, not because they were black. Tokenism smells as bad as bigotry, and so does any minority quota. We were first in the industry to make widespread use of women as station managers at airports, and they were promoted on merit. The vast majority of our station managers came from within the airline, but we brought in a few new ones, which had the effect of keeping the others on their toes. We adopted a practice of assigning promising newcomers to stations as interns; after learning the ropes, they went into management.

I'm proud of that record. I'm even prouder of the people to whom we provided opportunity and who proved themselves. People like Winnie Gilbert, who became a vice president and was one of the most effective, competent officers I had. She had started out as a line stewardess when Rickenbacker ran the airline and remembered well Captain Eddie's distaste for female employees—he was so biased that for years the only woman sales representative in the system, Alice Eckhoff, was carried on the payroll as "A. Eckhoff" so Rickenbacker wouldn't know he had a lady sales rep.

As vice president for In-Flight Service, Gilbert ran a department with a budget of well over $100 million and supervised a work force that grew to some six thousand. Diminutive, feisty, and attractive as well as an outstanding executive, Winnie had one weakness: She hated to fire anybody. We finally collided over one of her top subordinates, a man she had hired who was doing a lousy job.

I told her to get rid of him. She came up with more excuses than a losing football coach, and one day I called her in.

"Look, Winnie, I've heard you complain about this clown over and over again. He's incompetent and you know it. I realize he has personal problems, but you've given him every chance. Your counseling hasn't done one damned bit of good. You've been procrastinating for the past six months and I'm ordering you to fire him. You're a vice president and you'd better act like one."

She fired him, and from that day on I think she became not merely a good officer but a great one. She had been bloodied, yet she learned that sometimes butts have to be kicked even when you feel the pain yourself.

I had to admire the way she stood up for her sex without being belligerently feminist. At the first staff meeting she attended as a new vice president, the only woman in the room, she rose to get a cup of coffee. As she passed behind my chair, I said rather brusquely, "While you're up, I'd like some coffee, too." Winnie didn't say a word. She poured one cup for herself and marched back to her seat. I knew damned well she had heard me, but from the set of her jaw I also knew damned well she had just made her point.

At the next staff meeting, I was heading for my second coffee when she caught my eye with a glance that was like a radar signal. I said politely, "Winnie, would you like a cup?"

"Thank you, Frank," she said sweetly.

She was never afraid of me. I was trying to establish strong leadership, and in that kind of situation, some degree of fear seems to be inevitable—especially among the insecure. Yet leadership is not synonymous with dictatorship and the distinction is important. I've been accused of running a one-man airline; what I actually ran was a company where one man took the responsibility for making the big decisions.

When I first came to Eastern, I attended a staff meeting trying to decide whether to upgrade our 727 interiors. Higginbottom was presiding, and after listening to the pros and cons of spending about $38 million on the project, he passed around pieces of paper on which each officer was to record his vote.

What the hell kind of a debating society have I gotten myself into? I thought. *Sam's got all the input—he should decide.*

When I headed any kind of program at NASA, I had an appropriate staff study the problem. We'd go over its report, discuss all the facts and implications, and based on what I had been told I'd determine the course of action. That was the way I operated at Eastern, too; I made the final decision, but only after consulting with knowledgeable people, and I accepted the final responsibility for its outcome.

Too many times, particularly in the press, this style was interpreted as a one-man militaristic show. Wrong. Every major decision I made was based on input from many others, and I might add that when a program was implemented, I didn't interfere with the people assigned to carry it out. And that's how we arrived at the most innovative, daring experiment in the history of labor-management relations.

19

CREST OF THE WAVE

It was our success with the 1976 wage freeze that spawned the idea for what we eventually called the Variable Earnings Plan or VEP.

VEP was as much a philosophy as an economic experiment, for it was based on my belief that Eastern's people didn't just work for a company—we *were* the company, labor and management alike. We were the inhabitants of a tiny world, trying to coexist peacefully, and we had to share the risks of failure as well as the fruits of success.

From the day I'd taken over, I knew my biggest and most difficult task was to get labor costs down; there was no other way to survive under the smothering weight of a debt structure that was costing us millions. I also knew that the only way we had won the wage freeze was by combining it with a profit-sharing plan. The former proved that our people were willing to make sacrifices; the latter showed it was a rare union leader who'd give up anything without getting something in return.

The profit-sharing plan adopted in 1976 had given employees two options: They could share in the profits the company made, or they could receive warrants to purchase Eastern stock at a fixed price. The overwhelming majority chose the former, even though the profit-sharing plan was a five-year deal and the warrants were good for ten years.

VEP was a radical, controversial departure from the 1976 or any previous profit-sharing program because, in effect, it also provided for deficit sharing. Ironically, the man who helped me the most in translating what began as a vague idea into a specific program was a union man—Chuck Dyer of ALPA, who also happened to be a graduate of the Harvard Business School and was intrigued by VEP's far-reaching implications.

"It is," I emphasized to the staff, "deficit sharing as well as profit sharing. Eastern always projects a profit, but we seldom make what we said we'd make. It seems to me that if I were a banker holding our notes, I'd like to have some kind of backup to assure me that if the airline wasn't going to make it, the employees would subsidize it."

There was a momentary silence in the big conference room. Then someone blurted, "The employees?"

"Why not? Look, forty-four cents out of every revenue dollar goes for salaries, so that's a logical place to start. It's simple—if we make money, they'll share. If we don't, they'll share in that, too."

We worked out VEP's details at subsequent staff meetings. Once that was settled, I hit the evangelist trail again, holding meetings in every city where I'd explain how VEP would work and why it was essential to Eastern's future. Starting in 1978, each employee would receive 96.5 percent of his or her base pay, the company retaining 3.5 percent as a guarantee that it would earn at least two cents on every sales dollar. Management's contribution was 5 percent and my own was 7 percent.

If profits failed to reach that level, the withheld VEP funds would be used to bring profits up to the two-cent level. But if profits exceeded two cents, every employee would share in one third of all profits above that level—up to a maximum of 3.5 percent of base salary. In other words, we were guaranteeing a minimum 96.5 percent of the base and a maximum of 103.5 percent. It was a good deal for both company and employee.

We didn't pluck that 2 percent figure out of thin air. Our staff had taken a careful look at the future and determined that Eastern could not be a viable company unless it achieved an average annual profit of at least 2 percent of sales over the next ten years. Meeting interest payments, operating a modern fleet, and improving service and routes were all predicated on this inviolate goal. Every subsequent action taken, including demands on the work force, was guided by the 2 percent profit requirement and was approved by the board.

ALPA was the first union to go along with VEP, followed by the flight attendants. The IAM, representing the mechanics, was another matter. Jim Cates, president of Eastern's huge IAM District 100, actually saw some merit in the plan, but he warned me he was going to have a terrible time selling it to the other local officers, and especially to the two top international chiefs—IAM President Bill Winpisinger and Vice President John Peterpaul.

"I've already discussed it with them," he told me. "They're taking the position that if we adopt VEP at Eastern, the IAM will have to do it elsewhere. They think it's better to sacrifice our members rather than let the idea spread."

"Jim, I won't take no for an answer."

"Well," he sighed, "I'm going to Washington tomorrow and discuss it again with Peterpaul. I'll let you know when I get back."

I wasn't going to wait that long. I followed Cates to Washington and called the IAM's national headquarters after I figured Cates and Peterpaul had had time to talk. Winpisinger's office informed me the answer was still no.

"Where are Peterpaul and Cates now?"

"They're out to lunch."

"Where are they eating?"

"They didn't say."

I knew some of the restaurants Peterpaul frequented, so I got into a taxi and began making the rounds. I found them in the fourth one and sat down at their table uninvited. For almost three hours, I argued the case for VEP until Peterpaul, who was either impressed by my eloquence or merely exhausted, finally said the IAM's national leadership would support the program.

I still had to sell District 100, where Cates's second-in-command, Secretary-Treasurer Steve Hyrtzay, had far more doubts about VEP than Jim. I liked Steve. Like Cates, he was tough but a realist who simply wanted the best for his members; all you had to do was convince him what actually was best. After one disappointing session with an audience of mechanics, Hyrtzay commented that my arguments hadn't seemed to make much of an impression.

I said, "Steve, I'll come back a thousand times to convince these guys, and if I have to, I'll come back a thousand and one times."

I was talking to another IAM group and as usual, when I finished explaining the plan I asked for questions. A gnarled mechanic stood up.

"Yeah, Colonel, I've got a question. Why the hell should I trust a guy dumb enough to sit on top of a rocket built by the lowest bidder?"

I never got to answer the question because everyone was laughing so hard—including myself.

Hyrtzay fought for months before he finally agreed to put VEP to a vote. The winning margin wasn't a landslide—about eleven hundred out of the eight thousand votes cast—but I would have settled for a majority of one. With VEP secured, Eastern surprised the unions and not a few of our airline peers by pulling out of the industry's Mutual Aid Pact.

The pact, detested by every airline union since it had been instituted in 1961, was an industry buffer against strikes. It created a complex formula under which a struck carrier could receive payments from unaffected competitors—basically the extra profits the latter made on routes normally operated by the shut-down airline.

I pulled Eastern out of the Mutual Aid Pact for two reasons: First, for us it was a one-way street—we were too weak to take any strike, and the MAP compensation we'd receive would have been like taking aspirin for a terminal disease. Second, I figured the pact was doomed anyway; it was already under heavy attack in Congress. I wanted to sever Eastern from Mutual Aid before everyone was forced to.

Between 1976 and 1980, Eastern enjoyed the most profitable four-year period in its history. The figures speak for themselves: a $45.2 million net in 1976, $27.8 million in 1977, a record $67.2 million in 1978, and $57.6 million in 1979. Under VEP, employees received dividends amounting in some cases to several thousand dollars per person at the end of 1978, plus additional money from the 1976 profit-sharing plan.

Those were halcyon years, and for me personally the apogee of my airline career. We improved our service, modernized the fleet, established good relations with the unions, and achieved unprecedented management stability. Gradually, I had formed a new management team that I still consider to have been the best in the industry. Except for Jack Hurst, the team was formed from within Eastern itself.

The top officers included Russ Ray, whom I promoted to senior vice president for Marketing; Hurst, who rose to senior vice president for Technical Support, a post embracing not only facilities but properties, computer sciences, communications, and parking; Mort Ehrlich, senior vice president for Planning and one of the industry's most respected economists; Paul "Stoney" Johnstone, senior vice president for Operations Services, who had been our vice president for engineering; William Bell, senior vice president for Legal Affairs, a brilliant lawyer with a dry wit, whom we regarded as the staff cynic (when he retired, I replaced him with Dick Magurno, very much Bell's equal); Marv Amos, senior vice president for Personnel and Corporate Administration; and Tom Button, senior vice president for Flight Operations, whom I picked for the job after several others had a shot at it. When Charlie Simons retired, I promoted Wayne Yeoman, a former brigadier general with a doctorate in business from Harvard. He was a pilot who had flown fifty-three missions in Korea and had originally been hired by Floyd Hall—his duties were rather nebulous until I became aware that he had an unappreciated talent for finance.

On our vice presidential level, all were capable but four persons stood out: Winnie Gilbert, Rolf Anderson, Dave Kuntsler, and José Smith. Kuntsler was the one who got me into making television commercials for Eastern, something no other CEO in the airline industry had ever done before.

Actually, Russ Ray had suggested that I do a TV spot when I still was a vice president. The airline was sponsoring a televised golf tournament and Russ wanted me to film one of the commercials.

"No way," I told him. "I'll do anything for this company, except hawk wares."

Russ remembered that earlier incident when Kuntsler approached him with an idea for building a new advertising campaign around our improved service, with me doing the plugging. Russ told him I had already objected to playing pitchman, but he persisted. The two of them finally took their brainstorm to Ed Ney, president of Young and Rubicam, our ad agency.

Ney thought it was a lousy idea. "It's too risky," he said. "If Eastern's service turned sour, Frank's credibility would be destroyed—not only with the public but within the airline itself."

Ray and Kuntsler shifted strategy. They agreed there was risk, both external and internal, but they argued that any new ad campaign had to be aimed at Eastern's employees as well as passengers.

"If TV commercials are going to tell the public that Eastern's trying harder," Kuntsler pointed out, "employees will get the same message."

Thus evolved the concept of the eventual campaign: to emphasize our dedicated employees, to admit we were going to goof at times but also promise that we'd keep trying to improve. And Ney was finally sold on using me instead of a silk-voiced professional announcer or some show business celebrity. Then Kuntsler and the ad agency came up with a winner for an accompanying slogan: "We Have to Earn Our Wings Every Day."

I liked the slogan more than I did the idea of my participation. Subsequent surveys showed that "We Have to Earn Our Wings Every Day" ranked second only to United's famous "Fly the Friendly Skies" in quick public recognition. What also sold me were surveys we had taken prior to the new ad campaign, showing that the public perceived Eastern as a big airline that flew to a lot of places, but also one that was coldly impersonal and not very friendly. Putting me in the commercials, everyone argued, would really personalize Eastern.

I also liked the format—commercials that took the viewers into our cockpits, kitchens, baggage areas, reservations centers, and so forth. I laid down just one request: "I'll try not to hold you people up," I told the ad agency, "but I don't want you wasting my time, either. When we do a commercial let's do it right the first time."

I carefully memorized my lines so I wouldn't have to use cue cards; I didn't want to hear any "Borman—Take 50" crud, and thus I became known around the ad agency as One-Take Borman, which our director considered the equivalent of an Emmy Award. To be truthful, I wasn't that good—I blew my lines more than once—yet things ran smoother than I expected. The people doing the filming were real professionals who'd have everything ready before I showed up, and we worked fast enough to shoot two commercials a day.

Choosing the subject matter was a cooperative effort. Young and Rubicam would bring a dozen or so "storyboard" ideas to our own advertising staff and three would be picked by consensus. Every script was submitted to me for approval, but I can't remember vetoing a single one; my only input was to make minor changes if I thought some word was too hard to pronounce.

The biggest problem was the agency's wanting to shoot a commercial smack in the middle of a busy airport operation, or in a hanger when we were curing a sick airplane. The TV crew tried hard not to interfere, however, and they didn't disrupt things to any great extent. One anticipated problem that didn't develop was my known preference for ad-libbing.

This used to drive poor Bob Christian crazy. He'd labor hard at ghostwriting some speech I was supposed to give, only to have me glance at it, write out a few notes on three-by-five cards, and then talk off the cuff. Young and Rubicam at first was afraid I'd depart from the commercial scripts, but these fears were unfounded—in a thirty-second or one-minute spot, I didn't have time to wing it.

A lot of people assumed I ad-libbed in one of the campaign's most popular commercials, filmed in the kitchen of our principal caterer, Marriott. I delivered my assigned lines about our improved food service, picked up a juicy red apple from a table, tossed it into the air, and, after catching it, took a bite. Somehow the word got around that the apple wasn't in the script. It was a great touch, but it was the director's idea, not mine. His main concern was that I'd drop the damned thing.

Some of Russ Ray's own subordinates in marketing objected to the campaign. They were worried about our making promises we couldn't keep—promises like having spare airplanes assigned to the system, faster baggage delivery, better on-time performance, and friendlier service. I didn't agree.

"If we don't live up to our promises," I told them, "we aren't going to stay in business. We're telling everyone Eastern is a new airline, and we're going to live up to what we advertise."

The commercial I liked most wasn't made for television. It was an ad run in national magazines and featured several thousand employees, including myself, lined up in the shape of the Eastern Falcon logo—it was the most effective pictorial layout I've ever seen and I was very proud of it. It seemed to capture the airline's new spirit better than any words.

The TV commercials won me exposure matching that of my astronaut years, possibly even more. After they began running, I couldn't walk down the street of any city without being recognized. But such exposure was not without mixed blessings. One result was that passenger complaints, instead of being addressed to Eastern in general, would arrive in the form of letters addressed to me personally. A great many started out, "Dear Col. Borman: Well, you sure didn't earn your wings today. . . ." or "Your wings didn't flap on my recent flight. . . ."

One viewer took offense at the apple I picked up.

"When you finish explaining your clean and organized kitchen," he wrote, "you stand directly behind the apples, which are not covered, to continue your discussion. May I remind you that as one talks (exhales), micro-organisms are emitted into the air. Therefore it is a poor health practice to have a general discussion over uncovered food. Whether this poor practice is done only on the TV commercial or if it is permitted in your kitchen, I suggest it be terminated."

Short of asking Bill Marriott to have his kitchen staff wear surgical masks, there wasn't much I could do about this complaint. A truthful answer would have been that I was very much interested in Eastern's food service, but not from the standpoint of a health fanatic. A poor meal on one of our flights would drive me up the wall, yet it was one area in which I developed a certain measure of tolerance for occasional shortcomings.

I was having fun in those years, when the whole airline was doing so many things right and so few things wrong. Even crucial, dead-serious staff meetings brought laughs. Mike Fenello, vice president under Tom Buttion, reported one morning that a 727 had been damaged in a ground mishap.

"At thirteen-oh-three yesterday," Mike intoned dourly, "Aircraft Five-Fourteen damaged its right wingtip when it ran into Building Twenty-one."

There were two red faces in the room: mine because I was furious, and Buttion's because he found it hard to believe that one of his pilots had been careless. Before I could open my mouth, Bill Bell spoke up.

"Tom," he asked innocently, "was Building Twenty-one parked in the right place?"

I didn't like getting special treatment when I flew on Eastern, although I knew it was only human nature to handle a boss with care. Sometimes I even resorted to making my reservations under the pseudonym F. Bomar, hoping I could travel incognito. When I traveled alone, the easiest way to avoid any fuss was to ride in the cockpit, talking to the crew.

I got on one flight commanded by a captain whose list of suggestions, advice, grievances, and questions would have filled an entire chapter of this book. For almost two hours I listened patiently, and when he finally ran out of subject matter, I settled back in the jump seat. The co-pilot turned around. "Colonel Borman, I've got a question."

"Go ahead," I said wearily.

"You been gettin' any lately?"

The airline's unexpected success brought me personal attention. There was talk of my running for the U.S. Senate, talk that I quickly discouraged. When a reporter asked me if I'd be interested in political office, I gave him the same reply I made to every suggestion or even hint that I go into politics.

"The answer's no," I said. "And that comes from Susan Borman, too."

The subject of my leaving Eastern came up for real, in fact, early in 1977 when I was in Washington attending the annual Alfalfa Club dinner. I was president of the club that year and I was staying at the Capital Hilton. It was around noon the day of the dinner when a call came from the White House.

"President Carter would like to see you," the operator said.

I walked over to 1600 Pennsylvania Avenue, only two blocks from the Hilton, and was ushered immediately into the Oval Office, where Carter and Hamilton Jordan, his top aide, were waiting for me. Both were dressed in Levis, the President wearing brogans and a leather jacket. Very informal, I thought—so much so that I was a little startled.

"We'd like you to come to work for us," Carter said after the pleasantries were over.

Jordan added, "We think you'd make an excellent addition to this administration."

I asked for more details and Jordan left the room. Carter took my arm and steered me into the tiny private office he had set up just behind the Oval Office. We began talking.

"I can tell you it would be at the cabinet level," the President said.

"Which cabinet post, Mr. President?"

"First I want to know if you'd be willing to come. Then I'll tell you what job I'd like to offer you."

Shades of Nixon and Haldeman again. As politely as possible, I said, "I'm totally committed to Eastern, Mr. President. We've just begun rebuilding the airline and it would be impossible for me to leave at this time."

Carter pressed me to reconsider, but I kept assuring him I had an unfinished mission at Eastern, one I felt was a mandate. Yet it's a very tough thing to reject an offer from the President of the United States.

It was to happen again three years later, just before Ronald Reagan's inauguration. Ed Meese and Pendleton James, the White House personnel director, asked me to fly to California and discuss a possible high government post. The only question they asked was whether I'd like to be considered as a candidate for defense secretary. Eastern was in the throes of deregulation chaos by then and I said—not without some reluctance—that I wasn't interested because the airline was going through some rough times.

"We could go bankrupt because of deregulation," I told them, "and the last thing a new president would want is to have a major airline fail."

They said they understood and we parted on friendly terms. I did accept appointment to the President's Advisory Commission on Intelligence, but had to resign because it was making too many demands on my time. I think President Reagan was somewhat irked, but the airline was my priority.

Susan had regained her health and strength. Our own relationship had changed since her illness—I was depending on her more and more to help me at Eastern as I tried to establish rapport with employees. She was not merely my liaison with them, but theirs with me.

Her "enlistment," if you can call it that, had begun with the VEP campaign. I had been a little discouraged at some of the initial negative reactions to the plan, and one night I came home with an idea.

"I want to reach the wives of employees," I told Susan. "They hold the purse strings and I need to get the VEP message across to them as well as their husbands. Will you help me?"

"Sure, if you'll tell me how I'm supposed to help."

"Let's face it, we don't have the money to throw fancy cocktail parties around the system. But we have to get 'em together in a group somehow, so you can talk to them about VEP and what I'm trying to accomplish. And I'm not sure many would come to just hear a speech."

"Dutch treat luncheons," Susan suggested. "They'd be a little more festive, yet inexpensive and very informal."

They weren't bona fide dutch-treat affairs. We'd arrange for a Holiday Inn or Ramada to furnish brown bag lunches, with the wives picking up half the cost. We paid the rest and also paid for the meeting room. The luncheons were launched as a part of the VEP sales campaign but continued almost as long as I stayed at Eastern. After VEP was adopted, Susan often went around the system on her own. She was my personal ambassador and she was marvelous, with the charisma to talk to women in their own language and about their own concerns. When I was selling VEP, she'd set up one of her luncheons in the same city, explaining what the program meant to every Eastern family. After her brief talk, there'd be a discussion, and always she'd have one special thing to say: "Through me, I want you to know Frank."

She'd spend the entire afternoon with the wives, both union and non-union, and the luncheons achieved such popularity that we heard the IAM tried to get the mechanics' wives to boycott them; I know for a fact that this union's officials told their own wives, "You can't go to Mrs. Borman's luncheon." Most of them came anyway.

Gradually, not only were the wives listening to her but she was listening to them—they began to trust her. Susan would come home with everything from complaints to compliments, and sometimes she came home with touching stories of employees in trouble; the wives had started to confide in her. She got a letter from one wife in St. Louis whose husband had terminal cancer; she told Susan it would mean a lot to a dying man if he heard from the top boss. I immediately wrote him that he was not to worry about hospital bills, and that Eastern was going to take care of his family as best we could.

The ultimate compliment came from the husbands who began using Susan as a direct and fast conduit to me. She came into Cleveland on a solo visit after the city had been hit by a fierce blizzard. My phone rang shortly after her luncheon ended.

"Frank," she announced, "you got a lot of people madder than hell at you because their husbands' winter jackets haven't arrived and it's freezing here."

The jackets were shipped on the next available flight.

Susan always took along a supply of self-addressed postcards, which she'd hand out after her talk. "I can't answer all your questions," she'd admit disarmingly. "For example, I'm no expert on economic or financial matters. But Frank will have the answers to anything you want to ask on these cards. He cares about you and he's willing to listen to anything you'd like to say about Eastern, especially if you think management is doing something wrong. Or maybe you have some good ideas that would help the airline. I can assure you Frank will read them."

Read them I did. As might be expected, they included petty complaints that could have been handled by a local supervisor, and a number of imagined wrongs. But there also were a number of legitimate grievances that hadn't been redressed at the local level. Those postcards vented a lot of anger against the company in areas that otherwise might never have been brought to my attention.

A lot of management people laughed at this approach to grass roots thinking. A few of my own officers considered it naïve paternalism, while union leaders sneered at it as company propaganda. But when Ambassador Susan got rolling, the doubts and snickering stopped—it was working. I was deliberately trying to involve the whole family structure in the airline and I didn't give a damn if this was called paternalism, propaganda, or anything else. It kept me in touch with the people in the pits, the people doing most of the work. And what's more, it made the second and third echelons of management more responsive to those under their direct supervision—everyone knew the boss was listening.

Quite a gal, my wife. We were flying from New York to Miami one night, sitting in first class, when a flight attendant tapped my shoulder.

"Colonel, would you please come up to the cockpit with me?"

"Anything wrong?"

"Yes, but I'd rather tell you when we're up front, out of sight."

We squeezed into the 727's flight deck. "We've got a crazy man in the rear section," she told me. "He knows you and Mrs. Borman are on the flight and he's demanding that he talk to you, but I don't think you should go back there. He's a real sicko."

"Maybe I'd better talk to him," I offered.

"No, sir. Please stay here so he can't get to you."

I stayed, but before anyone could stop him the disturbed passenger sat down next to Susan, who waved the flight attendants off and began talking to him, calmly and softly. He rambled on and on about his unhappy life and how he intended to make one final splash by setting off a bomb in Washington.

"Now, if you'll go back to your own seat," Susan finally assured him, "tomorrow we'll arrange a press conference for you in Miami and you can tell everyone what's bothering you."

Like a docile child, he obeyed. Police took him off the airplane after we landed. The next day I got the ticket list, obtained his name, and then called the FBI's Miami office. It turned out he was on parole for a child abuse offense and had a history of mental problems.

There was a large, ugly cloud on the horizon even during these wonderful years of black ink and golden morale: the approaching

storms of airline deregulation. At first, I didn't believe it was inevitable, yet I couldn't ignore the possibility. I knew if the industry was
deregulated, Eastern with its high labor costs and huge debt was
going to be the most vulnerable carrier of them all. So I began
preaching cost-cutting sermons even when deregulation was just a
conversation topic at Washington cocktail parties.

Yes, I really did go around Building 16 turning off lights in un-
occupied offices. And ordered the water feeding the Rickenbacker
Memorial Fountain shut off because the electric pump was wasting
energy. And replaced the worn but very expensive drapes in my office with inexpensive shutters. I may have come off as a combination
of Jack Benny and the tightest Scotsman in Edinburgh, but I was
trying to get across the message that even the smallest economy gesture helped . . . that we couldn't afford *any* unnecessary expenditures.

We were hit by a heavy rainstorm that caused Building 16's roof
to leak so badly that the interior's costly burlap wallpaper began to
peel. It had to be replaced, but when the matter came up at a staff
meeting and someone innocently suggested that we look at some
new wallpaper samples, I balked.

"We won't be needing any samples," I snapped. "We'll call maintenance, have 'em strip off the old wallpaper, and just paint the
walls."

When we were faced with absolutely essential spending, I made
sure we got our money's worth. Airplane carpeting takes a beating
and has to be replaced periodically. The time-honored practice at
Eastern had been to order about 80,000 square yards of carpet material, cut it up, and install it. Sound logical? It wasn't, because too
often the airline would buy 80,000 yards of inferior material that
wouldn't stand up.

"From now on," I told Purchasing, "buy only a couple of hundred
yards and try the carpeting out on a Shuttle aircraft where it'll really
get the hardest use. If the material holds up, then buy whatever's
needed."

The biggest obstacles to economizing were the work rules required
under our labor agreements. Getting a union to eliminate or even
modify an unproductive work rule was like trying to take a credit
card away from a profligate mistress, and the IAM was the worst
offender.

Once a work rule got into a contract, it was set in granite. Many had deceptively innocuous beginnings, instituted on a very modest scale—usually to solve some minor problem at a single station. The next thing management knew, the work rule had spread throughout the system and was costing the airline a few million unnecessary bucks.

Before I came to Eastern, the airline had a maintenance base at Baltimore. Traffic was too light to justify the base, but when the decision to close it down was announced, the IAM protested. So rather than fire the Baltimore mechanics or transfer them to other bases, the company agreed to find them new duties: The mechanics were assigned the job of pushing the airplanes away from the gate.

Every other airline in the country required only one mechanic for this push-back task; he drove the tractor that did the pushing. The two guys who had already unloaded the bags then "walked the wings," guiding the tractor driver. Not at Eastern. When the IAM screamed about disrupting its Baltimore members, we ended up with three mechanics assigned to push-back: one on the tractor and two wing walkers. The two baggage handlers just went back into the terminal and sat on their butts until the next flight.

If this featherbedding had been confined to Baltimore, we could have lived with it. But the IAM insisted on applying the same work rule to every city we served. Imagine what this did at a station like Atlanta, where Eastern had forty-four gates—we had a whole damned regiment of mechanics doing nothing but pushing back airplanes. We actually needed multiple teams at the Atlanta hub, because during peak hours, the push-backs were only one or two minutes apart. Once the planes had left the gate, however, we had a horde of idle mechanics doing absolutely nothing.

We tried and tried to get the IAM to change the rule, but ran into a stone wall. Unions, I learned, don't give back anything they've already won. Yet this one work rule was costing us millions. I brought up the matter at a staff meeting shortly after I had met with Harding Lawrence of Braniff to discuss a possible merger.

"Harding told me Eastern would never make it," I recounted, "and he cited that one goddamned rule as evidence. So let's get rid of all three mechanics doing push-backs."

"And just how do you propose doing it?" someone asked.

"What's wrong with using reverse thrust? Let the airplane itself do the pushing."

Every technical man in the room began voicing objections, starting with our chief pilot. "The pilot can't see where he's going," he pointed out.

"He doesn't have to. He's already got a stick guy [the wand-waving ramp man] out there to keep him from running into anything."

Maintenance voiced concern that using reverse thrust in the ramp area would lead to foreign-object damage (FOD).

"We won't know that until we try it," I replied.

Paul Johnstone of engineering was worried about what would happen if you used reverse thrust on the 727, whose three engines are aft-mounted. "If you power back on a three-holer and then apply the brakes, you'll have the plane sitting on its ass," he predicted.

"Like I said about FOD, we won't know until we try it."

Several people still urged caution, and I agreed that we should check first with the engine manufacturers to make sure the procedure wouldn't cause problems. I welcomed the objections and doubts; I didn't mandate the reverse thrust push-back until there was a consensus that it deserved at least a tryout and it wasn't put into effect until we successfully experimented with the unprecedented technique in Miami.

As might be expected, the IAM raised unshirted hell, claiming we were trying to eliminate at least forty-one jobs.

"Nobody's gonna lose his job," I said. "Mechanics taken off push-back duties will be reassigned to other jobs, where they can start earning their pay."

Came the day the new procedure was to be used for the first time in Atlanta. Charles Buckland, our system director from Miami and a wonderful individual, was on hand to supervise the operation and he decided to serve as the stick man himself. Also present was the local head of the IAM, who announced he was not going to let it happen even if he had to lie down behind the aircraft's wheels to prevent it.

Buckland glared at him and waved his sticks for the push-back. The pilot applied reverse thrust and the plane began to roll back. The IAM guy hastily got out of the way just in time. Every airline in the nation adopted the reverse thrust technique except Delta—I guess because Delta didn't think of it first.

I was never to forget that incident at Atlanta, nor the stocky, loudly aggressive IAM representative who was behind the wheels.

His name was Charles Bryan.

20

THE WINDS OF CHANGE

The airline industry was dragged kicking and screaming into deregulation—and that included me.

I wish it hadn't, because I have come to believe that deregulation
was the best thing that ever happened to U.S. air transportation. Its
only real fault was the way it was implemented—virtually overnight,
without giving the established ·carriers a chance to adjust to new
rules dictated by a free-market environment they hadn't experienced
for fifty years.

The original intent of deregulation's supporters was to phase it in
gradually, and that's the way it should have been done. Either a
limited number of new carriers could have been granted market entry over the first five years, or unlimited entry could have been accompanied by some control over fares until the readjustment period
was over. If we had fought harder for such a logical phase-in, instead of opposing deregulation outright with no attempt to compromise, I think we could have gotten the benefits without as much
pain.

No one can judge deregulation's merits without understanding the
forces that led to its adoption. For half a century, the nation's reg-

ulated carriers had followed a steady pattern of technological progress, each generation of new aircraft bringing improved safety and
increased productivity. As the industry grew, operating costs rose
steadily, but they were always held in check by the greater efficiency
of bigger and faster equipment.

The technology/productivity formula was beautifully simple. Its
efficiency contained the forces of increased operating costs and kept
fares under control. A single 727 could do the work of six DC-3s
and perform it five times faster, while carrying people at lower yet
profitable fares.

But eventually the various factors that led to higher operating costs
chipped away at the formula until the buffer zone of efficiency shrank
almost to the vanishing point. First, a huge proportion of productivity gains began going to labor, shrinking the industry's investment
strength. One of the most damaging acts was ALPA's successful
campaign, right after World War II, to peg pilot pay scales to the
size and speed of the airplane—a perfect example of partially negating the technological advances. It was a small cloud that grew into
a giant thunderhead; from 1960 on, all airline wages went up so
drastically that the average airline salary was 40 to 60 percent higher
than the U.S. industrial average.

The second negating factor was inflation, an insidious trend that
started in the late 1950s and early sixties. The first 727 Eastern bought
cost about $4 million. The last one, purchased sixteen years later—
virtually the same airplane—had a $17 million price tag. In 1973,
we were paying around $117 million a year for a billion gallons of
kerosene. Five years later, our annual fuel bill was $1 billion for the
same amount of fuel.

So by the mid-seventies, technological improvements no longer could
hold these forces in check—the newest airplanes weren't capable of
increasing productivity enough to offset spiraling labor costs and
inflation. And this is what established the climate for deregulation.

The unions and most airline executives alike portrayed deregulation as an anti-labor measure, predicting that it would cost thousands of employees their jobs. It did, temporarily; yet if we had
continued to be a regulated industry, the results would have been
the same. Eventually we would have priced ourselves out of the air
market, jobs would have been decimated, and only the rich could
have afforded to fly. The one way the industry could have survived
in a regulated environment would have been for labor to restrain its

insatiable appetite, and this would have been like asking the sun to rise in the west. The unions were as satisfied with the status quo as management.

I fought deregulation simply because I perceived Eastern to be especially vulnerable when the winds changed. It was only too easy to see the effects of competition from carriers like People Express, with labor rates far below ours. We were paying a three-man 727 crew about five hundred dollars an hour; it cost People Express, operating the same airplane with the same crew complement, just over one hundred dollars an hour.

Nor did it take a crystal ball to recognize that if deregulation came, the east coast markets, embracing our prime routes, would be the first and hardest hit. This was the main reason I fought so hard for VEP even before deregulation; at the time, it was the only means we possessed of holding down labor costs.

Deregulation became law in October of 1978, but more than a year passed before the full effects were felt. Only one major airline CEO supported the legislation: Dick Ferris of United; the rest of the industry was a solid phalanx of opposition.

I testified in Congress against it, made speeches against it, and even debated Senator Ted Kennedy on national television.

When I was asked to testify before a Senate subcommittee on deregulation, I marched up to Capitol Hill with my own version of the adage "One picture is worth a thousand words."

The General Accounting Office, which was gung-ho for deregulation, had issued a report declaring that the airlines could cut fares as much as 55 percent by adding more seats. I zeroed in on that claim. Into the paneled, Greek-style hearing room, I had brought a large object covered with a red and yellow tarpaulin.

"The GAO assumption states that airlines could easily increase their productivity by simply increasing the number of seats in each aircraft, thereby permitting a reduction in fares," I said. "This is a great idea."

I paused, then added, "Take a look at what you'd get."

I pulled the tarpaulin off, unveiling a mockup of an aircraft interior with three rows of seats.

"The two front rows," I explained, "are set up in the comfortable configuration of current Eastern 727s and DC-9s. The third row is set up to get in the number of seats the GAO study says could be put on a DC-8 by airlines in price competition. What we have here is a GAO airplane. Senators, I'd like you to try that third row."

Amid laughter from the spectators and a few chuckles from the senators themselves, subcommittee chairman Howard Cannon of Nevada and Senator Barry Goldwater of Arizona tried to get into the seats, which were less than five inches away from the row in front of them. Cannon, a portly man who happened to be one of deregulation's staunchest supporters, looked like Oliver Hardy trying to squeeze into Stan Laurel's trousers. Goldwater, slimmer than his colleague, couldn't make it either.

"That's about standard for the GAO," he puffed as more laughter swept the room.

Some of the dire predictions we made came true. Mergers compressed the industry into a handful of megacarriers, yet this didn't really suppress competition—the industry is more competitive now than it has ever been. It's true that the explosive traffic expansion created by lower fares brought chaos, as we feared, but this wasn't deregulation's fault. Put the blame where it belongs: on the Department of Transportation (DOT) under its former secretary, Elizabeth Dole, and her fellow culprits—the Reagan administration and Congress.

This was the triumvirate that resisted using the Airport Trust Fund the way it was intended to be used. Every penny of the fund's accumulated $5.7 billion surplus earmarked for modernization of air traffic control and airport improvements, and paid for by taxes on airline tickets, was utilized to reduce the federal deficit on paper.

That money sat idle while the DOT allowed the Federal Aviation Administration's air traffic control system to deteriorate, unable to cope with the traffic growth. And the FAA, dominated by its parent agency, waited until the situation reached the crisis stage before it finally implemented a modernization plan and began hiring more controllers. The public and the press largely blamed the airlines for all the chaos. So, for the matter, did Dole and her DOT. Rather than accepting at least part of the responsibility, she went in the opposite direction—projecting an image of the DOT as the public's only real protector, demanding airline reforms, and threatening to punish the industry for its sins. It was nothing but political posturing, and the day would come when Eastern itself would be victimized by such posturing.

I've never blamed Eastern's problems on deregulation. Granted, it made our task more difficult and our lives more demanding, but we still could have lived with it if our unions had recognized that high labor costs were incompatible with a free-market environment. The pilots did, and to a lesser extent so did the flight attendants, but not the IAM.

VEP wasn't the only protective barrier I tried to erect. For two years prior to deregulation's full impact, I tried vainly to merge Eastern with another airline because I wasn't sure that with our labor costs we could make it on our own in a totally free market. I went to bat four times.

The first attempt was early in 1978, when Pan Am and Frank Lorenzo of Texas Air became embroiled in a bidding war for control of National Airlines, our major competitor in the Florida market and, like us, headquartered in Miami. Pan Am was desperate to get a domestic system that would mesh with its international routes and I wanted no part of that brand of competition—National was tough enough. So when Pan Am outbid Lorenzo (who made millions off the National stock he already owned), I put in a bid of our own.

Bill Seawell of Pan Am was furious—he had his hand on the pot, ready to rake it in, when I suddenly raised the ante. But Seawell was wrong in feeling that ours was just a nuisance bid. We really wanted National; in fact, over a year before I had talked to our Miami neighbor about a possible merger and got nowhere, so our bid was legitimate—we were doing pretty well financially then and could have financed the deal. Seawell was so determined to acquire National that he outbid us by paying about $90 million more for the stock than he'd planned to originally.

Another merger attempt, one that would have given our unions collective coronaries, came early in 1979 and involved Northwest. I contacted Don Nyrop and we met twice to discuss putting our airlines together. At the very first meeting, held secretly in Chicago at Nyrop's suggestion, I told Don I wanted him to run the merged companies as CEO and that I'd be the number two man. We conferred again in Miami; Nyrop by now was getting enthusiastic, for our route systems were beautifully compatible, and the prospect of linking our strong east coast and southern markets to Northwest's northern transcontinental and Pacific routes was mind-boggling.

"I'd like to discuss this with a few of my people," Nyrop said. "Then I'll call you and we can meet again."

The third meeting never came off. Three weeks later he phoned me.

"I'm sorry, Frank. I'm too concerned about Eastern's labor costs to go through with this. It's too much for us to swallow."

I said I understood his position and that I was sorry, too. I'm still sorry; it would have been one hell of a marriage, one made in heaven for both carriers.

The third merger prospect in the early days of deregulation was Braniff, then headed by Harding Lawrence. Like me, he had followed the axiom "If you can't beat 'em, join 'em," but Harding ended up welcoming deregulation like a kid handed a blank check in front of a candy store. He saw it as a chance to expand Braniff into a giant overnight; within two months after the Deregulation Act became law, Braniff had opened thirty-two new routes involving sixteen cities it had never served before, and incredibly it inaugurated service to all sixteen new points within a twenty-four-hour period.

When I sounded him out on a possible merger, the kid who had gone into the candy store had developed a stomachache—too much expansion too fast. Braniff was hurting, but you couldn't tell it from Harding Lawrence.

What fascinated me about Braniff was its South American routes; a merger would make Miami a gateway to that market. I called Harding and suggested we meet—typically, he insisted I come to Dallas. We were the marginal carrier and Braniff was the failing one, yet Lawrence wouldn't talk unless it was on his home ground.

I flew into Dallas and was met by a Lincoln Town Car driven by Harding's Italian valet. He drove me to Braniff's brand-new executive office building, where I was ushered into a private elevator and taken to Lawrence's spacious office. When I'd taken over Eastern's command, I had refused to use Floyd Hall's huge office with its private shower and settled for less ostentatious quarters. But compared to Lawrence's abode, Floyd's was spartan—Harding's even had a huge polar-bear rug and looked like something featured in *Architectural Digest*.

It was more of a luxury penthouse apartment than an office. I happened to glance out the window and saw some workers cleaning Harding's private swimming pool. He insisted that we not start talking until after his valet served an excellent lunch, and I couldn't help thinking that Harding Lawrence was living in another world. Even though Braniff was on the ropes, he seemed to be trying to convince me that his own born-to-the-purple style somehow reflected a healthy airline.

From the start of our discussion, he acted as if Braniff would be doing Eastern a favor if they merged. "Just the name Braniff," he intoned, "is worth more than you can imagine. Do you realize that even as we sit here there's a Braniff plane landing in Korea, another in Hong Kong, and a third in Hawaii?"

I realized it all right. I also knew those Braniff planes landing at various Pacific destinations were 747s and DC-8s with pitifully few passengers aboard. Lawrence's decision to complete in the Pacific against established carriers had proved disastrous. When I had first gotten a gleam in my eye for Braniff's South American routes, I'd been curious to see how it was really doing in the Pacific. We did a gate count the week Braniff started service from Portland/Seattle to Hawaii. The average was 14 passengers a day on a 375-passenger 747.

Harding let it be known that if we merged he wanted to remain as president and CEO. "But you'd actually run things," he assured me. "I'd like to stay on for six months before retiring."

His promise to retire six months after the merger was about the only tentative agreement we reached. Harding had an inflated idea of how much Braniff's stock and assets were worth and his price was unrealistically high. We never came anywhere near a meeting of the minds, but that's moot—the only way we'd have considered Lawrence's price tag was to convert his debt into equity and Braniff's banks said absolutely no.

The fourth merger attempt involved another made-in-heaven marriage: Eastern and TWA. I could have positively drooled over the prospects of combining our two domestic systems—Trans World's east-west and our north-south routes—and feeding them into TWA's profitable international routes.

TWA's chairman, Ed Smart, told me his directors weren't interested. I didn't reach first base with TWA President Ed Meyer, either, and I got the impression that TWA's management was more concerned with preserving its own status quo than strengthening its airline. I think Meyer in particular felt I'd end up running the merged carrier, and he wasn't prepared to give up his high place on the corporate totem pole.

When we announced on April 6, 1978, that Eastern was buying the French-built A-300, one would have thought we had spit on the American flag, insulted motherhood, and come out foursquare in favor of sin. Yet the outcry wasn't quite as loud as a lot of people expected, simply because the decision-making process was a carefully planned affair that had begun thirteen months earlier.

Many factors went into our choice, starting with the kind of airplane we needed. Our 727-QC fleet was a disaster; these planes were so fuel-inefficient that we were actually losing money flying them full. And our fuel costs were horrendous—they had almost tripled between 1973 and 1977. Our propjet Electras, used mostly as backup planes on the Shuttle, were obsolete and many of our DC-9s were aging and too small. Eastern's best aircraft were the 727-200 and the L-1011, but we didn't have enough of the former and we had too many of the latter.

Our staff studies outlined the kind of new airplane we desperately needed, namely:

1. A plane with a payload somewhere between the TriStar's capacity of 293 passengers and the 727-200's 149; the target was an airliner seating about 170.
2. A "new technology" aircraft that was fuel-efficient and quiet enough to meet all present and future noise standards.
3. A medium-range transport with New York–Miami nonstop capability, yet versatile enough to operate safely at short-runway airports like La Guardia and Washington National.
4. An airliner that could be delivered before 1980 so we could start replacing our geriatric planes as quickly as possible.
5. A two-engine airplane, because on Eastern's predominantly short- to medium-haul routes, it was too expensive to operate three-engine equipment—this was the superb 727's chief shortcoming.

Our shopping list contained two major limitations: First, there was no American-made transport available "off the shelf" to meet our five specifications, and second, we were going shopping with an empty wallet and damned little in our checking account.

Throughout the latter half of 1976 and early 1977, the three U.S. airframe manufacturers made sales pilgrimages to Miami. Lockheed was pushing a smaller version of the L-1011. McDonnell Douglas touted the DC-9 Super 80—a stretched DC-9 with a fuselage only three feet shorter than the original DC-8. Boeing had four interesting designs on its drawing boards: a stretched 727 called the 727-300; the 757, a two-engine concept that combined a longer 727-200 fuselage with a new type of wing airfoil and bigger engines; the 767, a two-engine widebody; and the 777, which was identical to the 767 but with three engines and a greater range.

None met all of our five requirements. The 757 came closest and Charlie Simons loved it, but as I told him, "It's too far down the line—Boeing hasn't even decided whether to build it." The Super 80 was intriguing. McDonnell Douglas always had the reputation of building "rubber" airplanes—taking an existing, proven design and stretching it into a bigger and better aircraft. The company had done this with both the DC-8 and DC-9; the Super 80 would be the fourth stretch job on the original DC-9 design. It would seat up to 173 passengers and McDonnell Douglas was promising to start deliveries in early 1980.

Simons thought the Super 80 was too small—its 173-passenger capacity could be achieved only with sardine seating, and the configuration we had in mind provided only 133 seats. Furthermore, our relations with McDonnell Douglas weren't very good at the time; during the Hall regime, Eastern had sued the manufacturer for delayed DC-9 deliveries. The dispute was settled amicably later, but when we first discussed the Super 80 with Sandy McDonnell, both sides were suspicious of each other.

It was Simons who suggested that we consider the A-300, already in service on Air France and Lufthansa. I was lukewarm initially—the airplane, a twin-engine widebody that carried almost 250 passengers, seemed far too large, even though it met the rest of our specifications. But Charlie insisted we should at least invite the French manufacturer, Airbus Industrie, into the competition and look at the airplane itself.

"Western Airlines came damned close to buying the A-300," Simons said, "and would have if Art Kelly [Western's president] hadn't gotten cold feet. He was worried about too much static from Congress and the unions if he bought a foreign-made airplane."

A French team headed by Airbus Industrie Vice President and General Manager Roger Beteille came to Miami for the first meeting. Although his English was halting, his presentation impressed me. Beteille was actually one of the A-300's designers, so he really knew the airplane and what it could do for us. We were interested enough to set up further meetings, but the biggest hurdle for Airbus to overcome was the plane's size.

"It's really too big for our needs," I pointed out.

Beteille said he understood, and then came up with an idea that floored us. "We'll make you a deal where you don't have to pay for the seats you can't use. If you want a hundred-seventy-passenger airplane, we'll price the A-300 as a hundred-seventy-passenger airplane. If traffic develops to the point where equipment the size of our A-300 is justified, only then will you have to pay for the additional capacity."

He wasn't being entirely altruistic. The French were anxious to get their foot inside the door of the American market, so totally dominated by U.S. airframe companies. European manufacturers hadn't had much luck in the past. Only United had bought the French Caravelle. The British had done a little better with their propjet Viscount and the BAC One-Eleven, but neither had made much of a dent against the overwhelming domination of Boeing, McDonnell Douglas, and Lockheed. Beteille knew, as we did, that selling the A-300 to Eastern would be an enormous boost to Airbus Industrie's prestige and potential future sales, not only here but throughout the free world.

Our technical people fell in love with this truly international product—the Germans built the fuselage, Britain supplied the wings, and the tail was made in Spain. It had Dutch components, too. All the French did, other than provide the basic design and the cockpit, was to assemble the A-300 at their Toulouse factory.

Helping Beteille negotiate was George Warde, a former president of American Airlines who had gone to work for the French firm as its chief North American representative. Jovial and a horse-trader at heart, Warde was a tough nut to crack at the bargaining table, but he knew the U.S. airline industry and understood Eastern's problems. The first time he showed up for the talks, I asked him bluntly, "Why should we buy your airplane?"

"Because if you don't, you're dead," Warde replied. He was operating from a tough stance, feeling that Airbus had given us a major concession with its proposal to make the full price of a 250-passenger airplane contingent on whether traffic increased. But he also knew how financially strapped we were and that we still had doubts about buying a foreign product. I figured Airbus might be willing to go one step further.

I had already gone to Toulouse and seen the A-300 being assembled in a building that looked more like a big hangar than a factory. The workmanship was superb, and the more I looked at the airplane, the better I liked it. So when I got back, I met with Warde and the president of Airbus Industrie, Bernard Lathiere, a delightful Frenchman whose exuberance was as natural as his accent. Both he and Warde were consummate salesmen, but they weren't prepared for what I threw at them. Only Simons knew what I was going to pull.

"You must realize," I began, "that Eastern's daily utilization of the A-300 would be far higher than what Air France and Lufthansa required."

"Of course," Lathiere smiled. "But . . ."

I interrupted, "So what I propose is that you lease us four A-300s at *no cost* for a period of six months, so we can evaluate the airplane on our own routes and under our own operating conditions."

From the look on Lathiere's face, one would have thought I had suggested moving the Eiffel Tower to Miami Beach. "Frank," he sputtered, "that's unheard of!"

"I realize that, Bernard, but it's the only way we can really judge your product, not merely from its operational abilities but from the standpoint of passenger acceptance. We may find considerable prejudice against a foreign-made aircraft, and if that prejudice exists, it's better we know now than when it's too late."

Simons jumped in for the kill. "What we're really proposing is a joint venture. If you think your product is that good, we'll be the ones to prove it for you. And it'll cost you a hell of a lot more to advertise the A-300 in the United States than to loan us four airplanes that'll be flying advertisements in themselves."

Lathiere's resistance crumbled and we had a tentative deal. Simons worked out the details while we shipped a number of pilots and mechanics to France for crew and maintenance training. Our four borrowed A-300s began flying on December 13, 1977, over high-density route segments and immediately started drawing raves from pilots, mechanics, and passengers. Those airplanes performed better than we had ever hoped. They compiled the best reliability record in our fleet and they were using between 20 and 30 percent less fuel per seat-mile than our Boeings and DC-9s. Overall operating costs were lower than what Airbus had promised and we knew we had ourselves one hell of an airplane.

I was sold, but for a while I was marching to the sound of my own drum. Our planning department was ambivalent—the staff would be for it one day and opposed the next. Even Simons got a mild case of cold feet. He began worrying that the A-300 was just too big, too controversial, and too expensive. He was a great financial man, but he had dealt with adversity for so long that he wore worry like a suit of clothes.

He tried his damnedest to get even more favorable terms. He first proposed that Airbus take in ten L-1011s as a trade-in on twenty-two A-300s. Warde turned him down, and Simons came back by offering preferred Eastern stock as partial payment. Warde said no again.

The financing deal Simons finally worked out was incredible. We ordered twenty-three A-300s at $25 million per aircraft. Including spare parts, it added up to a $778 million package—a sum that turned our lenders pale. When they refused to advance us that much cash, Charlie Simons wrought a few miracles.

He wangled from General Electric, eager to provide the A-300's engines, $45 million in subordinated financing and another $96 million worth of similar debentures from Airbus. Both loans contained a unusual provision: The interest rates could fluctuate depending on the airline's profits, between 9 and 9.45 percent on the Airbus notes and between 8 and 10.5 percent on GE's.

Airbus also agreed to accept another $66 million in four-year senior notes at just under 11 percent interest. The French then arranged for $250 million in export credit financing through a group of European banks, again at a very favorable interest rate of 8.25 percent. The final Airbus contribution was to credit Eastern with the total worth of the four A-300s we were operating on trial—about $100 million.

We signed the contract with three months still left in the trial period; the airplane was that good. Still on the agenda, however, was the task of forestalling criticism for buying a foreign airliner, and one of the first things I did was to obtain an appointment with George Meany, the crusty old curmudgeon who was Mr. American Labor.

Aging but still possessing the aura of a born leader, he sat there smoking a fat cigar that smelled like burning engine oil (I think every labor boss I ever dealt with smoked cigars). I told him we were buying the A-300 and I wanted him to know why. I went through our financial problems, assured him we had gotten a great deal, and said the new airplane was the only way we could compete. He asked a few questions, and he kept calling me either "young man" or "son," but from his enigmatic expression I wasn't sure I was getting through.

"Mr. Meany," I finally concluded, "I can understand why trade union people could get upset about this, but in the long run we'll be preserving American jobs. I'd rather buy an American-built airplane, but what we need and want right now isn't available."

Meany peered at me from behind a thick cloud of smoke and smiled. "Young man," he boomed, "I agree with you. If we can't be competitive in aerospace, we deserve to lose. Your deal sounds fine to me."

Covering all bases, I also talked to Bill Winpisinger, president of the IAM, about the Airbus contract. His chief concern was the reaction of the big IAM unit at Boeing and suggested I meet with some of the union's chief stewards in Seattle. I followed his advice, telling them just what I had told Meany and Winpisinger. They wouldn't have voted me man of the year, but I diffused most of their resentment.

For the public, press, and politicians, we devised a campaign built around the fact that the A-300 was not really an all-foreign product. Its American-made components accounted for one third of the airplane's dollar value—Goodrich made the tires, GE built the engines, and all the electronics came from U.S. firms. American labor actually supplied 50 percent of the total man-hours that went into every Eastern A-300 built.

Five months after we announced the Airbus contract, we signed with Boeing for twenty-one 757s and an option for another twenty-four, with deliveries beginning in 1983. It was a $560 million commitment—in less than one year we had bought some $1.4 billion worth of new airplanes, but we also had completed a modernization of Eastern's fleet that would take us into the 1990s, plus providing an insurance policy against such contingencies as rising fuel prices.

A penny-per-gallon jump in the cost of jet fuel added at least $10 million to the airline's direct annual operating costs. If the A-300 was fuel-efficient, the 757 was even more so—when this 174-passenger plane went into service five years later, we found it was consuming almost 35 percent less fuel than the 727-200, and by the time I left Eastern, the new Boeings had proven themselves the most economical aircraft in the carrier's history.

The gamble I took with that massive modernization program was to bring the unions down on my neck years later. I would be accused of plunging Eastern further into debt with this supposed spending spree, while simultaneously demanding more sacrifices from employees in a financial crisis ostensibly brought on by excessive aircraft purchases.

Of all the accusations made against me, this one angers me the most. Yes, buying new airplanes did add to an already oppressive debt load. But without those new planes, Eastern couldn't have survived even if deregulation hadn't come. Both the A-300 and 757 contracts were signed at a time when we were making some money, when we could not judge the catastrophic extent of low-cost competition with its fare wars, and when we absolutely had to modernize the fleet just to stay in business. In the ten years I headed Eastern, the size of our fleet increased by only three aircraft a year. Fleet modernization was primarily a replacement program, allowing us to dispose of the aging, fuel-gulping planes that were almost impossible to operate profitably. We sold thirty-five 727-QCs to Federal Express, while peddling fifteen Electras and several L-1011s to used-aircraft brokers.

I knew I might be hung out to dry for buying the 757 right after we'd gone into deep hock with the A-300. But I had to weigh that risk against what would happen if we stopped with the Airbus and tried to compete over the next decade with a fleet that was at least 60 percent obsolescent. At this time Delta was on a new-equipment splurge that by the mid-eighties would give it the most modern fleet in the industry, and it was doing so while we were still scrounging around for *used* aircraft that would be at least a slight improvement over what we had.

Boeing gave us a good deal on the 757. I was later to be accused of buying too many; actually I wished we had bought more, because their capacity saved us when air travel boomed in the era of discounted fares. And I shudder when I recall how close we came to not getting those airplanes.

The original contract was signed shortly after Congress passed a new tax bill permitting what was known as Safe Harbor Leasing. It enabled companies heavily in debt to sell their tax write-offs to profitable firms, the latter in turn using them to reduce their own taxes. Let's say we had a tax benefit worth ten dollars. Under Safe Harbor Leasing, we could sell that benefit to a company like GE for eight dollars—we'd have eight bucks in cash and GE would have ten dollars' worth of tax benefits.

Safe Harbor Leasing was the cornerstone of our 757 financing deal with Boeing. I'll never forget the day we reached an agreement with Tex Boullioun, the blunt-talking senior vice president of Boeing who was handling the original negotiations. There had been a total impasse after several days of futile discussion and Tex finally said, "I'm sorry but we're not getting anywhere and I have to catch a plane back to Seattle."

"Fine," I said. "I'll go with you to the airport."

I sat in the backseat, sandwiched between Boullioun and another guy from Boeing—I think Wayne Yeoman was driving. We kept talking and just as the car bounced hard over some railroad tracks Tex suddenly blurted, "Okay, Frank, you've got a deal." It was almost as if the jolt had loosened his resolve.

Two years later, the deal we made going over those railroad tracks got an even worse jolt. The media had begun criticizing Safe Harbor Leasing as a refuge for inefficient companies and Congress was set to repeal it. We had based all our long-range planning on the assumption that Safe Harbor would be around long enough for us to meet the financial commitments we had made in our reequipment program. One of the most decisive legislative battles in Eastern's history was fought by Jim Reinke, our vice president for Regulatory Affairs in Washington, and lobbyist Tom Korologos.

I tried to help them, spending weeks in Washington testifying before Congress and buttonholing influential senators like Russell Long of Louisiana. When I finished my pitch to him, he smiled encouragingly. "Well, Colonel, you've been very persuasive. You've convinced me and I'm with you."

I sighed in relief. Then he added, "Until the next guy comes along and he convinces me you're wrong."

Jim and Tom were magnificent—they kept working while other lobbyists were taking time off for cocktails and partying. Their doggedness finally paid off when Senator Bob Dole of Kansas agreed to see them one morning about 2 A.M. "Okay," Dole said, "tell me what you really need."

Reinke wrote down on the back of an envelope the gist of a provision that would phase out Safe Harbor Leasing gradually without killing it outright. Dole promised to support it and it was finally passed in that form. But while the revised law saved some of our 757s, it fell short of protecting all of them, and out to Seattle we flew on another mission born of desperation.

Boeing Chairman T. Wilson (the T. stands for Thornton, but Wilson was always called by his first initial) had his entire staff gathered to hear Eastern's presentation. T. happened to be the only friend I had in that big conference room—I was told later that his entire staff was unanimously in favor of canceling our 757 contract. I don't know how many minds I changed that day, but apparently I needed to impress only one man and that was T. Wilson.

I recounted how important the 757 was to Eastern's future. I said our destiny was linked irrevocably to growth—not the wild overnight expansion orgy of a Braniff but an orderly, carefully executed strategy that anticipated the future without waiting, vulnerable and unprepared, for the future to arrive.

The A-300 and 757, I explained, were just part of that strategy. The other components were route expansion, modernization of ground facilities, instilling new pride in every employee, and—the most difficult task of all—recasting the airline's high-cost image by enlisting labor's cooperation.

"I'm betting Eastern can do it," I concluded, "and I think Boeing can bet on it, too."

I left Seattle with Boeing's agreement to provide sufficient subordinate financing for the airplanes not covered under Safe Harbor.

When we were trying to decide what engine to put on the 757, we had a choice among three aspirants: Pratt & Whitney, General Electric, and Rolls-Royce. GE, which felt it couldn't give us the same kind of deal that had gone into the A-300, dropped out of the competition. The PW entry was a brand-new engine of considerable promise, but I had qualms about putting an unproven engine on a brand-new airplane. Yet our experience with Rolls had been so dismal that virtually the entire technical and marketing staffs lined up in opposition to our buying the British engine again.

"They're still government-owned and we can't depend on the government to support their product," an engineer told me.

I always felt the main reason for the engine's sorry performance was Roll-Royce's financial troubles when the RB-211 had still been in development. Yet I couldn't overlook the advice I was getting from people who knew more about turbine power plants than I did. The competition between PW and Rolls became so fierce that the latter's chairman came out of one negotiating session and remarked to me, "You know, that was just like a bloody Arab bazaar."

What intrigued me most about the Rolls sales campaign was an offer to provide export financing, something Pratt & Whitney couldn't match. So I told Sir Kenneth Keith, who was then president of Rolls,

"Look, before I agree to anything I'd like to talk to someone in the British government—as high up as I can go."

Keith arranged for me to meet with British Prime Minister James Callahan, who was in Washington on a state visit. I conferred with him at the British Embassy and laid the facts on the line.

"Mr. Prime Minister, your engine almost broke us earlier. I think you may well have the better engine now, but it's only going to be better if you'll give me your assurance that your government will support it from development on. The RB-211 that we put on our Lockheeds was woefully immature when we bought it. We can't handle another problem engine, particularly with one that's going on a two-engine airplane. So I need your personal guarantee that if we go with Rolls, the British government will back the product."

"You've got it," he said promptly.

I added, "Sir, I want one more thing from you. It's important that Rolls knows nothing about the outcome of this conversation. We're going to buy that engine, but as far as Rolls is concerned, I didn't get anything out of this meeting except a friendly, noncommital chat."

"And why should you want my promise of support kept secret?" he asked, mystified.

"Because, Mr. Prime Minister, I'd like to get a few more bucks out of Rolls first."

When we announced our choice of Rolls, the reaction within Eastern itself was that I had lost my mind. But the RB-211-535 turned out to be not only our most reliable and quietest engine, but overall perhaps the best turbine power plant ever put into airline service. It was so quiet that it enabled the 757 to become the only airliner permitted to take off from Washington National Airport after 10 P.M.

The judgment of the human ear in evaluating aircraft noise is decidedly suspect; it is about 99 percent subjective and 1 percent objective. By federal edict, we were ordered to put "hush kits" into our older DC-9 and 727 engines to meet new noise standards. It was an extremely expensive retrofit, yet it was impossible to tell the difference between an engine that had been modified and one that hadn't.

I was so convinced that not only Eastern but all the airlines were wasting money on retrofits that I arranged a demonstration. We invited a number of congressmen and local officials out to Dulles Airport and had different 727s stage a flyby—some had the hush kits installed, but others had engines we hadn't touched. Not a single spectator could identify which planes had been modified.

The modification order for the DC-9 was even more ridiculous. We took an unmodified model out to the noise-instrumented range at Yuma, Arizona, having argued to the FAA that the DC-9 didn't need any retrofit. It came within a half decibel of meeting the new criteria, but we still had to change all DC-9 engines covered by the retrofit order.

This wasn't the only time I fought city hall and lost. We wanted to use the A-300 on the Eastern Shuttle, where it would have been absolutely ideal. It not only would have done the work of two 727s, thus reducing congestion, but until the 757 came along it was the quietest airplane in our fleet. We got no static from either La Guardia or Boston's Logan International, but the FAA wouldn't let us bring the A-300 into Washington National.

We applied for permission in the waning days of the Carter administration and I had Langhorne Bond, the outgoing FAA administrator, convinced that the A-300, operated as a Shuttle aircraft with a light fuel load, would present no problems at National. But the Reagan administration took over before Bond could officially approve the operation and I had to campaign all over again. This time I was dealing with Drew Lewis, the new secretary of transportation, who passed the buck to newly appointed FAA chief Lynn Helms. He told me he wanted to reexamine Bond's approval.

"Why?" I asked. "We've already demonstrated to the FAA that the A-300 is quieter than any plane operating at National."

"Well, it's more a matter of safety than noise. It's a very heavy airplane and that could create safety problems."

He subsequently sent me a list of various technical reasons why the A-300 would be potentially dangerous operating at National. We refuted every one, but Helms came up with another objection. He claimed if we lost an engine during a turn on a downwind approach, the A-300 would become uncontrollable.

"Baloney," I snapped, "and I'll prove it to you."

First, we had Airbus set up the situation Helms described in a simulator. There was absolutely no indication that losing an engine downwind on a turn could cause control problems, even if the failed engine was on the side into which it was turning. Helms said a simulator might not be realistic enough, so we demonstrated the maneuver with a real A-300. Helms still refused approval, but when he left office a few months later, I tried again with Don Engen, his successor and a retired admiral who had won his wings in the Navy. He admitted, "It's obvious the A-300 would be acceptably quiet and safe at National, but politically we can't handle it, Frank. And that's why it won't be approved. There's too much community pressure against a big airplane that would bring more people in and out of the airport."

I appreciated his candor and that ended the matter.

That experience was just one reason why I abhorred dealing with politicians, especially when it involved noise. At Boston's Logan Airport, we suddenly were hit by a rule from the Port Authority that we could no longer taxi our aircraft to runways—they had to be towed. Taxiing, we were told, was too noisy and bothered the neighborhood. Incredibly, only Eastern's planes were involved, ostensibly because they were using taxiways closest to a noise-affected area.

The towing rule was not only ludicrous but economically catastrophic. It was bad enough that we had to revert to our push-back tractors, but those same tractors now would have to tow the planes right up to their takeoff positions. We discovered that some environmental activist plying his trade around Logan had gotten not merely to the Port Authority but to the governor of Massachusetts and his secretary of transportation, Fred Salvucci. But we also learned that wasn't the real motive behind the asinine order.

Eastern at the time was planning to build a new reservations center to serve the New England area. The choice of location lay between Rhode Island and a site in rural Massachusetts; our people preferred the former. When we protested the towing edict, we were told in effect that if we located the new reservations center at Logan, Eastern would have no further difficulties with noise complaints.

I was furious at this blatant political blackmail, but we didn't have much choice. So we agreed on Logan as the location of the center. It was no sooner in place and operating than Salvucci ordered the Port Authority to restore the towing requirement. This time we enlisted the aid of Tom McGee, the courageous Speaker of the House in the Massachusetts state legislature. I personally took him out to Logan and had him listen to taxiing aircraft in the area supposedly involving only Eastern's planes. The aircraft were so quiet you could hardly hear them.

McGee introduced a bill making it illegal for the Port Authority to force us to tow our airplanes, and it passed over the objections of the two men who controlled the Port Authority: Salvucci and his boss, Governor Michael Dukakis—the same Dukakis who at this writing would like very much to become President of the United States, presumably running on a platform that would include honesty and integrity in government.

We didn't need the machinations of politicians as Eastern braced for the first real onslaught of unregulated competition. We took advantage of the new law by spreading the Falcon's wings in several new markets: Miami–Haiti, Atlanta–San Francisco, Miami–San Francisco, St. Louis–Salt Lake City, and Fort Myers–New York. We inaugurated nonstop service between Atlanta and five other cities— Detroit; Cleveland; Savannah; Charleston, South Carolina; and Columbia, South Carolina. A bit later we challenged Delta on its prime Atlanta–Los Angeles route, an extremely difficult market to crack against an established carrier. I drew a lot of criticism for invading that particular Delta territory, as I did for trying to compete in the New York–Los Angeles market, but it was essential to develop Atlanta as a hub and without a western terminus the hub would have been a dead duck. By expanding to the west coast, we ended Eastern's north-south stagnation. For a while, I considered making St. Louis an east-west hub, but TWA was too firmly entrenched there and eventually we chose Kansas City, one of the best moves we ever made.

Being aggressive was the name of the game and we played it to the hilt. Route development is a risky business at best and some of the markets we entered were admittedly marginal, like Atlanta–Los Angeles. Yet I felt we at least should try, and if something didn't work out, all we needed was the discipline to admit we made a mistake, take our losses, and quit.

I think we were pretty well positioned for deregulation as the eighties began. We still were in debt, yet we had great employee morale and we had just completed the four most profitable years in the company's history. Eastern's public image was no longer that of an airline content merely to fly from A to B and the hell with how we did it.

We weren't afraid of innovation, either. We went from the industry's worst oversales record to the best, thanks to a gimmick that came from Dave Kuntsler's fertile mind. Like all airlines, we were plagued by the real parent of overbooking: no-shows, which in the Miami–New York market could reach as high as 30 percent on any given flight. The standard weapon against no-shows was to over-book deliberately in the same proportion as the anticipated no-shows. The computers weren't infallible, however, and if the oversales out-numbered the computer-predicted no-shows, we had more con-firmed passengers than seats.

Kuntsler came up with a plan called leisure class, aimed at people who didn't absolutely have to leave on a particular flight. If a flight was overbooked, we told leisure class passengers, "We've oversold, but because there will probably be no-shows, your chances of board-ing are good. If there's no coach seat available, we'll put you in first class at the coach fare. And if there's no seat available, we'll put you on the next flight to your destination and it won't cost you a cent." The key was honesty with the public.

The one area in which we remained vulnerable was our high costs. All the economy measures we took amounted to just nibbling around the edges—it was the kind of fat that required surgery more than dieting. And there wasn't anything I didn't try.

In looking for excess weight, I zeroed in on the two hotels we owned in Puerto Rico, heavily mortgaged and losing money. I had sent Wayne Yeoman over to talk to the unions about wage cuts—those two hotels had the highest labor costs per room in the Western Hemisphere. He told them we couldn't keep the hotels operating with their current contracts; the unions not only refused to coop-erate but went on strike. When they finally returned to work, we said, "Okay, we warned you we couldn't stay in business, so we're selling the hotels."

Easier said than done. There were no buyers, so we informed the two insurance companies holding the mortgages, Travelers and Con-necticut General, that they now owned the hotels.

"We won't take 'em," they protested.

I said that if they didn't, we were filing a bankruptcy petition in the Puerto Rican courts, and that did it—we dumped the hotels into their unwilling laps and good riddance.

I couldn't understand the unions' blind obstinance, preferring to let the hotels and their own jobs go down the drain rather than give us a reasonable contract that would allow a viable operation.

But then, I still had a few things to learn about unions.

The wave of deregulation competition struck, and my honeymoon period at Eastern was over.

21

THE STORM BREAKS

Deregulation's full impact on Eastern's fortunes and Charlie Bryan's rise to power as a union leader arrived on the scene virtually in tandem, twin omens of our troubled future.

It was Susan who first warned me that Charlie Bryan was a potential enemy—not just of mine but of Eastern's.

We were attending the IAM's annual convention in Las Vegas, shortly after Bryan's 1980 election as president of District 100. I was at the head table with the IAM national brass; my wife was sharing a table in the audience with Bryan and several others. Charlie had only one topic on his mind: Frank Borman.

He kept asking Susan about the *Apollo 8* mission in particular, about the fame and acclaim it had brought me. At first she was flattered at his interest, but his obsession with that single subject began to bother her.

She finally said, "Charlie, *Apollo 8*'s just history. It's all in the past. Frank's at Eastern now and NASA is a closed chapter in our lives. We're writing a new chapter."

Bryan never broke stride. He kept pestering and prodding her about the mission until she told him bluntly she didn't want to talk about it anymore. Then he made a final remark that chilled her.

"Frank Borman's had his *Apollo 8,*" Bryan said. "Now it's my turn—I'm gonna have mine."

When we went to our room later that night, I offhandedly asked Susan how she got along with Charlie. She told me what he had said, and added, "Frank, you've got a problem with that man."

I laughed. "Come on, he seems like a nice enough guy."

"You're wrong. He's obsessed with the idea that he's going to be in the same arena as Frank Borman. You don't even know him, Frank. He's a little guy who's suddenly been given a lot of power. He doesn't seem to give a damn about Eastern."

No more prophetic words were ever spoken.

Bryan's first act upon assuming office in January 1980 was to torpedo VEP, the linchpin of the defenses we had erected against the inroads of our new fare-slashing competitors. The pilots wanted the plan renewed and so did 87 percent of non-contract employees. But VEP was dead without the support of the IAM, and Bryan pulled the plug when he threatened to strike rather than to renew this key element in our efforts to control costs and build up our cash reserves.

His destruction of VEP was not unexpected. Bryan had run on an anti-VEP campaign against Jim Cates, who supported it openly.

I didn't help Jim's cause when I sent letters to employees and made several speeches urging that the expiring VEP program be renewed because it was absolutely essential to the company's survival in a deregulated climate. I never mentioned Cates's candidacy, but Bryan quite naturally went around accusing me of interfering in a union election. The end result was that I did the loyal Cates a disservice, although I doubt whether he could have beaten Bryan even if I had kept out completely. Bryan was a very effective campaigner, possessing tremendous rapport with the mechanics.

Admittedly he was a natural leader, but he also had the ability to seize on a single issue and ride it to power. It is a quality present in too many labor leaders and politicians alike, and the sharing of that quality is no coincidence—this is one of the major flaws in the American labor movement. Union leaders are more interested in internal politics than in the real world of economics; playing politics keeps them in power.

Bryan needed a single issue for his campaign and VEP was the instrument he chose, disputing the fact that it had worked and was vital to Eastern's future. He called it the "Variable Extortion Plan"— a catchphrase that won votes.

Bryan found achievement of power to be an ego-building exercise. In one of the first conversations I had with him after his election, he remarked suddenly, "You know, I feel I have a special calling with my union. When I appear at these meetings and I explain the issues to my people, they're all looking to me for salvation. Sometimes I really feel like Jesus and they're reaching out to touch me."

After he defeated Cates, someone slipped me a copy of a letter the loser had written to all members of IAM District 100. It was a plea for union unity after the bitter election, but it also included these words: "Mr. Frank Borman, whom I have the utmost respect for, was the company official in my opinion that did the most for Eastern Air Lines in the 32 years I have had an employee-employer relationship. Mr. Borman, I'm sure, will continue to work with the leaders of this district for the interest of all."

Bryan must have read the letter. Hopefully, if naïvely, I tried to cultivate his goodwill. First, I wanted to heal the wounds of the election and the death sentence his victory had passed on VEP. I knew I had to work with the guy for Lord knows how many more years, and I sought the same honest relationship I had enjoyed with Cates. I was anxious that he understand Eastern's precarious position, battling to compete successfully against the wave of new low-fare, low-cost carriers like People Express and Air Florida.

I invited Charlie to our weekend retreat in Key Largo, Florida, so we could relax and talk one on one, away from any business environment. Susan, despite her strong negative feeling about Bryan, was graciousness personified, and so was Charlie for that matter. I tried to persuade him that we could work together and how important his cooperation was to the airline.

"You have to understand, Charlie," I told him, "that it's no longer a case of them against us, management against labor. You're now a part of the whole picture and you're going to have to accept some responsibility in helping us meet the challenges of deregulation."

"Yeah, I absolutely agree," he assured me. But when I pressed him on specific ideas I had, cautioning that they could very well involve sacrifices on the part of his members, he refused to commit himself. That was Bryan; he could convince you that he had accepted what you told him as the gospel truth, and he was a master at portraying himself as a reasonable man, but getting him to promise anything definite was like mining coal with a nail file.

Immediately after his election, he had professed great admiration for me and called me a national hero. But I still began setting up a kind of buffer zone by cultivating the top honchos of the IAM, Bill Winpisinger and John Peterpaul. The better I got to know Bryan, the harder I wooed them—especially after I started getting vibes from both that they didn't think much of Charlie Bryan.

"Charlie hears voices," Winpisinger once grumbled to me during one of our recurring crises when Bryan was being his usual obstinate self.

I grew to like Winpisinger. He was a heavyset, cigar-smoking pragmatist with an unlimited vocabulary of four-letter words, who made outlandish statements just to unnerve his audience; I soon learned he didn't mean most of it. He was an occasional dinner guest at our house, and when I found out he was a racing buff, I took him to the Indianapolis Speedway Memorial Day races several times.

Peterpaul had begun his career as a mechanic at Mohawk Airlines. He was almost as profane as Winpy and just as pragmatic—a pair of typical old-style labor bosses, tough-talking and about as smooth as sandpaper. Under their hard-boiled crusts, however, ran a vein of vulnerability; they wanted to stay in power, which made them a little afraid of Charlie Bryan and his huge District 100. Bryan was in absolute command of nearly fourteen thousand mechanics, baggage handlers, and other ground workers who represented one third of our work force.

I came to trust Winpisinger and Peterpaul and they always assured me they were well aware that dealing with Bryan was an exercise in frustration—Charlie just kept saying no until he was sure that if he gave you anything, you had to give back something in return. This may be standard operating procedure in labor negotiations, but Bryan never could be convinced that Eastern had little or nothing to give back. In Winpisinger and Peterpaul, I felt I had two realistic men who could control him if push came to shove.

The new Bryan regime notwithstanding, I had at least some reasons for optimism. We were really challenging Delta on its home ground: Atlanta. By 1981, we finally were carrying as many business travelers through our Atlanta hub as leisure passengers—we were no longer primarily a vacation airline.

The cost of upgrading that crucial hub was heavy. We had to

spend millions on a new terminal but we would have been dead without it, and we came damned close to not getting the facilities. When the city had first decided to modernize and expand Hartsfield Atlanta International Airport, Hall and Higginbottom spent a small fortune on architectural designs for a terminal in the new complex. Then they decided Eastern couldn't afford it and canceled the project.

This would have left us out in left field, parked in the old terminal, while Delta was operating out of its own brand-new terminal. With the assistance of our lawyers, I had to do a lot of pleading before the city council agreed to give us the necessary space. In essence, any large expenditure was taking an airman's calculated risk, yet the alternative was standing still or contracting—and that meant financial disaster. Deregulation created an environment of growth; Eastern would not survive if we didn't move forward.

The one predictable thing about the airline industry, however, is its unpredictability. In August of 1981 came the strike of the Professional Air Traffic Controllers Organization (PATCO), the dumbest, most futile, and inexcusable walkout in the history of American labor relations. Yet, while it had the inevitable result of destroying that ill-advised union, the damage done to the nation's air transportation system was almost incalculable—the effects are still being felt seven years later.

I believe President Reagan was justified in firing the controllers and I publicly supported this action, even though the PATCO strike forced mandatory flight cutbacks that wrecked our traffic projections for months to come. The 1980–1982 recession demolished those projections even further, especially in the vital Florida market, which comprised our bread-and-butter routes.

All the airlines serving Florida were hit hard, and to fill empty seats fares were slashed—cuts we had to match. The 1981 price wars cost Eastern at least $100 million, with discounted tickets representing 70 percent of our sales. Only two years before, our discounted sales had amounted to less than 45 percent of total revenues. We were getting hit from every side; the cut-rate airlines were bad enough, but just before Christmas of 1981, Delta came in with a new round of fare cuts affecting the Florida market. The arithmetic was simple: Delta could afford them and we couldn't.

We lost $17.3 million in 1980—our first red ink in five years—and nearly $66 million in 1981. Contraction was tempting, but every study showed that would actually increase our losses. In fact, Eastern was a notoriously difficult patient on which to perform route surgery. We had a network so intricately woven that tampering with it would have been like pulling cans from the bottom of a stack.

In the spring of 1982 we pulled off a coup that stunned the industry. On April 16, the Civil Aeronautics Board—in the final stages of its deregulation phase-out—rejected Braniff's bid to sell its South American routes to Pan Am. The CAB's authority over international route cases was the last remaining gun in its regulatory arsenal, and Chairman Dan McKinnon was adamantly opposed to giving Pan Am a South American monopoly.

Pan Am, with White House support, lobbied furiously to win a reversal but McKinnon refused to budge, in the hope that another carrier would make Braniff an offer. The CAB was scheduled to meet on Monday, April 26, to make a final ruling on Pan Am's request for reconsideration—a ruling that McKinnon knew would have to go in Pan Am's favor unless someone else put in a bid for the routes.

For weeks, I had been urging Howard Putnam, Lawrence's successor at Braniff, to make a deal with Eastern. Putnam kept vacillating, and I was furious when I learned he already had a deal with Ed Acker at Pan Am while he was still talking to us. But on Sunday, April 25, Putnam called me and said the CAB had told him to find a buyer other than Pan Am.

We met in Eastern's New York office that same night. At 2:30 A.M. on Monday, we reached across a conference table and shook hands: For $30 million, Eastern had acquired Braniff's entire South American route system. Putnam and his lawyers caught an early morning Shuttle to Washington and presented the deal to the CAB by 9 A.M. while Pan Am was left holding the bag. I found out later that Air Florida Chairman Eli Timoner was preparing to make Braniff an offer that very day, not dreaming we were going to move as fast as we did.

We weren't out of the woods yet. Our agreement with Braniff called for us to start flying Braniff's routes on June 1. Sixteen days before that deadline Putnam called me, fatigue and defeat in his voice.

"Frank, we've run out of cash. I have to renege—we can't hold out until June first."

"When are you shutting down?"

"Tonight."

It would have been hard enough to take over those routes in two weeks; now we had twenty-four hours. Our CAB operating certificate was contingent on our starting service the day Braniff suspended service—if we didn't make it, Pan Am could have reopened the case.

We didn't even have our own people in the various South American bases—they were all staffed by Braniff personnel who'd be transferring to Eastern's payroll. I set up a telephone conference call embracing everyone who was going to be involved in launching service. I told them what had happened and added, "I know you're all eager, dedicated, and competent. I also know you're going to tell me it's impossible to get this done in one day. But I'm telling you there are a lot of eager, dedicated, competent people who *can* get it done, so if you decide you can't do it, I'll get someone who can."

Before the twenty-four hours were up, Eastern had started serving South America. Most of the credit should go to George Lyall, our vice president for the Latin American division in Miami, who did a fantastic job of coordinating the operations. He told me later, "You know, I don't think I'll ever forget that speech you made."

Braniff had a lot of pros down there, all of them native South Americans, and we didn't make the mistake of acting like invading gringos, telling them how to run things. We listened to *them*, not the other way around, and it worked. We did clean out some deadwood, but we kept most of the Braniff people and they proved to be excellent employees.

I caught hell from a segment of the media that challenged the wisdom of acquiring those routes. BORMAN TAKES EASTERN ON RISKY PATH, read one headline in *The Wall Street Journal*. The accompanying article pointed out that Braniff had lost $24 million on its South American operations over the past two years. It quoted an unnamed rival airline executive (I'll bet it was someone from Pan Am): "Borman sniffs space dust. Eastern has bitten off more than it can chew."

By the time I left Eastern, those routes were among the most profitable in our system. What the critics hadn't looked at was Braniff's inability to feed traffic into South America from its domestic system. Braniff had operated its South American division out of Miami, and Miami was a dead end for that airline domestically—it had nothing going into the city and had to rely on other carriers to supply the connecting traffic. And Braniff had served South America with aging, fuel-inefficient DC-8s.

For Eastern, Miami was the perfect North America—South America hub; virtually our entire system fed into it. And we put first-class equipment into our South American routes—L-1011s supported by 727-200s. We didn't have easy going at first; load factors were disappointing and the Peruvian government threw us a curve by limiting us to only three nonstop flights weekly between Miami and Lima, instead of the eleven we had requested. Later the government raised our authorization to eight weekly flights and traffic began increasing until we were more firmly established in the market than Braniff had ever been. By mid-1983, our South American system was producing 10 percent of Eastern's total revenues.

The minute we took over Braniff's routes, however, we also became the number one U.S. carrier of illicit cocaine being smuggled into the country. At the first inkling of trouble, I assigned Ernie Dunham, head of security at Eastern, to make certain the smuggling was stopped. But stopping it completely was difficult because the rewards of drug traffic were so great.

We tried our best to cooperate with both the Drug Enforcement Agency and the Customs Service, which were having their own problems—a jurisdictional war. We were tipped once that we had an L-1011 coming in from South America with a load of cocaine. DEA asked us to leave the shipment on board so its agents could keep the plane under surveillance while it was being unloaded. Before they could act, a local Customs official impounded the aircraft and removed the drugs.

We were faced with a stiff fine until I had a face-to-face meeting with Commissioner of Customs William Von Rabb and explained the situation. I also assured him we were doing everything possible to stop the smuggling.

We put seals on every compartment that could possibly be opened. We had guards positioned around every plane the instant it landed and they stayed there until it took off again. No one could get near the aircraft without signing in and out with the guard.

We shut every conceivable loophole, yet the drugs still kept coming into Miami. Once we flew German shepherds, trained to sniff out drugs, down to Bogotá, Colombia. Within a week, all had been poisoned. We had base managers in South America threatened so often that we had to switch them to other jobs.

Eventually, it became clear that some of our own employees had to be involved. They had worked out fantastic schemes for hiding drug shipments, like putting bags of cocaine behind the wall panels in lavatories. We even found one shipment in an L-1011's electronics bay. The most widely used method was to wait until all regular luggage from a South American flight had cleared Customs. Then cocaine-filled suitcases were removed from behind air conditioning panels in the baggage compartments, mixed with luggage from domestic flights, and picked up in the domestic baggage area by accomplices. It was no small-time operation, either; between 1981 and 1985, according to federal authorities, the airline's smuggling ring brought in between 5,400 and 16,200 pounds of cocaine with a street value of $250,000 a pound.

During the course of our investigation, Dunham asked the IAM to cooperate because the finger of suspicion was pointing directly toward a group of its members: the baggage handlers. The IAM's answer was "It's your problem—we don't condone it but we won't help you solve it."

It took eighteen months for the DEA, the FBI, and Eastern to uncover the ring. A grand jury indicted twenty-two Eastern baggage handlers and low-level supervisors, all stationed at Miami International Airport. Another fifty who weren't indictable were fired.

The smuggling ring wasn't the only mystery with which we had to contend. Early in 1980, a number of flight attendants reported the appearance of red facial and body spots on their skins—all after working A-300 flights between JFK Airport in New York and Miami. Some complained of becoming warm and flushed, followed by itching and burning. All assumed the spots were blood and panic set in.

At least sixty flight attendants were affected, some two or three times, and we ended up with a total of 120 separate instances. The spots showed up not only on faces but on hands, thighs, and chests.

The Transport Workers Union made a big issue out of the mystery, first claiming that the "bleeding" was the result of altitude sickness; the TWU contention was that Eastern was deliberately operating the A-300 at higher-than-normal altitudes, and was trying to save money on fuel by decreasing aircraft pressurization.

Pure bunk. So was the union's charge that we had threatened to fire any flight attendant who talked to the press about the spots. When we disproved the altitude theory, the TWU voiced additional suspicions: The "red sweat" had to be the result of the ovens on the A-300, or maybe chemicals used in aircraft cleaning.

We were just as puzzled as everyone else. No pilots or passengers were affected. The first attendants reporting spots to Dr. David Millett, Eastern's director of flight medicine, said they had disappeared after several hours. After Millett finally obtained actual samples, preliminary laboratory tests showed they were not blood, nor could they be identified as anything else. The test results were so inconclusive that we enlisted the aid of several prestigious organizations: the Centers for Disease Control in Atlanta, the National Institute for Occupational Safety and Health in Cincinnati, NASA, Columbia University's College of Physicians and Surgeons, the Air Force and Duke University.

Their verdict was unanimous: They didn't know what caused red sweat any more than we did. We got plenty of theories—an allergic reaction to makeup; hemophilia; chromhidrosis (colored perspiration) caused by genetic factors or bacterial infection; a combination of exertion, altitude changes, and dehydration; even mass hysteria. What we didn't get was a solution.

Then Millet uncovered a curious pattern. The affected flight attendants had all been on overwater A-300 flights that required lifejacket demonstrations. Not a single case had been reported on A-300 trips that flew entirely over land. With this lead, we examined the demonstration lifejackets that had been obtained recently from a new supplier, and discovered that the red spots were particles of red paint, so poorly applied that the paint flaked off.

We changed over to another type of demonstration jacket and the red sweat mystery was solved, although not to the satisfaction of the union. Millett informed me that despite all evidence pointing to the demo jackets, the TWU was never fully satisfied with this explanation. Apparently it preferred to think there had to be something wrong with the working conditions on an A-300 flight.

In retrospect, red sweat was a rather minor crisis, yet one symptomatic of labor's inherent distrust of management. At the time, I found it disturbing that any union, in the face of proven scientific evidence, still could regard those demo jackets as some kind of management cover-up of a more sinister cause. It seemed to portend trouble.

There was every reason to feel concern as 1982—a year when growth and service improvement were combined with mounting losses—drew to a close. The 1982 red ink alone amounted to nearly $75 million. The other set of figures I kept looking at were labor and operating costs of such competitors as People Express and Air

Florida—their pilots, flight attendants, and mechanics were earning approximately half of what we were paying their Eastern counterparts. Our 2 percent profit requirement had not been met for two years. Unless we could return to profitability promptly, Eastern was doomed.

Before the year ended, we had managed to wring one concession out of Bryan and the IAM. He finally agreed to replace VEP with a plan called the Employee Investment Program. Under EIP, mechanics would continue to have 3.5 percent of their wages withheld, but Eastern had to guarantee that the money would be repaid—at 10 percent interest—within a set time frame, regardless of our profit/loss status.

It was the best we could do in a bad deal, but it prevented a strike and gave us some cash flow. I knew, however, that EIP fell far short of what VEP's renewal could have provided; the new plan simply added to debts that would have to repaid. All we really did was toss Bryan a bone to keep him happy until the next crisis came along.

We didn't have long to wait.

If there were one year in my life I would not want to live over, it would be 1983.

History will record that Eastern lost its battle to remain independent in 1986 when it became part of Texas Air. That's only technically correct; the first pages of that final chapter had actually been written three years earlier.

In January 1983, Eastern and the IAM were locked in bitter and futile negotiations for a new wage contract; the old agreement had expired many months ago. Bryan was demanding a 30 percent wage increase over the next thirty months retroactive to the beginning of 1982, plus improved fringe benefits mostly involving retirement pay. The whole package would have cost Eastern millions more than we could afford.

The IAM laid a sign-or-we'll-strike ultimatum on the table in face of the $75 million we had lost in '82 and the fact that 1983 projections looked even worse. In good faith, we responded with an offer that to my knowledge had never been tried before by any major corporation.

"If you don't believe we're in deep trouble," Marv Amos told Bryan, "we'll let any three experts of your own choosing look at the airline's books. Let them tell you what kind of raise this company can afford and we'll abide by their decision."

Specifically, he suggested that the experts consist of two business school professors and an IAM representative. Bryan's reply was made to the news media.

"It would be an exercise in futility," he declared. "In business schools they don't teach trade unionism. I'm not interested in having someone who runs a business school determine the destiny of my membership."

As negotiations hardened into an angry impasse, Bryan began citing management mistakes as the reason why his mechanics were being shortchanged. His major claim involved our decision to buy the 757.

"Some of the money that went for the 757s should have gone to pay raises for employees who have gone without any increase for nearly two years," he charged. He was to continue this refrain for the next three years, during every crisis and every confrontation, and his members believed him. What Bryan ignored were two salient facts: First, if we hadn't modernized the fleet when we did, we would had to pay much more later for both the 757 and the A-300. And second, if we hadn't purchased them, we would have been dead competitively.

Eastern bought those planes at bargain-basement prices—one expert estimated we paid perhaps 25 percent less than they would have cost in 1983 because of the manufacturers' discounts and Safe Harbor financing.

And naturally, Bryan never would admit to another reason for the huge equipment commitment; we were buying those airplanes to help compensate for the IAM's own inefficiencies—its unproductive work rules that were costing us millions. One example: At Delta, non-union mechanics were allowed to double as baggage handlers during peak periods, a practice that simply improved service to passengers and cut costs. At Eastern, a mechanic could be staring at three hundred pieces of unloaded luggage and would walk away in complete indifference—his union forbade any crossover of duties.

Bryan refused to believe anything Amos told him about our precarious finances. When Dwayne Andrews, the company's chief negotiator during the endless bargaining sessions, laid dollars-and-cents figures on the table, Bryan's response was to announce to the press, "I don't believe the gloom and doom forecasts placed before me. I think 1983 will be profitable for Eastern."

How the hell he reached this conclusion is known only to Charlie Bryan. He was apparently impressed with senior vice president of Planning Mort Ehrlich's projection of a modest 4 to 6 percent traffic increase for the year, but what totally escaped Bryan was Ehrlich's bottom-line forecast: a severe decline in yield. By 1983, 85 percent of Eastern's fares were discounted; we were being forced to match $49 fares between New York and Miami, and $198 round-trip fares on flights to the Northeast, Midwest, and west coast.

I couldn't keep up with the statements he kept issuing. At one stage he told reporters, "We've made recommendations for saving money that would help the company escape financial difficulty and still grant a substantial wage increase, but they've ignored them."

To this day, I'm completely unaware of any suggestion Charlie Bryan ever made that would have contributed one cent toward reducing costs. He resisted virtually all attempts to revise his expensive, archaic work rules and every concession he agreed to make was accompanied by a giveback demand that negated the concession.

He harped long and loud on the fact that Eastern had managed to post a $12.2 million profit in the last quarter of 1982, indicating, as he informed the press, that the airline had turned the corner and could afford to meet his demands. What he didn't tell the media was that the $12.2 million came from selling our Safe Harbor leasing and tax benefits to raise cash. Without this income, our losses would have been close to $90 million.

I grudgingly admit that Bryan's manipulation of the press was masterful. He could sound so reasonable, sincerely cooperative, and knowledgeable that many reporters swallowed whatever he told them—and conversely, our attempts to correct his "facts" were dismissed as company propaganda. Bryan skillfully portrayed himself as a responsible labor leader, loyal to his members yet always cognizant of Eastern's difficulties and willing to compromise. And when he knew he couldn't gloss over those difficulties, all he had to do was blame them on Frank Borman and Eastern's inept management.

For example, Bryan was flying one morning from Miami to New York on an L-1011 that developed engine trouble. The captain decided to land at Baltimore for repairs, but when it became apparent the engine couldn't be fixed for many hours, we ferried an A-300 into Baltimore that picked up the stranded passengers and landed them in New York's La Guardia Airport a few hours late.

Because many passengers were nervous when the TriStar landed in Baltimore routinely on two engines, we handed out coupons worth fifty dollars on any future Eastern flight—a kind of apology for their inconvenience and concern. Bryan took that incident and magnified it into a classic example of management stupidity. In speech after speech his version was that there had been a short delay in Baltimore, and that we'd handed out fifty-dollar coupons to a planeful of passengers who had paid only forty-nine dollars for their fares. He failed to mention that it hadn't been just a brief delay but a major mechanical problem requiring a long wait for a replacement aircraft, or that people paying forty-nine dollars constituted about 5 percent of the passengers aboard.

"Isn't it stupid," he'd tell his audience, "that we were selling forty-nine-dollar tickets and giving people a fifty-dollar refund, which meant we were paying them a dollar for being on the flight?"

Wayne Yeoman, our senior vice president for Finance, had been on the same plane. Wayne went to a retirees' meeting at which Bryan was the speaker and heard him tell that story. After the speech, Yeoman accosted him.

"Charlie, I was on that flight and you know damned well it didn't happen that way," Wayne said angrily. "Your story is just complete misrepresentation."

Bryan must have told that same story fifty times and never changed a word, even after Yeoman's protest.

When Bryan refused to budge in his wage demands, I tried to get management's message across, not merely to the mechanics but to the other unions and non contract employees. In videotapes and speeches by me and other top officers, we outlined the company's money problems. I wasn't preaching anything new—I had been telling everyone the same things since before deregulation.

The future of the airline and of its forty thousand employees was based on a fragile structure, consisting of three pillars: the equipment program, without which we couldn't compete; the banks that financed the program; and the reduction of labor costs, so that we could resume profitability and ensure continued financial support from the lenders.

It was during these critical negotiations that Charlie hired a young Washington labor consultant named Randy Barber as District 100's economic adviser, although "personal guru" would have been a better job description. Bryan was difficult enough on his own, but when he came under Barber's influence he became even worse. I have only gut instinct to go on, but I'm absolutely convinced that Randy planted in Bryan's mind the belief that Charlie should run Eastern himself.

Charlie wouldn't listen to anyone in management, to the other unions, or to his own IAM superiors. But he did listen to Randy Barber. From the time these two joined forces, a propaganda pattern emerged: All of Eastern's problems were the result of bad management. There wasn't anything Bryan didn't criticize, from route development to fares, from the fleet modernization program to scheduling. It made no difference that neither Bryan nor Barber had any experience or knowledge of airline operations. It made no difference that all but a handful of major carriers also were swimming in red ink, including such stalwarts as American, United, and Delta. If we cut fares to match the competition, Bryan would claim the cuts weren't necessary. If we tried to hold the line on fares, Charlie would tell the press that Eastern wasn't being competitive.

Negotiations continued throughout February. We finally called in a federal mediator, who got nowhere; meanwhile the airline continued to hemorrhage—in the first two months of '83, Eastern lost over $44 million. When the mediator tossed in the towel early in February, the IAM set a strike date of March 13.

As the strike deadline neared, the FBI picked up a rumor that the union had taken out a contract on me. I figured the rumor was an act of intimidation, not a real threat, but the FBI took it seriously enough to insist that I wear a bulletproof vest, and off-duty policemen were assigned to protect Susan and me, as well as our grandchildren. Actual violence was committed against dissident IAM members. One mechanic known to be pro-company had his trailer riddled with bullets. And a former union official who had vocally supported policies like VEP lost most of one hand in a shotgun ambush. The union claimed the latter incident involved a personal feud, but the victim swore he had been shot because he was pro-company.

Publicly, Bryan denounced violence, although he never took internal action against it. But he condoned subtler anti-company tactics aimed at pressuring management into settlement on his terms. One strategy was a deliberate slowdown that affected service on L-1011 flights, and this was achieved by using the aircraft's ovens in an effective display of union muscle flexing.

Mechanics would report that numerous ovens needed repair, then would delay repairs or refuse to make them at all with the excuse that there wasn't time. We strongly suspected that many ovens were being damaged deliberately, and when we began to run short of cooking units to the point of delaying flights or serving cold meals, we asked for a court injunction against the slowdown. A judge denied the injunction because he said we couldn't prove either sabotage or willful procrastination on repairs.

Finally one night, in sheer frustration, our vice president for Maintenance loaded all the out-of-service ovens on trucks and took them to a subcontractor for repairs. Bryan charged us with violation of a union contract provision that forbade outside repairs on any aircraft component, and the judge upheld his position. We had to bring back the ovens and the slowdown continued.

In a last-ditch effort to prevent a strike, I gave my blessing to a final offer: We agreed to grant a 32.2 percent wage increase over the next thirty months, commencing in 1983, and asked Bryan to submit the offer to his members for a vote. Bryan agreed, but announced he would recommend rejection because the wage boost was not retroactive to January 1982.

We were beaten before a single vote was cast, yet I tried to offset Bryan's irresponsible ruthlessness by sending a personal letter to all IAM members explaining why the offer was the best we could make, and bluntly warning that a strike would be catastrophic for them as well as everyone else.

"If you turn down this contract," I wrote, "it will mean the end of Eastern as we know it."

Charlie, furious that I had gone over his head to his own constituency, took us to court again with the charge that under the Railway Labor Act, management had no right to deal with a union except through its elected representatives. When the judge finally got around to ruling against Bryan, his decision was meaningless—my letter hadn't swayed many votes anyway.

The vote was overwhelmingly for rejection, as expected. Long before the vote was taken, Bryan had ordered his members to boycott meetings at the various stations where company officers, including myself, tried to present the cold financial facts.

Rejection of our offer meant the setting of a new strike deadline: March 23. By now, however, Bryan's obstinancy in the face of what obviously was a major crisis had alienated the entire airline, including the other unions.

Even prior to his setting the final deadline, from all sides had come pleas for me to stand firm against the IAM even if it meant a strike. The pilots assured me they'd cross the picket lines. Three thousand flight attendants signed a petition pledging to support the company if the mechanics walked out. Non-union employees promised to work at whatever extra jobs were required—from aircraft cleaning to sweeping out hangars. So, for that matter, did the pilots.

Even travel agents called, volunteering to work at Eastern for free during the strike. Shirley Sabin, a St. Petersburg Beach agent, announced she had lined up twenty to thirty agents in her area and was busy organizing similar help from the 240 agencies in the Suncoast Travel Industry Association.

Every fiber in me wanted to take on Charlie Bryan and I had Eastern solidly behind me. Now we had to consider the consequences of taking a strike. I sent financial people to Northwest, an airline that had been strike-afflicted more than any other carrier, to get some idea of how long we could expect our cash to last in the event of a strike without going bankrupt. We brought in a firm of bankruptcy experts to advise the Board of Directors on the pros and cons of filing under Chapter 11 if the mechanics went out.

We evaluated selling Eastern's prime asset, the east coast Shuttle, just to raise enough cash to withstand a long strike until the IAM caved in. Our calculations showed we had enough cash to withstand a strike for twelve days. With every intention of telling Charlie Bryan to go to hell and strike, I flew to New York for meetings with the banks. Eastern had a $200 million line of credit and I asked them to release $110 million.

I said, "With this money, we can take a strike for at least thirty days. In that period, the mechanics will have missed two paychecks and I think some of them will start coming back, willing to accept a far less expensive settlement."

The banks turned me down. Operationally, we were ready—ten thousand pilots and flight attendants were primed to cross those picket lines, eighteen thousand non-contract employees were willing to get their hands soiled in the most menial work, and we had outside contractors lined up to perform basic maintenance.

Our directors were kept fully informed. They listened to the bankruptcy lawyers, the financial experts, and the vice presidents whose departments were operationally ready to take a strike. Then Jack Fallon, chairman of the board's executive committee, flew to Florida and spent a weekend with Susan and me; for hours we discussed the airline's dilemma.

We had overwhelming evidence that if the mechanics stayed out for more than twelve days, we'd end up in Chapter 7, which meant absolute bankruptcy, seizure of all assets, and a total shutdown. Fallon, a big, tough Irishman from Boston, had never backed away from a fight in his life. Nor had I. But to fight at this point would put Eastern out of business. As I drove Jack back to Miami, both of us in a low mood because we knew what the decision must be, he looked at my grim face.

"Frank," he said quietly, "we'll have to give in today so we can live to fight another day—it's that simple."

The last-minute negotiations were still going on in Washington on March 23 with the strike deadline set for midnight. I flew to the capital and walked into John Peterpaul's office at the IAM's national headquarters.

"John," I said, "your union is going to destroy our airline."

"There's nothing I can do," he insisted. "I don't control Bryan."

"Then what's it going to take to settle this?"

"What's on the table," he replied coldly.

I stood up. "Okay, John, but I want you to know whatever we give, you're gonna have to give back."

Peterpaul allowed himself a slight smile. "All right," he said. "We'll work with you if it comes to that."

I phoned our negotiators and told them school was out—go ahead and settle. The same night I flew back to Miami, as depressed as I've ever been in my life. I felt I had let down some twenty-eight thousand loyal employees and I rightly feared the consequences. I had no sooner arrived home and started talking disconsolately to Susan than a female reporter from a Miami television station rang the doorbell.

"Colonel," she asked, "what happened?"

"We were raped," I said bitterly, and closed the door.

To avoid the strike, we had to give a 32.2 percent wage increase, not only a bitter pill but an impossibly expensive one. Not counting the long-range fringe benefits and subtracting a few union concessions including retroactivity, the settlement added $170 million to annual costs.

The consequences of surrendering to Bryan ran beyond the effects on Eastern's fragile finances. I had made the mistake of promising to stand tall against the IAM's threats. I'd meant it, but when I had to break that promise to save the company, I lost credibility to an incalculable extent. I turned loyalty and faith into cynicism and distrust; in the end I was to pay dearly for this loss of confidence in what had been strong leadership. Nor could I blame any of Eastern's employees for becoming disillusioned. They'd been willing to march with me to the gates of hell and I'd let them down. The pilots in particular were hurt—they had already agreed to wage concessions, as had the non-contract employees—and they were as angry at me as they were at the IAM. The IAM settlement had the effect of creating a new attitude of militancy within the other unions.

On more than one occasion, I have been reminded that Bob Crandall of American, faced with a similar strike threat from his TWU mechanics when he demanded a two-tier wage structure for all employees, actually dared the union to walk out. Crandall, like us, had positioned American to maintain operations if his mechanics struck. Non-union employees had been trained to take over ground jobs and contingent maintenance contracts had been signed with fixed base operators at every station. The union backed down after Crandall warned the mechanics they wouldn't have any jobs to return to if they walked out, and he got his two-tier program.

While our pre-strike preparations were identical, however, there was one vast difference in our respective situations. American had more than $1 billion in liquid assets on hand and could have withstood any strike almost indefinitely. In contrast, Bryan shrewdly played on Eastern's financial weakness even as he denied that it really existed.

Now, after the humiliation of the '83 settlement, we had to forge a new strategy—one that would help us recover from surrendering to labor financial spoils that we couldn't afford.

For both me and the airline I loved, life would never be the same.

22

FROM BAD TO WORSE

Charlie Bryan's postsettlement comment to the press was a case of looking through rose-colored glasses.

"There's no question the company can afford it by virtue of the change in attitude on the part of the work force, the change in morale," he declared. "We're very confident the company is going to make a profit in the next three years."

I wasn't anywhere near that confident, but I recognized that our only hope lay in cooperating with the unions. Yet I also realized that nothing was more difficult than dealing with Bryan and the IAM from a position of weakness.

In April, with a default on our loans now only too possible and a $60.7 million loss recorded in the first quarter of 1983, I met with Bryan in Washington for about an hour and a half, an amicable but unproductive session during which I warned Charlie that we had a liquidity dilemma that the unions must help us solve. He agreed we had a problem, but he did not commit himself to a solution. Then he informed the press that we had buried the hatchet.

The meeting led to formation of a management-labor committee to explore ways out of the mess. Bryan was a member of the committee, but every time we met he remained vague on any promises of cooperation, and the committee kept spinning its wheels. I set up a luncheon meeting attended by company executives, directors, and IAM officials including Charlie. When it ended, Bryan told reporters that employees were generally aware of the problems Eastern was facing.

"Regardless of what their [the company's] intentions may be," Bryan assured his listeners, "the result is going to be one of affirmative employee action."

"What action will your union take?" he was asked.

"We're in the middle of talks and discussions," he said.

Yes, there were many talks and discussions. They achieved nothing. Bryan's chief contribution was to continue his campaign of "it's all the fault of mismanagement," even as the management he vilified kept trying everything to keep the airline afloat.

In May, the banks froze our credit line and we found ourselves $90 million short of meeting immediate payroll and other operating expenses. I had no choice but to ask Eastern's employees for help—namely, to put 10 percent of their wages into company debentures, a gesture that I figured would impress the lenders sufficiently to unfreeze our credit line. Almost 70 percent of the non-contract employees voted for the giveback plan and the pilots quickly followed suit. The flight attendants wavered, then went along.

Only the IAM balked; Bryan for months had been accusing me of manufacturing crises to force concessions out of the workers. I called him to my office.

"This is for real, Charlie," I warned. "The banks have cut off our credit and we'll be out of cash by the end of June."

He agreed to a radical suggestion: I proposed a joint meeting in Atlanta where we'd both speak to some 250 company and IAM officials from around the system.

On June 3, we convened this unusual session in a local hotel. The room was jammed, while rank-and-file IAM members stood outside and listened to the proceedings through an open door. I spoke first.

"Unless we improve the labor relations and the working relationships in this company, you can kiss it off," I told the tense and silent audience. "The demands of the free market call for—no, demand—a change in the relationships we have with the people in this room.

"I want a change in the relationship. I want a relationship that fosters mutual respect. That's the wave of the future, and unless we do that, we cannot guarantee the survival of this airline."

Bryan rose and called the past eighteen months of bitter labor negotiations "a fierce and treacherous experience for all of us." He continued, "What happened during the last year and a half at Eastern was a tragedy that fed off horrendous labor relations. But what management is telling you about the short-term situation is factual. The banks have cut us off."

This was Charlie Bryan playing the phony role he loved best: labor statesman. Then he damned near exchanged his new olive branch for a club.

"It's make-or-break time at Eastern Airlines for labor relations," he said ominously. "If we're betrayed again . . . I can tell you, if this is a hollow promise, an empty commitment, I don't think Eastern will ever, ever, have any labor peace—ever!"

With that one remark, he had almost destroyed the conciliatory mood in that packed room. I didn't want it to end that way and I hastily ended the meeting on an upbeat note: "What happened here today is historic. There is going to be a new era, and it's going to include new management techniques. I hope it will be a two-way street."

But deep in my heart, I knew that the "hollow promise," the "empty commitment," had been made by Charlie Bryan. He recommended to his members that they accept the new investment plan, then, after it was ratified, proceeded to insist that their contributions be voluntary, which made IAM cooperation meaningless.

Ratification by the three unions and the non-contract employees at least convinced the banks to loosen the purse strings temporarily. But by fall, we were back to square one, and once more I knew I had to go back and ask for more concessions.

As I had warned Peterpaul, I knew the IAM was going to have to give back much of what Bryan had pried out of Eastern. This became increasingly apparent throughout the spring and summer of '83. Competition on our north-south routes was getting stiffer than ever, with People Express expanding rapidly. So was Piedmont, and we were faced with the opposition carriers doubling their capacity even as they fought us with fare cuts.

Eastern was bleeding from every pore when I went to see Bill Winpinsinger.

"This is going to end in disaster," I told him. "We can't live with that damned IAM contract. I need someone who can deal with people like Charlie Bryan and make the unions realize the bind we're in. I'd hire him as a consultant, a kind of liaison man between management and labor. He definitely wouldn't represent management. He'd be sort of a permanent arbitrator or mediator."

Winpinsinger didn't hesitate. "If I were you, Frank, I'd get Bill Usery."

Usery's track record was superb. A big, bluff man with a reputation for absolute integrity, his background was pure labor. He had been Secretary of Labor in the Gerald Ford administration and had once been an IAM official. After he left the cabinet, he established a labor relations consulting firm with such prestigious clients as Westinghouse and General Motors. It was Usery, in fact, who helped forge the Toyota–General Motors partnership deal that also involved the United Auto Workers.

He accepted the job, possibly the most difficult in his illustrious career. Usery was to stay with the airline until I left, becoming not only a treasured friend but a man to whom I owe a large debt of gratitude.

Usery came to Eastern in the middle of not merely another crisis but one that threatened the airline's existence. By the fall of '83, we were in such grave straits that we couldn't meet the interest payments on our loans. The banks handed us an ultimatum: Cut labor cost by $200 million a year or be declared in default.

I wasn't worried about the pilots' cooperation. For the past two years, Eastern's ALPA local had been headed by Augie Gorse, a tough but reasonable negotiator whom I had grown to respect. He was a veteran Eastern captain, suspicious of the company when he was elected chairman of the Master Executive Council, but he was also a hard-nosed realist who became convinced I was playing straight with him. Gorse served two terms as MEC chairman, a unique achievement at Eastern, where the pilots had a habit of eating their own. Meetings were poorly attended and, as happens so often in unions, a small but vocal minority really called the shots. It took a strong leader to keep them in line without being recalled at the next election for being too cooperative with management. Of all the union officials I worked with, Gorse and another captain, George Smith, who succeeded Augie in mid-1983, were the best—they weren't pro-management but they *were* pro-Eastern.

For a long time, the flight attendants' TWU unit had even less stability than the pilots. It kept shifting between indecisive Pat Fink and Bob Callahan, a well-educated young man whose mind always seemed to be somewhere in left field. He had taught history before becoming a flight attendant, held news conferences in Spanish, and claimed he got his bargaining strategy out of a twenty-five-hundred-year-old book on Chinese warfare.

Both Fink and Callahan represented a hardworking, anti-management cadre that set union policy while the silent and sadly indifferent majority let them run the show. I'll say this for Charlie Bryan: He molded the mechanics into a loyal, cohesive army that followed his policies blindly. Eastern could have used the unity that Bryan inspired, and that was the greatest tragedy of his regime.

With the banks breathing down our necks again, I had to keep warning everyone that the alternative to wage concessions was bankruptcy. The danger in making such a blunt prediction is that it becomes a self-fulfilling prophecy. The airline industry is unique in that most customers pay in advance for a service they'll use later. A carrier that admits it's in serious trouble creates nervousness among the public, and passengers shy away from it.

By October of '83, we had begun to lose thousands of advance bookings as passengers switched their reservations to Delta, People Express, Pan Am, and Republic because of the adverse publicity. At one point, we stood to lose a third of fall and winter bookings from travel agents who frankly explained their clients were concerned that Eastern wasn't going to be around very long. That's exactly what had happened at Braniff.

I can't overemphasize the damage done by my loss of credibility, the erosion of the employee confidence that had once been such a strong asset. Throughout those last unhappy years at Eastern, it was painful to recall the happier times when I had enjoyed trust and loyalty, yet could give it back in equal proportions. I never stopped trying to give it back, but gradually it ceased to be a two-way street; only the non-contract workers never faltered in their faith.

I especially remembered the time a blizzard hit the east coast, snarling operations for two days. Our people really hung in there, most of them sleeping at the airports and working long hours to get the mess untangled. They were absolutely magnificent and I was so grateful that I hit eight cities in forty-eight hours to thank them personally. We had an esprit de corps, an unshakable morale, unsurpassed by any airline.

Now, in midfall of '83 with another crisis looming, I turned to silver-haired William Julian Usery for help.

Eastern had lost $129 million in the first nine months of the year. I asked the three unions to take a 20 percent pay cut—15 percent in actual reductions and the rest in vacation time givebacks. The alternatives, I emphasized, were Chapter 11 or a complete shutdown and liquidation of the airline under Chapter 7.

Bryan threw down the gauntlet. He now was seeking control of the airline and refused even to consider any concession unless I resigned. Some of his own members urged him to let them at least vote on the wage cuts, but Charlie maintained his intransigence. Pat Fink, whose TWU flight attendants were negotiating for a new contract, went along with Bryan and threatened to strike. The *Miami Herald,* normally willing to lend Charlie its ear, declared in an editorial, "That object in the union leaders' hands isn't a white flag of surrender; it's a tourniquet that they, and only they, can apply to stop EAL's hemorrhaging."

Bill Usery went to work, his most immediate task being to cool off the flight attendants before they could strike. It wasn't easy, because in her own way, Pat Fink was almost as hard to deal with as Bryan.

"She has a very difficult problem in arriving at decisions," Bill wryly confided to me, in one of his classic understatements. Patience, however, is one of Usery's greatest virtues. One of his techniques is to wear down the negotiators in marathon sessions until both sides, in sheer weariness, decide to compromise. Yet Usery always appeared as fresh as a man who has just had twelve hours of uninterrupted sleep.

He was almost sixty years old when he came to Eastern and I marveled at his stamina. Not until later did I find out how the old fox did it. He'd keep both parties up most of the night talking, then, when heads were starting to nod, he'd announce, "I've got an important meeting that might help solve things. I'll be back in about three hours, so you guys keep talking."

And while the bedraggled negotiators were steadily running out of gas, Usery would sneak off for a three-hour nap. Then he'd return, fresher than anyone in the room, ready to bang heads together.

Usery quickly earned the Eastern unions' confidence by convincing them that he wasn't representing either side. He found the pilots bitter. George Smith, who had just succeeded Gorse, told Bill that what ALPA resented was our giving the concessions the pilots had made over to the mechanics to prevent the strike.

Usery encountered the same belligerence toward both me and the IAM among the flight attendants' negotiators—a "Charlie Bryan got his, so we want ours" attitude. And the biggest obstacle facing Bill was the emergence of disbelief in Eastern's financial condition.

Usery proposed to the three unions that an outstanding, totally impartial firm look at the airline's books. He recommended Lazard Frères for the special, unprecedented audit. ALPA and the TWU agreed, but Charlie Bryan balked, insisting that Locker/Abrecht, the accounting firm the IAM was using, do the audit.

Usery solved this latest impasse by suggesting that both firms be hired, so the company ended up paying for two audits. The accountants quickly came up with identical verdicts: Eastern was in a deep hole and only the unions had the shovels to dig the airline out. The Lazard Frères report was more detailed; it went beyond confirming my near-bankruptcy alarms by outlining specific measures that must be taken, both immediately and over the long term.

They were adopted in large part, but only after some marathon sessions between Usery and the unions. I stayed out of them at Usery's request, although he kept me advised throughout the proceedings. Actually, management didn't get involved much because I had given Bill a blank check, virtually assuring him that I'd go along with whatever he worked out.

He had to haul in some pretty big guns before he wrested an agreement out of Bryan. The crucial meeting in Charlie's office began at 4 P.M. and lasted until almost 3 A.M. Bryan had with him Randy Barber, Peterpaul of the IAM, one of the Locker/Abrecht partners, and Brian Freeman, a former Treasury Department official who had helped put through the Lockheed and Chrysler government loan-guarantee programs and was now Peterpaul's economic adviser. Usery was flanked by Fred Bradley of Citibank, and Ray Minella from Merrill Lynch, the airline's investment banker.

What Bryan finally agreed to was the plan recommended by Lazard Frères and accepted by the other unions. It called for a $367 million cut in labor costs for 1984 only, to be achieved by:

1. Taking 18 percent of each employee's salary (22 percent of the pilots') and putting it into Eastern stock, a $292 million saving that also gave employees 25 percent of the company
2. The unions' promising to increase productivity by $75 million

From all three groups Usery obtained a pledge to return to the negotiating table toward the end of 1984, at which time both management and labor would review Eastern's finances and take whatever steps were necessary to improve the company's position. This was the key element in the Lazard Frères report, a recognition that the $367 million package—actually less than what the firm felt was needed—was strictly a temporary relief measure and might fall short because it was partially dependent on unspecified productivity improvements.

Lazard Frères had emphasized that reducing labor costs could not be a one-year deal; further concessions might be required if the airline failed to achieve profitability. Usery would say later, "No one believed the company could overcome its financial problems in one year."

To make sure Bryan accepted this fact of life, Bill asked him to sign a letter of understanding to that effect, thus adhering to the promise that the Lazard Frères plan was subject to renewal by the end of 1984. Bryan did sign, along with the other union leaders, after Usery sweetened the pot: Four union people would go on Eastern's Board of Directors, one each from the IAM and TWU and two representing both the pilots and non-contract employees.

Usery's reasoning seemed sound at the time. We were asking employees to make sacrifices, and Bill felt strongly that putting union people on the board was the best way for them to understand company problems. The precedent already had been set at Chrysler when Lee Iacocca invited Douglas Fraser of the United Auto Workers to serve as a director. Fraser's presence played a major role in Chrysler's recovery.

That's what worried me. I knew Fraser to be one of the most intelligent, responsible, and respected men in the American labor movement. I also knew Charlie Bryan was no Doug Fraser. Nevertheless, I welcomed Usery's proposal. More than anything else, I wanted labor peace based on union recognition of deregulation's economic realities.

Usery's plan was one part of a formula designed to create a new era of labor relations at Eastern, an environment of mutual cooperation and respect. Promised productivity improvements were another key aspect. So was a joint pledge to try to find ways to restructure our $2.3 billion debt. So was an agreement for a labor-management review of employee relations programs twice a year. My misgivings notwithstanding, I hoped that a new era really had begun and would continue if everyone kept the promises that had been made.

Management tried. The one area in which we couldn't live up to expectations was debt restructure, something Bryan insisted was possible. It wasn't, simply because the interest we were paying on our debt averaged only 9.8 percent; the prime rate in October of 1983 was 11 percent and had been much higher.

I insisted that officers, including myself, accept the same wage cuts as everyone else. I badly wanted a three-year agreement and argued vehemently for it. Bryan and Peterpaul said it was politically impossible, but assured me that long before 1984 ended, everyone would agree to extension. So I signed on behalf of management, hoping for the best.

We went into 1984 and the first thing that fell short was the promised $75 million in savings from greater productivity. The IAM led the way in that broken promise. The only thing Bryan would agree to was experimenting with new work rules at our new Kansas City hub. They were so successful that we asked Charlie to extend them throughout the system. "No way" was his answer.

This from the same man who had proclaimed solemnly to the media, "Our intention is to make Eastern the best airline in terms of productivity."

I still can remember another statement Bryan made after the Usery-forged pact in which the three unions pledged a 5 percent productivity increase to achieve the promised $75 million in savings. "That five percent commitment we made is peanuts," Charlie assured reporters. "We're going to exceed that by so much, people will think that five percent goal is ridiculous!"

The actual productivity gain achieved by the three unions in 1984 amounted to $22 million, and most of this came from the pilots. The IAM's contribution consisted largely of Bryan's telling his members to work harder, by such means as limiting lunch hours and breaks to allotted times. The work rules themselves generally remained unchanged.

The flight attendants didn't come close to the 5 percent goal. Then, in their usual game of musical chairs, the flight attendants threw Pat Fink out of office and brought back Robert Callahan, who celebrated his election by announcing that the productivity promise didn't apply to the new administration.

"I didn't make the commitment for the productivity gains," he informed Usery, "and I don't know anything about it."

ALPA's leadership at Eastern also changed shortly after the TWU's switch. The new MEC chairman was a co-pilot named Larry Schulte. Once he got into power, Schulte became as militant as Bryan.

Bryan, of course, was the IAM's selection to go on the board, and the TWU picked Callahan. ALPA and the non-union employees got two outsiders as their directors: Tom Boggs, a Washington lawyer and lobbyist who was the son of the late congressman Hale Boggs, and Arthur Taylor, onetime president of the Columbia Broadcasting System.

We kept our pledge to improve labor relations. The company started an employee involvement program aimed at encouraging people to tell management how they could perform their jobs better. We spent a lot of money hiring top consultants to make sure the program maintained total objectivity—we didn't want anyone to feel that criticism of a company policy or method was going to bring recriminations.

We did get some good suggestions, constructive criticism, and workable ideas. The trouble was that most of them came from the non-contract employees. Where the unions were involved, the program that had so much potential never really got off the ground. Time and again, we'd try some new idea or procedure, often suggested by employees themselves, and the union would object to it, usually on the grounds that it wasn't in the contract. A lot of worthwhile productivity gains went out the window, thanks to this attitude.

We badly needed new carpeting in the hallways of Building 16; the old carpeting looked as if it had been run over by a division of fifty-ton tanks. We bought the carpeting from a firm that offered to install it for practically nothing, but the IAM's representative on our labor-management committee said, "No, that's our work." We had to argue with them for hours over whether we should have the carpeting laid by mechanics being paid fifteen dollars an hour, or by the company that sold us the material.

During the '83 negotiations, a union official I had always considered one of the more responsible ones led a gang through our hangar at Atlanta, cutting hoses and destroying other equipment. I couldn't begin to count the number of times during some labor dispute that we found the radiators of ground vehicles punctured by ice picks.

One of the most disappointing aspects of my tenure was the lack of integrity I found in Eastern's unions when disciplinary action against a member was plainly warranted. Unions tend to protect mediocrity anyway, but they also countenanced sloppy work and even proven dishonesty.

We had one case involving numerous thefts from one of the maintenance shops. An investigation narrowed the suspects down to a single mechanic who was put under surveillance. He was nailed carrying a big thermos jug off the premises, and inside the jug was a thirteen-pound length of expensive stainless-steel chain.

The culprit claimed he had been framed by fellow workers who didn't like him. "I didn't know there was anything in my jug when I took it out of the shop," he insisted. Despite the obvious implausibility of his not noticing thirteen extra pounds, the IAM accepted his story and fought against his dismissal.

We had a captain with a long history of abusing women. He had been disciplined several times, and when he beat up a flight attendant we fired him. ALPA took his case to an arbitrator who ruled in the pilot's favor. Then one night his wife shot and killed him after he began punching her. The same union lawyer who had defended him remarked, "Well, he finally got what he deserved."

Protecting members is one thing, a statutory responsibility in the purest analysis. But blind protectionism carried to the extreme of lying is another matter, which is exactly what happened when we tried to administer a program against alcoholism.

We had a tough yet a reasonable approach to this problem. The inviolate rule was immediate dismissal if you were caught drinking on the job—a drunken mechanic working on complex aircraft equipment could wind up killing people. But if anyone with an alcohol problem asked for help, this was provided instantly. The unions challenged this policy, winning an arbitrator's ruling that we couldn't fire anyone with a history of alcoholism even if he was seen drinking on duty—we had to rehabilitate him.

I could live with even that ruling, but from the day it was issued the unions claimed alcoholism was involved in every case requiring disciplinary action. We'd catch some guy stealing and the union would immediately identify him as an alcoholic needing rehabilitation, so we couldn't fire him.

Unions rose to power in the thirties and forties largely because of management's arrogant indifference to the welfare and even the human dignity of employees. Workers needed protection against management's sins, yet the pendulum swung back, as it does with most

reform movements, and management and consumers became pitifully vulnerable to labor's excesses. Organized labor has lost much
of its clout, especially in the deregulated airline industry, and I think
this trend will continue—not merely because shortsighted union
leadership is based on a stay-in-power structure, but because the
economic and social factors that led to labor's emergence have changed
so drastically.

Eastern's unions have found this out the hard way but, tragically,
not soon enough. The atmosphere of confrontation that Charlie Bryan
spawned in the 1983 crisis spread to the other unions in another
year of financial distress, and the "new era" of labor-management
cooperation proved to be a mockery.

23

TRYING TO GO UP A DOWN ESCALATOR

Fifteen minutes after his election to the Board of Directors, Charlie Bryan emerged from the directors' meeting and greeted the press with a rosy forecast. Eastern, he said, would show a profit in the second quarter and "I fully expect all quarters coming up to be profitable."

When this pronouncement hit the papers, the board was ready to hang him. Bryan's statement was in possible violation of the Securities and Exchange Commission's disclosure rules—corporate directors aren't supposed to make financial predictions based on information available only to directors.

Dick Magurno, senior vice president for Legal Affairs, quickly had a private chat with Bryan concerning director protocol. Charlie thereupon issued a lame statement of "clarification" through a spokesman—it said his remarks "weren't based on information available to him as a director." He was telling the truth; the financial discussion at the board meeting had been on the gloomy side.

Shortly after he went on the board, he joined with all but one director to give me a five-year contract as CEO. The contract, my first at Eastern, was the board's idea; ironically, it was prompted mostly by Bryan's own previous demands for my resignation and amounted to a vote of confidence.

The lone dissenting vote came from Arthur Taylor, one of the four union-designated directors, who often enlivened board meetings. Once we were listening to Mort Beyer, an outside financial consultant, tell us that Draconian measures were needed to keep Eastern solvent. Taylor objected to the word "Draconian" as offensive.

"It comes from Count Draco of Transylvania, who was reputed to drink the blood of victims he murdered," he pontificated. "This was the origin of the Count Dracula vampire legend."

At the next board meeting, Mort casually mentioned that he had looked up "Draconian" in a dictionary.

"It's origin is Greek," Beyer lectured gently. "Draco was an Athenian statesman and lawyer who drew up an extremely harsh code of law."

That was the last word heard on the subject from Mr. Taylor.

Like most CEOs of companies in trouble, I didn't enjoy annual shareholder meetings. But I had a compensating factor that some didn't enjoy: the support of a board I believe was the finest in the industry, perhaps in any industry. Throughout all these tumultuous years, the directors held steadfastly to their own unwritten rule—do what's best for Eastern. The debt of gratitude I owe them can never be repaid.

I believed strongly in employee involvement and so did many union members. I thought the guy running a lathe or pounding sheet metal should have an opportunity to tell us how he could do his job better. Bryan's interpretation of involvement—influenced, I'm sure, by Randy Barber—was that the unions should have a say in major company policy decisions, including what markets we should serve and what fares we should charge.

In a further move to improve labor relations, we instituted a profit-sharing plan (contingent, naturally, on our making money), and I hired a new vice president for Labor Relations: Jack Johnson, who came to Eastern from Goodrich, where he had an exemplary reputation. He replaced Dwayne Andrews after Dwayne had a heart attack and had to slow down.

Johnson was a good man with a superb intellect, a love for his work, and a very human approach to dealing with labor—he was very much on the employees' side, wanting to do right by them as long as it was within the limits of the company's ability.

The "new era" at Eastern followed on the heels of the worst year in the airline's history. Its 1983 losses added up to a $183.7 million bloodbath. Bill Usery's efforts helped staunch the flow, but by the time he came into the picture, he was merely playing catchup ball. That was our problem—we never did overcome the effects of the 1983 agreement.

The other major debilitating factor was the low-cost competition. Every new onslaught of fare cuts adversely affected our critical per-seat yield—the average amount we were getting for carrying each passenger one mile. While our *direct* operating costs actually compared favorably to those of American and Delta, our per-seat yield was considerably lower. One financial expert estimated that if Eastern had matched Delta's yield in 1984, we would have generated an extra $452 million in incremental revenues.

There was no point in waiting until the end of the year to ask the unions for an extension of the 1983 pact. In July of '84, quietly and without making any public announcement, I had Usery and Johnson pass the word to the unions that we needed to keep the wage cuts in effect for at least another year. They refused to go back to the bargaining table then, and they refused to discuss the matter for almost another six months.

We ended 1984 almost $38 million in the red, despite a small profit in the last two quarters. As far as Bryan, Schulte, and Callahan were concerned, the unions had done their duty and they demanded full restoration of wage cuts for 1985.

This was impossible. Going back to the old wage scales would have added $22 million a month to the payroll, increasing 1985's labor costs by $264 million. And coming up was a grim deadline: By December 31, 1984, we had to submit to our lenders a new business plan that included final determination of the next year's labor costs. This annual projection was required under our loan covenants—in effect we were supposed to assure the banks that we were maintaining a certain degree of financial stability. With no such assurance on hand, we would be in technical default.

In November, Bill stepped up efforts to get the unions in for serious talks, as they had promised in the letter of agreement they'd signed when they exchanged wage concessions for 25 percent of the airline and union representation on the board. They might as well have written their signatures in disappearing ink. Bryan and the others finally agreed to negotiate, but every meeting produced the same answer: Give us back those wage cuts.

With no sign of progress as the December 31 deadline arrived, I unilaterally announced that the wage investment program would stay in effect during 1985 to avoid default.

The unions reacted furiously, charging that I had sprung this on them without warning. Nonsense. Usery and I had been telling them for six months we'd have to extend; now they regarded it as an open declaration of war.

The action achieved the purpose for which it was mostly intended—the unions reluctantly came back to the bargaining table. But "reluctantly" is an inadequate description of Charlie Bryan's mood. He distributed to the press a bulletin he had sent to his members, claiming that by extending the wage agreement without employee approval I had violated that agreement.

"This treacherous act by Frank Borman represents a total absence of credibility and the ultimate betrayal of the trust of our members and your union leaders," Bryan declared. "We must remember that Eastern Airlines did not betray the employees; Frank Borman did."

I read his statement in *The Wall Street Journal* and could only remember the solemn promise Bryan had made to review Eastern's finances before ending the investment program. I remembered Peterpaul and Bryan telling me to my face, when I pleaded for a three-year pact, not to worry—we'd get extensions before 1984 ended. I remembered Bryan's grandiose assurances of mammoth productivity gains that never materialized.

Assured that negotiations were resuming, the lenders granted a one-month extension to work out another agreement. The talks dragged on during the whole of January and into early February 1985. I let Usery do the talking, and Bill finally moved negotiations off dead center by agreeing to recommend to the company that the wage cuts be restored just for the month of January.

Usery told me that in the unions' eyes this would "right the wrong" they felt had been inflicted on them by my unilateral order, and that they'd then be willing to discuss how to proceed from there. I agreed, but as the new deadline of January 31 approached, the unions were still balking. On the night of the thirty-first, I drove to the Miami Airport Hilton, where they were meeting. Usery glumly told me the pilots and flight attendants might be coming around, but Bryan had refused.

I went into the room, Usery following me like an ambling bear. Peterpaul was there and so were Bryan and Barber. I told them if we had to go into default, Chapter 11 was inevitable, with Chapter 7 not far behind.

Peterpaul had the grace to look uncomfortable; Bryan seemed unmoved.

The next day, Eastern went into technical default. The banks held back any action because the negotiations were still going on, but it wasn't until February 11 that Bryan joined the pilots in agreeing to retain the wage cuts for the rest of the year. We weren't entirely out of the woods; the machinists voted down the agreement the first time around and the flight attendants also rejected it. At Bryan's urging, the IAM reversed itself in a second vote, and we didn't need TWU approval—winning two out of three was sufficient for the lenders to waive default. Once more we had bitten the bullet.

Extension not only won us some breathing room with the banks, but gave us a chance to see some black ink for a change, at least for most of 1985.

By midyear, I decided we needed a president who would take over the day-to-day business of the airline while I concentrated on solving financial problems. It was something Bill Usery had been urging, too. "You shouldn't be the center and focal point of so much controversy," he advised. "This might restore faith and confidence in many areas with the unions."

There was another reason why his advice and my thinking coincided: I was then fifty-seven and had always planned to retire three years down the road. It was time to reduce an oppressive work load; the question was choosing the right man to succeed me as president while I retained the board chairmanship and CEO post. In effect, I'd be grooming him for the top job.

In April 1984, I had hired a new senior vice president for Engineering and Maintenance named Joe Leonard—not as a potential successor, however, because I wasn't even thinking of one at the time. I hadn't been satisfied with our maintenance operation, and after a widely publicized incident involving one of our L-1011s—a near-ditching in the Atlantic—I decided changes had to be made. The TriStar had lost power in all three engines, a multiple malfunction traced to faulty installation of oil rings. There had been sloppy work by inadequately supervised mechanics.

Marv Amos, our in-house headhunter, came up with Leonard's name. He had had a long tenure at Northwest and was in charge of American's huge maintanence base in Tulsa when we contacted him. Don Nyrop gave Leonard exceptionally high marks.

Joe shaped up Eastern's maintenance in a hurry. He wasn't afraid to kick butts, but everyone liked him. He was the kind of hands-on operator we needed; the board accepted my recommendation before the year was out and named him president and chief operating officer.

Also, in September of '85, we hired Jerry Cosley away from TWA as our new senior vice president for Corporate Communications. Cosley, a veteran in airline public relations, was the most skilled practitioner of that art I ever met.

We got a little breathing room in '85 and we used it to spring one of the most unique concepts ever developed by a major carrier: the Moonlight Special.

The idea came from Jerry Schorr, vice president for Cargo Sales and for my dough the best air-cargo man in the industry. Against the opposition of the planning department he had been trying to sell a way to recapture some of the overnight cargo business we had lost when we got rid of the 727-QCs. He finally took his case to me one day in the spring of '85. He told me that Consolidated Freight, a big freight-forwarding company, had been using United DC-8s to carry its cargo, but the planes were now grounded because they couldn't comply with noise regulations.

"Consolidated can't use United's DC-10s," Schorr explained. "Their galleys are in the bellies and that doesn't leave enough room for freight. We could grab Consolidated's business by leasing them the bellies of a few A-300s—our galleys are in the cabin. My plan is to establish a hub somewhere, like the one Federal Express operates at Memphis, only we'd be carrying passengers as well as cargo. Fly 'em overnight from major stations into the hub, reload the passengers and cargo according to final destination, and we'd have a damned profitable operation. The beauty of it is that we could charge really low fares because these late-night flights would be carrying freight anyway."

We finally picked Houston as the ideal hub for two reasons: Its location cut down the number of airplanes needed and the weather was favorable. Continental had just about run us out of Houston, but putting the Moonlight Special in there enabled us to challenge its low-fare flights.

We started on April 1, dispatching a fleet of A-300s at midnight from a dozen cities including New York, Miami, Chicago, Atlanta, and Los Angeles into Houston. The first night was a near disaster. We had underestimated the number of ground tugs needed to handle the flights and everything ran late. Two flights were delayed coming in and that fouled up matters even more. Our people at Houston didn't panic, however; they rented additional tugs for the second night and from then on the Moonlight Special was a model of efficiency—and it was profitable.

Passenger business exceeded all expectation, load factors averaging well over 90 percent. Everyone was surprised at the number of people willing to fly all night at bargain-basement fares. We charged ninety-eight dollars for a cross-country trip, at least 20 percent less than any competitor's fare, and we still made money. The cargo more than paid operating expenses and the passenger revenue was pure gravy.

Such factors as the wage concessions and the success of the Moonlight Special contributed to a healthy $73.8 million profit for the first nine months of 1985. This "health," however, was more like the rosy flush of an oncoming fever. By the third quarter, we were forced to dip into the employee profit-sharing reserve. To show a profit that quarter, we had to withdraw more than $52 million from the reserve or Eastern would have been nearly $29 million in the red. Fare wars, which had abated during the first six months, started up again. Yet it was hard to plead poverty when the books showed we were almost $74 million in the black as of September 30, and the unions began pressing for restoration of full wages, with the flight attendants demanding increases as well.

And that's when a new round of disastrous fare wars struck Eastern again like a sledgehammer, eroding our yield even further. At years's end, Eastern's 1985 profit amounted to only $6.3 million for the full twelve months. I could see more trouble ahead, but I wasn't prepared for one trouble that did develop.

In March 1986, the Federal Aviation Administration notified Eastern that it was being fined $9.5 million for violating government regulations covering aircraft maintenance practices.

It was, and at this writing still is, the largest civil penalty ever levied against an air carrier.

It also happened to be the phoniest.

I refused to pay it and challenged the FAA to take us to court, but we never got a chance to prove our case. Shortly after I left the airline, the new management decided to pay the fine rather than go through lengthy litigation. I wish Eastern had fought it out in court, because it would have unmasked the whole sorry mess for what it really was: a despicable example of politics and bureaucracy at their worst. To this day, I find it hard to believe that the FAA and its parent agency, the Department of Transportation, got away with it.

The story began late in 1985 when a team of FAA inspectors began a "special audit" of Eastern's maintenance. We weren't the only carrier being checked out. It had been a bad year for airline safety, with nearly two thousand crash fatalities worldwide, and the media was in a feeding frenzy on the subject. The U.S. record itself didn't warrant the general hysteria; in this country there were four fatal accidents involving scheduled carriers during 1985 with a death toll of 197; all but 60 of those deaths, however, occurred in a single crash—a Delta L-1011 caught in wind shear while landing at Dallas–Fort Worth.

But there also had been the crash of a nonscheduled Arrow Airlines DC-8 carrying American troops, killing all aboard. American Airlines had already paid a record $1.5 million penalty for alleged maintenance violations, so the press and congressional spotlight was on the whole industry—not to mention the FAA and DOT themselves.

I wasn't surprised that Eastern was targeted for an investigation. The near-ditching incident, plus our known financial difficulties, had made us suspect. Yet, I was confident we had cleaned up our act after that L-1011 embarrassment. Some thought we should have fired the mechanics responsible, but I felt management was partially at fault—we had changed certain engine maintenance procedures without making sure the word had filtered down to the mechanics directly involved. Under Joe Leonard the gaps had been plugged, so when FAA Administrator Don Engen phoned me to announce the special inspection, I told him we'd welcome his team.

The special inspection team arrived, headed by George Mattern, who, we learned, had virtually no experience in dealing with airline operations. His background was almost entirely in general aviation. I couldn't believe the FAA had put him in charge of the Eastern investigation, but I tried to provide his team with an environment of wholehearted cooperation.

"We have no secrets," I assured them. "You have access to everything. We're proud of our operation and if you encounter the slightest problem, notify Joe Leonard or myself and we'll take care of it."

Through the several weeks of the inspection, I met periodically with the team personnel as well as having occasional sessions with the regional officials who came down from Atlanta to check on progress. Not once did I hear anything but positive remarks. "Your people are really cooperating," I was told frequently. Now and then they would point out some minor problems and we corrected them immediately. I was grateful for the attitude of Mattern's team because his own inexperience worried me.

We were talking one day about Eastern's maintenance check schedules. He said in perfect seriousness, "You know, if you did everything you were supposed to do with an airplane exactly when you were supposed to do it, you'd never have a delay, you'd never have a canceled flight, and you'd never have a maintenance write-up."

I stared at him. "George, you've got to be kidding. Do you honestly believe that following a rigid maintenance schedule will eliminate every mechanical malfunction?"

"I certainly do."

I sighed. "Well, George, if you really feel that way there's no use discussing the subject."

The inspection team took six weeks to complete its probe. Its members had dispersed to other assignments when Joe Ames, an enterprising and knowledgeable reporter on the *Miami News*, decided to get a jump on the team's report. He phoned Jack Barker, veteran public affairs officer for the FAA's Southern Region in Atlanta. Barker himself was an old pro, highly respected by the media and industry alike—he had been around Atlanta so long it was a standard gag that Sherman had left Jack behind in Atlanta after marching through Georgia. Barker, who had always leveled with us and the press, talked freely to Ames; on February 6, 1986, I sat in my office reading the story Ames had written under the banner headline FAA FINDS NO WEAKNESS WITH EASTERN.

The story itself quoted Barker as saying that the only major deficiencies uncovered by the six-week, in-depth investigation were in record keeping.

"Any corrective action that the FAA deemed necessary has already been taken," Barker added. He said the inspection had turned up no glaring weakness in Eastern's operations or maintenance that he knew of, although he cautioned that in a thorough probe like the one conducted, "it's virtually impossible that there won't be some violation—it's such a complex business."

Over the years, we had established good rapport with the FAA's

Southern Region administration, particularly regional director Jonathan Howe. He was extremely capable, with an excellent technical background—he knew airplanes and he knew the airline business. He was tough but fair, and that's all we asked. Howe had visited Miami several times during the course of the investigation and was right on top of its progress. If the team had uncovered anything serious, Howe would have been climbing all over us.

A week after the Ames story appeared, FAA Administrator Engen phoned me from Washington. His opening remark stunned me.

"Frank, I've seen the report from the investigating team and it isn't good."

"What the hell are you talking about?" I demanded. "Haven't you seen the story in the *Miami News*? It says the FAA gave us a clean bill of health except for some discrepancies in record keeping."

"The story's wrong. This is serious, but I think we can fix it if you're willing to make some changes. Jonathan Howe will be coming down to Miami shortly. He'll bring a solution that'll be acceptable to everyone."

"What kind of solution? Look, Don, I need more explanation than what you've given me."

"Jonathan will give you the details. We can work this out."

I briefed my staff on the unexpected turn of events and we waited anxiously for Howe to arrive.

But Howe never showed up. He actually flew to Miami on the scheduled morning, but the minute he got off the plane, I learned later, he was told to call Engen immediately. Howe got right back on the FAA airplane and flew to the capital without seeing me. The first indication I had that the supposed "solution" had fallen through came in another call from Engen.

"Frank, Jonathan won't be coming down. I've had to replace him."

"What's going on? You called me earlier to say he's coming. He's due here in thirty minutes for an eleven o'clock meeting. We're all waiting for him."

"I know, but there've been some major changes."

I could sense the embarrassment in his voice as he added, "I can't talk about it now. There's been a major development."

There was another FAA official I respected—Tex Melugin, director of the Southwest Region. I asked Engen to send him to Miami and Tex arrived the next day, accompanied by Howe's temporary replacement. Based on the inspection team's report Melugin was ready to ground the airline, but after we went over its allegations and I challenged the majority of its conclusions, Tex began to have second thoughts. Before he left, we agreed to the wording of a relatively mild FAA statement that had Eastern admitting some technical violations and assuring the public that we were cooperating with the agency to correct them.

Under the law, the FAA could penalize an airline up to $1,000 per violation, multiplied by the number of times the carrier flew an aircraft contrary to the FAA regulation. For example, if we operated an airplane with an illegal part for 100 flights, that added up to 100 separate violations with a potential maximum fine of $100,000. In our case, the FAA threw the whole damned book at us: 78,372 individual violations adding up to a $9.5 million penalty.

The statement Melugin and I agreed on was never released. Instead, without waiting for Eastern to examine the allegations thoroughly and respond to them, the FAA leaked the proposed fine to Dick Witkin of *The New York Times*. Witkin had the decency to check with us before printing the story, but our immediate comment had to be vague—it took weeks to sort out the FAA's voluminous charges and analyze them for validity. In fact, Jerry Cosley's first reaction to Witkin's query was "Dick, I don't know a damn thing about it."

The rest of the media jumped on the bandwagon. Poor Jack Barker, apparently in hot water with his superiors for the quotes he had given Ames, changed his tune. "Well, there are still some loose ends in the inspection," he said lamely.

Cosley took due note of that hedging and remarked at a staff meeting, "Barker went with the facts and now somebody's changing the facts." Somebody sure was, as we discovered when we examined the FAA's charges in minute detail. Of the 78,372 alleged violations, almost 49,000 or about 63 percent involved Eastern's C check, a major periodic maintenance inspection and interim overhaul procedure.

We had four maintenance checks, A through D. The C check was exceeded only by D in thoroughness and the time allotted, amounting to everything but a major overhaul. C checks were usually accomplished annually, the maximum schedule being once every four hundred days, although some airplanes received C checks every two hundred days. The procedure pulled an aircraft out of service ("downtime") for twenty-four hours.

To improve the fleet's reliability, we had decided to schedule all C checks every 366 days. The revision was aimed at our 727s but also included the A-300s and DC-9s. At the same time, we increased the downtime of each airplane from twenty-four hours to three days, in effect upgrading the C. It not only improved reliability but enhanced safety. And we notified the FAA of the change.

When the agency socked us with some forty-nine thousand supposed violations involving the revised C check, we had been following the new schedule for more than a year. In that time, not once had the FAA advised us that we were doing anything wrong. Now it was claiming we had put the procedure into effect without adequately justifying it. When I pointed out that the FAA had had a year in which to ask for more detailed justification and had found no fault with the 366-day schedule for our DC-9s and A-300s, all I got was a collection of shrugged shoulders.

Another alleged violation concerned some of our older 727s in service. We had discovered tiny cracks appearing along the door frames. We had alerted the FAA and also advised Boeing of what we were doing to fix the problem. Boeing sent a service bulletin to all 727 operators recommending that they follow Eastern's repair methods, but not all carriers complied. Whereupon the FAA issued an airworthiness directive (AD) that made the repairs mandatory. We immediately checked with Boeing to make sure our procedures achieved the repairs required by the AD, and Boeing assured all 727 customers that if they had followed the service bulletins, they were in compliance. Now the FAA was charging we had failed to obtain the agency's confirmation that the service bulletin and AD were identical. Yet Eastern had originated the fix that led to both the service bulletin and the AD.

More than nineteen thousand violations concerned two 727s that we had unknowingly operated with a small crack in an actuator support beam on the main landing gear assembly. One of them had the gear partially collapse while taxiing. We investigated this mishap and discovered that the faulty component had come off a non-Eastern aircraft we were maintaining for another 727 operator. Somehow the refurbished but still cracked actuators had been put into a bin holding new parts and wound up on our two 727s while they were being overhauled.

Yet the business of the "unjustified" C check schedule and just those two 727s flown with an illegal component added up to some

68,000 of the 78,372 violations and accounted for about $9 million of the total fine. The remaining violations were mostly minor discrepancies in record keeping, sins every carrier has committed in trying to record all the work performed on aircraft whose components number in the millions—there are nearly 3 million individual parts in a 727, for example, and between 4 million and 5 million in an A-300 or L-1011.

Some of the violations were not only petty but in many instances weren't even true. One concerned a JFK mechanic, Nicholas Contes, who according to the FAA had been illegally authorized by Eastern "to perform required inspection of flight control systems, hydraulic systems, doors and external doors and openings of A-300 aircraft although Contes has never received training on the A-300."

We presented documented evidence showing that Contes, who had been first a line maintenance mechanic and then an inspector for thirty years, was more than qualified. Our own maintenance training manual, approved by the FAA, required not only experience but on-the-job training, which Contes had fulfilled in spades. But the FAA refused to admit he was not only qualified but a superior inspector.

Eastern was cited for numerous violations of an FAA airworthiness directive requiring ashtrays to be installed inside lavatories. According to the inspection report, we had operated an A-300 from December 3 to December 19, 1985, on ninety flights with the "Aft lavs E and F missing inside ashtrays." We showed that the missing ashtrays actually had been replaced on December 5. We further pointed out that the ashtrays in question were not the ones covered by the AD—the A-300 had another inside ashtray that complied with the AD. We didn't get to first base.

Another violation involved a 727 that the FAA claimed had been operated on some three hundred flights with a fastener (rivet) missing from the forward-entry door frame. The report didn't specify which rivet was missing; our own inspection records showed there was a fastener gone but this had been replaced the same day. The FAA charged that we had operated this 727 in an unairworthy condition, a ridiculous assertion—one missing fastener out of the scores that go into a door frame does not constitute an unsafe condition.

We refuted at least two thirds of the violations list, which included 695 *unspecified* items. We especially zeroed in on the C check paperwork complaint, because it had prompted the bulk of the $9.5 million fine.

The FAA's announcement of the fine accused us of changing the C check schedule to save money. It actually cost us *more,* because the downtime per aircraft was tripled and maintenance costs rose correspondingly. Meanwhile, the press was crucifying us; the headlines and accompanying stories quite naturally put the emphasis on the stiff penalty and the FAA's grossly overgeneralized and unsubstantiated claims, and that one figure—78,372 violations—stood out like Braille. Witkin was one of the few reporters who carried our rebuttal in detail, but that was the problem—the average reporter and consequently the public could not really grasp the complex technicalities of our case. When it came to effective public relations, the FAA had a distinct advantage—the very size of that fine made Eastern appear guilty.

Fed up with the bad publicity and not wanting to take on the awesome power of the federal bureaucracy, I met with Engen to propose a compromise. I offered to pay a fine of slightly over $3 million, a sum I considered more than fair inasmuch as our own study of the FAA's charges showed we hadn't sinned anywhere near even $3 million. Engen paused and said he needed time to consider this.

The next day he informed me the compromise was unacceptable.

I said, "Okay, go ahead and sue us."

I am convinced that Engen bowed to pressure from Transportation Secretary Dole and her top deputy, James Burnley, who eventually succeeded her. Dole herself was under heavy pressure from Congress and the media. After four years in which the air traffic control system should have been built back up to strength, the ATC system was still floundering with a thousand fewer controllers than before the 1981 strike, even though traffic had increased 20 percent. The failure had to be blamed on Dole—her DOT controlled ATC funding.

The media's blitz on air safety applied more pressure, and Dole reacted as only a politician will react: She went into a "getting tough" act that was more of a public relations campaign than a legitimate air safety crusade. To improve her own image and that of the DOT, she crucified Eastern, and if the $9.5 million fine had ever been subjected to the glaring spotlight of a court battle, I believe we could have proved it.

Don Engen had to share the blame, although I understood the difficult position he was in—subservient to a politically motivated cabinet officer afraid to accept responsibility for the damage her own ineptness had inflicted on U.S. air transportation. He was never able to admit the FAA's failures because that would have reflected back on Dole, so he went around trying to convince everyone that the ATC system wasn't in trouble. He kept insisting that it wasn't capacity-limited when it was so obviously splitting at the seams.

Long before the fine controversy, he flew down to Miami one day to discuss capacity, and I asked him how he liked his job.

"I don't like to complain," Engen said, "but I just can't stand being micromanaged by people who don't understand aviation. I don't know how long I can take it."

I knew what he meant. Interference from the transportation secretary's office was worse under Dole than with any of her predecessors.

I knew Elizabeth Dole fairly well; from the time she took office, she had sought my advice on industry matters, and I thought we had a good relationship. Once she phoned me at our weekend home in the Florida Keys to discuss airport security problems. Another time she asked me to set up an industrywide meeting aimed at limiting peak-hour congestion, an agreement that required Justice Department exemption from antitrust laws. We won the Justice Department's approval and achieved moderate if temporary success in spreading some peak-hour schedules.

But any goodwill we had banked with the FAA and DOT bureaucracies dissolved under the 1985 heat of criticism directed against them. We were still reeling from the penalty publicity when the Defense Department announced it would no longer use Eastern for any reason, because of unsafe maintenance practices—a page right out of the fiction the FAA had just written.

After I angrily protested to Engen, he phoned Deputy Secretary of Defense William H. Taft, informing him that Eastern had a fine safety record and urging him to withdraw the order. Taft quickly complied.

More than two years later, I continue to see references to the $9.5 million fine in stories on air safety—each mentions a bald indictment, carrying an implication of guilt in the face of contradictory evidence the government ignored. Also ignored was the fact that over the past decade, Eastern had compiled one of the best safety records in the industry.

There is sentiment developing to give the FAA back its independence, removing it from the DOT's influence and authority. This needs to happen. The loss of that independence turned what had once been an effective, efficient organization into a political football.

Don Engen himself finally quit. Although he never publicly repeated what he had told me about the frustrations of working under Dole and the DOT, he reportedly made similar statements privately. I wish he had demonstrated the courage to confront Dole and her subordinates when the chips really were down and Eastern was being vilified.

What also hurt was the timing of this hatchet job. It took place just as our financial woes worsened and we faced a final confrontation.

It was clear by mid-1985 that Eastern's finances had decayed to the point of desperation.

Our plans to "live and fight another day," as Jack Fallon had put it, had failed. Even though we had extended the airline's life for two years, and despite the fact that our revenue growth was above the industry's average, we hadn't been able to achieve the fundamental goal of competitive labor rates.

So late in '85, faced with increasing union truculence and seeing no way to achieve the 2 percent profit goal set a decade before, we began to search again for a merger partner.

We tried TWA again—its pilots were urging an Eastern-TWA marriage. No dice. I approached Ed Colodny of USAir, who told me, "Labor's out of control at Eastern—I don't think we could ever work with your unions." I met with Steve Rothmeier, Nyrop's successor at Northwest. We were supposed to hold a second meeting but Steve canceled it after studying the financial and labor data I had sent him. "I just looked over your balance sheet," he said. "With your labor situation, there's no use in our even having lunch."

I got the same response when I went outside the airline industry and talked to Bill Marriott. Ditto Fred Hartley of Union Oil, the Hilton chain, and Texaco—the latter two contacted by Fallon and Gilpatrick of our board.

In December of '85, Frank Lorenzo of Texas Air phoned.

"I'd like to talk to you about your SODA program," he said. SODA (System One Direct Access) was the computerized reservations system that we sold to travel agents. It was damned good, too—not quite as sophisticated as American's SABRE, but still one of the industry's best.

There was a move on within the industry to link all carriers except American and United into a single computer system so they could compete with SABRE and United's APOLLO. When I met with Lorenzo in New York, we talked about the possibility of putting our two systems together as a start—we both favored a complete consolidation eventually, bringing in carriers like TWA, Delta, USAir, and Pan Am.

It was a friendly chat with no immediate agreement, but the discussion led naturally into my confessing that Eastern was looking for a merger partner.

"If I can't get some breathing space from our unions," I told Lorenzo, "I'd like to talk to you about selling the airline. Eastern's a good property, but we have intransigent unions and we don't have the financial resources to fight back."

Lorenzo said cautiously, "I wouldn't be interested in doing anything unless it's a friendly arrangement. But if you want to talk further, just give me a call."

At the time, I regarded Texas Air as an ace in the hole, but also as a card buried so far down in the deck that I didn't think I'd ever have to play it. I must say, however, that Lorenzo impressed me. Very honest and direct, he hated small talk and expected you to get to the point fast.

It was no coincidence that the futile merger search coincided with another deadline: submitting our annual financial plan to the lenders, a prospect I faced with the unbridled optimism of a kamikaze pilot. The slump that had begun in the final quarter of 1985 was carrying over into 1986.

I knew I'd be facing labor's wrath if I asked for any concessions. The atmosphere at Eastern was one of increasing hostility and suspicion, culminating in two mysterious incidents of bugged executive offices. We found a microphone hidden in an unused telephone receptacle in Dick Magurno's legal department, and then discovered another mike in the ceiling of Joe Leonard's office. An FBI investigation failed to determine who had planted the listening devices.

At the board's suggestion, we had hired a respected financial consulting firm—AVMARK—to look over Eastern's books and advise us on ways to restore profitability. We figured another objective analysis by outside experts might carry more weight with the unions.

Early in January, Mort Beyer, AVMARK's president, met with the directors and bluntly informed us the airline must cut labor costs by up to $700 million a year. He specifically recommended a minimum 20 percent wage slash for all union and non-contract employees and said the only alternative was to file for Chapter 11.

The AVMARK report emphasized that we could no longer appease Eastern's lenders with temporary, stop-gap concessions that never stayed in place long enough to achieve long-range viability. This was something I had known since the inception of VEP but couldn't sell to labor.

AVMARK's insistence on more permanent concessions was based on a cold-blooded appraisal of the airline's labor costs compared to those of other carriers. Wages and benefits accounted for just under 40 percent of Eastern's total expenditures; the industry average was 35 percent, and for our low-fare competitors, People Express and Continental, the figure reached as low as 18 percent.

The bottom line of this differential was that we had to fill 88 percent of our seats just to break even on a ninety-nine-dollar fare between New York and Miami; People Express needed only a 50 percent load factor at the same fare.

AVMARK's castor oil approach was going to be unpleasant medicine for the unions to swallow, yet basically all we were asking was that they give back some of the gains they had already achieved— many of them, like the IAM's 1983 mugging, won at a time when the company couldn't afford increases. A 20 percent wage cut was going to be tough, but that 20 percent figure was deceptive.

From the start of full deregulation in 1979 through 1985, the average annual wages and benefits paid to Eastern's employees had increased by 9 percent per year. That was the wage and benefit structure *even counting all the wage concessions, employee investment programs, productivity gains, and so on,* a structure still well above the industry average, and one erected in spite of the fact that Eastern, more than any other carrier, had to play the deregulation game on a playing field that wasn't level. The bulk of low-cost competition throughout the industry during this time was aimed at Eastern's vulnerable routes. It was this single factor more than any other that made our labor costs unbearable.

Faced with a growing conviction that a showdown was almost inevitable—not merely with labor but with the lenders as well—I commissioned Merrill Lynch to try to find us a merger partner, preferably a non-airline company. The effort failed.

By mid-January we were making no progress with the unions; even Bill Usery couldn't get them to budge. So I met with Lorenzo at the Marriott Hotel in Fort Lauderdale. I said I still hoped to reach an agreement with labor, but if that failed, it was a choice between selling the airline or going into Chapter 11.

Lorenzo was understandably concerned that I might be setting him up as a bogeyman to scare Eastern's unions. They had a right to be scared. When Lorenzo had acquired failing Continental and couldn't get concessions from its unions, he had put the airline into Chapter 11. In a bold effort to save it, he abrogated all labor contracts. Labor never forgave him. Later TWA's unions blocked Lorenzo's attempt to take over that carrier by agreeing to give Carl Icahn handsome concessions—the same ones they had refused to give TWA's previous management. That's how much they feared Frank Lorenzo.

"I want to know if you're serious about selling Eastern, or are you just using me as a bargaining chip?" Lorenzo asked me.

I told him, "Frank, our directors have authorized me to do one of three things: Fix the airline, sell it, or go into Chapter Eleven. Of those three choices, I prefer to fix it. But I give you my word that if our unions won't cooperate, we'll negotiate with Texas Air in good faith. Chapter Eleven, I assure you, would be our last resort."

"I'll accept your word," Lorenzo said.

There was one other suitor who showed a glimmer of interest. Peter Crisp, one of Eastern's directors, informed me that an investment firm had urged People Express to talk to me, ostensibly about merger. I didn't regard this as very welcome news; People Express itself was in deep trouble, mostly from a gluttonous expansion program culminating in an ill-advised purchase of ailing Frontier Airlines. But our executive committee thought we had a fiduciary responsibility at least to hear what People Express had to say, so I met with its chairman, Donald Burr, in Washington.

We talked about our respective airlines and their problems for two hours. Burr finally said, "Well, we don't have anything to offer, but keep us in mind if you need help."

As a viable partner, People Express ranked somewhere below a mom-and-pop grocery store located next door to a Safeway. I couldn't figure out the reason for the feelers until I heard later that after our talk, Burr had gone back to the investment firm with a proposal: that our board sign an agreement whereby People Express would manage Eastern.

It was a ridiculous idea. People Express didn't have the resources or depth of executive talent to manage itself, let alone a carrier three times its size. Burr's plan never got off the ground, and that left only Texas Air in the wings, waiting for a cue it didn't really expect to hear.

I stayed out of the negotiating pits, leaving that chore up to Bill Usery and Jack Johnson. Deliberately, I didn't disclose my talks with Lorenzo because I hoped an agreement would be reached before we had to face the prospect of seriously entertaining a Texas Air bid. But I did warn that Eastern might be up for sale, just as I warned of a Chapter 11 filing.

The longer negotiations dragged on with no progress, the more likely selling the airline appeared. Usery thought our best chance for agreement rested with the pilots and the flight attendants. He saw no immediate hope of cracking through the IAM's hardened stance.

As our hopes of reaching agreement with the unions seemed to fade, the talks with Texas Air assumed more serious proportions. Merrill Lynch represented Eastern in the negotiations, and Lorenzo was a hard bargainer who strove for every advantage. Yet he was no chiseler. His final offer was $9.50 a share for Eastern's outstanding stock, more than $3.00 above the current market price; it was a $607.5 million deal.

The national leaders of all three unions understood Eastern's difficult position, and I should know—I conferred with them personally during these crucial two months and found them a hell of a lot more realistic then their local officers in Miami. ALPA's president, Hank Duffy, talked with me privately and again with Larry Schulte present, both sessions giving me encouragement that the pilots would stand by the airline.

I trusted Duffy, a soft-spoken man of intelligence and integrity, more than I did Schulte. Larry's expressed views seemed to depend on whose company he was in at the time—he'd tell you whatever he thought you wanted to hear. In some ways I actually had more respect for Bryan, who at least had the charisma to lead, to stand up for his convictions.

Usery and I also met with John Law, president of the TWU, and John Kerrigan, who headed the union's airline division. Like Duffy, they knew the score at Eastern and promised to cooperate. They bemoaned the fact they had to deal with Eastern's weak, very fractured local, which the ineffective Callahan was running like a zoo.

The IAM was our biggest worry. Usery and I met at least three times with Bill Winpisinger before the February 23, 1986, deadline set by the lenders for new labor concessions. On each occasion I warned him that Bryan seemed absolutely irrational, apparently willing to see Eastern go down the drain rather than give in.

And on each occasion, Winpisinger assured me, "Don't worry— when it comes time to step in, I'll handle Charlie."

I got the same promise from John Peterpaul. At this point, I honestly believed we had Bryan blocked, with both international officials pledged to go over Charlie's head if necessary and take to the membership whatever proposal the company made.

My biggest concern, in fact, was Frank Lorenzo. As Eastern approached the lenders' February 23 deadline, Lorenzo became increasingly suspicious of my motives. Once he called me in an angry panic over a report that Pan Am had put out feelers on a merger with Eastern.

"You're going to be hearing all kinds of rumors these days," I told him. "Don't worry about them. We've got a deal, our board's committed to it, and we'll live up to our word. Frank, we're going to try to fix it first, and if we can't, you're next."

But the continuing impasses in our labor talks simply fed Lorenzo's fears that both sides were stalling in hopes of getting some kind of agreement more palatable than selling. Neither Fallon nor I could convince him that the unions were doing the stalling, not the company.

Friday, February 21, ended with not one of the unions budging. They were meeting in three separate locations and Usery was commuting between them, a negotiator in perpetual motion.

Saturday morning I asked all the union leaders, local and international, to meet me in Building 16's auditorium, where I again warned of those three choices: Fix it, sell it, or Chapter 11. As forcefully as I could, I said that the prospect of selling was only too real and that Texas Air, our lenders, and Eastern had mutually agreed on midnight Sunday as a deadline for settling with the unions.

Eastern's board met the same day to discuss details of the Texas Air bid and be briefed on the union negotiations still going on. The status of the three unions differed. The flight attendants' contract had expired and no agreement on a new pact had been reached yet. A new pilots' contract was also in the negotiating process, so both the TWU and ALPA were being asked to incorporate the proposed 20 percent wage cut into new agreements. But the IAM's contract still had more than a year to run and this was the biggest stumbling block: Bryan was standing on the principle that he was unwilling to reopen an existing agreement.

During a board recess, Charlie told a *New York Times* reporter he preferred a Texas Air takeover to reopening the IAM contract. Then he added these immortal words:

"It might be surprising the relationship that could develop between Lorenzo and our organization. For all his faults, Lorenzo is a businessman who has demonstrated he knows how to make money and how to run a successful company. I can work with Frank Lorenzo."

The directors adjourned the Saturday meeting and scheduled another for 2 P.M. Sunday.

The final countdown had begun.

24

NIGHT OF THE FINAL COUNTDOWN

The longest journey of my life was not *Apollo 8*'s trip to the moon and back.

It was the five-mile, fifteen-minute drive from our home in Coral Gables to Building 16 on Sunday evening, February 23, 1986. I had been driving that route for sixteen years, but on this warm, beautiful night my pickup truck must have been driving itself—I was too busy thinking.

The board had recessed for dinner following the Sunday afternoon session and was scheduled to reconvene at 7:30 P.M. At the earlier meeting, Wayne Yeoman had spent most of the time outlining the details of Lorenzo's offer. Several directors invited me to join them for dinner, but I declined. I went home, showered, had a quiet meal with Susan, and left around 6:45.

I had slept hardly at all on Saturday night—the same insomnia had preceded the Gemini and Apollo missions. And the cause was the same. It had been fear for my family on the space flights. Now it was fear for another family: forty thousand Eastern employees.

Optimism wrestled with pessimism in the arena of my thoughts as I drove almost blindly toward Miami International. Throughout the day, Usery had been reporting "no progress" from the three union negotiating conclaves. Yet I kept thinking of the promises Winpisinger and Peterpaul had made. Peterpaul, in fact, was in Miami for an IAM convention. I knew the hotel where they were meeting and I had Winpisinger's home telephone number if I had to play those last two aces.

My confidence rose slightly as I neared the airport. I even began mentally comparing what I faced now with the space missions of the past.

It's the same thing, I thought. I've never gone into a mission without at least three alternatives. If the primary goal can't be attained, you go to an alternate mission. If that's out of reach, you abort, which is a failed mission but at least you're alive. This time fixing the airline is the primary mission, selling it is the alternate mission, and Chapter 11, God forbid, is the abort.

The lobby of Building 16 was deserted, and it struck me how incongruously peaceful everything seemed only a few hours before an airline Armageddon. Later, the lobby would be packed with Eastern employees, lawyers, and investment bankers, but right now it gave the impression that this was just another sleepy Sunday evening when the airline's heartbeat was throbbing anywhere but in that silent, empty building.

I rode the elevator to my office on the ninth floor. Three people were waiting for me: Lynn Fowler, my loyal executive assistant; Wayne Yeoman; and Dick Magurno. For about twenty minutes, Wayne, Dick, and I discussed the forthcoming meeting and the prospects for saving the airline. Usery popped in to brief us on how the negotiations were going. He thought the pilots and flight attendants were going to come around, but he still wasn't sure of the IAM.

Yeoman was worried. "I've done business with Charlie Bryan for years, Frank," he said. "I'd bet a very large sum of money that he won't do the responsible thing tonight."

"I wouldn't take your bet," I agreed, "but I've got Winpisinger's promise he'll keep the son of a bitch in line. Peterpaul's, too."

Tempering any optimism, however, was the midnight deadline agreed to by Texas Air, our lenders, and ourselves. We had less than six hours in which to reach agreement.

At 7:30 P.M., we went down to the auditorium.

The meeting began with further discussion of the Texas Air offer, concentrating on some of the conditions Lorenzo had attached to the proposed merger. They weren't unreasonable, but one of them gave Texas Air freedom to back out of the deal if Eastern's cash balance fell to the $80 million level. One director asked what the balance would drop to if either the pilots or flight attendants went on strike.

"A strike would result in a cash drain of three point five to four million dollars a day," Wayne Yeoman replied. "It wouldn't take very long to hit eighty million."

More talk as the minutes and hours dragged on. I finally rose.

"If the board does not accept the Texas Air offer," I said quietly, "and the company fails to get agreements with the unions, it will be forced to file for Chapter Eleven tomorrow. I suggest that management be authorized to do just that if the agreements are not reached. Our cash as of today is thirty million dollars below our forecast, and I think it would be appropriate now to discuss any concerns the board has with the Texas Air offer."

The big room was silent. Jack Fallon posed a question to Patrick Murphy, the bankruptcy consultant we had hired to advise us on Chapter 11 proceedings.

"I'd like to ask Mr. Murphy if he believes Eastern could survive under Chapter Eleven," Fallon said.

Murphy, a quietly competent man who had earned our respect, cleared his throat a little nervously—he was under the same pressure as every other man in that room.

"Counsel is proceeding with preparations to file a Chapter Eleven petition, if necessary," he began. "But my advice to this board is the same as it has been for the last two years. Namely, Chapter Eleven is a last resort."

Once again, an almost uncomfortable silence hung over the room like an invisible fog. The very words "Chapter Eleven" had a sobering air of sheer desperation.

Around 9 P.M., we got word that the pilots were nearing an agreement. The meeting was recessed for an hour and I walked over to Bryan. "Charlie, come up to my office."

I already had a strong hunch Peterpaul was going to bail out of his promise. I had seen him briefly on Saturday and he'd seemed strangely noncommittal, even nervous. I asked Bryan to wait in the outer office while I made a phone call. I had a premonition of disaster even as I dialed the IAM's hotel and asked for Peterpaul. The operator couldn't find him and I finally got some union official.

"I'm trying to contact John Peterpaul."

"Oh, he's already checked out. He's on his way back to Washington."

I hung up, sensing real trouble, and asked Bryan to come in.

"Charlie," I began, "we've been at this since '83 and you have to recognize it can't go on. I have every reason to believe the pilots and flight attendants are going to give us what we need. I know it's more difficult for you because your contract is not open. But I also know you have a sense of history. We have a very good opportunity to cure this airline, and if you just understand this, in the long run you'll come out a far stronger, more admirable person, if you just do the difficult. Choose the harder right instead of the easier wrong, and let's go forward,"

He looked at me. "Frank, you just don't understand that you're trying to run the company down and I can't go along with that."

After twenty minutes I finally gave up and asked him to wait outside. When the door closed behind him, I called Winpisinger's home. He answered and I wasted no time.

"Winpy, Peterpaul's gone."

He growled, "Yeah, I know. I couldn't reach him either. Is Charlie with you?"

"He's right outside my office."

"Put him on."

I hesitated. "Winpy, this is it."

He repeated brusquely, "Put Bryan on."

I called Charlie in and left him alone in my office, talking to the man who was supposed to be his boss. For a torturing fifteen minutes I waited in the outer office. When Bryan emerged, he wore a smug look on his fleshy, dark-complexioned face.

"Winpy wants to talk to you."

I picked up the phone. "Well, did you get it fixed?"

"There's nothing I can do," he replied.

"What do you mean, you can't do anything? You told me . . . ."

He interrupted, "Bryan tells me some of the directors are on his side and your whole board is fractured."

"Winpy, that's an absolute lie! Nobody's on his side. The guy is crazy—you told me yourself he hears voices. He's going to destroy this airline if you don't act."

"I'm sorry, but the way we're constituted, there's nothing I can do."

I said hoarsely, "You know this is the end of Eastern."

"So be it" was his cold-blooded answer.

I knew then the battle was lost. Winpisinger had reneged and Peterpaul had run. Neither wanted to risk losing Charlie Bryan's support. Both had the legal authority and political clout to overrule a local president—as a matter of fact, the airline's contract was with the international union, not the local—yet both stood aside.

The board meeting finally reconvened at 10:30 P.M., an hour and a half away from the deadline. By now we had word that the pilots had reached an agreement, but the TWU negotiations were still up in the air and the IAM wasn't budging. The directors heard an analysis of the Texas Air offer by representatives of Salomon Brothers and Merrill Lynch, and at this point, Charlie Bryan finally spoke—up to then all he had done was engage in whispered conversations with Randy Barber and two union attorneys sitting behind him.

"I've had a discussion with the chairmen of the audit and finance committees [directors Peter Crisp and Harry Hood Bassett, respectively] and I would like the board to be informed of what we talked about," Bryan said.

Bassett and Crisp told us they had met with Bryan during the recess, but had failed to convince him the company was in dire straits. Added Crisp, "We urged Mr. Bryan to reconsider in view of the fifty-seven years of this airline, and the fact that his decision would impact all the company's employees. We reminded him it seemed to be a tragic end for such fine people. We're very hopeful that something positive may still come out of this talk with Mr. Bryan."

Nineteen pair of eyes turned to Bryan.

I said, "I'd like Mr. Bryan to tell the board right now whether he'll participate along with the other unions."

Bryan snapped, "I'll tell the board what I choose to tell them. This board is going to make the decision, not Charlie Bryan. I know what the problems are" —he looked right at me— "and what the limits are. If the board hopes I'll respond to this kind of hysterics, it's mistaken!"

Blind rage swept over me. I walked over to Bryan.

"Charlie, are you or are you not going to cooperate?"

He just sat there, our eyes meeting like a pair of dueling swords. But he said nothing.

"Well, you've just destroyed this airline!" I snarled. "If you force the company to be sold, I'll pin it right on you!"

"And I'll tell 'em you did it!" he shouted back.

Director Karl Eller, my old high-school football teammate, calmed me down with a question.

"I'd like to ask, what are the financial implications of the concessions being asked of the IAM?"

"About a hundred ten million dollars is involved," I replied. "But I have to remind you that if all the unions do not participate, the airline will be forced to sell or go into bankruptcy. I have absolutely no hope that Eastern can make it without the same concessions from the IAM as from other employees."

Bryan, his face florid, said tartly, "When the IAM amended its contract on October seventeenth, 1985, I didn't complain about the other two unions. Let me remind you that the IAM has made recommendations for cost savings over the past several months, but we've never been given the opportunity to implement them."

I confined my retort to a terse "That's nonsense." Then I threw down the gauntlet again. "I think it's time for the board to decide whether to accept the Texas Air offer or file a petition for protection under Chapter Eleven of the bankruptcy laws."

Director Wesley Posvar, visibly upset with Bryan's obstinance, urged him to consider what was at stake. "Agreeing to wage concessions is very important for the unions and for the industry," Posvar said. "The unions are moving into a new era of responsibility, and obviously if unions don't face up to the national economic situation, all airlines are going to be in trouble in the future. I believe Mr. Bryan's position this evening is of very grave harm to the futures of a lot of people."

I applauded mentally and said aloud, "Eastern has something good going here and something good is now going down the drain. This company cannot survive if it does not restructure its wage scales."

That was all Bryan needed.

"Year in and year out," he declared, "the unions have been asked to trust management. Each year has been a crisis situation and the unions were told there were still enormous problems. It's time for management to trust the employees to find ways to improve productivity and reduce costs."

I didn't bother to remind the directors of what Bryan had omitted—the IAM's long history of obstructionism and empty productivity claims. Never had Charlie Bryan made a concession without demanding something from management. And he was about to prove it once more.

All I said in response to Bryan's tirade was "Without restructured agreements with labor, I repeat, this company cannot survive, and Mr. Bryan has told us he will not participate. I'd like to ask Bob Callahan if he'll check on the status of the TWU negotiations."

Callahan left the room. By now, midnight was almost upon us and Howard Turner, a lawyer representing Smith, Gambrell and Russell—Eastern's general counsel—kept popping in and out of the meeting. He was talking to the Texas Air merger team in Atlanta. More discussion, and Jack Fallon finally had his craw full of talk. The deadline was at hand.

"I think the board has deliberated long enough," Fallon announced. "I'd like to ask for a motion on the offer from Texas Air. And I might add this will be the most serious vote taken in Eastern's history. We've worked very hard to get ourselves into a position to vote. I deeply regret that this great airline is in this position and that the relationships between labor and management are such that they can't work together. However, it's our responsibility to do what's best for the stockholders and employees."

He paused, and seemed almost on the verge of tears. "I'd like to have us say a silent prayer before we vote."

Dick Magurno then came into the meeting to report that the ALPA agreement was ready to be signed although it wasn't official yet, and that the TWU and the company were "within an inch of reaching agreement." This put the ball right back in Bryan's court; the board had yet to vote on the Texas Air bid and Turner rushed back into the room to announce that Texas Air was willing to extend the deadline to 4 A.M.

He also told us that Texas Air was willing to remove the $80 million cash minimum and some other conditions that had concerned the board. Now we had some breathing room, but after a flurry of discussion on the ramifications of selling the airline, it was clear the board's sentiments had swung in favor of the Texas Air deal. Director Julian Scheer tried one last-ditch effort to break through Bryan's armor plate.

"Mr. Bryan," he asked, "are you fully aware that this board is going to sell the airline? If so, I'd like you to say for the record that you still refuse to participate."

Bryan launched into one of his patented discourses.

"Although the IAM will not agree to the company's proposals," he declared, "we have proven that we are saving labor costs. . . . The IAM will continue to save labor costs and improve productivity, and if the board decides to sell or bankrupt the company, you can't point to me and say, 'It's your fault.' I am against any activity tonight to sell Eastern or any decision to file for bankruptcy."

I couldn't believe what I had just heard. The IAM hadn't achieved lower labor costs; it had bled us dry for years. The IAM hadn't given us productivity gains; it had made a handful of small gestures in that direction, all drops in the proverbial bucket.

I didn't have to answer Bryan because Crisp said angrily, "Mr. Bryan, you have said that you will vote no tonight to the sale, and you indicated to me that there is no basis whatsoever that you would agree to come along with the other unions to fix it. It is obvious to me that the responsibility for forcing the board to sell the company is clearly yours!"

Both Posvar and Fallon pointed out that Bryan had removed the first option—the fix—and left the board with only the other two options. Pilot representative Boggs asked Fallon if, in the talks with Texas Air, there had been any discussion of Borman and top management's resigning. Fallon replied that, to his knowledge, Texas Air wanted the management team as much as it wanted the airline. (This may have been true at the time; Fallon was being honest but he wasn't clairvoyant.)

"I think the board should wait for twelve hours before making a decision," Boggs said.

Fallon, exasperated, reminded him that "delaying a decision would eliminate the Texas Air offer and force Eastern into Chapter Eleven."

"The board must make a decision tonight," Fallon warned.

Bryan had been holding a whispered conversation with Michael Connery, a lawyer with the firm that represented the IAM. Connery was nodding as Bryan suddenly said that he and Connery wanted to have a private meeting with Bassett and Crisp.

There was a brief adjournment. I went outside the building and stood by the Rickenbacker Memorial Fountain, placed there in tribute to the old curmudgeon who had headed Eastern for so many years. That stubborn, wonderful old man—a man whose political convictions made Calvin Coolidge seem like a liberal, a World War I flying ace, a true giant among the early airline pioneers. It was his airline I had inherited and now was about to lose. The moon was almost full and it was easy to read the plaque mounted on the front of the fountain:

EDWARD VERNON RICKENBACKER
"CAPTAIN EDDIE"
1935—EASTERN AIR LINES—1963
DEDICATED TO HIS INSPIRED LEADERSHIP
OF EASTERN AIR LINES AND THE AVIATION INDUSTRY

Above those words was a sculptured relief of Rickenbacker's stern, hawk-nosed face. I kept looking at it. I just couldn't stop looking at it. Standing there alone in the moonlight, never had I felt so close to this tortured, troubled airline. Never had I wanted so badly to save it. That simple little memorial outside Building 16 brought mental pictures of Eastern's past: the glory years of dashing air-mail pilots . . . the ubiquitous DC-3s and the graceful Constellations with their triple tails . . . the garish, circuslike FLY THE GREAT SILVER FLEET painted above the fuselage windows . . . the giant blue-and-silver jetliners that revolutionized air travel . . . and the people of Eastern . . .

The *people.*

They were the airline.

I returned to the meeting and found that Bryan had thrown down a gauntlet of his own. Bassett advised the directors that the IAM had offered to take a 15 percent wage cut. As Bassett explained it, Bryan claimed the IAM already had contributed 5 percent through productivity gains and Charlie's arithmetic showed that 5 percent plus 15 percent added up to the 20 percent we were getting from the other two unions.

Then Bassett dropped the other shoe. Bryan had attached a condition.

"Mr. Bryan's offer," the stone-faced Bassett said, "is contingent upon the appointment of a board committee to search for a new chief executive officer within a reasonable period of time."

Well, I thought, *at least it's out in the open.* You could feel the tension in the room. I rose, trying to keep my voice calm.

"Any allegation that the IAM already has given five percent is nonsense," I said.

Boggs said he didn't believe Bryan's proposal for a board search committee meant the offer was contingent "on Colonel Borman's leaving."

The hell it wasn't, and if the well-meaning Boggs didn't realize this, he was the only one in the room who didn't. Bryan had just played his trump card.

I said, "If the IAM will give twenty percent like the other employees, I'll submit my resignation this evening under those conditions. I will not submit my resignation if the IAM will only give fifteen percent, because that supposed five percent simply doesn't exist."

I looked at my watch. It was past 2 A.M. and I continued, "I believe the board must make its decision on the sale to Texas Air, and in view of Mr. Bryan's contingency condition, I think it's best that I abstain from any vote."

I went out to the lobby, trembling with emotion. It was starting to get crowded, but I shook off questions from employees who had come to wait for the verdict. Eventually, I was left alone off to one side, trying to gather my thoughts, and who charges out of the auditorium but Mike Connery, one of the lawyers advising Bryan. The minute he spotted me, he came running up.

His opening line: "Colonel, you've got to go in there and quit."

I just glared at him. For some reason, I can't forget what he was wearing—lizard shoes and wide red suspenders.

"What the hell are you talking about?"

"I'm offering you a deal. All you have to do is quit."

"And just who are you representing?"

"Charlie Bryan."

"Look," I said coldly, "I've already offered to resign and I'm sure the board will either accept it or reject it."

"You have to go back in there and make them accept it."

"I can't make them do anything, Connery. I just told you—I'll resign if we get the same break from the IAM as we're getting from ALPA and TWU."

He kept pleading and insisting. I finally walked away from him, disgusted, and went outside to the Rickenbacker Fountain again, wondering what was going on at the meeting. From the subsequent press reports and the rather impersonal official minutes I saw later, plenty.

One director called Bryan's offer "flaky."

"You can't allow a demand for the chairman's resignation to become a part of labor negotiations," he declared. "You do that and you lose control of the company."

Another director—Dave Wallace—said that if the board bought Bryan's offer, Borman's head in exchange for a 15 percent cut, "I'll join Borman in resigning because this would be such a reprehensible action that I could no longer sit on the board."

In one final effort to save Eastern, the directors put forth a counter-proposal: creating a new post of board vice chairman, to be appointed by a directors' committee, presumably with labor represented (obviously a tempting carrot for Bryan). When the counter-offer was put on the table, Julian Scheer emphasized that it was conditioned in the IAM's agreeing to full concessions.

Karl Eller snapped, "Before I'd agree to such a proposal, I'd have to hear Frank Borman tell us if he has any objections to it."

I was called back to the auditorium, listened to the counter-offer, and told the directors, "If the IAM accepts a twenty percent cut, I'll certainly agree to the appointment of a vice chairman to be selected by a board committee."

I wasn't really optimistic about this last-second compromise succeeding, but at least Charlie would be getting something he knew the board didn't really want to give him.

Bryan went off for another huddle with Bassett, Crisp, and Boggs, Barber and Connery accompanying him. He returned and Bassett glumly announced that Bryan had rejected the compromise.

The ball game was over. Jack Fallon called for an immediate vote. I left the room and went up to my office, where I sat waiting for word that the vote was over, my mind numb and drained.

Around 3 A.M., I was called back to the auditorium. As I walked in, the directors rose and applauded. Those waiting in the lobby heard the clapping and thought agreement had been reached with the IAM. It hadn't been reached—the airline, as I was quickly informed, had been sold. I appreciated the tribute, but that applause was the emptiest sound I ever heard.

Dimly, I heard someone read a resolution the board had passed, expressing "its deep appreciation to Mr. Frank Borman and his management team for their dedication and valuable contributions to the corporation and for their untiring efforts in its behalf." I was grateful for this, too, but at this point personal praise meant nothing.

The vote to sell was 15–4; all four union directors, Bryan included, had voted against the merger. A number of directors clustered around me, shaking my hand and murmuring words of sympathy. I scarcely heard them.

Still in a daze and badly shaken, I came out of the auditorium and was surrounded immediately by thirty or forty employees. I couldn't focus on individual faces.

With an effort, I cleared my throat.

"I'm sorry to say we have just sold our airline," I began. "But I would like to say . . ."

I stopped. I was fighting to propel more words out of my constricted throat. But I could manage only five more.

"I'll talk to you later," I said in a choked voice.

Vaguely, as if I were in a dream, I heard people saying things to me. . . . "Don't worry, Frank, we'll make it work. . . . It wasn't your fault, Colonel. . . . Hang in there, Mr. Borman. . . ." I was in too much of a state of shock to associate voices with faces.

I went from the lobby up to my office and called Susan.

"We sold the airline," I muttered. "I'll be home in a few minutes."

As it had earlier that evening, the truck drove itself. I was in a fog, conscious only of bitterness and frustration. For the first time in my life, I hadn't accomplished a mission.

When I got home, I started to tell her what had happened and self-control snapped.

The tough astronaut who had flown two of the space program's riskiest missions and been feted by rulers throughout the civilized world . . .

The man who had been offered cabinet-level jobs by three presidents of the United States and twice addressed joint sessions of Congress . . .

The man who had conducted more than one delicate diplomatic mission abroad . . .

The stern airline executive accused of running Eastern like a Marine drill instructor . . .

This was the same guy who now put his tired head on his wife's shoulder and cried.

EPILOGUE

Two years have passed since that unhappy night . . . two years in which I've finally achieved some sense of detachment from the event.

With detachment, I hope, has come a better perspective of my role in what happened. I feel more sorrow than bitterness that the Eastern I loved became a demoralized airline, still torn by labor strife.

That is not what either Frank Lorenzo or I wanted. His plan was to operate Eastern indefinitely as a separate entity, but only if the unions gave him competitive labor rates.

I'll let others judge the legacy I left behind. I can only pray that the people of Eastern will remember me as a man who tried to save their jobs by exchanging temporary adversity for long-range security. Maybe they will, if a couple of letters I received after I left the airline are any indication. They were from two national labor leaders. The first wrote: "I know that you understand my sincere admiration for the principles and integrity that you brought to your job. From my dealings with you, I know of your genuine feelings for the employees of Eastern and especially the pilots. Your selfless actions at the end of the whole buyout episode are something that I will remember and treasure for the rest of my life."

The letter was signed by Henry Duffy, president of the Air Line Pilots Association.

The second letter said: "Speaking for myself, I know you did your very best on behalf of Eastern's shareholders to whom your first responsibility lay, but more importantly I know you've always maintained a sincere consideration and interest for the welfare of Eastern's employees. I also know that many of them do not fully understand that now. However, as time passes, they will come to realize that you, in fact, were always working in their best interest."

It was signed by John Kerrigan, international vice president of the TWU and director of its Air Transport Division.

Men like Duffy and Kerrigan know I am not anti-labor and never have been. I do believe, however, that it is futile to deal with the type of intransigent union leaders we had at Eastern unless you're dealing with them from a position of financial strength.

I don't mean that when management is strong, it can't also be fair and cooperative. But this doesn't require an actual partnership with labor. The events leading to Eastern's sale might make anyone attempting this kind of arrangement a bit leary. When we put union officials on our board and encouraged employee participation, it was widely praised as "the wave of the future." It was exactly the opposite, because men like Bryan really wanted control instead of cooperation.

Companies that have made unions a part of a private-enterprise government—i.e., the board of directors—have done so largely out of economic necessity, like Chrysler. The success of such a partnership depends almost entirely on the caliber of the labor leader given such immense responsibility, for such a person must subordinate loyalty toward a union constituency to the overall welfare of the company.

This is the inevitable conflict that so often precludes labor as an effective participant in the actual governing of a corporation. It is a conflict that I don't think most labor leaders can handle. Not because they don't want to, not because they may not recognize the inconsistency or ambiguity of their position, but because they're afraid they can't stray from the mandate given them by their members and still stay in power. In my experience, the overriding motivation of the local union leaders I dealt with, with the exception of Augie Gorse and Jim Cates, was power. Gorse and Cates were the only ones willing to put the long-term needs of their members over their own power bases. The overriding motivation of management is for the corporate entity to stay alive, not the individual to stay in power, for an airline actually becomes a living entity. This involves a very different set of values.

As I write these final words, I do not know what will happen to the airline that was my world for sixteen years. But I must admit to a sense of *déjà vu*. Another DOT-instigated safety investigation, producing more headlines than factual evidence of serious sins. A union propaganda campaign destroying the company's reputation. The media once again in a feeding frenzy. And Charlie Bryan, the man who caused Eastern to be sold in the first place, still peddling his anti-management venom.

This is where I came in. And went out.

When I was working on the redesign of the Apollo spacecraft and flew so often between Houston and California, my course took me over New Mexico.

On one flight, I happened to look down at a beautiful little city thousands of feet below and thought, *That would be a great place to live someday.*

The city was Las Cruces. I resigned from Eastern on July 1, 1986, and Las Cruces is now my home.

Our son Fred was responsible for our moving to New Mexico. When his spinal injury had forced him to leave the Army, he eventually established a car dealership in Miami. Fred didn't like Florida, however, and finally bought a dealership in Las Cruces. Three months after Eastern was sold, he called to suggest that we settle there— "It's the world's best-kept secret," he joked.

I still miss Eastern and its people. Jerry Cosley once told me the most poignant moment after the sale was seeing my pickup truck, parked in its usual spot, with a sign on the windshield: FOR SALE BY OWNER.

I'm now a consultant in Las Cruces. Edwin is a major and a qualified helicopter test pilot, while Susan has started her own interior decorating business. And we have four wonderful grandchildren.

And I'm flying again. I acquired a Chipmunk, a British-built aerobatic plane that's sheer fun to fly—it takes me back to my Air Force days, when flight meant freedom from the prosaic.

Funny thing about that Chipmunk—I've always wanted one but had a devil of a time finding the right airplane, until two Atlanta-based Eastern captains helped me out. They located a Chipmunk in fine condition, flew it to Atlanta, modified it, and advised me to buy it.

One of them told me, "It's the least we can do for you, Colonel, after all you did for Eastern."

And I'll accept that as my airline epitaph.

•

INDEX

Soviet Union (*continued*)
  tour of, 237, 242–256
Soyuz 1 (Soviet spacecraft), 179
Space Station Task Force, 261
Spacesuits, 119–120, 122, 127–128, 135–136, 198
Space walks, 156–165, 166
Speas, R. Dixon, 329
Speas report, 329–330, 335
Sputnik 1, 72, 77
Stafford, Fay, 298
Stafford, Tom, 75–76, 96, 98, 125, 126, 127, 150, 156–165, 240, 256
  Gemini 6 and, 141–144
Star City (Soviet cosmonauts' training center), 246–249, 251, 257
STOL (short takeoff and landing) aircraft, 282
Supersonic transport (SST), 265
Swigert, Jack, 258

T-6 training plane, 41, 42
T-33 jet, 52, 59, 60, 61, 62, 76, 77, 110, 115
T-38 Talon, 85, 110
Taylor, Arthur, 402, 406
Taylor, General Maxwell, 28
Teague, Olin, 179, 180, 221
Texas Air, 420, 421, 424, 425–426
  takeover of Eastern by, 384, 428–438
TF-102 Delta Dagger, 80, 81–82
Thompson, Floyd, 171, 174
Thunderstorm penetration techniques, 60–62
Titan II rocket, 78, 98–99, 100, 103, 111, 112, 132, 133
Titov, Gherman, 243, 245, 250, 251, 252, 255
Trans-earth injection (TEI), 213, 215
Trans-lunar injection (TLI), 197, 202–203
Transport Workers Union (TWU), 328, 382, 383, 392, 396, 398, 401, 402, 409, 431, 433, 436, 440
TU-144 (Soviet SST), 265
Tupolev, Andrei, 255
TWA, 271, 359, 410, 420, 421

United Airlines, 355, 388, 421
USAF Experimental Flight Test Pilot School, 75–76
USAir, 420, 421
U.S. Department of Transportation (DOT), 356, 412–420

Usery, William Julian, 396, 397–401, 407, 408, 409, 423, 424, 425, 428
USSR, *see* Soviet Union
USSR Academy of Sciences, 239

V-2 rockets, 72, 99
Van Allen radiation belt, 203–204, 220
Variable Earnings Plan (VEP), 338–341, 347–349, 357
Vietnam War, 195, 234, 235, 236
  tour to improve POWs' treatment, 262–263, 267–269
Von Braun, Wernher, 99, 100, 137, 184, 195, 197, 220, 223
Voskhod 2 (Soviet spacecraft), 118

Wasp (aircraft carrier), 120, 147, 148, 149, 150, 165, 167
Wall Street Journal, 306, 380, 408
Warde, George, 362, 363, 364
Washington Post, 238
Watergate scandal, 227, 238
Webb, James E., 104–105, 107, 127, 151, 173, 179–180, 185–186, 190, 220
West Point (U.S. Military Academy), 24, 25–26, 28–38, 65, 66–73, 235
WHEAL (We Hate Eastern Airlines), 270, 271
White, Edward Higgins, II, 96, 98, 102, 114, 115, 118–120, 123, 153, 156
  death of, 170, 171, 172, 173, 174, 294, 295
White, Pat, 170, 294, 298
  suicide of, 176, 295–296
Wilson, T., 367–368
Winpisinger, Bill, 340, 365, 377, 395–396, 425, 428, 430–431
Witkin, Dick, 107, 179, 415
Woodward, Harper, 318, 319

X-15 (rocket-powered aircraft), 84, 107
X-20 (Dyna-Soar space vehicle), 77–78

Yeager, Chuck, 84–85, 86, 91, 107
Yeoman, Wayne, 342, 373, 387, 427, 428, 429
Young, Barbara, 298
Young, John, 95–96, 102, 113, 116–118, 132, 134, 165
Young and Rubicam, 342–344

Zahn, Toni, 283, 333
Zero-G plane, 79
Zond 5 (Soviet spacecraft), 189